# ILLUSTRATED HANDBOOK OF
# GARDEN PLANTS

# ILLUSTRATED HANDBOOK OF
# GARDEN PLANTS

A practical guide to 3000 popular plants: characteristics, properties
and identification, illustrated with more than 950 stunning photographs

ANDREW MIKOLAJSKI

CONSULTANT JOHN SWITHINBANK

LORENZ BOOKS

*for Finetta*

This edition is published by Lorenz Books, an imprint of Anness Publishing Ltd, Blaby Road, Wigston, Leicestershire LE18 4SE; info@anness.com

www.lorenzbooks.com; www.annesspublishing.com

If you like the images in this book and would like to investigate using them for publishing, promotions or advertising, please visit our website www.practicalpictures.com for more information.

*Publisher:* Joanna Lorenz
*Managing Editor:* Judith Simons
*Executive Editor:* Caroline Davison
*Project Editors:* Claire Folkard & Mariano Kälfors
*Designer:* Michael Morey
*Production Manager:* Steve Lang
*Editorial Reader:* Richard McGinlay

### ETHICAL TRADING POLICY

Because of our ongoing ecological investment programme, you, as our customer, can have the pleasure and reassurance of knowing that a tree is being cultivated on your behalf to naturally replace the materials used to make the book you are holding. For further information about this scheme, go to www.annesspublishing.com/trees

A CIP catalogue record for this book is available from the British Library.

Previously published as *An Encyclopedia of Garden Plants*

### PUBLISHER'S NOTE

# Contents

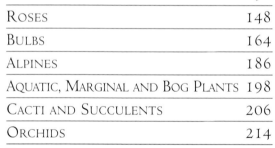
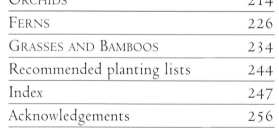

# INTRODUCTION

This directory is intended to be of practical value to gardeners. Plants are grouped according to type (trees, shrubs, perennials, etc.) and the descriptions are designed not only to allow for identification but to suggest how the plants can be used in the garden.

The number of plants available is constantly expanding, and it is obviously impossible to keep pace with every new introduction. One of the aims of this book is to bring together tried and tested plants, which have already proved their value in gardens and can be expected to perform reliably for many years to come alongside newer introductions that are likely to appear on the market. A few unusual plants are included (for instance *Berberis temolaica*, *Lonicera* × *tellmanniana* and *Phillyrea angustifolia*), plants which need no special cosseting but simply deserve to be better known. It is often only the difficulties of producing stocks in large quantities that have kept them out of gardens.

This border has been designed in a "hot" colour scheme with a combination of red-flowered and purple-leaved plants, both hardy and tender.

The summer-flowering *Itea ilicifolia*, though hardy, benefits from the shelter of a warm wall.

## Hardiness

All the plants in this book have been assessed for their hardiness, and for the US, the range of zones where they can be grown outdoors is given (see page 246). Most (apart from cacti and succulents and orchids) can be grown outdoors in most temperate areas, and are able to withstand lows of -15°C (5°F). Plants described as "borderline hardy" will need some form of protection from the coldest weather, either by growing them in a warm, sheltered spot (for instance in the lee of a sunny wall) or by covering them in winter with a dry mulch of straw or other similar material. However, severe lows in themselves are less detrimental to plants than cold, drying winds.

Hardiness in any case is relative, and the ability of many plants at least to survive cold is largely dependent on how hot the weather is the previous summer. Deciduous trees and shrubs, herbaceous bulbs that disappear below ground in winter have an in-built mechanism for surviving unfavourable weather. During hot, dry periods, plant growth stops altogether. As the soil dries out, roots delve deeper in search of moisture, while bark thickens in the heat. The result is a tough, sturdy plant with an extensive root system that is better able to withstand severe cold than one that has grown sappy through excess moisture during the growing season. These plants are able to survive colder winters than usual, simply because the preceding summer was a hot one. Winter temperatures in certain regions with a Mediterranean climate for instance can drop as low as they do in temperate areas, but plants such as olives are able to survive simply because of the long hot summers that ripen the wood. Hence the necessity of growing plants of borderline hardiness in a microclimate where they can ripen sufficiently. The same applies to many bulbs, which are adapted to long dry summers and indeed need a good summer roasting in order to flower successfully.

# How to use the directory

The directory section is divided into fourteen plant categories: Trees; Conifers; Shrubs; Perennials; Annuals and Biennals; Climbers; Roses; Bulbs (including corms and tubers); Alpines; Water Plants; Cacti and Succulents; Orchids; Ferns; and Grasses and Bamboos.

Each category features genus introductions in alphabetical order, accompanied by concise information on cultivation. These are followed by a selection of plant entries also organized alphabetically according to their most common and internationally accepted names.

A plant entry might be a species, hybrid or group of hybrids, a variant, or a cultivar. As well as a brief description, information is given on height and spread; best time of interest for flowers, foliage and fruits/berries/hips; and hardiness/zones.

*Erigeron* 'Quakeress'

## ERIGERON
Fleabane

Useful daisy plants, suitable for a sunny border, these suit cottage garden-style plantings. There are a large number of hybrids; only the species described is well-represented in gardens.
*Cultivation* Best in fertile, moist but well-drained soil in sun. Taller varieties may benefit from light staking.

### E. karvinskianus
(syn. *E. mucronatus*)
**Wall daisy**
This spreading species has dainty white flowers from late spring to autumn. H to 30cm (1ft), S 1m (3ft). Hardy/Z 8–9.

### E. hybrids
The following hybrids flower throughout summer but can also flower intermittently at other times. They are all hardy/Z 2–7. **'Dignity'** has violet-blue flowers. H and S 45cm (18in). **'Dunkelste Aller'** (syn. 'Darkest of All') has deep purple flowers with yellow eyes. H 60cm (24in), S 45cm (18in). **'Gaiety'** has mid-pink flowers. H 60cm (24in), S 45cm (18in). The deservedly popular **'Quakeress'** has white flowers flushed with pale lilac-pink. H 60cm (24in), S 45cm (18in). **'Schneewittchen'** (syn. 'Snow White') has pure white flowers, which turn pink as they age. H 60cm (24in), S 45cm (18in).

**Caption**
A full botanical name is given with each photograph

**Genus name**
This gives the botanical name for a group of related species

**Common name or names**
These apply to the whole genus, if given

**Genus introduction**
This is a general description of the genus and may give the number of species or state that the genus is monotypic (there is only one species in the whole genus). There is also some information on preferred conditions and natural habitat, country or countries of origin, and occasional advice on how the plants can be used in the garden.

**Cultivation**
This section gives the level of sun or shade that the plants described in the selection either require or tolerate as well as advice on the type of soil in which they should be grown.

**Hybrids**
Occasionally, there is one entry for a group of hybrids.

**Varieties and cultivars**
The descriptions of cultivars, forms, subspecies, and varieties appears within the main plant entry. Heights and spreads are only included if they differ from those of the main plant entry.

**Main plant entry**
This gives the current botanical name of the plant in bold and can refer to a species, hybrid or hybrids, a variant, or a cultivar.

**Synonym or synonyms**
If given, this provides the synonym or synonyms for the main plant entry. A synonym is an alternative name for the same plant.

**Common name or names**
If given, this provides the common name or names for the main plant entry.

**Hardiness ratings/Zones**
This gives the plant's temperature tolerance as either tender, down to 5°C (41°F); half-hardy, down to 0°C (32°F); or hardy, down to -15°C. Plants described as "Borderline hardy" will need some form of protection from the coldest weather. A slightly different system is used in the US and Canada. Zones are based on the average annual minimum temperature for each zone. The smaller number indicates the northernmost zone it can survive in and the higher number the southernmost zone the plant will tolerate. In some cases only one zone is given for a plant entry. See page 246 for details of zones and a zone map.

**Height and spread**
This gives the average expected height and spread, though growth rates may vary, depending on location and conditions. If the height and spread are the same, then only one measurement is given. Metric measurements always precede standard measurments.

# How plants are named

All living things are classified according to the binomial system, devised by the Swedish taxonomist Carl Linnaeus (1707–78) in his *Species Plantarum* (1753). Under the rules of this system, plants have Latin names consisting of the genus name (e.g. *Viburnum*) followed by the species epithet (e.g. *davidii*). Some genera comprise only one species, while others are vast. *Euphorbia*, for instance, is made up of some 2000 plants, annuals, perennials, shrubs and trees as well as some cactus-like plants, and is widely distributed. (Such genera are sometimes rather grandly described as "cosmopolitan".)

All members of a genus are assumed to have some relationship to each other (though this may not necessarily be immediately apparent to the naked eye) and different species can often be crossed with each other. At the higher level, some genera seem to be related to each other (roses, pyracanthas and rowans, for instance, which all have cup-shaped flowers in their wild state), suggesting some common ancestry, though much remains conjectural or relies on the evidence of fossilized remains.

Plant names can be a complex and confusing matter, and few gardening subjects have aroused such controversy in recent years as the naming of chrysanthemums.

## Naming plants

Nomenclature is not an exact science, and although there are certain internationally agreed rules, how they are put into use is often a matter of individual prejudice. Botanists and taxonomists frequently disagree over which name certain plants should bear, and in many cases there can be no "right" answer, since much depends on individual opinion. Hence the advisability of retaining synonyms, which can be as valid as the name officially sanctioned. The well-known mile-a-minute plant (here *Fallopia baldschuanica*) has

migrated several times between *Polygonum* and *Fallopia*, with ports of call at *Bilderdykia*. The most radical and controversial changes in recent years involved those to *Chrysanthemum*, which properly is made up exclusively of annual species from the Mediterranean. The perennials (which include the many garden forms that are such a feature of the autumn garden, the so-called florists' chrysanthemums) have been assigned to *Dendranthema*. However, so deeply entrenched is the name *Chrysanthemum* that it has been widely retained both within the nursery trade and in a number of plant dictionaries, this one included.

It occasionally happens that two plants thought to be distinct, with two separate names, are discovered to be, in fact, one and the same, and here a decision has to be taken as to which name has precedence.

## Cultivars

Many plant species have the genetic potential to assume different characteristics to adapt to changes in the environment. In the wild, the

habitat will favour seedlings best suited to the prevailing conditions, while the rest will not survive. Hence any population of a particular species in the wild will look more or less the same.

In the more controlled conditions of a garden, the genetic potential becomes manifest, since gardeners are able to germinate and grow on a larger proportion of the seed. All manner of variations can arise: double flowers, albino forms, plants with variegated leaves, etc. Such forms, if they have garden potential and are sufficiently distinct from the species, are given names and known as cultivars (a contraction of "cultivated varieties") or selections of the species, and the name is put in single quotes as, for instance, *Viburnum tinus* 'Eve Price'.

## Hybrids

Certain species can be crossed with each other to produce hybrids. This can occur in nature, but is more usually deliberately practised by plant breeders. Hybridization generally results in robust plants with bigger flowers. For instance, at Bodnant in Wales, *Viburnum farreri* was crossed with *V. grandiflorum* to produce *V. × bodnantense* (the cross indicating that the plant is a hybrid). Outstanding seedlings were given names, including 'Dawn' and 'Deben'.

Hybrids can be back-crossed with one of the parents, to consolidate a particular feature, or can be crossed with other species or hybrids. Some garden forms have such complex parentage that it becomes meaningless to try to ascribe them to one or other species or hybrid group. Indeed, if precise records were not kept, the ancestry of a plant can only be guess-work. Such plants are styled with the genus name followed by the cultivar name, e.g. *Campanula* 'Burghaltii'. Many roses and rhododendrons come into this category.

In general, garden forms can only be propagated vegetatively (cloning). Seedlings will revert back to the parent species (or one of them). Over time, the quality tends to deteriorate: repeated vegetative propagation is like photocopying a photocopy of a photocopy. Hence only the most vigorous of the older cultivars will stand the test of time, and there is good reason for replacing them with newly created hybrids. Many gardeners regret this, but while there is every reason to wish to preserve species that may be under threat in the wild to maintain the biodiversity of the planet, the disappearance of certain garden forms from cultivation does not represent a comparable loss.

Garden forms usually do not survive in the wild, but some species have been known to "escape", as with *Rhododendron ponticum*, from the Mediterranean, which has colonized areas of the UK and Ireland, to the extent that it has become a weed.

## Name changes
As previously mentioned, nomenclature is never precise and can lead to disputes amongst botanists. For instance, the genera *Berberis* and *Mahonia* were formerly united in a single genus, and members of the two will in fact hybridize, suggesting that there is some close relationship between them. Many botanists would like to see them reunited. Recent research into cacti and bamboos has resulted in reclassification, and some species formerly considered to belong to separate genera are now thought to be related, and some species have been switched from one genus to another.

Name changes result in synonyms. A new name is not necessarily more valid than the old, and merely represents the opinion of whoever has come up with the new name. Although many gardeners despair at what seem like constant changes, there is usually a good reason for a change (even though agreement may not be universal). Sometimes it is best to be practical. *Chrysanthemum* is a case in point.

Names of cultivars that have been bred abroad and given foreign names are often given translated names (or even new names) once imported. There are arguments for and against this: on the plus side, it results in names that are easier to remember and spell; on the down side, it leads to potential confusion. Modern rules require translated names to be set in a different font and without quotes.

Hybrids with the same parentage are sometimes given group names. This usually happens when all the seedlings share similar characteristics and, while varying, make good garden plants. A case in point is *Lilium* African Queen Group, plants of which all have orange flowers, but with differing intensity of colour. Conversely, the same name is sometimes ascribed to two different plants, as is the case with the clematis 'Princess of Wales', a name that applies to two cultivars, one honouring Alexandra, wife of Edward VII, the other Princess Diana.

The breeding of orchids has been scrupulously recorded. This hybrid **Cymbidium** Summer Pearl **'Sonya'** has complex parentage.

# Choosing plants for your garden

Choosing plants on aesthetic grounds alone – for form or flower colour, for instance – is not really a successful method of gardening, though nearly all gardeners fall victim to some ravishing specimen spotted at a garden centre or garden show. Since not all plants will thrive in the same conditions, it makes sense to limit your choice to what will do well in your garden. One of the most important lessons for any gardener is that you cannot grow what you want wherever you please.

### The aspect

Light is essential to all plants as it provides the energy that is needed to manufacture food during daylight hours, so providing the right levels of light is crucial if the plants are to thrive. For this reason, one of the first considerations is the aspect of your garden. You will need to study your garden to work out which areas are sunny, shady or in partial shade at different times of the day. In their natural environment, some plants will grow in dense shade on

The plants chosen for this scheme, including *Artemisia* and *Sisyrinchium*, are perfectly adapted to hot, dry conditions.

the forest floor while others are exposed to intense bright sunlight for long periods of time. This wide diversity of natural habitat explains why so many of the different ornamental plants we grow require different conditions. The ability to adapt to unfamiliar conditions is a major reason for the popularity of many common plants.

### The soil

It is worth finding out whether your soil is acid or alkaline, since not all plants will do equally well in both (though the majority are indifferent). The most reliable method is with a chemical soil testing kit, or you can make an educated guess by looking to see what is growing successfully in the surrounding countryside, or in other people's gardens if you live in a built-up area. Geological maps also indicate the presence of limestone or silt, for instance.

Equally important, perhaps more so, is the soil profile. The ideal – a loam that binds easily into crumbs, allowing for both moisture-retention and free drainage of excess water – suits nearly all plants. Stiff clays, cold and heavy to work, are usually nutrient high, suiting bog plants and others adapted to reliably wet conditions. Dry, sandy soils, easy to work and quick to warm up in spring, are nutrient poor but are the ideal medium for many of the Mediterranean plants and herbs. All soils can be improved by digging in

Dainty *Iris sibirica* is one of the many irises that appreciate a damp site. It looks exquisite grown near to water.

organic matter, in the form of garden compost or well-rotted farmyard manure, greatly increasing the range of plants you can grow.

If a plant is doing well in your garden, either plant more of the same, or some of its near relatives or others that enjoy the same conditions. The reverse is also true. If you have trouble establishing a particular plant, you are also unlikely to succeed with others of its ilk.

## Designing with plants

A garden is more than just a collection of plants, and relies for much of its impact on the way these are grouped together. If you have a flair for design, devising effective groupings may be no problem. If you do not, there are any number of strategies you can adopt that will lead to pleasing combinations.

When choosing plants for beds and borders, formal gardens for instance tend to dictate themselves. A formal rose garden will clearly feature roses, with only the "filler" plants left debatable. An island bed

is meant to be viewed from all sides, so the tallest plants will usually go in the centre and smaller ones around the edges. Try planting a small tree such as *Malus floribunda* to create plenty of height.

Most gardens will feature single-sided borders, and the secret of a successful design is planning for a long period of interest. A border will not remain attractive for more than a month if all the plants flower briefly, at the same time. The plants you choose should also not only look pleasing when flowering, but also when out of bloom. A series of plants that bloom at different times can lead to an uncoordinated appearance of plants in flower dotted

amid swathes of foliage at varying stages of growth. If you have space you can easily devote separate borders for spring, summer and autumn/winter interest. Otherwise, try a mixed border incorporating many different kinds of plants arranged in bold groups, rather than as isolated specimens. If you want to cut down on the regular replanting work, you can also use dwarf shrubs as backbone plants, then include flowering ground-cover plants, such as hardy geraniums and spring bulbs, to provide flowers over a long period.

The following pages should help you find useful suggestions as to which plants to place where.

Here, tulips and primulas provide the interest before the standard roses come into bloom.

A classic mixed border, combining roses, lilies, and a range of easily pleased perennials against a backdrop of clipped yew.

# Trees

A tree completes a garden. Whether it
is grown for its flowers, fruits,
foliage or overall appearance, a tree
adds dignity and style to any garden.
From mighty oaks to the more
manageable Japanese maples, there is
a tree for every type of garden,
whether you have rolling acres or a
suburban plot. Even if you have only
a courtyard, balcony or roof garden,
there are trees suitable for containers.
Careful selection is necessary,
however. Remember: a tree often
outlives the gardener.

A flowering tree makes a splendid eye-catcher at the peak of its glory,
dominating the garden.

# What is a tree?

Trees comprise a large and diverse group of plants that defies precise botanical classification. What distinguishes a tree from other forms of plant life is in fact no more than its overall appearance. Most people understand a tree as having a single woody trunk and a branching crown, while shrubs produce a number of stems from ground level. However, many trees can develop as multi-trunked plants, while certain shrubs become tree-like on maturity. Climatic factors also play a part: certain plants are unequivocally trees when growing at the foot of a mountain, for instance, but behave as shrubs at the mountain top, where strong winds will have a dwarfing effect, resulting in a thick trunk and gnarled branches. In isolation on open ground, trees will branch from ground level (or very near it) and be clothed in leaves; in forests, where the planting is denser and they are competing for light, they tend to develop tall, slim trunks, branching only near the top to form the characteristic leaf canopy. Generally, trees are assumed to have a height greater than 3m (10ft) and shrubs to be below that. But some weeping trees have a much shorter trunk than that and can in no way be mistaken for shrubs.

Trees occur in a range of plant families and have adapted to most environments except deserts and tundra. Most belong to the largest group, the angiosperms (all flowering plants). Gymnosperms include conifers and cycads, while even the most primitive plant group, the ferns and mosses (pteridophytes), includes the tree ferns (but treated as a fern in this book). Most trees are deciduous, shedding their leaves in autumn and experiencing a period of dormancy

The weeping willow is particularly alluring in spring, when its delicate, pale green emerging leaves cast dappled shade.

over winter, though some are evergreens that in favourable climates will be more or less permanently in growth. Evergreen trees tend to be less hardy than deciduous trees.

Essential to the planet's ecology, trees store carbon dioxide and produce oxygen, and the material they shed – leaves and twigs – breaks down in the soil to release nitrogen, carbon and oxygen to feed the next generation of plants. Their roots help prevent soil erosion, which is why they are often planted in railway cuttings and to retain the banks at the sides of motorways, and the vast amount of water stored in a mature tree helps prevent local flooding. Trees also provide food and shelter for a wide range of mammals, birds and invertebrates.

Most trees grown in gardens today are either species or very closely related to naturally occurring forms. A few have been extensively hybridized, however, most notably the Japanese maples (forms of *Acer palmatum* and *A. japonicum*) and flowering cherries (*Prunus*), resulting in a vast number of highly desirable garden plants.

## Trees in the garden

Even the smallest of gardens should include at least one tree. Trees give an air of maturity and permanence to any plot, quite apart from whatever ornamental qualities they may possess, and have the additional benefit – inestimable to environmentalists – of attracting wildlife into the garden. Birds will perch and sometimes nest in the branches, as well as feed off any autumn fruits or berries. Trees also attract pollinating insects when in flower, and harbour a wide range of invertebrates in their bark. Before making a choice, however, you need to consider the impact the tree will make on the rest of the planting. Deciduous trees that cast dappled shade in summer but are bare in winter can be underplanted with dwarf spring bulbs for early interest, followed by shade-loving perennials later on, but the shade cast by evergreens will be too dense to allow much other plant life to thrive. In a very small garden, a narrow, columnar tree, such as *Prunus* 'Amanogawa', is often the best choice.

Trees have a range of ornamental qualities, but whether you are planning an avenue of mighty oaks or have room for only a small tree, think long and hard over which species to plant. Most trees will outlive you. If it is flowers that you want, you could scarcely do better than look to the magnolias, with sumptuous, waxy, chalice-like flowers in spring; for more delicacy, a flowering cherry (*Prunus*) could fit the bill. In favoured areas, a catalpa or paulownia would provide spring flowers, while *Acacia dealbata* (perhaps trained against a warm wall) will flower in late winter. Rather less exotic, but equally attractive in their way, as well as being tough and hardy, are the rowans (*Sorbus*) and hawthorns (*Crataegus*).

Many trees have a second period of interest in autumn when the fruits ripen. Crab apples (*Malus*) are among the best, and their red, yellow or orange fruits, as well as looking good and attracting birds, can be cooked or made into a preserve. Rowans also have spectacular trusses of berries, which often change colour or turn translucent as the temperature drops in winter.

That elusive moment when the leaves of deciduous trees change colour in autumn just before they are shed is one of the most keenly anticipated events in the gardening calendar. The display will vary from year to year, depending on the conditions of the season. One reliable performer is the katsura tree (*Cercidiphyllum japonicum* var. *magnificum*), whose leaves turn brilliant orange and then give off the scent of burnt toffee as they fall to the ground. Many of the acers produce glorious autumn colour, particularly the Japanese maples, as do amelanchiers, rowans and beeches (*Fagus*).

Trees that have attractive bark are interesting in every season of the year. The birches are especially noted for this feature.

Many trees are surprisingly effective in winter, and not only the evergreens such as hollies (*Ilex*) or *Quercus ilex*. *Prunus serrula*, for instance, has shiny mahogany red bark, while that of *Betula utilis* var. *jacquemontii* (to name only one birch from a genus outstanding for this very feature) is a gleaming white. Site them where they will be dramatically lit up by the winter sun.

If space is restricted, a surprising number of trees will do well in containers. Not the large forest trees, obviously, but any of the evergreens that take kindly to pruning, such as bay (*Laurus*) or holly, as well as more modest trees, such as Japanese maples (stylish in glazed Eastern-style pots). Citrus and acacias make a good choice for a conservatory or porch.

Fruit trees have two-fold attractions: breathtaking when in flower in spring, they earn their keep by providing edible crops in autumn.

The trees described below are deciduous unless otherwise indicated.

## ACACIA
### Wattle
The main drawback of this delightful genus is that few wattles are hardy enough to grow as freestanding specimens in any but favoured climates. In the right spot, however, they make airy, elegant trees, laden with scented flowers. They are sometimes used as pavement trees, to spectacular effect. In cold areas they can be grown in conservatories (porches), but need cutting back to restrict their size. The genus also includes some shrubs.
*Cultivation* Moderately fertile, lime-free soil in full sun, with shelter from strong winds.

### A. dealbata
**Mimosa, silver wattle**
This evergreen Australian and Tasmanian species has silver-grey, fern-like leaves and masses of fragrant, fluffy yellow flowers in late winter to early spring. It is suitable for training against a warm wall. H 15m (50ft), S 10m (33ft). Borderline hardy/Z 9–10.

## ACER
### Maple
This is a huge and important genus, and there is a maple for every garden, large or small. *A. pseudoplatanus* (sycamore) is almost a weed in some gardens, but that should not blind you to the

*Acacia dealbata*

beauties of the other species. Maples suit a woodland planting or lightly shaded area.
*Cultivation* Acers tolerate most soil types, although *A. rubrum* does best in lime-free soil. Japanese maples like a leafy, fertile but well-drained soil. Smaller species are best in light shade. *A. palmatum* cultivars are particularly susceptible to frost, which can damage the young growth, and they do best in a sheltered spot.

### A. capillipes
The young stems of this erect, deciduous Japanese species are reddish. The leaves open red, mature to mid-green and turn crimson and orange in autumn. The grey-green bark is striped white. H and S 10m (33ft). Hardy/Z 6–9.

### A. × conspicuum 'Phoenix'
This is grown mainly for the beauty of its green bark, which turns vivid pink with silver stripes in winter. The autumn display is also good, with the leaves turning a bright golden-yellow. H 5m (16ft), S 3m (10ft). Hardy/Z 6–9.

### A. davidii
**Snake-bark maple, Père David's maple**
Native to China, the species has (usually) spreading branches. The leaves are tinged bronze as they emerge and turn red and purple in autumn. The grey bark is striped white. It does best in semi-shade. H 6m (20ft), S 3m (10ft). Hardy/Z 6–8.

*Acer × conspicuum 'Phoenix'*

**'George Forrest'** has larger, red-stalked, dark green leaves, but the autumn colour is not as good. H 4m (13ft), S 2m (6ft).

### A. griseum
**Paperbark maple**
Also native to China, this slow-growing species is one of the most outstanding members of a fine genus. The leaves turn a brilliant red before they fall in autumn, but the principal interest is the cinnamon-red bark, which peels to reveal a richer colour beneath. H and S 10m (33ft). Hardy/Z 6–8.

### A. japonicum
**Japanese maple, full-moon maple**
The Japanese maples, which also include selections of *A. palmatum* (see below), are among the most attractive of all small trees, staying fairly compact and ending up as broad or broader than they are tall. They all have spectacular autumn leaf colour. The species is a spreading, rather shrubby tree. H and S 10m (33ft). Hardy/Z 6–8. **'Aconitifolium'** (syn. 'Filicifolium') is a slow-growing tree or large shrub, generally broader than it is tall. The soft green, deeply cut leaves turn vivid orange-red in autumn. H 5m (16ft), S 6m (20ft).

### A. palmatum
**Japanese maple**
The species, which is native to Korea and China as well as to Japan, is a rounded tree or shrub

*Acer griseum*

*Acer japonicum 'Aconitifolium'*

displaying glorious autumn colour. H 8m (25ft), S 10m (33ft). Hardy/Z 5–8.
*A. palmatum* f. *atropurpureum* (syn. 'Atropurpureum') is notable for the vibrant purple of its leaves, in spring and autumn. H 8m (25ft), S 10m (33ft).
*A. palmatum* var. *dissectum* makes a dome-shaped tree with elegant ferny foliage, which turns red or yellow in autumn. It has a number of cultivars with coloured or variegated leaves. H and S to 4m (13ft) but usually less. Acers in the **Dissectum Atropurpureum Group** have similar colouring to *A. palmatum* f. *atropurpurem* but with very finely dissected leaves, giving the plant a more filigree appearance. Slow-growing, they eventually make attractive, dome-shaped, spreading trees. H and S 4m (13ft). **'Dissectum Nigrum'** (syn. 'Ever Red') has finely dissected, blackish-purple leaves and forms a low, rounded bush. H 3m (10ft), S 4m (13ft). **'Fireglow'** (syn. 'Effegi') carries rich burgundy-red leaves, which turn orange-red in autumn. This requires some sun to enhance the leaf colour. H and S to 3m (10ft). **'Kagiri-Nishiki'** (syn. 'Roseomarginatum') has pale green leaves margined with pink, later turning cream. H and S 3m (10ft). **'Katsura'** has the typical palm-shaped leaves of the species. Pale orange-yellow when young, they mature to a rich bronze, then redden in autumn. H 1.2m (4ft), S 2.5m (8ft). **'Ôsakazuki'** carries mid-green leaves, which turn brilliant orange, crimson and scarlet in autumn. H 5m (16ft), S 2.5m (8ft). The red-tinted leaves of **'Rubrum'** turn bright red in autumn. H 5m (16ft), S 2.5m (8ft). **'Sekimori'** has very finely divided, filigree foliage,

*Acer palmatum* f. *atropurpureum*

which is bright green, turning red or yellow in autumn. H and S to 3m (10ft).

**A. platanoides**
**Norway maple**
This fast-growing acer offers startling autumn colour, which is usually yellow but sometimes red. H 25m (80ft), S 15m (50ft). Hardy/Z 4–7. **'Crimson King'** has rich red-purple foliage. H 15m (50ft), S 5m (16ft). **'Drummondii'** is less vigorous with mid-green leaves that are variegated with creamy-white. H 12m (40ft), S 5m (16ft).

**A. rubrum**
**Red maple, scarlet maple, swamp maple**
This species has leaves that turn rich red-orange in early autumn. H 20m (65ft), S 10m (33ft). Hardy/Z 4–9. **'Scanlon'** is a slow-growing, densely upright form with good autumn colour. H 15m (50ft), S 5m (15ft).

**A. shirasawanum 'Aureum'**
**Moonglow maple**
A round-headed, slow-growing tree, with distinctive butter-yellow

*Acer palmatum* 'Rubrum'

leaves, which turn red in autumn. It needs some sun to colour the foliage but can scorch in full sun. H and S to 6m (20ft). Hardy/Z 6–8.

## AESCULUS
**Horse chestnut, buckeye**
A spectacular show of late-spring flowers is just one of the attributes of these majestic trees. Most are for big gardens only, although *A. pavia* is well worth considering for a smaller plot. *Cultivation* Grow in moist, fertile, well-drained soil in full sun.

**A. hippocastanum**
**Common horse chestnut**
This giant of a tree, which is native to south-eastern Europe, has mid-green leaves. The white, candle-like flowers are spectacular in late spring. H 25m (80ft), S 20m (65ft). Hardy/Z 4–7.

**A. × neglecta 'Erythroblastos'**
**Sunrise horse chestnut**
This slender, slow-growing, conical hybrid has red leaf stalks and leaves that emerge cream and pink, then turn yellow before maturing green by midsummer. H 10m (33ft), S 8m (25ft). Hardy/Z 7–8.

**A. pavia**
(syn. *A. splendens*)
**Red buckeye**
A shrubby, North American species, this has mid-green leaves and upright panicles of bright red flowers in late spring to early summer. H 3m (10ft), S 2.5m (8ft). Hardy/Zone 6–9.

## ALNUS
**Alder**
One of the few genera adapted to boggy conditions, alders are often planted near to water.
*Cultivation* Alders will grow in any fertile soil in full sun.

**A. glutinosa**
**Common alder**
This species has purplish catkins (pussy willows) in late winter. Dark green leaves emerge from sticky buds in spring. H 25m (80ft), S 10m (33ft). Hardy/Z 4–7.

## AMELANCHIER
**June berry, snowy mespilus, serviceberry**
These are charming trees for the spring garden, the dainty flowers appearing around the same time as tulips. They also provide good autumn colour and fruits that will attract birds. They make good specimen trees but are small enough for a mixed planting.
*Cultivation* Grow in a lime-free soil in sun or light shade.

**A. × grandiflora 'Ballerina'**
A profusion of starry white flowers appears on this spreading, shrubby hybrid in spring. The leaves turn red and purple in autumn. H 6m (20ft), S 8m (25ft). Hardy/Z 4.

**A. lamarckii**
This beautiful small tree bears copper-red young leaves, which turn orange and red in autumn.

*Aralia elata*

The white spring flowers are followed by black berries. H 10m (33ft), S 8m (25ft). Hardy/Z 4–8.

## ARALIA
**Angelica tree**
The genus includes some of the most elegant and architectural trees for the small garden. The species described makes a good specimen, but it can also be used in mixed plantings when young.
*Cultivation* Grow in partial shade, but they will tolerate full sun if the soil is reliably damp.

**A. elata**
(syn. *A. chinensis* of gardens)
**Japanese angelica tree**
This has spiny stems and coarsely toothed leaves, which turn yellow, orange or purple in autumn. White flowers appear in late summer to autumn. H and S 10m (33ft). Hardy/Z 4–9.

*Aesculus hippocastanum*

Betula albosinensis var. septentrionalis

## ARBUTUS
### Strawberry tree, madroña, manzanita

A genus with many attractions, not the least of which are the charming, strawberry-like fruits that give the trees their common name. (The fruits are edible, if on the insipid side.) The lily-of-the-valley-like flowers, which appear at the same time as the ripening fruits, are also beautiful. Add peeling bark to the list of attractions, and the surprise is that they are not more widely planted. There are two main reasons for this: not all are reliably hardy, and some will grow well only in acid soil.
*Cultivation* Most strawberry trees need lime-free soil in a sheltered position; *A. unedo* tolerates lime.

### A. × andrachnoides

This evergreen hybrid has peeling, reddish-brown bark and clusters of small ivory-white flowers, which are borne between autumn and spring. Fruits appear only occasionally. H and S 8m (25ft). Hardy/Z 8–9.

Arbutus unedo 'Rubra'

### A. unedo

This evergreen species has a spreading, sometimes rather shrubby habit. It is native to south-eastern Europe and the Middle East. The white flowers appear in autumn, at the same time as the strawberry-like fruits from the previous year ripen. The red-brown bark, which peels in shreds, is also an attractive feature. H and S 6m (20ft). Borderline hardy/Z 8–9. The form 'Rubra' reaches the same size as the species, but has deep pink flowers.

## BETULA
### Birch

The genus includes some of the best garden trees. They are hardy and easy to grow in addition to being graceful and quick growing. Most have attractive, usually white, bark and good autumn leaf colour. They are among the most reliable trees for alkaline soils.
*Cultivation* Birches will grow in any fertile soil in sun or light shade; they also tolerate poor soil.

### B. albosinensis var. septentrionalis

In a genus renowned for the beauty of its bark, this form of *B. albosinensis* (Chinese red birch) is outstanding for that feature. Creamy white when young, on mature specimens (those 15 or more years old) it develops a pinkish bloom and peels to reveal a mahogany red underlayer. The oval leaves are deep green, turning yellow in autumn and persisting on the tree until early winter. In favourable conditions trees can exceed the dimensions indicated, but only after 20 years or so. H 10m (33ft), S 6m (20ft). Hardy/Z 6–8.

### B. ermannii
### Erman's birch, gold birch, Russian rock birch

The species is native to Russia (the Kamchatka peninsula), Japan and Korea, and is valued by gardeners because of its beautiful peeling white bark, which is sometimes tinged pink or cream. This feature is particularly apparent on multi-stemmed trees. H 7m (23ft) or more, S 4m (13ft) or more. Hardy/Z 5–8.

Betula utilis var. jacquemontii

The vigorous 'Grayswood Hill', which has an attractive conical habit of growth, has pure white bark. H 7m (23ft) or more, S 4m (12ft) or more.

### B. pendula
### (syn. B. alba, B. verrucosa)
### Silver birch

This familiar tree, which is native to Europe and northern Asia, has slightly drooping branches and greyish-white bark, which cracks attractively on mature specimens. It may not always be long-lived in gardens. H 25m (80ft), S 10m (33ft). Hardy/Z 3–8. Notable selections include 'Youngii' (Young's weeping birch), which is less vigorous and has more pendulous branches. H 8m (25ft), S 5m (15ft). Hardy/Z 3–8.

### B. utilis var. jacquemontii
### (syn. B. jacquemontii)

This naturally occurring variety of the Himalayan birch has white bark, which makes it an outstanding plant for the winter garden. The oval leaves turn yellow in autumn. Many of the plants sold in the trade under this name are raised from seed collected in the Himalayas, so habits and growth rates can vary, but most will not exceed the dimensions indicated in 20 years. H 12m (40ft), S 5m (16ft). Hardy/Z 6–8. Selected seedlings include 'Grayswood Ghost', which has glossy leaves, the fast-growing 'Jermyns', which has rounded leaves and large catkins (pussy willows), and 'Silver Shadow', which has large,

drooping, dark green leaves; all three forms have particularly brilliant bark. H 12m (40ft), S 5m (16ft).

## CATALPA
### Indian bean tree

Catalpas are among the most impressive flowering trees, bearing orchid-like flowers in mid- to late summer. The large, soft leaves are also appealing, particularly in the coloured-leaf forms. Suitable trees for sheltered, sunny gardens, they are hardier than is commonly supposed, although flowers are not always freely borne in cold areas. They can also be grown as foliage plants in mixed borders and cut back hard annually in spring, which produces luxuriant foliage, albeit at the expense of the flowers. The common name refers to the seedcases, which dangle from the branches from late summer onwards.
*Cultivation* Grow in any fertile soil in sun. Provide protection from strong winds.

### C. bignonioides
### Southern catalpa, smoking bean

Native to the south-eastern United States, this has long seed pods hanging from the branches in autumn. Its most striking feature, however, are the panicles of orchid-like flowers, which are white marked with yellow and purple-brown. A mature catalpa in full flower is an impressive sight in midsummer. The large, soft green leaves are also handsome, making this a highly valued shade tree in hot climates. Flowering is

Catalpa bignonioides 'Aurea'

*Cercidiphyllum japonicum var.*
*magnificum*

reliable only during hot summers.
H and S 15m (50ft). Hardy/Z
5–9. **'Aurea'** is less vigorous. The
soft yellow-green leaves, tinged
bronze as they unfurl in spring,
benefit from some shade from
direct sun. Given that this tree is
more reluctant to flower than its
parent, plus the fact that it is
slightly tender, in cool climates it
is best treated as a pollard or
coppice and enjoyed for its leaves
alone. H and S 10m (33ft)
unpollarded.

# CERCIDIPHYLLUM

The genus contains a single
species, which is native to western
China and Japan. It is a choice
tree for the garden grown for its
spectacular autumn foliage.
*Cultivation* These trees do best in
woodland conditions – in fertile
soil in light dappled shade – and
although they are tolerant of lime,
the best autumn colour occurs on
acid soil.

× *Citrofortunella microcarpa*

*C. japonicum* var. *magnificum*
(syn. *C. magnificum*)
**Katsura tree**
This rare Japanese upright species
has rounded leaves that turn
yellow, orange and red in autumn
and smell of toffee when they fall
to the ground. H 10m (33ft),
S 8m (25ft). Hardy/Z 5–9.

# CERCIS

All six species in the genus are
small trees, with rounded leaves
and pea-like flowers in spring.
*Cultivation* The trees need fertile
soil in a sunny, sheltered spot
where the late-spring flowers will
not be damaged by frosts.

*C. siliquastrum*
**Judas tree**
The connotations of the common
name (this is supposedly the tree
from which Judas hanged himself)
do not militate against its garden-
worthiness. The species, which is
native to south-eastern Europe
and south-western Asia, is quick-
growing and produces dark pink
flowers on the bare wood in
spring. The kidney-shaped, blue-
green leaves turn yellow in
autumn. The tree can be trained
against a wall. H and S 10m
(33ft). Hardy/Z 8–9. The
shrubby form *C. siliquastrum* f.
*albida* has white flowers and pale
green leaves.

# × CITROFORTUNELLA

The trees in this hybrid genus
(a cross between *Citrus* and
*Fortunella*) are easy to grow, being
hardier than most *Citrus*.
*Cultivation* Grow in neutral to
acid soil in full sun. Container-
grown plants can be clipped to
keep them within bounds.

× *C. microcarpa*
(syn. × *C. mitis*)
**Calamondin**
This evergreen tree bears fragrant
white flowers at the same time as
the fruits from the previous
season are ripening. H 3m (10ft),
S 2m (6ft). Half-hardy/Z 9.

# CORNUS
**Dogwood**
The dogwoods are among the best
trees for a small garden. Some are
grown for their overall appearance

*Cornus alternifolia 'Argentea'*

and hence make good specimens,
while others have striking spring
flowers and good autumn leaf
colour. The genus also includes
many shrubs and a few perennials.
*Cultivation* They need fertile soil,
preferably lime-free, in sun or
light shade. The species described
need neutral to acid soil.

*C. alternifolia*
(syn. *Swida alternifolia*)
**Pagoda dogwood, green osier**
This species from eastern North
America is usually grown in the
variegated form **'Argentea'** (syn.
'Variegata'), one of the most
beautiful of small trees. It has a
distinctive tiered habit, but it is
slow-growing and takes several
years to develop its characteristic

'wedding-cake' appearance.
Careful staking is necessary
initially to establish an upright
leader. H 3m (10ft), S 2m (6ft).
Hardy/Z 4–8.

*C.* **'Eddie's White Wonder'**
This conical tree or large shrub
has white flowers in late spring
and leaves that reliably turn
orange, red and purple in autumn.
H 6m (20ft), S 5m (16ft).
Hardy/Z 6–9.

*C. kousa*
White flowers in summer are
followed by red fruits on this
elegant species, native to Japan
and Korea. The wavy-edged leaves
redden in autumn. H 7m (23ft),
S 5m (16ft). Hardy/Z 5–8.

*Cercis siliquastrum*

Crataegus laevigata 'Crimson Cloud'

# CRATAEGUS
## Hawthorn

Despite their ubiquity as roadside plants, hawthorns make excellent garden trees, particularly in exposed situations and on poor, limy soils. They are tough and hardy and make excellent hedges, particularly in country gardens.
*Cultivation* Grow hawthorns in any fertile soil, preferably in full sun. They can be grown in exposed positions.

### C. laevigata
(syn. *C. oxyacantha*)
**Common hawthorn, may**
Widely seen as a hedgerow plant in northern Europe, this bears white flowers in spring. These are followed in autumn by red haws, a valuable food source for birds. H and S to 8m (25ft). Hardy/Z 5–8. 'Crimson Cloud' is a distinctive selection, producing brilliant red flowers with white centres, which are a strong contrast to the glossy,

Crataegus laevigata 'Paul's Scarlet'

dark green leaves. H and S 5m (16ft). 'Paul's Scarlet' is one of the most popular of the hawthorns, but its double, deep pink flowers, produced in vast quantities, are usually sterile and haws are seldom produced. H and S 5m (16ft). Hardy/Z 5–8.

### C. × lavallei 'Carrierei'
This spreading, densely branched hawthorn has glossy green leaves that turn red in late autumn and winter. Clusters of white spring flowers are followed by orange-red fruits. H 7m (23ft), S 10m (33ft). Hardy/Z 5–7.

### C. persimilis 'Prunifolia'
(syn. *C. prunifolia*)
A compact, spreading hawthorn of garden origin, this bears clusters of white flowers in spring, which are followed by bright red fruit. The glossy, deep green leaves are tinted orange and scarlet in autumn. H 8m (25ft), S 10m (33ft). Hardy/Z 6–7.

# EUCALYPTUS
## Gum tree, ironbark

A familiar sight in many urban areas, eucalyptus are widely planted as pollution-tolerant street trees. Although potentially very large, they respond well to pruning. The foliage of most species changes shape as the tree matures, the juvenile leaves being generally considered the more attractive. Cutting back stems regularly ensures that trees retain their youthful appearance.
*Cultivation* Grow in any well-drained soil in full sun. (Some sources specify acid soil, but many species tolerate chalk.)

### E. gunnii
**Cider gum**
This evergreen from Tasmania is one of the most versatile of garden trees. Not only can it be allowed to develop freely as a single- or multi-stemmed tree, but it can also be kept within bounds by hard pruning so that it can be grown as a shrub in a mixed border. Pruning also encourages the ready production of juvenile foliage, which is coin-shaped and a gleaming pewter grey. Unless cut back, mature trees can become unstable. H 20m (65ft), S 6m (20ft). Borderline hardy/Z 8–10.

### E. pauciflora subsp. niphophila
(syn. *E. niphophila*)
**Snow gum, alpine snow gum**
This slow-growing evergreen tree is grown for its brilliant, peeling, cream and grey bark, which is shown to best advantage when the plant is grown as a multi-stemmed tree. The bluish-grey juvenile leaves are oval; adult leaves are sickle shaped. To retain the juvenile foliage, treat as a pollard. H and S to 6m (20ft). Hardy/Z 9–10.

### E. perriniana
**Spinning gum**
An evergreen species from Australia, this has flaking, white,

Eucalyptus gunnii

Eucryphia glutinosa

green or grey bark and bluish-green, rounded juvenile leaves, while adult leaves are lance-shaped. It is best treated as a pollard. H 5.5m (18ft), S 2m (6ft). Borderline hardy/Z 9–10.

# EUCRYPHIA

These trees deserve to be better known. Not only are the myrtle-like flowers beautiful, but they also appear late in the season, when few other woody plants are flowering. A mature eucryphia in full flower is an impressive sight. Choose among the species carefully because some are particular as to soil type.
*Cultivation* Plant in neutral to acid soil in sun or light shade in a sheltered spot. *E. × nymansensis* 'Nymansay' tolerates chalk.

### E. glutinosa
**Nirrhe**
This slow-growing small tree or shrub from Chile is an excellent flowering tree for an acid site. The large white flowers cover the plant in mid- to late summer. In mild areas the tree is evergreen; in cold areas the leaves turn rich orange-red before falling in autumn. H 10m (33ft), S 6m (20ft). Hardy/Z 8–10.

### E. × nymansensis 'Nymansay'
This columnar, evergreen hybrid is better known than *E. glutinosa*, probably because it tolerates alkaline conditions and has fragrant flowers. H 5m (16ft), S 2m (6ft), ultimately probably larger. Borderline hardy/Z 8–9.

*Fagus sylvatica 'Purpurea Pendula'*

# FAGUS
## Beech

The 10 species in this genus have a number of uses. While most – magnificent though they are – grow too large for the average garden, some are more modest and make fine specimens. Beech also makes a splendid hedge. While not evergreen, the faded leaves hang on the branches over winter in a most appealing way. The autumn colour of all beeches can be spectacular.
*Cultivation* Grow in any soil except wet, sticky clays. Forms with coloured leaves do best in full sun, but other forms prefer light shade.

### F. sylvatica
#### Common beech

This large European species is widely planted in parks and large public gardens. It can be unstable as a large specimen and its branches are brittle, especially in strong winds. It is, however, the parent of a number of handsome

*Fortunella japonica*

selections. Those listed are both hardy/zone 4–7. The excellent **'Dawyck Gold'** is a narrow, conical, slow-growing tree with leaves that are bright yellow as they unfurl in spring, becoming paler by summer. The dead leaves are held on the tree over winter. For the best leaf colour, plant in a sunny position. H 6m (20ft), S 2m (6ft). **'Purpurea Pendula'**, the weeping copper beech, is popular as a specimen in gardens both for its elegant habit and its rich purple leaves, which turn red in autumn. H up to 5m (16ft) (but often less), S to 2.2m (7ft).

# FORTUNELLA
## Kumquat

The four or five species in the genus are popular for their orange-yellow fruits, which, unlike other types of *Citrus* (to which *Fortunella* is related), can be eaten whole. Kumquats are native to southern China, and they make good conservatory (porch) plants.
*Cultivation* In frost-free climates they will grow in any well-drained soil in full sun or light shade, but elsewhere they need protection from frost.

### F. japonica
(syn. *Citrus japonica*, *C. macrophylla*)
#### Marumi kumquat, round kumquat

This small evergreen tree or shrub carries fragrant white flowers from spring to summer. These are followed by edible, oval, golden-yellow fruits, each up to 4cm (1½in) long. When grown in a container under glass the dimensions will be smaller than indicated here. H 3m (10ft), S 1.5m (5ft). Tender/Z 9.

# GLEDITSIA

Few trees have the charm of gleditsias, which look graceful all year round. In areas where there are hot summers the stems turn almost black, creating a sensational contrast with the lime green leaves. They are excellent as specimens or underplanted with prostrate ceanothus.
*Cultivation* Grow in any well-drained soil in sun or light shade. They are tolerant of pollution.

*Gleditsia triacanthos 'Sunburst'*

### G. triacanthos
#### Honey locust

This popular species, from North America, is usually represented in gardens by **'Sunburst'**. The leaves of this cultivar are bright yellow on emergence, changing to pale green by the end of summer. This does best in a sunny position, where it can be sheltered from strong winds, and it is definitely a better choice for a small garden than the more vigorous *Robinia pseudoacacia* 'Frisia', which it super-ficially resembles. H 12m (40ft), S 10m (33ft). Hardy/Z 5–9.

# HIPPOPHÄE
## Buckthorn

These attractive small trees and shrubs make good windbreaks or barrier plantings, but they also combine well with other plants in mixed borders, providing a good

foil to flowering shrubs and herbaceous perennials.
*Cultivation* Buckthorns will grow in any well-drained soil, including sandy soil, in sun or partial shade. They are well adapted to coastal conditions and will withstand strong, salt-laden winds.

### H. rhamnoides
#### Sea buckthorn

The spiny shoots of this native of Europe and temperate Asia are clothed in long, silver-green leaves. Small yellow flowers in spring (almost lost among the branches) are followed by showier orange berries in autumn. Male and female flowers are borne on separate plants, so for reliable berrying, plant members of both sexes. H and S 6m (20ft). Hardy/Z 3–8. **'Freisendorf Orange'**, **'Hergo'** and **'Leikora'** are female; **'Pollmix'** is male.

# IDESIA

The genus, from China and Japan, contains only one species, an elegant, understated plant, which is probably at its best as a specimen in a minimalist-style garden or in light woodland.
*Cultivation* Idesias need neutral to acid soil in sun or light shade.

### I. polycarpa

This is an unusual, spreading tree, with heart-shaped leaves, usually tinged bronze as they open in spring. Male and female flowers are carried on separate plants, so for the bright red berries that are a feature on female plants in autumn, trees of both sexes must be grown. H and S up to 12m (40ft). Hardy/ Z 7–9.

*Hippophäe rhamnoides*

*Idesia polycarpa*

Ilex aquifolium 'J.C. van Tol'

# ILEX
## Holly

Indispensable plants in any garden for their healthy, glossy leaves, the hollies are either trees or shrubs depending on age and how they have been pruned (if at all). If you inherit a garden with a large holly, think twice before ousting it – it will undoubtedly be of venerable age. Holly also makes an excellent hedge. Berries will be produced only on females, which will need a pollinating male nearby, so choose carefully among the cultivars. (*I. aquifolium* 'J.C. van Tol' is self-pollinating.) Those listed here are evergreen.
*Cultivation* Grow in any fertile soil, in sun or light shade. Variegated forms produce their best leaf colour in full sun. They are tolerant of atmospheric pollution and wind.

### I. aquifolium
**Common holly, English holly**
Seedlings of the species, which is native to northern Africa and western Asia as well as to Europe, often appear in gardens, but the many cultivars generally make more attractive plants. The following selections are all hardy/Z 7–9. 'Aurea Marginata Pendula' is a slow-growing, rounded, weeping tree with purple stems and spiny, glossy, bright green leaves that are margined with creamy yellow. It is a female form, producing red berries in autumn. It is an outstanding plant for year-round interest. H and S up to 3m (10ft). The male **'Ferox Argentea'** carries very prickly dark green leaves margined with cream. H 6m (20ft), S 4m (13ft). **'J.C. van Tol'** is self-fertile, with bright red berries among the plain leaves. H 6m (20ft), S 4m ((13ft). **'Silver Milkmaid'**, a female cultivar, has an open habit and leaves with white margins. The berries are scarlet. H 6m (20ft), S 4m (13ft). **'Silver Queen'** (syn. 'Silver King'), which is a slow-growing male form, also has white-edged leaves. It has a dense, upright habit of growth. H 10m (33ft), S 4m (13ft).

## KALOPANAX

The genus, which is native to China, Korea, Japan and parts of Russia, contains a single species, which, while not exactly beautiful, nevertheless makes a striking statement in the growing season with its maple-like leaves and, in winter, its barbed branches.
*Cultivation* Grow in any fertile, well-drained soil either in sun or light shade.

### K. septemlobus
(syn. *Eleutherococcus pictus*, *E. septemlobus, Kalopanax pictus*, *K. ricinifolius*)
**Castor aralia, tree aralia**
This spreading tree has lobed, dark green leaves and large heads of small white flowers, which appear in autumn and are followed by small black berries. H and S 10m (33ft). Hardy/Z 5–9. The leaves of *K. septemlobus* var. *maximowiczii* are more deeply lobed. H and S 10m (33ft).

## × LABURNOCYTISUS

This curiosity would be a talking point in any garden, although it is not an entirely beautiful tree. It is a hybrid of *Chamaecytisus purpureus* and *Laburnum anagyroides*, grafted on to laburnum seedlings. It retains some of the characteristics of both its parents.
*Cultivation* Grow in any well-drained, moderately fertile soil in full sun.

### × L. 'Adamii'
This tree is grown for its laburnum-like flowers in late spring or early summer. Some are yellow (like laburnum), others purple (like *Chamaecytisus*), while a third group are purplish-pink, flushed yellow, all colours appearing simultaneously. H 8m (25ft), S 6m (20ft). Hardy/Z 6–8.

## LABURNUM
### Golden rain

These decorative trees with their long pendulous flowers have one drawback, which is a serious one for many gardeners: all parts of the plant are poisonous. Effective as they are as specimens, laburnums are at their most attractive when planted in avenues and trained as a tunnel. In a small garden, they can be very effective when planted as a pair and trained to make an archway.
*Cultivation* Plant in any well-drained soil in sun or light shade.

Kalopanax septemlobus var. maximowiczii

### L. × watereri 'Vossii'
This laburnum, a naturally occurring hybrid of *L. alpinum* and *L. anagyroides*, is one of the best-loved trees, with its racemes of golden-yellow flowers, which are followed by pea-like seed pods. Initially upright, it becomes more rounded on maturity. H and S 8m (25ft). Hardy/Z 6–8.

## LAURUS
### Bay laurel, sweet bay

The small genus, which contains two species, is a typical plant of the Mediterranean littoral. In colder areas bays are usually grown as shrubs, principally for their leaves, which, while not edible in themselves, can be used to flavour a variety of dishes. Bay looks effective in containers and incomparably stylish when arranged in pairs to frame a doorway. It is also a good choice for a seaside planting.
*Cultivation* Plant in any well-drained soil in sun or light shade.

Ilex aquifolium 'Aurea Marginata Pendula'

Laburnum × watereri 'Vossii'

Laurus nobilis

Choose a sheltered spot in all but the warmest gardens because cold, drying winds can kill it.

### L. nobilis
### Bay laurel
This handsome evergreen foliage plant has glossy mid- to dark green leaves. The flowers, produced in spring, are inconspicuous. Although it can be grown as a standard, it is often pruned to a shape, such as a cone or ball. H 12m (40ft), S 10m (33ft). Borderline hardy/Z 8–10.

## LIGUSTRUM
### Privet
Most of the privets are shrubs, planted mainly as hedging, although they are widely considered inferior to many other evergreen hedging plants. The genus includes a number of fine trees, which are tough, tolerant plants.
*Cultivation* Grow in any garden soil in sun or shade.

### L. lucidum
### Chinese privet
The evergreen species, which originates in China, Korea and Japan, has oval, glossy, dark green leaves and white flowers in late summer. It can be kept smaller than the dimensions shown by regular clipping. H and S 10m (33ft). Hardy/Z 7–10.

## MAGNOLIA
Sumptuous and stately, magnolias are among the most handsome of garden trees, as well as being among the hardiest. Drawbacks of some of the species are their enormous size, slowness of growth and reluctance to flower until some 20 or more years after planting. Fortunately, most of the modern selections are free from these vices. All magnolias make incomparable specimens and are best appreciated when grown in isolation. A few are shrubs.
*Cultivation* Grow in well-drained, humus-rich soil in sun or light shade. Not all magnolias will tolerate chalky (alkaline) soil.

### M. campbellii
The species is found in a range from the Himalayas to China. The large, cup-and-saucer-shaped flowers, to 30cm (12in) across and either white or pink, emerge in late winter to early spring before the glossy green leaves. H to 15m (50ft), S to 10m (33ft). Hardy/Z 7–9. The vigorous **'Charles Raffill'** is a well-known selection, with claret-stained, white flowers, opening from rose pink buds. H 10m (33ft), S 5.5m/18ft.

### M. 'Elizabeth'
A conical tree, this bears fragrant, goblet-shaped, pale yellow flowers, to 15cm (6in) across, in mid- to late spring. The leaves are attractively tinged with bronze when they emerge. This needs acid soil. H 10m (33ft), S 6m (20ft). Hardy/Z 5.

### M. grandiflora
### Bull bay, laurel magnolia
One of the few evergreen magnolias, the species is native to the south-eastern United States. Sadly, it is less hardy than some other species. In an open situation, it makes a magnificent, broadly conical tree, with long, glossy, dark green leaves and citrus-scented, waxy-textured, creamy, white, cup-shaped flowers, which are borne in late summer. It is tolerant of lime, and it may be grown against a wall in cold areas. H 18m (60ft), S 15m (50ft), less when wall-trained. Borderline hardy/Z 7–9. The selection **'Victoria'** is hardier than the species but has smaller flowers. The leaves are brownish-red beneath. Hardy/Z 6.

Magnolia campbellii

### M. 'Heaven Scent'
This lovely spreading tree hybrid bears a profusion of fragrant, goblet-shaped, white flowers, heavily flushed with deep pink outside, from mid-spring to early summer. The leaves are glossy dark green, lighter green beneath. This needs to be planted in acid soil. H 10m (33ft), S 6m (20ft). Hardy/Z 5.

### M. 'Pickard's Schmetterling'
### (syn. M. 'Schmetterling')
A spreading tree, this bears goblet-shaped, rich pinkish-purple flowers in mid-spring. The flowers open as the leaves emerge. H 10m (33ft), S 6m (20ft). Hardy/Z 5.

### M. × soulangeana
The hybrid of *M. denudata* and *M. liliiflora* has given rise to a large range of garden-worthy plants, all with goblet-shaped

Magnolia × soulangeana 'Amabilis'

Magnolia 'Pickard's Schmetterling'

flowers from mid-spring and a candelabra-like habit as they mature. The plants are moderately tolerant of lime. The following are all hardy/Z 5–9. The slow-growing **'Amabilis'** has pure white flowers. H and S to 6m (20ft). The flowers of the conical **'Brozzonii'** are heavily flushed with purple on the outside and white within. They are produced over a long period from mid-spring to early summer. H and S to 8m (25ft). The large flowers of **'Rustica Rubra'** (syn. 'Rubra') are a dramatic deep purple. H and S to 6m (20ft).

### M. sprengeri
This slow-growing species, which is native to China, carries large, cup-shaped, white or pink-tinged flowers in early spring before the leaves appear. It has a compact habit. H 20m (65ft), S 10m (33ft). Hardy/Z 7–9.

Magnolia sprengeri

Malus 'Evereste'

Mespilus germanica 'Nottingham'

## MALUS
### Crab apple

As well as a plethora of fruit-bearing trees (forms of *Malus domestica*), this genus includes a number of trees of purely ornamental value, although even with these it is worth bearing in mind that the fruits, small and hard though they are, can be cooked or made into jellies. These ornamental trees are smaller than the flowering cherries, to which they are, therefore, a useful alternative, and, having a more 'rustic' appearance, they suit cottage-style gardens.
*Cultivation* Grow in any ordinary, fertile garden soil which is not too wet, in sun or light shade.

#### M. coronaria
##### Wild sweet crab apple

The species, native to North America, is usually represented in gardens by the form **'Charlottae'**, an attractive small tree. Fragrant, semi-double, pink flowers are borne in late spring, and these are followed by yellowish-green fruits. The leaves take on good autumn colour. H and S 9m (30ft). Hardy/Z 5–8.

#### M. 'Evereste'

In spring this conical small hybrid bears a profusion of large white flowers, opening from reddish-pink buds. The fruits, which develop in autumn as the leaves turn yellow, are bright orange to red. H 7m (23ft), S 6m (20ft). Hardy/Z 4.

#### M. floribunda
##### Japanese crab apple

A spreading species from Japan, this bears pale pink flowers in late spring and small yellow fruits in autumn. H and S 10m (33ft). Hardy/Z 5–8.

#### M. 'John Downie'

This is one of the finest crab apples, and the best for making jelly. The cup-shaped, white flowers, borne in late spring, are followed by quantities of egg-shaped, orange and red fruits. H and S 6m (20ft). Hardy/Z 5–8.

#### M. × robusta 'Red Sentinel'

This hybrid produces a wonderful display of deep glossy fruits, which stay on the tree for most of the winter. H and S up to 7m (23ft). Hardy/Z 4–8.

#### M. tschonoskii

A notable introduction from Japan, this strong-growing, erect species bears pink-flushed, white flowers in spring. Fruits ripen to glossy yellow (with a red flush) in autumn as the leaves turn orange, red and purple. H 12m (40ft), S 7m (23ft). Hardy/Z 5–8.

#### M. × zumi 'Golden Hornet' (syn. M. 'Golden Hornet')

A small, rounded tree with deep pink buds that open to white flowers in late spring. They are followed by a good crop of bright yellow fruits. H 10m (33ft), S 8m (25ft). Hardy/Z 5–8.

## MESPILUS
### Medlar

Although medlars have been known since the Middle Ages, they are not grown commercially, so most people are unaware of the unique delights of the fruits, which are edible only once they have been frosted (or 'bletted') on the plant. The flowers, in late spring, are also attractive. The one species in the genus makes a charming specimen.
*Cultivation* Grow in well-drained soil in sun or light shade.

#### M. germanica

This medlar is found growing wild in forests and woodlands in south-eastern Europe and south-western Asia. The white flowers, borne in late summer, are followed by rounded brown fruits. As an added bonus, the leaves turn yellow-brown in autumn. H 6m (20ft), S 8m (25ft). Hardy/Z 6–9. The most widely grown selected form is **'Nottingham'**, which is less thorny than the species and has larger leaves.

## MORUS
### Mulberry

These handsome trees are sometimes found in old cottage gardens: they can live for several hundred years. Although the raspberry-like fruits are edible, mulberries are grown more for their stately overall appearance.
*Cultivation* Mulberries need fertile, humus-rich soil in full sun. For the best fruiting, provide some shelter from strong winds.

#### M. alba
##### White mulberry

The shiny, heart-shaped leaves of this mulberry turn yellow in autumn as the fruits ripen from white through red to black. The species is native to China. H and S 10m (33ft). Hardy/Z 5–9. **'Pendula'** is a weeping form, ideal for a smaller garden. Unfortunately, it does not fruit freely. H 3m (10ft), S 5m (16ft). Hardy/Z 5–9.

Morus alba 'Pendula'

## PAULOWNIA

Only one species of this fairly small genus of deciduous trees is at all common, and the climate of your garden will determine how you grow it. Where summers are long and hot, it can make an excellent specimen, but in colder areas, where it is less likely to flower, it is best treated as a pollard, when the huge leaves make it an exotic-looking foliage plant for a mixed border.
*Cultivation* This needs well-drained fertile soil in full sun with shelter from wind.

#### P. tomentosa
##### Foxglove tree, empress tree, princess tree

The most usual common name of the species, which is native to central and western China, derives from the upright spires of foxglove-like, mauve flowers. Unfortunately, the overwintering flower buds are generally killed by frosts in cold climates. In areas with hard winters, therefore, it is usually best enjoyed for the hairy young shoots and leaves and cut

Paulownia tomentosa

Populus alba

back hard annually in early spring. The leaves on coppiced plants will be up to 60cm (2ft) across. H to 12m (40ft), S 10m (33ft) (uncoppiced). Hardy/Z 6–9.

## POPULUS
### Poplar, aspen, cottonwood
Lombardy poplars are a familiar roadside tree in Europe, but the genus contains many other handsome species, although the majority are suitable only for larger gardens. Poplars are fast growing and are useful for providing a barrier in a relatively short time. All have invasive roots, however, so take care not to plant them near buildings whose foundations they could damage.
*Cultivation* Most poplars will grow in any garden soil, including wet, sticky clay (as long as it is not waterlogged), in an open position.

### P. alba
### White poplar, abele
The species, from central and southern Europe, central Asia and northern Africa, is recognizable from the white, woolly undersides of the leaves (turning yellow in summer), which create a charming effect as they flutter in the breeze. H to 40m (130ft), S 15m (50ft). Hardy/Z 4–9. **'Richardii'** is a more compact form, with leaves that are golden-yellow above and white beneath. H 15m (50ft), S 12m (40ft).

### P. × candicans 'Aurora'
This decorative, slow-growing hybrid forms a pillar-like tree with oval leaves that are splashed with white, cream and pink. Some shelter is desirable if the leaves are not to scorch. Pollarded, it makes a pretty specimen in a small garden. H 15m (50ft), S 6m (20ft). Hardy/Z 5–9.

### P. nigra
### Black poplar
Although handsome, the species is eclipsed in popularity by the selected form **'Italica'** (Lombardy poplar), an elegant, narrowly columnar tree. It tends to be short-lived in cultivation and seldom reaches the dimensions indicated. H 30m (100ft), S 5m (16ft). Hardy/Z 3–9.

*Prunus* 'Pandora'

## PRUNUS
### Ornamental cherry
This large genus contains evergreens and deciduous plants, shrubs as well as trees. Apart from the fruiting varieties (cherries, plums, apricots, peaches and almonds), there are a huge number of ornamental ones, many being hybrids of Japanese origin. A cherry orchard is a spectacular sight when in flower in spring, and an ornamental cherry should be among the first choices for a flowering specimen.
*Cultivation* Grow ornamental cherries in any well-drained, moderately fertile soil in full sun. A little lime seems to suit them.

### P. 'Amanogawa'
### (syn. P. serrulata 'Erecta')
This is an upright ornamental cherry with, usually, semi-double, shell-pink flowers in late spring. The leaves, which are tinged with bronze when young, redden in autumn. It is an ideal specimen for a small garden, but is also effective when planted in pairs or

*Prunus* 'Hillieri'

avenues. H 8m (25ft), S 4m (13ft). Hardy/Z 6–8.

### P. 'Hillieri'
A spreading tree, this hybrid bears clusters of soft pink flowers in mid-spring. H and S to 10m (33ft). Hardy/Z 6.

### P. 'Okame'
This cherry is laden with clusters of carmine-pink flowers in spring. The leaves turn orange and red in autumn. H 10m (33ft), S 8m (25ft). Hardy/Z 5–8.

### P. 'Pandora'
This makes a spreading tree, with deep pink buds in early spring opening to paler pink flowers. Good autumn leaf colour adds to its attractions. H 10m (33ft), S 8m (25ft). Hardy/Z 6–8.

### P. sargentii
### Sargent cherry
A spreading species from Japan, Korea and Russia whose pale lilac-pink flowers are followed by cherry-like fruits that ripen to a glossy crimson. The leaves are a magnificent crimson and orange in autumn. It may grow too large for most gardens. H 25m (80ft), S 20m (66ft). Hardy/Z 5–9.

*Prunus* 'Shirofugen'

### P. serrula
### (syn. P. tibetica)
### Tibetan cherry
This species from western China is usually planted for its gleaming mahogany red bark which peels off in strips to produce an eye-catching feature in winter. Site where the tree will be well lit by winter sun. H and S 10m (33ft). Hardy/Z 6–8.

### P. 'Shirofugen'
One of the best of the cherries, this makes a spreading tree. The abundant double white flowers, which open from pink buds and age to pink, are fragrant. They may not appear until early summer. H 8m (25ft), S 10m (33ft). Hardy/Z 6–8.

### P. 'Spire'
### (syn. P. 'Hillieri Spire')
This upright, vase-shaped tree is a good choice for a small garden, and a possible alternative to the roughly similar 'Amanogawa'. It has pale pink flowers, which appear with the leaves in mid-spring, and good autumn colour. H 10m (33ft), S 7m (23ft). Hardy/Z 6–8.

### P. × subhirtella 'Autumnalis'
### Autumn cherry
This cultivar, which was developed in Japan, is probably the finest winter-flowering tree, producing flushes of pink-tinged white flowers throughout winter, during mild spells. The peak display usually occurs right at the end of winter, shortly before the equinox. The leaves turn yellow in autumn. H and S to 8m (25ft). Hardy/Z 6–8.

*Prunus* × *subhirtella* 'Autumnalis'

## PTEROCARYA
### Wingnut
This Asiatic genus consists
of towering trees that make
handsome specimens where there
is lots of space. The common
name relates to the winged seeds,
which dangle in strings from the
branches in autumn.
*Cultivation* Wingnuts need fertile,
well-drained soil in sun, in a
position where they will not be
exposed to late frosts, which can
damage young foliage.

### P. stenoptera
### Chinese wingnut
A fast-growing tree, this is particularly happy near water. Once
mature, it produces greenish-
yellow catkins (pussy willows)
in early summer. The glossy green
leaves turn yellow in autumn at
the same time as the winged nuts
develop. H 30m (100ft), S 15m
(50ft). Hardy/Z 7–9.

## PYRUS
### Pear
"Pears for your heirs" is a familiar
saying among the gardening
fraternity – in other words,
fruiting varieties will not produce
any worthwhile crops until some
years after you have planted them.
Apart from the fact that this is
not strictly true, the genus does
include a number of attractive
ornamental trees, which reward
the gardener from the word go.
*Cultivation* Grow in fertile, well-
drained soil in sun or light shade.

Pyrus calleryana 'Chanticleer'

Pyrus elaeagnifolia

### P. calleryana
### Chinese pear, callery pear
This Chinese species is usually
represented in cultivation by the
selection **'Chanticleer'**, a conical
ornamental tree with white
flowers in spring followed by
inedible brown fruits. The leaves
redden attractively in autumn.
H 15m (50ft), S 6m (20ft).
Hardy/Z 5–8.

### P. elaeagnifolia
A dainty specimen when young,
this is an unusual species from
Asia Minor that deserves to be
better known. Its thorny branches
are covered with attractive, grey-
felted leaves. White flowers in
spring are followed by green
fruits. H 12m (40ft), S 8m
(25ft). Hardy/Z 5–9.

### P. salicifolia 'Pendula'
### Weeping willow-leaved pear
This is the form of the species
that is, deservedly, most
commonly encountered, and it
makes a delightful and elegant
specimen in a small garden. The
narrow, silver-grey leaves are borne
on pendulous branches, and
creamy white flowers appear in
spring. H 5m (16ft), S 4m
(13ft). Hardy/Z 5–9.

## QUERCUS
### Oak
All the oaks are magnificent trees,
and you shouldn't be put off by
their final size. They stay small
for quite a long time and can be
pollarded to keep them within
bounds, even if this prevents them
from achieving their full

Quercus ilex

splendour. Oak trees are also
important for wildlife, providing
shelter for an enormous range of
insects, birds and small mammals.
*Cultivation* Oaks should be grown
in ordinary, well-drained soil,
preferably in a sunny, open site.
They tolerate light shade, but
need space to expand.

### Q. ilex
### Holm oak
This majestic evergreen does
particularly well in coastal
situations. The variable leaves,
often lance-shaped are silver-grey
when young, darkening to a glossy
green as they age. H 25m (80ft),
S 20m (65ft). Borderline
hardy/Z 7–9.

### Q. robur
### (syn. Q. pedunculata)
### Common oak, English oak
The large species has the
characteristically lobed leaves and

clusters of acorns in autumn.
H 35m (120ft), S 25m (80ft).
Hardy/Z 5–8. More manageable
in smaller gardens are some of the
selections, including the shrubby
**'Compacta'**, which is very slow
growing. H 5m (16ft), S 4m
(13ft). Also slow growing is
**'Concordia'** (golden oak), a
small, rounded form carrying
bright yellow-green leaves in
spring. H and S 10m (33ft).
The neatly upright **'Hungaria'**
resembles *Populus nigra* 'Italica'
(Lombardy poplar) in outline.
H 9m (30ft), S 1.5m (5ft).

## ROBINIA
These handsome trees are often,
rather ill-advisedly, recommended
for small gardens. Most make
quite large plants and grow rapidly.
A safer bet if space is at a premium
is the shrubby *R. hispida* (rose
acacia) at 2.5m (8ft) in height.
*Cultivation* These trees need well-
drained soil in a sunny, sheltered
spot. Avoid excessively windy
sites: the branches are brittle and
snap easily.

### R. pseudoacacia
### False acacia, black locust
The species from the United
States is less widely grown than
the selected form **'Frisia'**, a
golden-leaved variety, which has
become one of the most popular
of all garden trees, although it

Quercus robur

can eventually grow quite large. Unlike other yellow-leaved trees and shrubs, it holds its colour well through the summer, making a splendid foil for purple-leaved shrubs. The shoots are very thorny and brittle. H 15m (50ft), S 8m (25ft). Hardy/Z 4–9. At the other end of the scale, **'Lace Lady'** is a compact, even bonsai-like form, which is good for a container. H and S 45cm (18in).

## SALIX
### Willow
The genus contains creeping shrubs as well as some quite large trees. Willows offer a variety of attractions for the garden. Many are grown for their catkins (pussy willows) or brightly coloured young shoots – regular annual or biennial hard pruning ensures a good supply of these – and weeping varieties look attractive growing at the water's edge. Some willows are also prized for their handsome summer foliage.
*Cultivation* Willows need reliably moist soil, ideally in full sun.

### S. alba
#### White willow
The fast-growing species, from Europe and western Asia, is a spreading tree with a large number of garden forms, some with coloured stems, which are best coppiced or pollarded. H 25m (80ft), S 10m (33ft), but considerably less if cut back hard annually. Hardy/Z 2–8. **'Hutchinson's Yellow'** has clear golden-yellow stems. *S. alba* subsp. *vitellina* **'Britzensis'** (scarlet willow, coral-bank willow) has brilliant orange-scarlet shoots. *S. alba* var. *sericea* (syn. *S. alba* 'Splendens'; silver willow) is also best if cut back hard, but in this case to create a vase-like clump of silvery foliage.

### S. babylonica var. pekinensis 'Tortuosa'
(syn. *S. matsudana* 'Tortuosa')
This bizarre tree is grown exclusively for the interest of its twisted stems, at their most striking in winter. H 15m (50ft), S 8m (25ft). Hardy/Z 5–8.

### S. caprea 'Kilmarnock'
(syn. *S. caprea* var. *pendula*)
#### Kilmarnock willow
This is a weeping miniature, with cascades of silver-white catkins in late winter. The tree is created artificially by grafting a prostrate plant on to rootstocks of varying height. H 1.5–2m (4–6ft), S 2m (6ft). Hardy/Z 5–8.

### S. daphnoides
#### Violet willow
The species, an upright, fast-growing tree, is found from

*Robinia pseudoacacia 'Frisia'*

Europe to central Asia. The young shoots are purple. H 8m (25ft), S 6m (20ft). Hardy/Z 5–9. The superior selection **'Aglaia'** has bright red shoots and silvery catkins before the dark green leaves appear. H 8m (26ft), S 6m (20ft).

### S. 'Erythroflexuosa'
(syn. *S.* 'Golden Curls', *S. matsudana* 'Tortuosa Aureopendula')
This spreading tree has twisting stems and leaves, which are useful in flower arrangements. Pale yellow catkins appear in spring. It can be kept smaller by regular cutting. H and S 5m (16ft). Hardy/Z 5–9.

### S. integra 'Hakuro-nishiki'
(syn. *S.* 'Albomaculata')
This willow is actually a shrub that is usually sold grafted on to a clear stem to create a round-headed miniature tree. The leaves, which follow the slender catkins, are strikingly variegated with pink and cream. They keep a good colour well into summer. This graceful tree is a good choice for a container. The height varies according to the rootstock. H to 1.5m (5ft), S to 1m (3ft). Hardy/Z 5–8.

### S. × sepulcralis var. chrysocoma
(syn. *S.* 'Chrysocoma')
#### Golden weeping willow
The fast-growing weeping willow is possibly the most familiar of all willows, and it is an evocative sight when the tips of its arching branches trail in water. It is equally attractive when bare in winter as when it is clothed in its bright green, lance-shaped leaves in summer. H and S 15m (50ft). Hardy/Z 6–8.

*Salix integra 'Hakuro-nishiki'*

Sophora microphylla

Sorbus mougeotii

Sorbus scalaris

# SOPHORA

An interesting genus, *Sophora* contains both deciduous and evergreen trees and shrubs and some perennials. In many ways they are plants for the connoisseur, and they do look rather exotic with their wisteria-like flowers. They are good as specimens or, in cold areas, trained against a warm wall.
*Cultivation* Grow sophoras in fertile, well-drained soil in a sunny, sheltered spot.

## S. japonica
### Japanese pagoda tree, Chinese scholar tree
The tree, which is native to China and Korea, is grown for its late summer flowers, which are white and scented, although these appear only after a hot summer and on mature trees. The leaves turn yellow in autumn. H 30m (100ft), S 20m (65ft). Hardy/Z 5–9.

## S. microphylla
### (syn. *Edwardsia chilensis*)
### Kowhai
A spreading species from New Zealand and Chile, this evergreen tree bears rich yellow, pea-like flowers in mid- to late spring, followed by dangling seed pods. Train against a warm wall in frost-prone areas. H and S 8m (25ft). Borderline hardy/Z 8–10.

# SORBUS
## Rowan
The rowans are splendid plants for cold gardens. They are hardy and provide a valuable food source of berries for birds in winter. Attractive flowers and outstanding autumn colour add to their appeal.
*Cultivation* Grow in any well-drained soil in sun or light shade. Most rowans tolerate winds and urban pollution.

## S. aria
### Whitebeam
A large number of cultivars have been developed from this European species. **'Lutescens'** has a more conical habit than the species and is thus better suited to small gardens. The leaves are covered in creamy-white hairs and are particularly brilliant as they emerge in spring. The heads of white flowers that appear in late spring are followed by dark red berries. H 10m (33ft), S 8m (25ft). Hardy/Z 6–8.

Sorbus aria 'Lutescens'

## S. aucuparia
### Mountain ash, rowan
The species, which is a conical to rounded tree with good autumn colour, is found in Europe and Asia. **'Sheerwater Seedling'** is a narrowly upright selection with white flowers in spring followed by orange berries. The leaves turn red or yellow in autumn. H 10m (33ft), S 5m (16ft). Hardy/Z 4–7.

## S. cashmiriana
### Kashmir rowan
Native to the western Himalayas, this is a light, airy tree with finely toothed greyish-green leaves. The pink-flushed flowers are followed by round white berries, which remain on the tree after the leaves have fallen. H 4m (13ft), S 3m (10ft). Hardy/Z 5–7.

## S. commixta
This compact tree, from Korea and Japan, is generally grown in the form **'Embley'**, which fruits

Sorbus cashmiriana

rather more freely. The white spring flowers are followed by an abundance of brilliant orange-red berries at the same time as the leaves turn red. H 10m (33ft), S 7m (23ft). Hardy/Z 6–8.

## S. 'Joseph Rock'
This upright hybrid has white flowers in spring followed by bright yellow fruits in autumn as the leaves colour brilliant red. This is the best yellow-fruited variety, but is susceptible to fireblight. H 10m (33ft), S 7m (23ft). Hardy/Z 7–8.

## S. mougeotii
This unusual small tree or shrub is native to mountainous regions of northern Europe. The broad leaves have greyish hairs on their undersides. The fruits, sometimes lightly speckled, turn red in autumn. H 4m (13ft), S 3m (10ft). Hardy/Z 6–7.

## S. 'Pearly King'
The glossy dark green foliage of this spreading hybrid colours yellow or red in autumn. White flowers in spring are followed by pinkish berries. H and S 6m (20ft). Hardy/Z 6–8.

## S. sargentiana
### Sargent's rowan
Native to south-western China, this rowan is one of the most outstanding members of the genus. The large, crimson, sticky leaf buds make a strong statement in late winter, emerging as matt green, feathery leaves that turn brilliant orange-red in autumn. Masses of red berries develop from the clusters of white spring flowers. H and S 10m (33ft). Hardy/Z 7–8.

Sorbus thibetica 'John Mitchell'

## S. scalaris
### (syn. S. aucuparia var. pluripinnata)
### Ladder-leaf rowan
This Chinese species makes a spreading tree or large shrub, with glossy green leaflets that turn red and purple before they fall in autumn. The white flowers, which appear in late spring to early summer, are followed by red berries. H and S to 10m (33ft). Hardy/Z 6–8.

## S. thibetica 'John Mitchell'
### (syn. S. aria 'Mitchellii')
A notable selection of a Chinese species, this has leaves that are covered with white hairs on their undersides in spring, making a brilliant effect in the wind. They turn yellow in autumn, when the green berries ripen to red. H 20m (65ft), S 3m (10ft). Hardy/Z 5–7.

## S. vilmorinii
### Vilmorin's rowan
An outstanding specimen for a small garden, this tree is native to south-western China. Arching branches carry glossy green, fern-like leaves, which turn red and purple in autumn. The white flowers, produced in late spring to early summer, are succeeded by berries that are initially red but turn to white flushed with pink as winter advances. H and S 5m (16ft). Hardy/Z 6–8.

## STYRAX
These graceful trees are delightful, but the cultivation requirements restrict their use to woodland gardens.
*Cultivation* These trees need fertile, well-drained, humus-rich, lime-free soil in light shade with shelter from wind and late frosts.

Sorbus vilmorinii

## S. japonicus
### Japanese snowbell
An elegant species from China, Korea and Japan, this bears fragrant, bell-shaped white flowers in summer. The leaves turn yellow or red in autumn. H 10m (33ft), S 8m (25ft). Hardy/Z 6–8.
'Pink Chimes', with pink flowers with yellow stamens, is rare and worth looking out for. H 9m (30ft), S 7m (23ft).

## S. obassia
### Fragrant snowbell
The species, from China, Korea and Japan, has bell-shaped white flowers in summer amid dark green leaves that turn yellow in autumn. H 12m (40ft), S 7m (23ft). Hardy/Z 6–9.

## TILIA
### Lime, linden
Avenues of these long-lived trees are often a feature of stately homes and they were also commonly planted in town squares. Although the scent of the inconspicuous flowers is incomparable, their suckering habit made them unpopular for a while. The following selections are improvements that make excellent garden plants. Pollard or pleach them to restrict their size, albeit at the expense of the flowers.
*Cultivation* Grow lime trees in any moderately fertile, well-drained soil (preferably alkaline), in sun or light shade.

## T. cordata
### Small-leaved lime
The upright European species flowers in midsummer, and the heart-shaped leaves turn yellow in autumn. H 25m (80ft), S 15m (50ft). Hardy/Z 4–8.
'Winter Orange' is a desirable selection with golden-orange young stems that are a feature in winter. Cut back hard for the best winter display. H 25m (80ft), S 15m (50ft) (unpollarded).

## T. × europea
### (syn. T. intermedia, T. × vulgaris)
### Common lime
This long-lived and vigorous tree is a hybrid of T. cordata (small-leaved lime) and T. platyphyllos (large-leaved lime) and is too large for most gardens. It has dark green leaves and, in midsummer, clusters of pale yellow flowers. H 35m (120ft), S 15m (50ft). Hardy/Z 4–7. 'Wratislaviensis' is a more modest size, but its distinction is obvious only at maturity, when the bright yellow young leaves contrast vividly with the older green ones, creating a spectacular golden halo effect. H 20m (65ft), S 12m (40ft). Hardy/Z 5.

## TRACHYCARPUS
### Chusan palm, windmill palm
The hardiest of all palm trees, this remarkably tough evergreen makes an exotic-looking specimen.
*Cultivation* These palms will grow in any well-drained soil in sun or light dappled shade. It is important to provide shelter from strong winds.

## T. fortunei
### (syn. Chamaerops excelsa of gardens)
This evergreen is the only palm hardy enough to be grown outside in northern Europe. Its exact origins are unknown, but it is widely naturalized in China and Japan. It is grown for its stiff, pleated, fan-like leaves and, on mature specimens, its fibrous bark. It needs a position sheltered from cold winds, and young plants should be protected from the worst winter weather with horticultural fleece. In favourable situations it can grow larger than the dimensions indicated. H 4m (13ft), S 2.5m (8ft). Borderline hardy/Z 8–10.

Trachycarpus fortunei

# Conifers

The backbone of the garden, conifers are a diverse group of plants ranging from mighty giants such as the redwoods to dwarfs suitable for rock and scree gardens, troughs and windowboxes. Mainly evergreen, tough and hardy, they give year-round pleasure, providing backdrops to the transient flowers of summer and coming into their own in autumn and winter as their firm outlines begin to dominate the scene. Conifers embrace a wide range of colours, from blue-grey through many shades of green to vivid golden yellow.

This collection of conifers indicates something of the variety of textures and forms to be found in this fascinating plant group.

# What is a conifer?

Conifers are a fascinating group of plants. Within the plant kingdom, they belong to a division called gymnosperms – plants that produce naked seed. The word conifer itself means "cone-bearing". Other gymnosperms include palms and cycads. Conifers are assumed to be "lower" or more primitive plants than the angiosperms (all flowering plants), which produce covered seed.

Conifers do not flower in the conventional sense. In spring, male and female cones, not necessarily conspicuous at this stage, appear together with new shoots and leaves. Male and female cones can be borne on separate plants (such species are described botanically as dioecious) or on the same plant (monoecious). The cones are either held erect on the branches or hang down; in many cases, the female cones are a conspicuous and decorative feature. The males ripen and shed their pollen grains then wither and drop. The pollen adheres to the sticky surface of the female cone's ovule (the structure on which fertilization takes place). The female cone develops as a woody structure, whose scales part to release the ripe seed, between a few months to two and a half years after pollination, depending on the species. Conifer seed usually has a papery "wing" attached to it and is wind-borne.

A few conifer genera, however, generally assumed to be younger in evolutionary terms for this reason, have fleshy berries instead of cones, notably yew (*Taxus*), juniper (*Juniperus*) and the nutmeg yew (*Torreya*). Seed dispersal is through the gut of whatever animal feeds on the berries. Included here is the maidenhair tree (*Ginkgo biloba*), not strictly a conifer, but the sole survivor of a prehistoric division of plants.

Dwarf conifers planted close will gradually merge with one another to create a living sculpture. A spiky phormium provides strong contrast.

What distinguishes conifers from other plants in most people's eyes are the leaves, which are usually needle-like (botanically, linear or acicular) or scale-like. Most are stiff and hard and have a waxy surface that stops water evaporating – essential to the survival of the plant in freezing conditions. The needles are usually mid- to dark green, but some are yellowish and others have a glaucous bloom that makes them appear blue (extreme cold usually intensifies the blue). The leaves can be carried in two ranks opposite each other on the stem in a comb-like arrangement; alternative arrangements include whorls (three or more arising from a single point), spirals or loose bundles. Spruces (*Picea*) have leaves that are set singly, but densely; some species have decidedly bristly branches.

Most conifers grow strongly upright, naturally forming tall, slim obelisks or cone shapes, good examples being the Serbian spruce (*Picea omorika*) and the Japanese cedar

(*Cryptomeria japonica*). A few, such as the Kashmir cypress (*Cupressus torulosa* 'Cashmeriana'), have pendulous, "weeping" branches. Many, such as the Scots pine (*Pinus sylvestris*), become spreading with age, developing a characteristic broad crown. A few conifers, however, are prostrate plants that hug the ground. Some dwarf forms make dense mounds or cone shapes.

Many conifers are resinous and have sticky, aromatic stems. Though some are so well-clothed with foliage that the central trunk is barely visible, if at all, others shed their lower branches as they mature. This can reveal striking bark. The black pine (*Pinus jeffreyi*), for instance, has black bark that is deeply fissured (split) and greyish shoots.

Changes in the names given to conifers down the years have resulted in some potential confusion. Certain common names have remained in use in spite of revisions to the botanical name. Not all conifers commonly referred to as cedars belong to the genus *Cedrus*: botanically, the Japanese cedar is *Cryptomeria japonica*, and the white cedar *Thuja occidentalis*. The swamp cypress belongs to the genus *Taxodium*, not *Cupressus*. Nor are all firs *Abies*: some belong to *Pseudotsuga*.

## Conifers in the garden

These plants are – or can be – a mainstay of the garden, providing solid masses of colour (in rather subdued tones it is true) throughout the year. They earn their keep as a backdrop to showier but transitory spring- and summer-flowering plants, but come into their own when the earth is bare in winter and their shapes, textures and colours dominate. With heights ranging from 1m (3ft) or less for a dwarf conifer such as *Picea pungens* 'Globosa' to the 90m (300ft) of the giant redwood, there is a conifer for every garden. When choosing a small conifer, however, make sure that dwarf really does mean dwarf. Some varieties sold as dwarfs are actually better described as slow-growing: they stay reasonably compact for a number of years, but eventually make huge trees, and are a viable option only provided that you are prepared to discard them once they outgrow their allotted space.

Some of the bigger conifers make dramatic specimens provided there is adequate room for them. Many of the cedars (*Cedrus*) are excellent for this purpose, as also are the spruces (*Picea*) and cryptomerias. For a deciduous tree, the maidenhair tree (*Ginkgo biloba*) would take some beating, with its unique fanlike leaves that turn butter yellow in autumn, as well as its fissured bark.

Dwarf conifers planted close together will grow into each other, like a living sculpture, besides making excellent ground cover. Some

Conifers and heathers are a classic combination, and can provide welcome colour during the coldest months of the year.

form dense mats, particularly the prostrate junipers (*Juniperus*). In such plantings, they are often combined with heathers, a combination that should not be dismissed, despite its ubiquity: subtle effects can be achieved through a judicious mix of foliage and flower colours. Dwarf conifers are also excellent in rock gardens, providing height and structure among mat-forming

alpines, and are also suitable for troughs and containers, either with other dwarf plants or on their own.

Certain conifers, such as yew (*Taxus*), *Thuja* and false cypress (× *Cupressocyparis*), make excellent hedging plants that provide thick, impenetrable screens. The deciduous larch (*Larix*), however, makes a very effective windbreak, filtering the wind when the branches are bare.

Dramatically lit by the winter sun, this group of conifers exhibit a great variety of subtle colours at a time when the showier plants have finished their display.

Abies amabilis 'Spreading Star'

Abies balsamea 'Nana'

Abies grandis

Abies koreana

## ABIES
### Silver fir

These trees are found in Europe, North Africa, Asia and North America. Most grow too large for the average garden, but there are some dwarf and slow-growing forms. *A. koreana* is very popular, and there are compact forms of that which can be planted in borders and rock gardens. Most silver firs are conical.

**Cultivation** Silver firs will grow in most fertile soils, but not in shallow chalk or excessively dry soil. They like a reasonably open situation as long as it is not exposed to harsh winds.

### A. amabilis
**Pacific silver fir, beautiful fir**

The species is not widely grown, but the selection **'Spreading Star'** makes excellent ground cover, as its name implies. The glossy dark green needles smell of oranges when they are crushed, and the cones are deep purple. H 50cm (20in), S to 5m (16ft). Hardy/Z 6–8.

### A. balsamea
**Balsam fir, balm of Gilead**

Although this, too, is unfamiliar in gardens, it has a number of notable cultivars. All are hardy/ Z 4–7. Those classified as **Hudsonia Group** are dwarf trees, usually compact and rounded in form, although there is some variation. H to 60cm (2ft), S 1m (3ft). **'Nana'**, a good rock garden conifer, makes a dome-shaped

bush, which is tolerant of some shade. The aromatic, shiny green, needle-like leaves, shorter than those on the species, are arranged in two ranks on the stems; the cones are purplish-blue. H and S 1m (3ft).

### A. cephalonica
**Greek fir**

This rare tree is, at 30m (100ft) in height, unsuitable for most gardens, but the selection **'Meyer's Dwarf'** (syn. 'Nana') is more manageable, forming a low, spreading, flat-topped, shade-tolerant mound that is good in a rock garden. The needle-like leaves are glossy green and are shorter than on the species; the cones are greenish-brown and resinous. H 50cm (20in), S 1.5m (5ft) or more. Hardy/Z 6–8.

### A. forrestii
**Forrest fir**

This medium-sized to large conifer is from Yunnan, China, and it forms a narrow, cone-

shaped tree. The needles, carried in a comb-like arrangement, are dark green above and silvery white beneath; the cones are violet blue. This is a quick-growing tree, but it can be unreliable in areas where prolonged cold spells occur. H 10–20m (33–65ft), S 3–6m (10–20ft). Hardy/Z 7.

### A. grandis
**Giant fir, grand fir**

Native to western North America, this is one of the most majestic of the species, making a tall, slim, cone-shaped tree. The needle-like leaves smell of oranges when they are crushed; the cones ripen from green to reddish brown. Vigorous and quick-growing, this makes a handsome specimen tree. H to 80m (270ft), S to 8m (25ft). Hardy/Z 7–9.

### A. koreana
**Korean fir**

This is one of the most attractive of the silver firs, notably for its impressive violet cones that age to brown, which are produced even by young specimens. The needles are dark green with white undersides. Use it as a specimen tree or in mixed planting; it associates well with a wide range of garden plants. H 10m (33ft), S 6m (20ft). Hardy/Z 6–8.

### A. procera
(syn. *A. nobilis*)
**Noble fir**

From the western United States, this forms a cone-shaped tree, which matures to a broader, irregular obelisk. The greyish-green needles, sometimes with a bluish cast, are arranged in

Abies cephalonica 'Meyer's Dwarf'

Abies procera

two ranks. Mature trees have silvery-grey, fissured bark; the cones are green. The noble fir makes an attractive specimen, particularly when young; it is sometimes used as a Christmas tree. It is wind-tolerant and reliable at high altitudes. H to 45m (150ft), S to 9m (30ft). Hardy/Z 6–8.

## ARAUCARIA

The southern hemisphere is the main home of these striking trees, which have, triangular leaves that are larger than those of most conifers. Only *A. araucana* is in general cultivation, and mature specimens are often found in the gardens of Victorian houses, to which they bring an exotic flavour. Other species are well worth considering for a warm climate or as conservatory (porch) plants.
*Cultivation* Araucarias do well in a fertile soil in a sunny but sheltered position.

### *A. araucana*
### (syn. *A. imbricata*)
### Chile pine, monkey-puzzle-tree
This tree, which comes originally from Chile and Argentina, is slow growing at first but accelerates as it approaches maturity. It develops a broad, dome shaped crown on a tall trunk. The female trees have impressive spiky cones, almost pineapple-like in appearance: large and rounded, they take up to three years to ripen. H 25m (80ft), S 10m (33ft). Hardy/ Z 7–10.

### *A. heterophylla*
### (syn. *A. excelsa*)
### Norfolk Island pine)
A good conservatory (porch) plant when young, this will eventually outgrow most conservatories. It has an appealing tiered habit and fan-like branches. It occasionally serves as a Christmas tree in Latin countries. H to 45m (150ft), S 8m (25ft). Tender/Z 9–10.

## CALOCEDRUS
### Incense cedar
Incense cedars are a small genus of large conifers from the Far East and parts of western North America. Only the species described is widely grown.

*Cultivation* Any good soil in sun or light shade is suitable, but avoid exposed positions.

### *C. decurrens*
### (syn. *Heyderia decurrens, Libocedrus decurrens*)
Native to the western United States, this tree tends to vary in habit in gardens. In Europe it forms a tall, elegant spire, whereas specimens in the wild are often more spreading, since the habit influenced by climatic differences. The needles are glossy dark green. The maroon bark is fissured and flakes off, and the cones are yellowish-brown, aging to red-brown. It is resistant to honey fungus. H 30m (100ft) or more, S 6m (20ft) or more. Hardy/ Z 6–9.

## CEDRUS
### Cedar
A small genus, but perhaps containing the most magnificent of all conifers when mature. They are generally suitable only for large gardens but are worth considering if you are prepared to remove them once they start to get too large. They make ideal lawn specimens.
*Cultivation* Cedars are tolerant of most soils, including chalk (alkaline), and do best in a sunny open site.

### *C. atlantica*
### Atlas cedar
Originating from the Atlas Mountains in North Africa, this species is less common in gardens than some of the following selections. All are hardy/Z 7–9. 'Aurea' has bright, golden-yellow leaves. H 40m (130ft), S 10m (33ft). *C. atlantica* f. *glauca* (blue Atlas cedar) is one of the most handsome forms. Initially cone-shaped, it develops a more spreading crown. The needles, white when young but becoming bright glaucous blue, are arranged in clusters; the cones are light green. H to 40m (130ft), S to 10m (33ft). Plants in cultivation are normally sold under the name Glauca Group (indicating that they may vary). 'Glauca Pendula', also glaucous blue, has an arching leader and pendulous branches,

Cedrus atlantica 'Aurea'

Cedrus atlantica f. glauca

and it develops as a tent-like structure. It can be kept small by cutting back the central leader, which will persuade the horizontal branches to spread more widely (they may need support as a result). H and S to 15m (50ft), more or less.

### *C. deodara*
### Deodar cedar
This graceful, though potentially large, conifer originating from the Himalayas has a weeping habit. H 40m (130ft), S 10m (33ft). Hardy/Z 7–9. The more modestly sized 'Aurea' is an improvement, having the same broadly conical outline, with weeping branches,

but with the added distinction of bright yellow needles. A slow-growing tree, it is a good choice for a specimen in a small garden. H 5m (16ft), S 2.5m (8ft).

### *C. libani*
### Cedar of Lebanon
A tree for a stately home, this species originates from the near Middle East. It forms a conical tree that spreads with age, making a dramatic outline. The needle-like leaves are dark greyish-green; the cones are greyish-brown. Heavy snowfalls can cause problems to mature specimens, which may need surgery. H and S to 30m (100ft). Hardy/Z 7–9.

Cedrus atlantica 'Glauca Pendula'

Chamaecyparis lawsoniana 'Aurea Densa'

Chamaecyparis obtusa 'Nana Gracilis'

# CHAMAECYPARIS
## False cypress

This is a useful genus, from East Asia and North America, with a huge range of cultivars. There is a cypress for every garden, and the range includes giant forest trees as well as smaller forms that can be used as specimen trees, for hedging and as dwarf plants for the rock or scree garden.
*Cultivation* The soil should ideally be neutral to acid, but cypresses tolerate chalk. An open, sunny site is best.

### C. lawsoniana
(syn. *Cupressus lawsoniana*)
**Lawson cypress**
Although this conical tree, native to North America, is too large for most gardens, it has given rise to a bewildering number of cultivars of widely diverging habits. All are hardy/Z 6–9. Among the best dwarfs is **'Aurea Densa'**, which is ultimately rounded and one of the outstanding golden-leaved cultivars. H 2m (6ft), S to 1m (3ft). **'Bleu Nantais'** is another good blue-green, slow-growing, cone-shaped, dwarf cultivar. H and S to 1.5m (5ft). Both these have needle-like leaves that become scale-like. Taller varieties include the conical **'Ellwoodii'**, which is one of the most popular grey-green varieties. H 3m (10ft).

### C. obtusa
(syn. *Cupressus obtusa*)
**Hinoki cypress**
This Japanese species is less tolerant of lime than some species, and it is not widely planted, yielding to its many attractive cultivars. All are hardy/Z 4–8. **'Crippsii'** (syn. 'Crippsii Aurea') is a rich gold when grown in full sun,

Chamaecyparis lawsoniana 'Bleu Nantais'

making a fine specimen. H 15m (50ft), S 8m (25ft). **'Nana Gracilis'** is a dwarf, forming a rough pyramid. The scale-like, glossy green leaves are held in plates. H and S 2m (6ft) or more.

### C. pisifera
(syn. *Cupressus pisifera*)
**Sawara cypress**
Seldom found in cultivation, this Japanese species has given rise to a number of useful cultivars, all of which are hardy/Z 5–8. **'Boulevard'** is a popular selection, which will thrive in moist soil, and has bright silver-blue, feathery leaves. H 10m (33ft), S 4m (12ft). **'Filifera Aurea'** is a delightful conifer, with elegant, drooping, whippy branches. It is a good choice for a small plot because it is too slow-growing to pose a problem in most gardens, despite its eventual height. H 12m (40ft), S 5m (15ft).

# CRYPTOMERIA
## Japanese cedar

Despite the common name, this monotypic genus (there is only one species) is found in China as well as Japan, albeit in two distinct forms. Unusually among the conifers, Japanese cedars will tolerate pruning and can even be coppiced or trained. They look good in a Japanese-style garden, especially when they are grown to develop a gnarled trunk. Japanese cedars are among the most beautiful of all conifers.
*Cultivation* These trees will grow in any well-drained, preferably fertile, soil in sun or light shade.

### C. japonica
The species can reach a height of 25m (80ft) and is roughly columnar in shape. There are a huge number of cultivars available, suitable either as specimens or for use in rock gardens. All are hardy/Z 6–9. **'Bandai-Sugi'** is a slow-growing rounded dwarf form with blue-green foliage that bronzes well in cold winters. H and S 2m (6ft). The intriguing **'Cristata'** (syn. 'Sekka-sugi') has leaves that are curiously fused together, so that they resemble coral. H 8m (25ft), S 5m (15ft). **'Elegans'** is potentially large and

Cryptomeria japonica

will form a broad obelisk; the trunk is often attractively curved. The wedge-shaped leaves are soft and bluish-green when young, turning a rich, glowing bronze in autumn. Plants sold as **Elegans Group** may vary. H 20m (65ft), S 6m (20ft). **'Lobbii'** makes a handsome specimen in a large garden, forming a tall, slender, conical tree. The needle-like leaves are arranged in spirals. On mature specimens the thick, fibrous bark peels away. The cones age to brown. H 25m (80ft) or more, S to 6m (20ft).

Cryptomeria japonica 'Lobbii'

× *Cupressocyparis leylandii* 'Golconda'

× *Cupressocyparis leylandii* 'Leighton Green'

## × CUPRESSOCYPARIS

The chief value of this much maligned hybrid genus between *Chamaecyparis nootkatensis* and *Cupressus macrocarpa* lies in the trees' speed of growth. They are often planted as hedging where a pollution-resistant screen is needed quickly, and they do in fact make a splendid, tough, tight hedge, but only if cut regularly. Allowed to grow freely, they can soon get out of hand.
*Cultivation* Grow in any well-drained soil in sun or light shade.

### × *Cupressocyparis leylandii*
**Leyland cypress**
This is the hybrid most commonly sold as hedging, but it has a number of named varieties that can fulfil other purposes. All are hardy/Z 6–9. 'Golconda', one of the most decorative, forms a narrow cone shape. The scale-like leaves, carried in flattened sprays, are brilliant golden yellow; the cones are rounded. H to 35m (120ft), S to 5m (16ft), but tolerant of clipping. 'Leighton Green' develops as a tall, narrow, cone-shaped tree with bright green foliage. Although it is no less

suitable for hedging than other cultivars, it is perhaps best as a specimen because it produces a stronger central leader than the other cultivars and thus makes a slimmer, more elegant tree. The cones are freely produced. H to 35m (120ft), S to 5m (16ft).

## CUPRESSUS
**Cypress**
The characteristic tree of the Mediterranean, these are among the stateliest of conifers. They are not always easy to grow away from their native habitat, but they can be used as fine specimens or for hedging. They resent transplanting, so always look for young specimens rather than mature trees. The broadly similar *Chamaecyparis* is more reliable.
*Cultivation* Grow in any fertile, well-drained soil in full sun.

### *Cupressus arizonica* var. *glabra* (syn. *C. glabra*)
**Smooth cypress**
From the south-west United States, this is a good specimen where space in a garden is limited. It forms a regular cone shape. On young specimens the bark is

smooth, reddish-purple and flaking; it thickens and turns to greyish-brown on older trees. The scale-like leaves are glaucous bluish-grey and aromatic; the cones are dark brown. H to 15m (50ft), S to 5m (15ft). Hardy/Z 7–9.

### *C. macrocarpa*
**Monterey cypress**
From Monterey Bay, California, this was once widely used for hedging, but it has largely been superseded by × *Cupressocyparis leylandii*. Excellent cultivars have been developed from the species, however. Both those listed here are borderline hardy/Z 7–10. 'Donard Gold' forms an elegant obelisk that gradually becomes conical. The bright yellowish-green leaves are aromatic when crushed; the cones are rounded and maroon- to dark-brown. H to 30m (100ft), S to 12m (40ft). 'Goldcrest' is a highly desirable smaller version. H 5m (16ft), S 2.5m (8ft).

## GINKGO
**Maidenhair tree**
This deciduous tree is a living fossil, the sole survivor of a family of trees from 200 million years ago, once serving as a food source for dinosaurs during the Mesozoic era.
*Cultivation* Ginkgos are easy to grow in any moderately fertile soil in sun. They are also tolerant of urban pollution.

### *G. biloba*
This long-lived, ornamental deciduous tree makes an eye-catching specimen. Initially upright in habit, it becomes more spreading on maturity. Its distinction lies in its unique, fan-shaped, light green leaves, which turn butter yellow before falling in autumn. The fruits (not cones) are plum-like. H to 30m (100ft), S to 8m (25ft). Hardy/Z 5–9. The selection 'Fastigiata' (sentinel ginkgo) is narrower and more column-like. H 30m (100ft), S 5m (16ft).

*Cupressus arizonica* var. *glabra*

*Cupressus macrocarpa* 'Donard Gold'

*Juniperus chinensis 'Aurea'*

# JUNIPERUS
## Juniper

Junipers are usually represented in gardens by the cultivars and hybrids rather than by the species. Many are rock garden plants, while others look good grouped in island beds. They also do well in troughs and containers. On female plants, berry-like fruits develop and are used in the production of gin or to flavour game dishes.
*Cultivation* Any well-drained soil in sun or light shade is suitable. Junipers tolerate pruning.

### J. chinensis
#### Chinese juniper

The species is not notable in itself, but has given rise to many attractive cultivars. **'Aurea'** (Young's golden juniper), a slow-growing male selection that forms a narrow obelisk, has aromatic, dull golden-yellow leaves, which are wedge-shaped initially, but become scale-like as they mature. Many cones appear in spring, and the tree produces its best colour in sun. H to 20m (65ft), S to 6m (20ft). Hardy/Z 5–9.

### J. communis
#### Common juniper

This variable species is found throughout the northern hemisphere. Selections include **'Hibernica'** (Irish juniper), which makes a distinctive, narrow cone-shape, the foliage having a bluish-green cast; the berries, initially green, ripen to black over three years. H 3–5m (10–15ft), S 30cm (1ft). Hardy/Z 3–7.

### J. 'Grey Owl'
(syn. *J. virginiana* 'Grey Owl')

This is a splendid, spreading conifer, with silver-grey leaves and violet berries. H 3m (10ft), S 4m (13ft). Hardy/Z 3–9.

### J. horizontalis
#### Creeping juniper

A ground-hugging conifer from North America, the species forms a mat of greyish-green leaves, which are needle-like when young, becoming scale-like with age, with dark blue berries. H to 30cm (1ft), S 2m (6ft) or more. Hardy/Z 3–9. There are many attractive cultivars, all suitable for ground cover. **'Blue Chip'** (syn. 'Blue Moon') is glaucous blue. H 50cm (20in), S 3m (10ft). **'Douglasii'** is bluish-green, turning rich purple in autumn. H 30cm (1ft), S 3m (10ft). **'Golden Carpet'** is bright yellowish-green. H 30cm (1ft), spread 3m (10ft).

### Juniperus × pfitzeriana
(syn. *J.* × *media*)

This dwarf conifer is a hybrid probabl between *J. chinensis* and

*Juniperus communis* 'Hibernica'

*J. sabina* (the hybrid is thought to occur wild in Inner Mongolia). The cultivars listed are hardy/Z 4–9. **'Pfitzeriana Glauca'** forms a spreading, flat-topped bush clothed in glaucous blue to silver foliage. The berries are dark purple initially, developing a paler bloom as they ripen. The natural habit develops best if the plant is given sufficient space. H 1m (3ft), S 2m (6ft). **'Sulphur Spray'**, which has yellowish-green foliage, can become table-like on maturity. The dark purple berries develop a bluish bloom as they ripen. This is one of several plants in this hybrid group that are more or less indistinguishable from one another, including the widely grown **'Pfitzeriana Aurea'**. H 1m (3ft), S 2m (6ft).

# LARIX
## Larch

A genus of deciduous conifers with often brilliant autumn colour. Larches are usually grown as forestry trees but are useful for windbreaks.
*Cultivation* Grow in any moist garden soil in an open situation.

### L. decidua
#### European larch

As the common name implies, this is a European species, which develops a spreading crown with age. The pale green leaves turn red and yellow before falling in autumn. H to 30m (100ft), S to 6m (20ft). Hardy/Z 3–6.

### L. kaempferi
#### Japanese larch

Largely similar to *L. decidua*, this has purplish-red shoots that are conspicuous in winter, making it more garden-worthy. Both have a number of cultivars. H 30m (100ft) or more, S to 6m (20ft). Hardy/Z 5–7.

# METASEQUOIA
## Dawn redwood

The genus consists of a single species, one of the few deciduous conifers. It is a remarkable tree, known until 1941 only from fossilized remains. It is best by water, appreciating damp conditions, but is also tolerant of drier soils. It can be used as a specimen in a lawn.
*Cultivation* Fertile, preferably moist soil, in sun or light shade, suits the dawn redwood. On drier soils it is usually less vigorous.

### M. glyptostroboides

Native to China, this rapidly grows into a narrow cone-shaped, almost columnar tree. The feathery leaves are light green in spring, turning pink, red, then brown in autumn, the best colour

*Juniperus horizontalis*

Metasequoia glyptostroboides

being produced on mature trees.
H to 40m (130ft), S to 5m
(16ft). Hardy/Z 5–10.

## PICEA
### Spruce

Found throughout the northern
hemisphere, spruces are widely
planted as Christmas trees,
*P. abies* being the usual choice.
There is a wide range of garden
varieties, some with grey, yellow
or blue foliage. Most are
symmetrical in shape, and there
are many dwarf forms suitable
for rock gardens.
*Cultivation* Neutral to acid,
slightly moist soil is the ideal,
in an open site. Late frosts can
cause damage.

Picea abies 'Gregoryana'

### P. abies
#### Christmas tree, Norway spruce

The species, which is native to
Scandinavia, is a conical tree
and the traditional choice for
Christmas trees in Europe.
H 40m (130ft), S 6m (20ft).
Hardy/Z 3–8. **'Gregoryana'** is
an attractive dwarf selection that
makes an impenetrable mound
of dark green foliage. It is one
of the most compact of all dwarf
conifers. H and S 60cm (2ft).

### P. glauca
#### White spruce

Although the species, which
comes from North America, is
rarely grown in gardens, it is
represented in cultivation by its
many cultivars. Those listed here
are hardy/Z 3–6. *P. glauca* var.
*albertiana* **'Conica'** is a dwarf
selection of a naturally occurring
variant from the Canadian Rocky
Mountains. As its name suggests,
it makes a tight cone of bluish-
green, seldom bearing cones. H
to 4m (13ft), S 2m (6ft). The
slow-growing **'Alberta Globe'** is
another, even smaller clone, also
bluish-green but making a dome.
H and S 1m (3ft).

### P. omorika
#### Serbian spruce

This large conifer comes from
Bosnia and Serbia. Initially
narrowly conical, it matures to
a broad obelisk. The dark green
foliage sometimes has a bluish
cast; the bark cracks in squares
on maturity. The cones are purple,
ripening to brown. It tolerates
alkaline soils and urban pollution.
H 20m (65ft), S to 3m (10ft).
Hardy/Z 5–8.

### P. pungens
#### Colorado spruce

Originating in the United States,
the species is the parent of many
notable garden plants. All are
hardy/Z 3–8. **'Globosa'** forms
a dome or mound shape and has
bristle-like, glaucous green foliage,
arranged radially. H and S 1m
(3ft). **'Montgomery'** is silver-
blue, making a broad-based
cone. Slow-growing, it should
be among the first choices for
a specimen tree in a small garden.
H 1.5m (5ft), S 1m (3ft).

Picea pungens 'Globosa'

## PINUS
### Pine

Most of the straight species are
unsuitable as garden plants,
magnificent though they are,
since they are nearly all too large
for the average plot. Selection
by nurserymen has produced a
number of useful clones that are
more manageable, however. The
needles, which are sometimes
quite long, are held in characteristic
bundles. Dwarf pines associate well
with heathers in a border display.
*Cultivation* Any well-drained soil
in sun is suitable, but pines are
not tolerant of pollution.

### P. mugo
#### Dwarf mountain pine

This useful conifer from central
Europe is less widely grown than
its many garden-worthy clones,
many of them dwarf and ideal for

Picea pungens 'Montgomery'

Pinus mugo 'Corley's Mat'

a rock garden. H to 3.5m (11ft),
S to 5m (16ft). Hardy/Z 3–7.
**'Corley's Mat'**, as its name suggests, makes a prostrate, spreading
carpet. H 1m (3ft), S 2m (6ft).
The slow-growing **'Mops'** is almost spherical. Resinous brown
buds are borne in winter. H and
S 1m (3ft).

### P. sylvestris subsp. scotica
#### Scots pine

A majestic conifer, this is widely
distributed throughout northern
Europe and eastern Asia. It grows
as a cone-shape but develops a
characteristic spreading crown
with age. A distinguishing feature
is its grey-green, twisted needles.
An exceptionally hardy conifer,
it is effective when planted in
stands in exposed sites. H to
30m (100ft), S to 9m (30ft).
Hardy/Z 3–7.

Pinus sylvestris subsp. scotica

*Sequoia sempervirens 'Adpressa'*

## SEQUOIA
### Californian redwood

The single member of this genus is one of the tallest and oldest living things on the planet, with specimens dating back 2000 years and achieving heights of more than 100m (325ft). There are a few more modest selections, but even these need space.
*Cultivation* Well-drained, fertile soil is needed, in sun or light dappled shade. Growth is slower in shade.

### S. sempervirens

This is a gigantic conifer from coastal California and Oregon. The smaller **'Adpressa'** develops a broadly conical habit, with horizontal upper branches and lower ones that sweep down to the ground. The foliage is creamy white at first, aging to grey-green. This selection is slow growing and may with time exceed the dimensions given here; it does best in a damp climate. H 9m (30ft) or more, S to 6m (20ft). Hardy/Z 7–9.

## SEQUOIADENDRON
### Giant redwood, big tree, Sierra redwood, wellingtonia

A close relative of *Sequoia*, the giant redwood is also a genus of one species. Although less tall than the Californian redwood, it is the world's largest tree by mass.
*Cultivation* Grow in fertile, well-drained soil in a sunny, open site.

### S. giganteum

Native to California, this forms a cone shape, more spreading with age; the lower branches sweep down, then curve upwards. The scale-like leaves, arranged spirally, are awl-shaped, suffused with grey and aromatic when crushed. The bark is thick and fissured. A magnificent specimen tree, although it is obviously suitable for large gardens only, it can achieve a great age. H 80m (260ft) or more, S to 10m (33ft). Hardy/Z 6–9.

*Sequoiadendron giganteum*

## TAXODIUM
### Swamp cypress

Swamp cypresses are among the most beautiful and elegant of all conifers. Unfortunately, their eventual size rules them out for all but the largest gardens.
*Cultivation* These trees need reliably moist or even wet soil, ideally acid, and a shaded spot.

### T. distichum
### Swamp cypress, bald cypress

This large, deciduous (though sometimes semi-evergreen) conifer comes from the south-eastern United States. It forms a tall cone shape that becomes untidy as it matures. The needle-like leaves, which redden in autumn, are carried in two ranks, as on yew. Mature plants produce the best colour. Purple male cones hang down and are a feature in winter; the female cones are inconspicuous. Near water it produces special breathing roots, which look like knees emerging from the ground around the trunk. H to 40m (130ft), S to 9m (30ft). Hardy/ Z 5–10. The slender *T. distichum* var. *imbricatum* **'Nutans'** is more modest. H to 20m (70ft), S to 6m (20ft).

## TAXUS
### Yew

This is an extremely valuable genus of conifers for the garden, with a range of foliage colour and habit. Yew is widely used for

*Taxodium distichum*

hedging and topiary work, since, unlike most other conifers, it tolerates pruning and even seems to thrive on it. Even mature specimens will recover well if cut back hard. A further distinction is that these conifers produce fleshy berries (usually red) rather than woody cones, helping to brighten up the winter garden. All parts of the conifer are toxic; in some areas, there are restrictions on planting, particularly where cattle are grazed.
*Cultivation* These tolerant conifers can be grown in any but swampy ground, in sun or shade.

### T. baccata
### Common yew

A long-lived conifer, this is widely found in Europe and also in North Africa and Iran. Typically, it has blackish-green leaves, carried in a comb-like arrangement on the stems; male and female flowers are produced on separate plants, with berries, each containing a single seed, following on the females. Uncut, the yew forms a broad, spreading cone shape with dense horizontal branches. H to 20m (65ft), S to 10m (33ft), if unpruned. Hardy/Z 6–7. **'Fastigiata'** (Irish yew), a female (and hence berry-producing) selection, is a familiar graveyard tree, forming an obelisk, pointed at the crown, but spreading with age. The stems are

*Taxus baccata 'Fastigiata'*

*Taxus baccata 'Repandens'*

strongly upright. It can be kept
within bounds by pruning and
can also be wired into a narrower,
more formal shape. H to 10m
(33ft), S to 6m (20ft). The
selection **'Fastigiata Aureomargin-
ata'**, also strongly upright, is a
golden-foliaged female, which
forms a broad obelisk. The leaves
are actually dark green; only the
margins are yellow. H to 5m (16ft),
S to 2.5m (8ft). **'Repandens'**
does not produce a strong vertical
leader but forms a mat of spreading branches near ground level.
It makes good ground cover and
is best without extensive pruning
that might affect its natural habit.

*Taxus baccata 'Standishii'*

H to 60cm (2ft), S to 5m
(16ft). **'Standishii'** forms a slim,
tightly packed column of
yellowish-green, needle-like leaves
carried on strongly upright stems.
It is one of the most decorative
of all yews and, due to its limited
size, is an excellent choice for a
small garden. It requires full sun
and makes a good container plant.
H 1.5m (5ft), S 60cm (2ft).

## THUJA
### Arborvitae
These excellent conifers are
similar to *Chamaecyparis* and
are often mistaken for them, a
distinction being that *Thuja* has
aromatic foliage. They are just
as good for hedging. Varieties
include a number of coloured
foliage forms.
*Cultivation* Any but waterlogged
soil is suitable, in full sun or light
shade, although yellow forms are
best in full sun.

### T. occidentalis
#### Eastern thuja, northern
white cedar
Although this species is not widely grown, it is the parent of a vast
number of cultivars. **'Ericoides'**
is a dwarf form, growing into a
broad, sometimes rounded,
obelisk. The spreading, scale-like
leaves are green in summer, turning rich brown, sometimes purple,
in autumn. As the name suggests,
it combines well with heathers
and is good in a rock garden. H
and S 1.2m (4ft). Hardy/Z 3–8.

### T. orientalis 'Aurea Nana'
(syn. *Platycladus orientalis* 'Aurea
Nana')
This is an appealing dwarf
selection of a much larger species
from China and Iran. It makes an
egg-shaped plant, with yellowish-
green, scale-like leaves held in
irregular, vertical, fan-like plates;
they tinge bronze in cold weather
in autumn. The cones are flagon-
like and bluish-green, maturing
to grey. An excellent choice for a
small garden, it associates well
with heathers and other yellow-
leaved shrubs. H and S to 60cm
(2ft). Hardy/Z 6–9. **'Sieboldii'**
(syn. *Platycladus orientalis*
'Sieboldii') also makes an egg-
shaped plant and holds its mid-
green, aromatic leaves in similar
fashion. It combines well with
heathers or other low-growing
conifers. H and S 2m (6ft).

### T. plicata
#### Western red cedar
A large conifer originating from
western North America, the
species forms a cone-shaped tree,
broadening at the crown with age.
It is an excellent specimen for a
large garden. The scale-like leaves
are carried in two ranks on stems
that hang downwards at their tips.
The spread of the Western red
cedar can exceed the dimensions
shown because where the stems

*Thuja occidentalis 'Ericoides'*

trail on the ground, they can self-
layer, a habit that has produced
some vast specimens in the wild.
It is suitable for planting as a
hedge. H to 35m (120ft), S 9m
(30ft) or more. Hardy/Z 6–8.
The conical **'Atrovirens'** is slightly
slower growing than the species.
H 8m (25ft), S 2m (6ft). **'Irish
Gold'** usually stays fairly dwarf.
The foliage is bright yellow-green
with lighter patches. H and S 2m
(6ft), although it can reach a
height of 20m (65ft).

*Thuja orientalis 'Aurea Nana'*

*Thuja plicata 'Irish Gold'*

# Shrubs

Shrubs encompass a wide range, from tree-like plants (which can substitute for trees in small gardens) to more diminutive ones that can be used in rock gardens or as ground cover. Most are grown for their often spectacular flowers, but others have less obvious attractions – showy berries or good leaf colour in autumn, attractive winter stems, or an appealing habit. Judiciously chosen, shrubs give an air of permanence to any planting.

Shrubs are the mainstay of any garden and this large garden of trees and shrubs will virtually look after itself.

# What is a shrub?

Shrubs are woody plants and can be evergreen or deciduous. That definition also applies to trees, but most gardeners would never confuse the two. In general, shrubs are usually compact plants with a height and spread no greater than 3m (10ft), and usually branching from the base. This habit, however, can also be observed in trees; equally there are some shrubs that can be grown with a single upright trunk and look to all intents and purposes like miniature trees. Some slow-growing plants, such as hollies (*Ilex*) and bay (*Laurus*), will be shrubby initially (and can be treated as shrubs in gardens) but will end up as trees in the fullness of time.

In the wild, shrubs are found in a huge range of habitats, from coastal areas to high altitudes, open plains to woodland: hence the need to consider carefully any plant's cultural preferences when making a choice. The different habits of growth represent a response to climate. Plants from coastal areas, for instance, tend to be tough,

Magnolias can be either be classified as trees or shrubs depending on the species. This *Magnolia × loebneri* 'Leonard Messel' in bloom is however a shrub, and here combines well with the flowers of a Camellia japonica hybrid.

stunted-looking and scrubby, the better to weather salt-laden winds, while woodland shrubs are more rangy, as they crane their necks towards the available light. You do not need to imitate nature slavishly in your garden, however, since many seem to perform well in a variety of conditions.

The shrubs grown in gardens today comprise both species and hybrids. Some genera have been extensively hybridized to produce a vast range of plants, most notably roses – dealt with in their own section in this book – and rhododendrons, which include dwarf plants suitable for a rock garden as well as others that end up as huge tree-like specimens. Shrubs such as *Fuchsia* and – to a lesser extent – *Hydrangea* and *Ceanothus* are other genera that have attracted the attention of hybridizers.

## Shrubs in the garden

These useful plants are the backbone of many a planting, particularly in a small garden, where there is

frequently little or no space to grow trees.

A shrub border can be a low-maintenance option for a driveway, or indeed any other area of the garden where there is space to be filled. A mixture of evergreens and deciduous shrubs will provide a shifting focus of interest; apart from the seasonal flowers and berries for which most shrubs are grown, variegated evergreens will provide year-round interest. Be sure to include some winter-flowering shrubs, such as *Viburnum tinus*, *Mahonia × media* and *Lonicera fragrantissima*. There are too many spring-flowering shrubs to mention, but for interest after midsummer, you could look to the hydrangeas, fuchsias, *Buddleja davidii* and *Ceratostigma willmottianum* (of modest size, but a real eye-catcher when starred with its sky blue flowers). *Parrotia persica* has vivid autumn leaf colour.

Many shrubs are utility plants and make ideal hedging material, the shrubby honeysuckle (*Lonicera nitida*)

Massed heathers need little attention, and provide weed-suppressing ground-cover besides making a sea of colour.

and privet (*Ligustrum*) both providing good dense screens. *Aucuba* and Portugal laurel (*Prunus lusitanica*) have larger, more handsome leaves, but cannot be clipped quite so tightly. Some camellias make excellent flowering hedges, and it is also possible to mix plants for an informal look appropriate to rural gardens (such hedges will also attract wildlife).

There is a whole host of shrubs suitable for planting in light woodland. If you have acid soil, a rhododendron garden can be spectacular (perhaps also including other acid lovers such as *Pieris* and camellias), but there are plenty of lime-tolerant alternatives, such as *Photinia*, if you garden on alkaline soil. On a very open, windswept site, heathers are the obvious choice.

For a specimen, choose architectural plants such as a yucca or those with spectacular flowers, such as a tree peony (provided the site is reasonably sheltered). Forms

Rhododendrons, combining well here with conifers and other evergreens, have flowers that range from small and delicate to magnificent and gloriously coloured, along with exquisite foliage.

of *Viburnum plicatum* have a striking tiered habit that is appealing even when the plant is bare in winter.

Prostrate shrubs can be used as ground cover, particularly those with stems that will root where they touch the ground. *Ceanothus*

*thyrsiflorus* var. *repens* would be a delight when smothered with its clear blue flowers in early summer, but is not so long-lived or as shade-tolerant as such humbler alternatives as cotoneasters and periwinkle (*Vinca*).

Some shrubs lend themselves to pruning and training, and these are ideal in a formal scheme, either to punctuate geometrically shaped borders or to line the edge of a path. Box is the classic choice for a low formal hedge, and larger specimens can be clipped to ball, cone or cube shapes. Rather faster growing is privet – a coarser plant, it is true, but of surprising elegance when trained as a standard. *Viburnum tinus* and *Prunus lusitanicus* are comparably stylish alternatives.

All of these shrubs are also excellent in containers, as are the spotted laurel (*Aucuba japonica* 'Crotonifolia') and hydrangeas. Many others will also thrive in pots, and this gives you the opportunity to grow any that would not thrive otherwise in the soil type in the open garden.

## Pruning

Many woody plants benefit from pruning occasionally, but few actually need it regularly, and a good many are best with minimum intervention. You should be guided by the way the plant is performing in your garden.

If necessary, winter- and spring-flowering shrubs can be pruned immediately after flowering, which gives them ample time to produce sufficient new growth for flowering the following year. Summer-flowering shrubs (which generally flower on wood made in the current season) can be pruned in early spring. All deciduous shrubs can also be pruned in winter, often a good time, since the stems are bare then and it is easy to see what you are doing.

As a matter of routine, cut out all diseased, damaged or obviously dead wood. You should also remove entirely any plain green shoots on variegated shrubs. You can then trim the rest of the growth, but be selective. Cut out some of the older wood to the base (this is always less productive and more disease-prone than younger growth) and shorten the remaining stems, cutting weak shoots back hard, but vigorous ones only lightly. You will probably be able to leave some shoots unpruned.

In cold districts the topgrowth of some shrubs (for instance some fuchsias) will die in winter, and this should be cut back hard in spring. Certain other shrubs, notably *Buddleja davidii*, can also be cut back hard annually, though this is by no means essential.

Abelia × grandiflora

# ABELIA
These evergreens are greatly
valued for their graceful habit
and late flowers, which last from
summer to late autumn.
**Cultivation** Grow in any well-
drained soil in full sun or light
shade. In cold areas, they prefer
a warm, sheltered site, ideally
against a wall.

## A. × grandiflora
Of garden origin, this shrub has
slightly scented, white flowers
from midsummer to autumn.
H and S 2m (6ft). Borderline
hardy/Z 6–9. **'Gold Spot'** (syn.
'Aurea', 'Gold Strike', 'Goldsport')
has golden-yellow leaves. H and S
2m (6ft).

Abelia × grandiflora 'Gold Spot'

# ABELIOPHYLLUM
There is only one species in the
genus, and it is a real connoisseur's
plant and something of a rarity in
gardens. It is slow-growing, takes
some years to settle down to
reliable flower production and
is difficult to propagate. Like
wisteria, it is hardy but needs a
hot spot to ripen the wood
sufficiently for good flowering.
Left to its own devices, it is a
sprawling shrub, seen to best
advantage when wall-trained.
Frost can damage the flowers.
**Cultivation** Grow in fertile,
well-drained soil in a sheltered
site, ideally trained against a
warm wall.

## A. distichum
In late winter to early spring this
deciduous Chinese species has
dainty, sweetly fragrant white
flowers, something like forsythia
but much smaller. H and S to
1.5m (5ft). Hardy/Z 5–9.

# ABUTILON
Flowering maple, Indian
mallow
These elegant shrubs produce
appealing lampshade-like flowers
from late summer into autumn.
They are sometimes trained as
standards and used as dot plants
in park bedding schemes. They
are also good in containers, either
on their own or as the central
feature in a mixed planting.
**Cultivation** Grow in any fertile,
well-drained soil in full sun in a

sheltered spot. In cold areas, wall-
training is an effective way of
improving their hardiness. The
species described is a very lax
grower, needing the support of
wires or of other shrubs.

## A. megapotanicum
Trailing abutilon
The evergreen or semi-evergreen
species has orange-red and yellow,
lantern-like flowers and maple-like
leaves. H and S 2m (6ft).
Borderline hardy/Z 8–9. The
leaves of **'Variegatum'** are mottled
with yellow. This makes a good
standard.

# ARTEMISIA
Wormwood
These aromatic subshrubs are
ideal for mixed borders, white and
grey gardens and herb gardens.
They make excellent 'fillers' in
rose gardens or, indeed, anywhere
where you need to fill space in
summer. The genus also includes
a number of perennials.
**Cultivation** Artemisias will grow
in poor, dry, well-drained soil in
full sun. Prune in spring to keep
plants neat.

Abutilon megapotanicum 'Variegatum'

## A. abrotanum
Southernwood, lad's love,
old man
This deciduous or semi-evergreen
species is an effective filler in
a number of situations. The aromatic, silvery-grey leaves are very
finely divided. The grey-yellow
flowers borne in late summer are
insignificant. H 70cm (28in),
S 50cm (20in). Hardy/Z 6–9.

Artemisia abrotanum

*Aucuba japonica*

## AUCUBA

Tough, tolerant evergreens, aucubas thrive in quite deep shade and make excellent hedging. Female plants have red berries in autumn, but there are also self-fertile forms. It is easy to take them for granted, but few shrubs look so stylish in containers, which is, perhaps, the best way of growing them.
**Cultivation** Aucubas grow in any soil that is not waterlogged, in sun or shade.

### *A. japonica*
**Spotted laurel**
To all intents and purposes, this is the only species grown, generally in one of its variegated

*Ballota pseudodictamnus*

forms. **'Crotonifolia'** (female) is the best, with leaves generously mottled with yellow. H and S 2m (6ft). The plain green *A. japonica* f. *longifolia* (female) is worth looking out for, however and has elegant, narrow, glossy leaves with wavy edges. H and S 2m (6ft). Hardy/Z 7–10.

## BALLOTA

These often sub-shrubby plants are excellent in a Mediterranean-style garden or as an edging to a border, where they are a good foil to more flamboyant plants. They look their best in hot, dry conditions and revel in the reflected heat of a gravel garden.
**Cultivation** Grow in sharply drained soil in full sun.

### *B. pseudodictamnus*
This woolly-leaved species is of greatest interest when it is in flower in summer. The individual flowers, tiny and lilac-purple, are not striking in themselves, but they are held in woolly, beige-green calyces in 'bobbles' on the stem and complement the grey-green evergreen leaves. H 45cm (18in), S 60cm (2ft). Borderline hardy/Z 7–9.

## BERBERIS
**Barberry**
An important genus, tough and hardy, that includes both evergreens and deciduous species, all with spiny stems. Although some are almost too familiar as hedging, there are also some very choice species that are well worth seeking out. The forms with coloured leaves make excellent specimens.
**Cultivation** Any soil is suitable. The evergreens are shade-tolerant. Deciduous types grown for their leaf colour are best in sun or only light shade. Overgrown and straggly plants can be cut back hard in spring.

### *B. darwinii*
This evergreen species from Chile is one of the best for hedging. Showers of rich orange flowers are produced in mid- to late spring, followed by blue-black fruits. H 2m (6ft), S 1.2m (4ft). Hardy/Z 7–9.

### *B. 'Goldilocks'*
One of the best evergreens, this slow-growing hybrid has drooping racemes of glowing orange flowers in spring (and sometimes in mid-summer). The flowers are followed by blue-black fruits. H 4m (13ft), S 3m (10ft). Hardy/Z 7–10.

### *B. temolaica*
A very handsome deciduous berberis, this slow-growing plant is difficult to propagate but is well worth looking out for. It has glaucous green leaves on whitened stems, lemon-yellow spring flowers and egg-shaped autumn fruits. Plants can be cut back hard annually or every two years for the interest of its winter stems. H and S 1.5m (5ft). Hardy/Z 5.

### *B. thunbergii*
This variable deciduous shrub has a number of interesting selections, all of which do best in fertile soil. The purple leaves of *B. thunbergii* f. *atropurpurea* turn orange in autumn. H and S 1.5m (5ft). **'Aurea'** has soft yellow leaves and is best in some shade. H and S 1m (3ft). **'Helmond Pillar'** is a

*Berberis temolaica*

distinctive upright selection with dark purple-red leaves. H 1.5m (5ft), S 45cm (18in). The popular and distinctive **'Rose Glow'** has purple leaves swirled with pink and cream turning lipstick red in autumn. H 1.5m (5ft), S 1.2m (4ft). On **'Silver Beauty'**, the leaves are mottled with creamy white. H 60cm (2ft), S 1m (3ft). Hardy/Z 5–9.

*Berberis thunbergii* f. *atropurpurea*

Buddleja alternifolia

# BUDDLEJA

The heavily fragranced flowers of these medium-to-large deciduous shrubs are irresistible to butter-flies. *B. davidii* is almost a weed in some gardens, seeding itself freely even in cracks in walls, paving and gravel drives, but there are also other species, many beautiful. They are reliable plants for the back of a border.
*Cultivation* Grow in any, even poor, soil in full sun. Buddlejas thrive in alkaline soil. Some species can be pruned hard in late winter to early spring, but this is not essential.

## B. alternifolia

This handsome plant, originally from China, has pendent racemes of deliciously scented mauve flowers in early summer. Its size is easily controlled by pruning. H and S 4m (13ft). Hardy/Z 6–9. The form **'Argentea'** is even more desirable. It has silver-grey

leaves and is very effective both as a standard and as a specimen. H and S 2.4m (8ft).

## B. crispa
**(syn. *B. sterniana, B. tibetica*)**
This handsome Chinese species makes a fine subject for a warm wall, the additional heat enhancing the woolliness of its grey leaves. The lilac-coloured flowers are scented. H and S 3m (10ft). Borderline hardy/Z 9.

## B. davidii
**Butterfly bush**
The most familiar of all the buddlejas, this bears long spikes of fragrant, usually mauve flowers in mid- to late summer. It is essential in a wild or ecological garden, because of its attraction to butterflies. H and S 3m (10ft), if unpruned. Hardy/Z 7–9. There are several selections, all of which can be pruned hard in late winter to early spring, including **'Black Knight'**, which has rich reddish-purple flowers; **'Nanho Blue'** with rich lavender-blue flowers; and **'Peace'**, which is a reliable white selection.

## B. × weyeriana
A curious hybrid of *B. globosa* and *B. davidii*, this plant bears flowers that show the characteristics of both parents, being arranged in tapering, ball-shaped clusters. The flowers are a muted orange flushed with mauve, a refreshing addition to any mixed planting in high summer. H 4m (13ft), S 3m (10ft), but less if pruned hard annually. Hardy/Z 6–8.

# BUXUS
## Box
These are indispensable evergreen plants in the garden for dwarf hedging. New plants can be easily raised from cuttings. Box thrives in containers.
*Cultivation* Grow in any reasonable soil in full sun or light shade. Clip hedges in mid-spring and late summer.

## B. sempervirens
**Common box**
The species most commonly used for hedging, this would eventually make a tree if left unpruned (albeit over several generations), although the plants seen in gardens are usually considerably smaller than the dimensions indicated. H and S 4m (13ft). Hardy/Z 6–9.
**'Elegantissima'** is a delightful selection, with small leaves that are variegated with cream. H and S 1.5m (5ft). **'Suffruticosa'** is a very slow-growing dwarf form, also with small leaves and a tight habit. It is the traditional choice for knot gardens. H 1m (3ft), S 1.5m (5ft).

# CALLISTEMON
## Bottlebrush
Native to Australia, the evergreen bottlebrushes bring a quirky, exotic touch to gardens with their vivid, brush-like flowers. In general, callistemons are not reliably hardy and are best grown in only fairly mild climates or in sheltered spots in frost-prone gardens.
*Cultivation* Grow callistemons in lime-free, preferably acid, well-drained soil in full sun, against a warm wall in cold areas. They are suitable for growing in containers under glass.

## C. citrinus
**Crimson bottlebrush**
This species has a profusion of spikes of red flowers from early to midsummer. H and S 5m (16ft). Half-hardy/Z 9–10. **'Splendens'** has flowers of a more vivid scarlet. H and S 2m (6ft).

## C. viminalis 'Captain Cook'
This low-growing form produces an abundance of large red flowers from spring to summer. H and S 1.2m (4ft). Half-hardy/Z 10.

Buxus sempervirens 'Suffruticosa'

# CALLUNA
## Heather, ling
This genus of heathers consists of a single species, but there are a huge number of cultivars, all evergreen and producing their spikes of bell-shaped flowers between midsummer and late autumn (some have a shorter flowering season within that overall period). Some also have coloured foliage, which provides interest over a longer period. Grow them on their own in heather beds or combine them with dwarf conifers or the other heath genera, *Dabeccia* and *Erica*. Heathers are good in containers.
*Cultivation* Grow in a sunny, open site in well-drained, humus-rich, acid soil. Clip after flowering.

## C. vulgaris
The following selection indicates something of the scope of the hybrids now available. All are hardy/Z 5–7. **'Alba Rigida'**

Buddleja davidii 'Black Knight'

Buddleja davidii 'Nanho Blue'

Callistemon citrinus

*Calluna vulgaris* 'Alison Yates'

(syn. 'Rigida Prostrata') has white flowers. H 15cm (6in), S 30cm (12in). **'Alison Yates'** has white flowers and silver-grey foliage. H 45cm (18in), S 60cm (24in). **'Annemarie'** has double, rose pink flowers. H 50cm (20in), S 60cm (24in). **'Anthony Davis'** has white flowers and grey-green foliage. H 45cm (18in), S 50cm (20in). **'Arran Gold'** has purple flowers and bright golden-yellow foliage, which turns lime green flecked with red in winter. H 15cm (6in), S 25cm (10in). **'Beoley Gold'** has white flowers and bright golden-yellow foliage. H 35cm (14in), S 60cm (24in). **'County Wicklow'** has double, pale pink flowers. H 25cm (10in), S 35cm (14in). **'Dark Beauty'** has blood-red flowers and dark green foliage. H 25cm (10in), S 35cm (14in). **'Darkness'** has bright crimson flowers and dark green foliage. H 25cm (10in), S 35cm (14in). **'Elsie Purnell'** has double, pale

pink flowers and greyish-green foliage. H 40cm (16in), S 75cm (30in). **'Firefly'** has pinkish-lilac flowers and orange-red summer foliage, darkening to brick red in winter. H 45cm (18in), S 50cm (20in). **'Foxii Nana'** has mauve flowers. H 15cm (6in), S 30cm (12in). **'H.E. Beale'** (syn. 'Pink Beale') has double, pink flowers. H and S 60cm (24in). **'Hammondii'** has white flowers. H and S 75cm (30in). **'Hammondii Aureifolia'** has white flowers and foliage tipped with yellow in spring. H 30cm (12in), S 40cm (16in). **'J.H. Hamilton'** has double, dark pink flowers. H 10cm (4in), S 25cm (10in). **'Joy Vanstone'** has pink flowers and yellow-gold foliage, which turns orange in winter. H 50cm (20in), S 60cm (24in). **'Kerstin'** has mauve flowers and greyish-lilac foliage, the new growth tipped with light yellow and red in spring. H 50cm (20in), S 45cm (18in). **'Kinlochruel'** has double, white flowers. H 25cm (10in), S 40cm (16in). **'Mair's Variety'** (syn. 'Alba Elongata') has white flowers. H 40cm (16in), S 60cm (24in). **'Mullion'** has lilac-pink flowers and dark green foliage. H 20cm (8in), S 50cm (20in). **'Multicolor'** has mauve flowers and copper foliage flecked with orange and red. H 10cm (4in), S 25cm (10in). **'My Dream'** (syn. 'Snowball') has double, white flowers, which are good for cutting. H 45cm (18in), S 75cm (30in). **'Orange Queen'** has lavender flowers and golden-yellow foliage, which turns bronze in autumn and orange in winter. H 30cm (12in), S 50cm (20in). **'Peter Sparkes'** has double, pink flowers. H 25cm (10in), S 55cm (22in). **'Red Carpet'** (syn. 'Marinka') has mauve-pink flowers and golden-yellow foliage, reddening after hard frosts in winter. H 20cm (8in), S 45cm (18in). **'Red Favorit'** has double, crimson flowers and dark green foliage. H 20cm (8in), S 70cm (28in). **'Red Pimpernel'** has crimson flowers. H 20cm (8in), S 45cm (18in). **'Red Star'** has double, deep lilac-pink flowers and dark green foliage. H 40cm (16in), S 60cm (24in). **'Robert Chapman'**

*Calluna vulgaris* 'Dark Beauty'

has lavender flowers and golden-yellow summer foliage, which turns orange in autumn and red in winter and spring. H 25cm (10in), S 65cm (26in). **'Roland Haagen'** has mauve flowers and golden-yellow foliage, turning bright orange with darker tips in winter. H 15cm (6in), S 35cm (14in). **'Serlei Aurea'** has white flowers and yellowish-green foliage, tipped with yellow in summer and autumn. H 50cm (20in), S 40cm (16in). **'Silver Queen'** has pale mauve flowers and silver-grey foliage. H 40cm (16in), S 55cm (22in). **'Silver Rose'** has lilac-pink flowers and hairy, silver-grey foliage. H 40cm (16in), S 50cm (20in). **'Sir John Charrington'** has mauve-pink flowers and golden-yellow summer foliage, which turns orange and red in winter. H 40cm (16in), S 50cm (24in). **'Sister Anne'** has mauve flowers and grey-green foliage, turning bronze in winter. H 10cm

*Calluna vulgaris* 'Darkness'

(4in), S 25cm (10in). **'Spring Cream'** has white flowers and foliage tipped with cream in spring, and yellow in autumn and winter. H 35cm (14in), S 45cm (18in). **'Spring Torch'** (syn. 'Spring Charm') has mauve flowers and foliage tipped with cream orange and red in spring. H 40cm (16in), S 60cm (24in). **'Sunset'** has lilac-pink flowers and golden-yellow summer foliage, turning red in autumn and winter. H 20cm (8in), S 45cm (18in). **'Tib'** has cyclamen purple flowers and dark green foliage. H 30cm (12in), S 40cm (16in). **'White Coral'** has white flowers. H 30cm (12in), S 40cm (16in). **'White Lawn'** has white flowers. H 5cm (2in), S 40cm (16in). **'Wickwar Flame'** has mauve-pink flowers and flame-orange foliage, deepening to brilliant orange-red in winter. H 50cm (20in), S 60cm (24in).

*Calluna vulgaris* 'Arran Gold'

*Calluna vulgaris* 'Hammondii Aureifolia'

*Calluna vulgaris* 'Wickwar Flame'

Camellia 'Cornish Snow'

Camellia 'Inspiration'

# CAMELLIA

This is a large genus, containing about 250 species of superb evergreen shrubs and small trees, made larger by the number of hybrids. Unfortunately for many gardens, they must have acid soil. On the credit side, they thrive in containers, so it is possible to enjoy these aristocrats of spring whatever your soil type. There are an increasing number of autumn-flowering camellias, which have been bred from *C. sasanqua*. Few of the species are in general cultivation: on the whole, they are not very hardy and are too large for most conservatories (porches). Hybrids can be divided into two large groups, cultivars of *C. japonica* and of *C. × williamsii*, although from the gardener's point of view, there is no appreciable difference between the two. There are two smaller groups: cultivars of *C. sasanqua* (which flower in autumn) and of *C. reticulata* (which flower in late winter to spring). Use camellias as specimens or in shrub borders. All have lustrous green leaves, making them splendid backdrops to other plants when out of flower. Some camellias

have flexible stems and can be wall-trained, to breathtaking effect once they are mature.

*Cultivation* Camellias must have lime-free soil (although they do not demand such a low pH as rhododendrons). The soil should be fertile and well-drained and, ideally, incorporate leaf mould. Camellias are best in light shade where early morning sun will not strike emerging flower buds in early spring. Make sure they do not dry out in late summer to early autumn, when plants are building the following season's flowers. They can be pruned after flowering.

## C. 'Cornish Snow'
This medium-sized shrub produces dainty, single white flowers opening from pink-tinted buds from midwinter to late spring. It needs a sheltered spot. H 3m (10ft), S 1.5m (5ft). Hardy/Z 7–9.

## C. 'Doctor Clifford Parks'
This desirable camellia bears semi-double, loose peony- or anemone-form deep red flowers in mid-spring. H 4m (13ft), S 2.5m (8ft). Half-hardy/Z 7–9.

## C. 'Inspiration'
A reliable, upright plant that has semi-double, deep pink flowers from midwinter to late spring. This is good when trained as a wall shrub. H 4m (13ft), S 2m (6ft). Hardy/Z 7–9.

## C. *japonica* cultivars
The following flower from mid- to late spring unless otherwise indicated. All are hardy/Z 7–9 unless otherwise stated. '**Adolphe**

Audusson' has semi-double, dark red flowers with white stamens in early to mid-spring. H 5m (16ft), S 4m (13ft). '**Akashigata**' (syn. 'Lady Clare') has very large, semi-double, deep salmon-pink flowers from early to late spring. It is suitable for wall training. H 1.5m (5ft), S 3m (10ft). '**Apollo**' (syn. 'Paul's Apollo') has semi-double, red flowers (sometimes marbled with white) with yellow stamens from early to late spring. H and S 3m (10ft). '**Ave Maria**' has formal double, pale pink flowers from early to late spring. This is a slow-growing plant, which is an excellent choice for a container. H and S 3m (10ft). '**Berenice Boddy**' has semi-double, pale pink flowers from late winter to late spring. It is exceptionally hardy and wind-tolerant. H and S 3m (10ft). '**Bob Hope**' has semi-double or peony-form blackish-red flowers. It is a good choice for a container. H and S 3m (10ft). The choice and unusual '**Bob's Tinsie**' has anemone-form flowers, the outer petals deep crimson, the inner petals crimson and white, from early to late spring. H 2m (6ft), S 1m (3ft). The compact and upright '**Doctor Tinsley**' has peony-form or formal double, pale pink flowers. H and S 3m (10ft). '**Elegans**' (syn. 'Chandler's Elegans') has anemone-form, soft pink flowers, sometimes spotted with white. It is slow-growing and best with minimal pruning. H and S 3m (10ft). '**Elizabeth Hawkins**' has anemone-form, bright red flowers in mid-spring. H and S 2m (6ft). '**Gloire de Nantes**' has semi-double, rich rose-pink flowers from late autumn to late spring, one of the longest flowering

Camellia japonica 'Ave Maria'

Camellia japonica 'Elizabeth Hawkins'

seasons of any camellia. H and S 3m (10ft). '**Grand Prix**' has semi-double, brilliant clear red flowers with yellow stamens. This looks magnificent when wall-trained. H and S 5m (16ft). '**Janet Waterhouse**' has semi-double or formal double, white flowers. H and S 3m (10ft). The reliably hardy '**Jupiter**' (syn. 'Paul's Jupiter') has single, bright red flowers with golden stamens. H 3m (10ft), S 2m (6ft). '**Kramer's Supreme**' has beautiful peony-form, bright red flowers in late autumn and in early to mid-spring. H 3m (10ft), S 2m (6ft). Borderline hardy/Z 8. '**Lady Loch**' has peony-form, pink flowers. H 3m (10ft), S 2m (6ft). '**Lavinia Maggi**' (syn. 'Contessa Lavinia Maggi') has formal double, white to pale pink flowers striped with pink and red from early to mid-spring. H and S 2m (6ft) or more. '**Nuccio's Jewel**' has peony-form, white flowers, flushed pink. This is a slow-growing camellia and a good choice for a container. H and S 3m (10ft). The dense and compact '**Rubescens Major**' has formal double or rose-form double, pinkish-crimson flowers with attractive darker veins in mid-spring. H and S 2.5m (8ft). '**Tricolor**' (syn. 'Sieboldii') has single or semi-double flowers striped in shades of red, pink or white in early spring. H and S 2m (6ft).

## C. 'Leonard Messel'
Semi-double to peony-form, pink flowers, veined with darker pink, are borne in early to late spring. H 4m (13ft), S 3m (10ft). Hardy/Z 7–9.

Camellia 'Doctor Clifford Parks'

*Camellia × williamsii 'Jury's Yellow'*

### C. reticulata
This species has a number of desirable cultivars, suitable for training against a warm wall. H and S to 4m (13ft) or more. Half-hardy/Z 9–10. **'Captain Rawes'** has large, semi-double flowers in mid-spring. **'Mandalay Queen'** has deep, rose-pink, semi-double flowers.

### C. sasanqua
This species is distinguished by its fragrant flowers, produced from late autumn to late winter. H and S to 3m (10ft). Borderline hardy/Z 7–9. The upright selection **'Narumigata'** has single, pink-tinted white flowers.

### C. 'Spring Festival'
This charming camellia has dainty, formal double, pale pink flowers from mid- to late spring. H 4m (13ft), S 2m (6ft). Borderline hardy/Z 8.

### C. × williamsii hybrids
The following is just a selection of the large number of fine hybrids available in this group. All are hardy/Z 7–9. The slow-growing **'Anticipation'** has very large, peony-form, deep rose-pink flowers from late winter to early spring. H 4m (13ft), S 2m (6ft). The exceptionally hardy **'Brigadoon'** has semi-double, soft silver-pink flowers with golden stamens in mid- to late spring. H 2.5m (8ft), S 2m (6ft). The prolific **'Debbie'** has peony-form, clear deep pink flowers from late winter to late spring. H 3m (10ft), S 2m (6ft). **'Donation'** has semi-double, pink flowers veined darker pink and with yellow stamens from late winter to late spring. It is deservedly one of the most popular of all camellias. H 5m (16ft), S 2.5m (8ft). One of the best whites, **'E.T.R. Carlyon'** has semi-double to rose-form white flowers in mid- and late spring. H 2.5m (8ft), S 2m (6ft). **'Golden Spangles'** has single, pinkish red flowers from mid- to late spring, but it is grown primarily for its leaves, which are generously splashed with yellow. H 2.5m (8ft), S 2m (6ft). **'J.C. Williams'** bears single, pale blush pink flowers in profusion in mid- to late spring. This is ideal for wall training. H and S 5m (16ft). **'Joan Trehane'** has rose-form, clear pink flowers from mid- to late spring. H 2.5m (8ft), S 2m (6ft). **'Jury's Yellow'** has anemone- to peony-form flowers, with creamy-white outer petals and creamy-yellow inner ones, from mid- to late spring. This is the nearest to a yellow camellia. H 2.5m (8ft), S 2m (6ft). **'Muskoka'** has semi-double, pink flowers veined darker pink, the number one camellia for a container. H 2.5m (8ft), S 2m (6ft). **'Rose Parade'** has formal double, rich deep rose pink flowers from early to late spring. H and S 3m (10ft). **'St Ewe'** has single, bright rose pink flowers with golden stamens in early to mid-spring. H 2.5m (8ft), S 2m (6ft).

## CEANOTHUS
### California lilac
No shrub has flowers of so true a blue as the *Ceanothus*. When the early forms burst into flower, it is a sure sign that summer is only just around the corner. There is also a valuable second group that flowers in late summer. There are deciduous and evergreen species, the evergreens being slightly more tender. In cold areas all are best grown as wall shrubs, but in more favoured spots they make truly spectacular specimens. The pink- and white-flowered types are of interest but less popular.
*Cultivation* Grow in any fertile, well-drained soil in full sun. They tolerate lime, but dislike shallow soils over chalk. In cold areas most do best as wall shrubs. Prune after flowering if necessary.

### C. 'Autumnal Blue'
A late-flowering plant, with clusters of powder blue flowers from late summer to autumn. One of the hardiest evergreens and ideal for wall training. H and S 3m (10ft). Hardy/Z 8–9.

### C. 'Cascade'
This evergreen is seen at its best when loosely tied to a wall, so that the arching stems, smothered in powder-blue flowers in late spring, can billow forwards. H and S to 2m (6ft). Half-hardy/Z 9.

### C. 'Dark Star'
Dark purplish blue flowers are carried in spring on this arching evergreen. H 2m (6ft), S 3m (10ft). Half-hardy/Z 8.

### C. 'Delight'
This evergreen variety, which has clusters of rich blue flowers in late spring, makes a good wall shrub. H and S 3m (10ft). Half-hardy/Z 9.

### C. × delileanus 'Gloire de Versailles'
An open, deciduous ceanothus, this would make a fine specimen in a sheltered spot. The pale blue flowers appear from midsummer to early autumn. H and S 1.5m (5ft). Hardy/Z 7. **'Topaze'** is more compact and has richer blue flowers. H and S 1.5m (5ft). Hardy/Z 7.

### C. × pallidus 'Marie Simon'
One of the few pink-flowered hybrids, this is a deciduous variety with pale pink flowers from midsummer to autumn. H and S 1.5m (5ft). Hardy/Z 9.

### C. 'Puget Blue'
This evergreen hybrid has masses of brilliant blue flowers appearing in early summer. H and S 2.1m (7ft). Borderline hardy/Z 8–10.

### C. thyrsiflorus var. repens
### Blueblossom
The species, one of the hardiest evergreens, is usually grown in this prostrate form, which is a wonderful carpeter for banks and large rockeries. Rich blue flowers cover the plant in late spring to early summer. It is shade-tolerant and looks splendid as groundcover under such airy, deciduous trees as gleditsias. H 1m (3ft), S 2.5m (8ft). Hardy/Z 8–9.

*Ceanothus 'Delight'*

*Camellia 'Leonard Messel'*

*Camellia 'Spring Festival'*

*Ceanothus 'Dark Star'*

Ceratostigma willmottianum

Cestrum elegans

Chaenomeles × superba 'Crimson and Gold'

# CERATOSTIGMA

A diminutive shrub, but of great significance, for this is probably the only late-flowering shrub that can provide flowers of this shade of blue. It tends to die back in hard winters but generally recovers. The species described should have a place in every garden. Its low habit makes it suitable for a mixed planting including perennials, annuals and grasses. The genus also includes the perennial *C. plumbaginoides*.
*Cultivation* Grow in any well-drained soil in full sun. In cold areas, cut back hard annually in spring.

## C. willmottianum

This deciduous Chinese species, which makes a twiggy bush, has small, vivid blue flowers in late summer to early autumn. H and S 60cm (2ft). Hardy/Z 7–10.

# CESTRUM

This small genus of generally tender plants contains one species that is hardy enough to be grown outdoors in cool gardens. The others make good conservatory (porch) plants in cold areas.
*Cultivation* Any fertile, well-drained soil is suitable. Grow in full sun, ideally in the shelter of a warm wall, and cut back hard annually in spring if the topgrowth dies back.

## C. elegans
(syn. *C. purpureum*)
An evergreen species originally from Mexico, this has clusters of reddish-purple flowers that appear

throughout summer. H 1.2m (4ft), S 1m (3ft). Tender/Z 10.

## C. parqui
**Willow-leaved jessamine**
This deciduous species from Chile has pyramid-like clusters of lime-green, star-shaped flowers, unspectacular in themselves but releasing a unique bubblegum-like fragrance at night in late summer. H 1.2m (4ft), S 1m (3ft). Borderline hardy/Z 7–10.

# CHAENOMELES
**Ornamental quince, japonica**
Essential shrubs for late-winter interest, these plants are charming as free-standing specimens and spectacular when trained against a wall. Selections with white, pink and red flowers are available, but the red-flowered types are the most popular.
*Cultivation* These plants are tolerant of any but waterlogged soil. They will grow in sun or shade and can be trained against north-facing walls.

## C. × superba
This multi-stemmed, deciduous hybrid group is usually represented in gardens by its selections, all of which flower on the bare wood in late winter. H and S 1.5m (5ft). All are hardy/Z 5–8. **'Crimson and Gold'** has red flowers with eye-catching yellow stamens. **'Knap Hill Scarlet'**, has large, bright red flowers. **'Nicoline'** has scarlet, sometimes semi-double flowers. **'Pink Lady'** has dark pink flowers.

# CHOISYA
A small genus of evergreens that have a neat, rounded habit making them excellent for creating a topiary effect without pruning, though older plants can become untidy. The leaves are highly aromatic, and they also bear fragrant white flowers in spring.

*Cultivation* Grow in any fertile, well-drained soil. Choisyas will tolerate some shade and are good for growing against a wall, but flower best in full sun.

## C. 'Aztec Pearl'
This compact shrub has fairly narrow, elegant dark green leaves

Choisya ternata

*Choisya ternata 'Sundance'*

and pink-tinged, white flowers that have a scent of almonds. H and S 1.5m (5ft). Hardy/Z 7.

### C. ternata
**Mexican orange blossom**
A handsome evergreen with glossy green leaves, this flowers mostly in spring with, often, a second flush in late summer or autumn. H and S 2.4m (8ft). Hardy/Z 7–9. The selection **'Sundance'** (syn. 'Lich') has bright yellow leaves. H and S 2m (6ft).

## CISTUS
**Sun rose, rock rose**
In Mediterranean countries these scrubby evergreen shrubs fulfil the same function as heathers in northern Europe. The flowers, which have a papery texture, like poppies, are short-lived, but

*Cistus × skanbergii*

follow one another in quick succession at the height of summer. A hot spot enhances the resinous quality of the stems, and hence the plant's aromatic property. They are perfect in a scree or gravel garden, basking in the reflected heat from the stones, combining well with shrubby herbs and *Genista*.
**Cultivation** Cistus need very well-drained soil of low to moderate fertility in full sun. Dead-head regularly to maintain flower production. In cold areas they may need winter protection.

### C. × hybridus
**(syn. C. coeris, C. × corbariensis)**
This tough hybrid has crinkled, papery, white flowers with a yellow blotch at the base of each petal in summer. H 1m (3ft), S 1.5m (5ft). Borderline hardy/Z 7–9.

### C. ladanifer
**Gum cistus**
This species has large white summer flowers, each petal of which is blotched with maroon at the base. H 2.4m (8ft), S 1m (3ft). Borderline hardy/Z 8.

### C. × pulverulentus
A hybrid cistus with pale pinkish-purple flowers. H and S 60cm (2ft). Borderline hardy/Z 7–9. The compact, spreading **'Sunset'** has glowing magenta flowers. H 60cm (2ft), S 1m (3ft).

### C. × skanbergii
A hybrid with small green leaves and pale pink flowers from early to midsummer. H and S 1m (3ft). Hardy/Z 8–9.

## CORNUS
**Dogwood, cornel**
These mainly deciduous shrubs and trees, native to northern temperate areas around the world, are excellent in cold, damp sites, associating very well with water features. Many can be cut back hard annually, which not only keeps them well within bounds but improves their winter stem colour, for which most are grown. They are highly effective in groups, a feast for the eye when lit up by low shafts of winter sun.

*Cistus × pulverulentus 'Sunset'*

**Cultivation** Dogwoods are tolerant of most soil types. They prefer sun but will do reasonably well in shade.

### C. alba
**(syn. Swida alba, Thelycrania alba)**
**Red-barked dogwood**
This suckering, deciduous species has clusters of small yellow-white flowers in early summer and good autumn leaf colour (red and purple). H and S 3m (10ft). Hardy/Z 2–7. **'Aurea'** has golden leaves and glowing red winter stems. H and S 3m (10ft).

**'Sibirica Variegata'** has leaves boldly variegated with creamy-white, excellent autumn leaf colour and red winter stems. H and S 3m (10ft).

### C. stolonifera
**Red osier dogwood**
This deciduous species is mainly seen in the form **'Flaviramea'**, which has mustard-yellow winter stems. H and S 1.5m (5ft). **'Kelseyi'** is a dwarf form with blackish-red winter stems. H 75cm (30in), S 1.5m (5ft). Hardy/Z 2–8.

*Cornus alba 'Sibirica Variegata'*

Cotinus 'Grace'

Cotoneaster lacteus

# COTINUS
## Smoke bush
The two species of impressive deciduous shrubs in the genus are usually grown in their purple-leaved forms, which also have spectacular autumn colour. They make large, rangy shrubs, but can be cut back hard for larger leaves, albeit at the expense of the flowers. The flowers are tiny, but carried in large panicles, looking like smoke from a distance – hence the common name. They are produced reliably only in hot summers. In cold areas it is better to cut the plant back hard annually for an improved foliage display. The purple-leaved forms are indispensable in a red or purple border. *Cultivation* Grow in reasonably fertile soil in full sun. Hard pruning in spring produces the best leaves, but this can be at the expense of good autumn colour.

### C. coggygria
**Smoke bush, smoke tree**
The plain green species is seldom grown. Far better known is the selection **'Royal Purple'**, grown principally for its coin-like, dramatic purple leaves, which turn vivid red in autumn. H and S 1.2m (4ft). Hardy/Z 5–9.

### C. 'Grace'
This familiar hybrid is similar to *C. coggygria* 'Royal Purple', but is larger and has oval leaves, which turn dark brownish-red in autumn. H 6m (20ft), S 5m (16ft). Hardy/Z 5–9.

# COTONEASTER
This is one of the most important shrub genera, containing both evergreen and deciduous species. Cotoneasters are tough, hardy, tolerant plants, which make excellent foils to a huge range of other showier plants. Some have sufficient distinction to work as specimens, but on the whole it is best to think of these as companions to other plants. Bees appreciate their creamy-white flowers in that bloom in early summer, and birds enjoy their autumn berries.
*Cultivation* Cotoneasters will do well in any reasonable soil in sun or light shade (evergreens cope with deep shade) and are tolerant of pruning.

Cytisus battandieri

### C. dammeri
This evergreen or semi-evergreen species is an outstanding ground-cover plant, carpeting the ground and thriving in many difficult garden situations. The plant flowers in early summer and bears scarlet berries in autumn. H 5cm (2in), S 1.2m (4ft). Hardy/Z 5.

### C. frigidus
This semi-evergreen species has the outstanding cultivar **'Cornubia'**, a tree-like shrub, bearing bright red fruit in autumn, that is good enough to use as a specimen in a small garden. H and S 5m (16ft). Hardy/Z 7–8.

### C. horizontalis
**Fishbone cotoneaster**
A versatile deciduous species, this can be grown as a wall shrub (or even up a tree trunk) or allowed to cascade over a bank, both of which methods display its unusual 'herringbone' habit, or it can be clipped to a table-like shape. It has excellent autumn leaf colour, along with an impressive display of vivid red berries. H 1m (3ft), S 2m (6ft). Hardy/Z 5–9.

### C. lacteus
This evergreen or semi-evergreen species is a dense shrub with an abundant crop of early summer flowers followed by orange-red berries. It is excellent hedging material. H and S 1.5m (5ft). Hardy/Z 7–9.

### C. salicifolius
**Willowleaf cotoneaster**
The species is seldom grown, but its excellent selections include **'Rothschildianus'**, a large evergreen notable for its abundant autumn crop of creamy-yellow berries. H and S 5m (16ft). Hardy/Z 7–8.

### C. × suecicus 'Coral Beauty' (syn. C. 'Royal Beauty')
This small evergreen with arching branches is covered with masses of bright red fruits in autumn. It is good for groundcover. H 60cm (2ft), S 1.2m (4ft). Hardy/Z 6–8.

# CYTISUS
## Broom
The genus contains about 50 species, found mainly in Europe, but also northern Africa and western Asia. These desirable, if usually short-lived, deciduous shrubs seem to pour out their pealike flowers in late spring to early summer. These are fragrant, usually yellow, and are followed by green seedpods. The brooms are excellent in gravel gardens or on any hot, dry site.
*Cultivation* Full sun and well-drained soil is essential, as is wall-training in cold districts. Brooms do not respond well to pruning or being transplanted.

### C. battandieri
**Pineapple broom**
A fascinating plant, this is beautiful in all its parts. The yellow flowers, which both look and smell like pineapples, appear in midsummer among the silky textured, silver-grey leaves. H and S 4m (13ft). Borderline hardy/Z 7–9.

### C. × beanii
Golden-yellow, pea-like flowers smother this sprawling hybrid in late spring or early summer. H 30cm (1ft), S 60cm (2ft). Hardy/Z 7–8.

### C. × praecox
This hybrid group has generally pale yellow flowers. H and S 1m (3ft). Hardy/Z 6–9. The form **'Warminster'** (Warminster broom) has masses of long-lasting, rich cream-coloured flowers.

Daboecia cantabrica 'Alba'

Daboecia cantabrica 'Rainbow'

Daphne bholua

# DABOECIA
## Heather

This genus contains two evergreen species, but only one is hardy, and most of the plants in cultivation are selected forms of this or hybrids with the other. They are best grown en masse in an open situation or in island beds with other heathers or conifers.
*Cultivation* Grow in preferably sandy, well-drained, acid soil in full sun. An open, scrubby site is preferable.

### D. cantabrica
#### Cantabrian heath, St Dabeoc's heath

This plant is normally represented in gardens by one of its many cultivars, all producing their urn-shaped flowers from early summer to mid-autumn. The following are all hardy/Z 5–8. **'Alba'** has white

flowers; plants sold under this name can vary. H 40cm (16in), S 70cm (28in). **'Atropurpurea'** makes glowing colonies of bronze-tinged foliage and has dark pinkish-purple flowers. H 40cm (16in), S 70cm (28in). The flowers of **'Bicolor'** can be white, pink or beetroot red (or streaked), different colours appearing simultaneously on the same stem. H 25cm (10in), S 65cm (26in). The purple flowers of **'Hookstone Purple'** appear only from midsummer. H 25cm (10in), S 65cm (26in). **'Rainbow'** is less eye-catching for its purple flowers than its colourful foliage, variegated with red and yellow. H 25cm (10in), S 65cm (26in). **'Waley's Red'** (syn. 'Whaley') has deep magenta flowers. H 35cm (14in), S 50cm (20in).

### D. × scotica
There are several outstanding members of this hybrid group. **'Silverwells'** has white flowers in summer and mid-green foliage. H 15cm (6in), S 35cm (14in). **'William Buchanan'** has purplish-crimson flowers which appear in mid- to late summer. H 35cm (14in), S 55cm (22in). Both are borderline hardy/Z 4–7.

# DAPHNE
Evergreen, semi-evergreen or deciduous, these delightful shrubs bear flowers with an exquisite fragrance. Some are rock garden plants, but the ones described here work well in mixed or shrub borders. Winter-flowering types

are best sited near a door where their fragrance can be appreciated to the full without the need to go too far outdoors.
*Cultivation* Grow these plants in any moist but well-drained soil in sun or light shade, ideally in a sheltered spot.

### D. bholua
This semi-evergreen species bears deliciously scented clusters of pink and white flowers in late winter. H 3m (10ft), S 1.2m (4ft). Borderline hardy/Z 8–9. The deciduous and hardiest variety *D. bholua* var. *glacialis* **'Gurkha'** bears purplish-pink flowers from mid- to late winter. Hardy/Z 8. **'Jacqueline Postill'** is evergreen and has deep purplish-pink flowers. H 3m (10ft), S 1.2m (4ft). Borderline hardy/Z 8–9.

### D. mezereum
#### Mezereon
A deciduous species, which suits a woodland garden, this produces pink or reddish, highly scented flowers in late winter. The red summer berries are poisonous, but equally attractive. H 1.2m (4ft), S 1m (3ft). Hardy/Z 5–8.

### D. tangutica
This small, evergreen species originates from western China. The fragrant white flowers, which are tinged with rose-purple, appear in late winter to early spring. H 60cm (2ft), S 45cm (18in). Hardy/Z 7–9.

# DESFONTAINEA

This genus of evergreen shrubs is usually represented in gardens by the species described here. When they appear, the flowers are something of a surprise, because in all other respects the plant looks just like a holly. This is an excellent specimen.
*Cultivation* Any well-drained, fertile soil suits these plants, but they need light shade and a sheltered spot. They do well in a mild, damp, maritime climate and will not thrive in dry conditions. In cold areas, grow against a warm wall.

### D. spinosa
Narrow, tubular scarlet and orange flowers hang among the branches in late summer. H and S 2m (6ft). Borderline hardy/Z 9–10.

Daboecia cantabrica 'Atropurpurea'

Daphne tangutica

Desfontainea spinosa

Deutzia longifolia

Elaeagnus × ebbingei 'Limelight'

Erica carnea 'Eileen Porter'

# DEUTZIA

These elegant deciduous shrubs are grown for their dainty flowers in late spring and early summer. They are ideal plants for a cottage garden-style planting or for a small garden.

*Cultivation* Grow in any moderately fertile soil in sun or light shade.

## D. × elegantissima

This hybrid has fragrant pink flowers. H and S 1.5m (5ft). Hardy/Z 5–8. Selections include the upright **'Rosealind'**, which has deep carmine pink flowers; **'Rosea Plena'** with double flowers that open pink and age to white and **'Strawberry Fields'**, which has large deep red-pink flowers. H 2m (6ft), S 1.2m (4ft).

## D. × hybrida

The hybrids in this group have clusters of star-shaped flowers. H 1.2m (4ft), S 1m (3ft). Hardy/Z 5–9. **'Mont Rose'** has deep pink flowers borne on arching stems. H 1.2m (4ft), S 1m (3ft).

## D. longifolia

The straight species has white flowers (usually striped purple on the back) in early to midsummer, but is better known through the selected form **'Veitchii'**, which has purple flowers on purple stems. H 2m (6ft), S 3m (10ft). Hardy/Z 7–9.

# ELAEAGNUS

The genus contains handsome evergreen and deciduous shrubs with a number of uses in the garden, either as specimens or as hedging. Some seem to prefer acid soil. Some also have the benefit of late autumn flowers, which are inconspicuous and parchment-textured, but highly fragrant.

*Cultivation* They suit any well-drained soil except shallow soil over chalk (alkaline soil).

## E. × ebbingei

A good plant for coastal gardens, this has evergreen leaves that seem to tolerate salt-laden winds, making it excellent hedging material. The leaves appear speckled with pewter grey. The autumn flowers are inconspicuous but ravishingly scented. H and S 3m (10ft). Hardy/Z 7–9. **'Limelight'** has leaves that are marked golden yellow in the centre. H and S 3m (10ft).

## E. pungens

This large evergreen species is seldom seen and is usually represented in gardens by **'Maculata'**, an excellent shrub for the winter garden, with leaves that are splashed with bright yellow. It has a tendency to revert to the plain green of the species. H and S 3m (10ft). Hardy/Z 7–9.

Elaeagnus 'Quicksilver'

## E. 'Quicksilver'

A truly outstanding deciduous hybrid, in time virtually a tree, this has narrow, silvery leaves, which are especially striking in spring. H and S 1m (3ft), ultimately larger. Hardy/Z 2–9.

# ERICA
## Heath

Also known as heathers, these are the familiar heaths, scrubby plants that can be used to carpet large tracts of land. They form the largest genus of heaths (the other two are *Calluna* and *Daboecia*), with some 700 or more evergreen species, and are particularly valued in the winter garden, although there are species that flower at other times of year. In smaller gardens ericas are excellent in island beds, either on their own (or with *Calluna* and *Daboecia*) or with dwarf conifers, with which they associate happily. They are also ideal container plants.

*Cultivation* Most heaths need acid soil, preferably sandy and well-drained, but *E. vagans* will tolerate alkaline conditions. If necessary, clip plants lightly after flowering. Tree heathers withstand hard pruning.

## E. australis
### Spanish heath

These are the shrublike tree heaths, straggly in growth but outstanding in flower. The species has lilac-pink flowers from mid- to late spring. H 2m (6ft), S 1m (3ft). Borderline hardy/Z 7–10. Selections include the more compact **'Riverslea'**, which has bright pinkish flowers, mostly in clusters of four. H 1.2m (4ft), S 1m (3ft).

### E. carnea
### Alpine heath, winter heath

This is an important species of carpeting heaths. The flowering season is from late autumn to mid-spring, with plants in milder climates being as much as two months earlier than those in colder areas. Generally they are in flower for six to eight weeks. The following selection of cultivars are all hardy/Z 5–8. **'Adrienne Duncan'** has lilac-pink flowers and dark green foliage tinged bronze. H 15cm (6in), S 35cm (14in). **'Ann Sparkes'** has rose-pink flowers deepening to lilac-pink from late winter to late spring and orange, bronze-tipped foliage, which turns crimson in winter. H 15cm (6in), S 25cm (10in). **'Aurea'** has pink flowers and gold foliage tipped with orange in spring. H 15cm (6in), S 35cm (14in). **'Challenger'** has magenta and crimson flowers and dark green foliage. H 15cm (6in), S 45cm (18in). The slow-growing **'Eileen Porter'** has magenta flowers. H and S 20cm (8in). **'Golden Starlet'** has white flowers and glowing yellow foliage, which turns lime green in winter. H 15cm (6in), S 40cm (16in). **'King George'** has pink flowers and dark green foliage. H 15cm (6in), S 25cm (10in). **'Myretoun Ruby'** (syn. 'Myreton Ruby') has pink flowers, which turn magenta then crimson, and dark green foliage. H 15cm (6in), S 45cm (18in). **'Praecox Rubra'** has lilac-pink flowers and foliage that is sometimes tinged with brown. H 15cm (6in), S 40cm (16in).

Erica carnea 'Rosy Gem'

'**Rosy Gem**' has lilac-pink flowers and dark green foliage. H 20cm (8in), S 45cm (18in). The vigorous '**Springwood White**' has white flowers. H 15cm (6in), S 45cm (18in). '**Vivellii**' (syn. 'Urville') has lilac-pink flowers, which deepen to magenta, from late winter to early spring and dark green, bronze-tinged foliage. H 15cm (6in), S 35cm (14in). '**Westwood Yellow**' has shell-pink flowers initially that darken to lilac-pink, and yellow foliage throughout the year. H 15cm (6in), S 30cm (12in).

### E. cinerea
**Bell heather, twisted heather**
These are the summer-flowering heathers, although some will continue well into autumn. The bell heather is typical of the genus and requires acid soil. The cultivars listed are all hardy/Z 6–8. '**Alfred Bowerman**' has magenta flowers. H 35cm (14in), S 45cm (18in). '**Blossom Time**' has also magenta flowers. H 30cm (12in), S 55cm (22in). '**C.D. Eason**' has bright magenta-pink flowers and dark green foliage. H 25cm (10in), S 50cm (20in). '**C.G. Best**' (syn. 'Graham Thomas') has salmon pink flowers. H 30cm (12in), S 70cm (28in). '**Champs Hill**' has dusky rose-pink flowers. H 35cm (14in), S 45cm (18in). Hardy/Z 5. '**Eden Valley**' has lavender-pink flowers with white bases. H 20cm (8in), S 50cm (20in). '**Fiddler's Gold**' has lilac-pink flowers and bright golden-yellow foliage, which is best in spring. H 25cm (10in), S 45cm (18in). '**Golden**

Erica cinerea 'Alfred Bowerman'

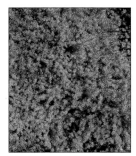
Erica cinerea 'Golden Drop'

**Drop**' has lilac-pink flowers and bright golden-yellow foliage, which is tinged copper in spring and turns copper red in winter. H 20cm (8in), S 60cm (24in). '**Golden Hue**' has amethyst flowers and pale yellow foliage, tipped with orange in winter. H 35cm (14in), S 70cm (28in). '**Golden Sport**' has deep carmine pink flowers and bright golden-yellow foliage. H 15cm (6in), S 30cm (12in). '**Heidebrand**' has flaming pink flowers. H 20cm (8in), S 30cm (12in). '**Hookstone White**' has white flowers. H 35cm (14in), S 65cm (26in). '**Lady Skelton**' has ruby red flowers. H 10cm (4in), S 15cm (6in). '**P.S. Patrick**' has bright reddish-purple flowers and dark glossy green foliage. H 30cm (12in), S 45cm (18in). '**Pentreath**' has rich reddish-purple flowers. H 30cm (12in), S 55cm (22in). '**Pink Ice**' (syn. 'Pink Lace') has rose-pink flowers and foliage that is tinged bronze when young and in winter. H 20cm (8in), S 35cm (14in). '**Stephen Davis**' has luminous red flowers. H 25cm (10in), S 45cm (18in). '**Summer Gold**' has magenta-pink flowers and bright golden-yellow foliage. H 30cm (12in), S 45cm (18in).

### E. × darleyensis
**Darley heath, Darley Dale heath**
These easy-to-grow hybrids have coloured young foliage and a long flowering period, usually from midwinter (sometimes earlier) until well into spring. Darly Dale heaths tolerate lime reasonably. The following selection of cultivars are all hardy/Z 7–8.

Erica × darleyensis 'Kramer's Rote'

'**Archie Graham**' has lilac-pink flowers. H 50cm (20in), S 60cm (24in). '**Arthur Johnson**' (syn. 'Dunwood Splendour') has pink flowers, which deepen to lilac-pink, and foliage tipped with cream in spring. H 60cm (24in), S 75cm (30in). '**Jack H. Brummage**' has lilac-pink flowers and foliage that is yellow-orange throughout the year. H 30cm (1ft), S 60cm (2ft). '**Kramer's Rote**' has magenta flowers and bronze-tinged foliage. H 35cm (14in), S 60cm (24in). '**Silberschmelze**' (syn. 'Molten Silver') has ash-white flowers and foliage faintly tipped with cream in spring. H 35cm (14in), S 80cm (32in). '**White Perfection**' has pure white flowers. H 40cm (16in), S 70cm (28in).

### E. lusitanica
**Portuguese heath**
This has the longest flowering period of any tree heath. The straight species has pink buds opening to white flowers from midwinter to late spring. H 1m

Erica lusitanica 'George Hunt'

(3ft), S 70cm (28in). Borderline hardy/Z 8–10. The selection '**George Hunt**' is smaller, with white flowers in mid-spring. Its chief merit lies in its yellow foliage, which lasts all year, making it an outstanding specimen plant. It is a frost hardy heath but needs a sheltered position. H and S 60cm (24in).

### E. vagans
**Cornish heath, wandering heath**
A vigorous, evergreen, bushy species that provides flowers in autumn (some selections coming into flower in late summer). Tolerates some lime and responds well to pruning. The faded flowers (if left on the plant) turn an attractive russet brown in winter. All are hardy/Z 6–8. '**Birch Glow**' has glowing rose-pink flowers. H 30cm (12in), S 50cm (20in). '**Hookstone Rosea**' has pale rose-pink flowers. H 35cm (14in), S 70cm (28in). '**Kervensis Alba**' has white flowers. H 30cm (12in), S 50cm (20in). '**Lyonesse**' has white flowers. H 25cm (10in), S 50cm (20in). '**Mrs D.F. Maxwell**' has deep rose-pink flowers and dark green foliage. H 30cm (12in), S 45cm (18in). '**Saint Keverne**' has bright pink flowers. H 30cm (12in), S 50cm (20in). '**Summertime**' has shell-pink flowers. H 15cm (5in), S 35cm (14in). '**Valerie Proudley**' has sparse, white flowers and bright lemon-yellow foliage. H 15cm (6in), S 30cm (12in). '**Viridiflora**' has small bluish-green or mauve flowers encased in green bracts. H 30cm (12in), S 55cm (22in).

Erica vagans 'Valerie Proudley'

*Euonymus fortunei* 'Emerald and Gold'

*Exochorda* × *macrantha* 'The Bride'

# EUONYMUS
## Spindle tree
This is a large genus of about 175 species of deciduous, semi-evergreen and evergreen shrubs, trees and climbers. The evergreen shrubs make excellent ground-cover and some can even be persuaded to climb walls. Deciduous types are among the best plants for autumn interest, having both spectacular leaf colour and showy fruits.
*Cultivation* Grow these shrubs in any reasonable garden soil, including chalk (alkaline soil). The evergreens tolerate shade.

### E. alatus
#### Winged spindle tree
The autumn fruits are the distinguishing feature of this deciduous shrub: bluish-purple, they split to reveal bright orange seeds, at the same time as the leaves redden but persisting on the branches for a while after the leaves have fallen. It is suitable for a wild garden or can be used in a hedgerow-type planting and will ultimately make a fine specimen. H 2m (6ft), S 3m (10ft). Hardy/Z 4–9.

### E. fortunei
This evergreen is exclusively grown in its variegated forms, of which there are a great many. The following are all hardy/Z 5–9. **'Emerald and Gold'** has leaves edged yellow. H 1m (3ft), S 1.5m (5ft). **'Harlequin'** is a dwarf plant, with mottled white and green leaves, useful as ground-cover if planted in groups. H and S 1m (3ft). Most handsome of all is **'Silver Queen'**, which has

leaves broadly edged with creamy white. It is slow-growing but worthwhile and spectacular as a climber. H and S 1.5m (5ft), more if wall-trained.

# EXOCHORDA
## Pearl bush
A genus usually represented in gardens in the form described here, a lovely, fresh-looking plant for late spring, associating happily with late-flowering white or cream daffodils.
*Cultivation* This is tolerant of all except waterlogged soils in sun or light shade.

### E. × macrantha 'The Bride'
The deciduous hybrid is only ever seen in this form, which is wreathed in white flowers in late spring, as its name implies. H and S 1m (3ft). Hardy/Z 5–9.

# FORSYTHIA
Indispensable spring-flowering shrubs, these deciduous plants bear bright yellow flowers before the leaves appear. They can be grown as specimens, and are also

*Forsythia suspensa*

excellent in a shrub or mixed border, especially with spring bulbs. The stems are good for cutting, which is a good method of keeping plants within bounds. Eye-catching when in full flower, but of less interest the rest of the time, plant them as unobtrusive backdrops to perennials or as a support for summer-flowering climbers such as clematis.
*Cultivation* Grow in any reasonable soil in sun or light shade. Remove older wood after flowering if necessary and shorten the previous year's growth by about one-third.

### F. × intermedia 'Lynwood'
This ungainly shrub is the best-known form, with rich yellow flowers on arching stems in early to mid-spring. H to 3m (10ft), S 1.5m (5ft). Hardy/Z 5–9.

### F. suspensa
#### Golden bell
An arching shrub with branches covered in bright yellow flowers in early to mid-spring. H and S 2m (6ft) or more. Hardy/Z 6–8.

# FOTHERGILLA
This small but interesting genus, containing only two deciduous species, is related to *Hamamelis*.
*Cultivation* Fothergillas need neutral or lime-free soil in sun or light shade.

### F. major
The pussywillow-like, fragrant flowers are a delight in early spring. Good leaf colour in autumn provides a second season of interest. H and S 2m (6ft). Hardy/Z 5–9.

# FREMONTODENDRON
## Flannel bush
A superb plant for a favoured spot in the garden, these Californian plants will reward you with a magnificent display of gleaming yellow flowers in summer. Contact with the stems and leaves can cause allergies.
*Cultivation* Fremontodendrons tolerate all soil types (except those that are waterlogged) but need a very warm position, such as against a heat-reflecting wall in cold areas. Some winter protection may also be necessary.

*Fremontodendron* 'California Glory'

### F. 'California Glory'
This hybrid, which is evergreen in all but the hardest winters, covers itself with gleaming buttercup-yellow flowers in summer. It is a fast-growing plant, but can be short-lived. H 3m (10ft), S 2m (6ft). Borderline hardy/Z 8–9.

# FUCHSIA
Thousands of hybrids have made this deservedly popular genus of evergreen or deciduous shrubs huge. They flower over a long period (from summer until the first frosts). Some have small, dainty flowers, like the species, but others are more flamboyant. They have a number of uses: in beds and borders, as wall shrubs, and in containers and hanging baskets (particularly pendent varieties). So-called hardy types can be cut back by hard frosts but will recover. From the gardener's point of view, fuchsias can be divided into two broad groups: hardy and tender. Hardy varieties (here defined as those that tolerate temperatures of -5°C/ 23°F or below) are excellent for cool borders. Smaller ones work well as edging plants and in rock gardens. Larger types can be used as specimens, trained against a wall or used for an informal flowering hedge, *F. magellanica* being especially effective for all these purposes. Tender varieties can be used as summer bedding and in containers planted for seasonal interest; those with trailing stems are ideal for hanging baskets. All are suitable for training as standards (trailing fuchsias will produce weeping standards). Most can be

Fuchsia 'Army Nurse'

Fuchsia 'Prosperity'

Fuchsia 'Dark Eyes'

Fuchsia 'Igloo Maid'

successfully overwintered if allowed to dry off at the end of summer before storage in a cool, bright, frost-free place. (The beautiful triphylla types, however, cannot always be relied upon to regenerate the next year.)
**Cultivation** Grow fuchsias in any well-drained soil in sun or light shade in not too cold a position. Protect hardy types over winter with a dry mulch. Cut back to ground level in spring.

### F. magellanica
### Lady's eardrops
This elegant species comes from South America and is one of the most reliable of all the fuchsias. From late summer until well into autumn, the red and bluish-purple flowers hang from the stems in a most appealing way. H 1.2m (4ft), S 45cm (18in), but considerably more where it overwinters successfully. Borderline hardy/Z 7–8. Desirable selections include *F. magellanica* var. *gracilis*, which is more slender in all its parts, with leaves daintily margined with

cream; *F. magellanica* var. *molinae*, which has smaller, pale pink flowers; and **'Versicolor'**, which has the advantage of beautiful leaves, coppery pink on emergence in spring, becoming grey-green.

### Hardy hybrids
These hybrids are all frost hardy/Z 7–9. **'Army Nurse'** has semi-double, blue-violet and deep carmine red flowers. It makes an excellent standard. H 1.5m (5ft), S 1m (3ft). **'Brutus'** is vigorous and has single, rich dark purple and cerise-red flowers. H and S 1m (3ft). The upright and bushy **'Genii'** has single violet-purple and cerise-red flowers among yellow-green leaves. H 1.5m (5ft), S 75cm (30in). **'Hawkshead'** is a popular cultivar, with single, pinkish-white flowers, which are tinged green. H 60cm (2ft), S 45cm (18in). **'Mrs Popple'** has single, deep violet and scarlet flowers. It is good as a hedge. H and S 1m (3ft). **'Prosperity'** has double, pale rose-pink and crimson flowers. H 1.5m (5ft),

S 1m (3ft). **'Riccartonii'** (syn. *F. magellanica* 'Riccartonii'), a good hedging fuchsia, has small purple and red flowers. H and S 1m (3ft). **'Tom Thumb'**, a compact form and good for a rock garden, produces masses of small, single, mauve-purple and carmine-red flowers. H and S 50cm (20in).

### Tender hybrids
These are all half-hardy to frost tender/Z 9–10. **'Alf Thornley'** has double, white and rose-pink flowers. H and S 1m (3ft). **'Chang'** has unusual, single, orange-red flowers, the sepals tipped green. H 1m (3ft), S 75cm (30in). **'Cotton Candy'** is an upright form with double, pale pink and blush-white flowers. H 1m (3ft), S 60cm (2ft). The trailing **'Dark Eyes'** has an abundance of perfectly formed, double, deep violet-blue and red flowers. H and S 1m (3ft). The trailing **'Frosted Flame'** produces large, single, barrel-shaped, bright red and white flowers over a long period. H 30cm (1ft), S 1m

(3ft). **'Gay Parasol'** has dramatic, dark red-purple and ivory-white flowers that open like a parasol. H 1m (3ft), S 45cm (18in). **'Golden Eden Lady'** has single, violet and pink flowers among yellow-green leaves. H 1m (3ft), S 75cm (30in). The trailing **'Igloo Maid'** is initially upright, then spreading, with double, white, pink-tinged flowers among yellow-green leaves. H 1m (3ft), S 60cm (2ft). **'Lord Lonsdale'** is unique, with single, salmon-orange and apricot-pink flowers and curled and crinkled foliage. H 1.5m (5ft), S 1m (3ft). **'Mantilla'**, a trailing, triphylla type, has long, single, rich carmine-pink flowers among bronze-tinged leaves. H 15cm (6in), S 75cm (30in). **'Monterey'** has elegant, long, single, salmon-orange flowers. H and S 1m (3ft). **'Royal Velvet'** has large, double, luminous deep purple and crimson flowers. H 75cm (30in), S 1m (3ft). **'Thalia'** is a triphylla type, with long, single, rich orange-red flowers among velvety leaves. H 45cm (18in), S 1m (3ft).

Fuchsia 'Brutus'

Fuchsia 'Chang'

Fuchsia 'Golden Eden Lady'

Fuchsia 'Mantilla'

*Genista aetnensis*

*× Halimiocistus sahucii*

## GENISTA
### Broom
These largely deciduous, airy plants, native to the Mediterranean, have showers of yellow pea flowers in spring or summer. The stems are leafless, giving a twiggy, even dead appearance in winter. They are not long-lived but are easily raised from seed. Essential plants for a Mediterranean garden or any planting in gravel. *G. aetnensis* can be a tree.
**Cultivation** Brooms thrive in well-drained soils of low fertility in full sun. They do not respond well to hard pruning.

### G. aetnensis
#### Mount Etna broom
A delightful deciduous shrub or small tree for a hot, dry garden, showering golden-yellow flowers

over lower plants in mid- to late summer. H and S 6m (20ft). Borderline hardy/Z 9–10.

### G. lydia
This deciduous species produces a mass of twiggy branches that are covered in deep yellow flowers in late spring and early summer. H 30cm (12in), S to 1m (3ft). Hardy/Z 6–9.

## × HALIMIOCISTUS
A group of usually evergreen hybrids, crosses between the genera *Halimium* and *Cistus*, both of which hybridize naturally in the wild. They have papery flowers that are saucer-shaped, and are excellent in a Mediterranean garden.
**Cultivation** Grow in any free-draining soil, ideally gritty and of low fertility, in full sun.

### × H. sahucii
A shrub with a long flowering season. The chalk-white flowers can be produced from early summer into autumn. H 45cm (18in), S 1m (3ft). Hardy/ Z 7–9.

### × H. wintonensis
A compact shrub, with white flowers marked with yellow and maroon at the base of the petals. H 60cm (2ft), S 1m (3ft). Borderline hardy/Z 7–9.

## HAMAMELIS
### Witch hazel
The genus contains some of the finest winter-flowering shrubs, which would no doubt be more widely grown were it not for their specific cultivation needs. Propagation is also difficult, and plants are slow-growing, so those offered for sale tend to be small and expensive. Besides their spidery, scented winter flowers, they also have outstanding autumn leaf colour.
**Cultivation** Witch hazels need rich, ideally lime-free soil in a sunny site that is sheltered from strong winds.

### H. × intermedia
This is a group of variable hybrids. H and S 4m (13ft), but only after many years. Hardy/Z 5–9. Selections include '**Arnold Promise**', which has bright yellow winter flowers and splendid autumn leaf colour; '**Diane**', which has red flowers and rich

autumn tints; and the rare '**Vesna**', with pale copper-coloured flowers and superb autumn leaf colour.

### H. mollis
#### Chinese witch hazel
One of the best of the witch hazels, this slow-growing species has scented yellow flowers in mid-winter. H and S 4m (13ft), for mature plants. Hardy/Z 5–9.

## HEBE
The large genus of scrubby evergreen plants from Australia and New Zealand contains about 100 species. They are grown for their (mainly) summer flowers, which are highly attractive to bees, and for their foliage. All hebes are excellent in seaside areas. Some have small leaves that cling to the stems almost like scales; these are the so-called whipcord hebes. The species with large, fleshy leaves are less hardy than others. Compact types are good in containers.
**Cultivation** Grow in any reasonable soil in full sun. Some of the taller hebes are remarkably tolerant of dry shade. The larger-leaved species can be pruned hard.

### H. 'Blue Clouds'
This excellent hybrid has long spikes of bluish-mauve flowers from early summer until well into autumn. H 1m (3ft), S 1.2m (4ft). Hardy/Z 8.

### H. cupressoides
This whipcord hebe has grey-green leaves and pale lilac-blue

*Genista lydia*

*Hamamelis mollis*

*Hebe 'Blue Clouds'*

Hebe cupressoides

summer. H and S 60cm (2ft). Borderline hardy/Z 9–10.

### H. 'Mrs Winder' (syn. H. 'Waikiki', H. 'Warlyensis')
This hebe has violet-blue flowers in autumn. The leaves often flush purple in cold weather. H and S 1m (3ft). Borderline hardy/Z 8.

### H. pinguifolia 'Pagei'
A dainty, spreading shrub, this has thick, silver-grey leaves and spikes of white flowers towards the end of spring. H 20cm (8in), S 60cm (2ft). Hardy/Z 8–9.

### H. rakaiensis
This small, green-leaved species grows in a compact bun-shape and produces its white flowers in early to midsummer. H 60cm (2ft), S 1m (3ft). Hardy/Z 8–10.

### H. speciosa 'La Séduisante'
This upright hybrid is aptly named. The rich, purplish-red flowers, carried on stems of the same colour, open from midsummer to late autumn. The leaves also have a purplish finish. H and S 60cm (2ft). Borderline hardy/Z 8.

## HELIANTHEMUM
### Rock rose, sun rose
The genus contains about 110 species of evergreen or semi-evergreen shrubs and subshrubs with brightly coloured flowers

Hebe pinguifolia 'Pagei'

from late spring to summer. *Cultivation* Grow in any free-draining soil in full sun. They thrive on soils of low fertility.

### H. hybrids
Most rock roses are of garden origin, varying in habit but generally hummock-forming. The following are hardy/Z 6–8. 'Ben Nevis' has yellow flowers with red centres. H and S 20cm (8in). 'Rhodanthe Carneum' (syn. 'Wisley Pink') has pink flowers. H 25cm (10in), S to 45cm (18in). 'Wisley White' has white flowers with yellow stamens. H 25cm (10in), S 45cm (18in).

## HIBISCUS
### Rose mallow
These shrubs have mallow-like flowers in late summer. The

flowers which appear in early summer. H and S 1.2m (4ft). Borderline hardy/Z 8–9. The selection 'Boughton Dome' is unique. It looks like a conifer, seldom if ever flowers and makes a neat bun shape without pruning. H 30cm (12in), S 60cm (24in). Hardy/Z 8–9.

### H. 'Great Orme'
An elegant hybrid, this has narrow green leaves and spikes of pale pink flowers, aging to white, from summer to autumn. H 1.5m (5ft), S 1m (3ft). Borderline hardy/Z 9–10.

### H. hulkeana
A species quite unlike any other, this has red-edged, toothed leaves and lilac-like flowers, which may be white, blue or mauve, in early

deciduous types described here are among the last woody plants to come into leaf, which happens in late spring. The genus also includes perennials and annuals. *Cultivation* Grow in any well-drained soil in a sunny, sheltered position.

### H. syriacus
A large number of cultivars have been developed from this upright deciduous species. The following are all hardy/Z 6–9. H 2.5m (8ft), S 2m (6ft). 'Oiseau Bleu' (syn. 'Blue Bird') is among the best known. It has violet-blue flowers with darker eyes. 'Totus Albus' is a rarity in having pure white flowers. It will add late interest to a white border. 'Woodbridge' has warm rose-pink flowers.

Hebe 'Great Orme'

Helianthemum 'Rhodanthe Carneum'

Hibiscus syriacus 'Oiseau Bleu'

Hydrangea arborescens 'Annabelle'

Hydrangea macrophylla 'Ayesha'

Hydrangea quercifolia 'Snow Flake'

# HYDRANGEA

The genus contains medium to large, mainly deciduous shrubs. Late-flowering shrubs are few, and hydrangeas fill the gap nicely. They are also some of the few deciduous shrubs that thrive in containers. Planted in half-barrels, they give distinction to any garden. Hydrangea flower heads take a number of forms: lacecaps have a central mass of tiny fertile flowers surrounded by larger sterile flowers; mopheads (hortensias) have domed heads of sterile flowers only; others have flowers in conical panicles. **Cultivation** All hydrangeas need rich, moisture-retentive soil. The larger, soft-leaved varieties need shelter from strong winds and hot sun, thriving in woodland conditions. Soil pH affects the colour of some hybrids: acid soil enhances blue flowers, while alkaline soil enhances pink flowers. Some selected forms of *H. paniculata* can be pruned hard annually for larger flowers.

## H. arborescens
Sevenbark
The species is less widely grown than its named selections, the loveliest of which is **'Annabelle'**, which produces large, cream-coloured flowerheads in late summer. H and S 1.5m (5ft). Hardy/Z 4–9.

## H. aspera
A rangy shrub, this has velvety stems and blue and white flowers in late summer. Best in lime-free soil in light woodland. H 3m (10ft), S 1.5m (5ft). Hardy/Z 7–9. The **Villosa Group** (syn. *H. villosa*) hybrids are characterized by pale purple flowers and make more rounded shrubs. H and S 1.2m (4ft) or more.

## H. macrophylla
Common hydrangea
The Japanese species is rarely seen in cultivation, but it is widely represented by many selected forms. The following are all hardy/Z 6–9. **'Altona'** (mophead) is a stiffly growing shrub, with flowers that are cerise pink on alkaline soils and mid-blue on acid soils. H and S 1m (3ft). **'Ayesha'** (mophead) has pale mauve or pale blue flowers. H and S 1.5m (5ft). **'Mariesii Perfecta'** (syn. 'Blue Wave'; lacecap) has blue (or mauve, depending on the soil pH) outer flowers

surrounding pink central ones. H and S 2m (6ft).

## H. paniculata
This species makes an upright, vase-shaped shrub and has conical flowerheads. It can be pruned annually to keep it within bounds. H 2m (6ft), S 1.2m (4ft), less if pruned annually. Hardy/Z 4–8. There are a number of fine cultivars, including **'Burgundy Lace'**, which has white flowers, aging to dull pink; **'Kyushu'**, which has pure white flowers; and **'Limelight'**, which has cool lime green flowers, the best colour being in shade.

## H. quercifolia
This species has conical flowerheads, like those of *H. paniculata*, but is distinguished by its oak-like leaves. H 2m (6ft), S 1.5m (5ft). Hardy/Z 5–9. **'Snow Flake'** has pure white flowers.

## H. serrata
(syn. *H. macrophylla* subsp. *serrata*)
The straight deciduous species seldom finds a place in gardens, but the named forms include some splendid plants for late summer-autumn interest, all hardy/Z 6–9. **'Bluebird'** (syn. 'Acuminata'; lacecap) has pale pink, pale purple or rich blue flowers and leaves that assume rich red autumn tints. H 80cm (32in), S 1m (3ft). **'Grayswood'** (lacecap) produces mauve central flowers surrounded by large white flowers that redden as they age. H and S 2m (6ft). **'Preziosa'** (syn. *H.* 'Preziosa'; hortensia) is outstanding, with rich red, mauve or blue flowers, depending on the soil pH. H ans S 1.5m (5ft). **'Rosalba'** (lacecap) has a row of white sterile flowers surrounding the central pink ones. H and S 1.2 m (4ft).

Hydrangea aspera

Hydrangea macrophylla 'Altona'

Hypericum 'Hidcote'

## HYPERICUM
### St John's wort
These valuable shrubs can be difficult to place in the garden because of the uncompromising yellow of the flowers. Try growing them in association with white groundcover roses. *H. olympicum* makes good groundcover.
*Cultivation* Grow hypericums in any well-drained soil in sun or light shade.

### H. 'Hidcote'
This is probably the most significant member of the genus. It has large, shining yellow flowers from midsummer onwards. H and S 1m (3ft). Hardy/Z 6–9.

### H. olympicum
The best species for groundcover, this is a sprawling shrub with golden-yellow flowers from midsummer onwards. Trim it with shears. It can also be grown in rock gardens. H 25cm (10in), S 30cm (12in). Hardy/Z 6–8.

### H. 'Rowallane'
This elegant hybrid needs a sheltered spot. Large, golden-yellow flowers are produced from early summer to autumn. H 2m (6ft), S 1.2m (4ft). Borderline hardy/Z 7–9.

## ILEX
### Holly
Hollies become trees eventually, but they are slow-growing plants and can be treated as shrubs in the garden, particularly if they are cut back regularly, a practice to which they generally respond well. Male and female flowers are carried on separate plants, so if

Hypericum olympicum

you are growing hollies for berry production, make sure there is a male nearby. Conversely, if you grow only males, don't expect any berries. Hollies make excellent hedges (given time) and can be clipped to shape.
*Cultivation* Hollies are tolerant of most sites and soils and will grow in sun or light shade.

### I. × altaclerensis
This is a large hybrid group. The heights and spreads shown are the ultimate size if plants are not pruned, but all can be controlled by regular pruning. Hardy/Z 7–9. The female 'Belgica Aurea' has leaves that are irregularly variegated with creamy yellow.

Ilex × altaclerensis 'Golden King'

H and S 3m (10ft). 'Camelliifolia' is a handsome plain green, free-berrying form. It has smooth leaves that develop a bronze hue in cold weather, and it is one of the best for hedging. H and S 5m (16ft). 'Golden King', a female form, bears large red berries and has gold-edged leaves. H and S 6m (20ft). 'Lawsoniana', a female, is unusual in that the leaf edges are green and the centres are splashed with yellow. H 2.4m (8ft), S 1m (3ft). 'Wilsonii' is a female that is grown for its abundant scarlet berries, rather than its plain green leaves. It will eventually reach tree proportions. H to 9m (29ft), S 5m (16ft).

### I. crenata
### Japanese holly
The species has small, rounded leaves, similar to those of box, and plants can be used for the same purposes. H 2.5m (8ft), S 2m (6ft). Hardy/Z 6–8. 'Mariesii', a female form, is very slow-growing, with black berries. H and S 1m (3ft).

## ITEA
These elegant rather than showy shrubs have fragrant flowers and handsome leaves. The species described here repays careful cultivation and makes a superb wall shrub.
*Cultivation* Grow in fertile, well-drained but not too dry soil in a sunny, sheltered site.

Itea ilicifolia

### I. ilicifolia
This beautiful evergreen shrub from China has shining, holly-like leaves and racemes of greenish flowers in late summer. It is an excellent support for yellow-flowered clematis. H and S 3m (10ft). Borderline hardy/Z 7–9.

## KALMIA
The genus contains seven species of hardy, evergreen shrubs for an acid site. Kalmias are excellent used in conjunction with heathers or in light woodland.
*Cultivation* Grow in reliably moist, lime-free soil in either sun or light shade.

### K. latifolia
### Calico bush, mountain laurel
The species bears white, pink, purple or red flowers in midsummer, which provide a fine contrast to the glossy leaves. H and S 3m (10ft). Hardy/Z 5–9.

Kalmia latifolia

## KERRIA
### Jew's mallow

These spring-flowering, deciduous shrubs, bearing desirable yellow flowers, have a curious, upright, suckering habit. Not the most winsome plants, they are tough and reliable, equally good with daffodils and in a shrub border. There is only one species.
*Cultivation* Kerrias are tolerant of all but waterlogged soils in sun or light shade.

### K. japonica

The species from China and Japan is seldom seen in gardens. It has single yellow flowers from mid- to late spring. H and S 2m (6ft). Hardy/Z 5–9. **'Golden Guinea'** is a rare but worthwhile single form with larger flowers than the species. H 1.5m (5ft), S 1m (3ft). Much more often grown is **'Pleniflora'**, which has double, button-like flowers. H to 2m (6ft), S 1m (3ft).

## KOLKWITZIA
### Beauty bush

The single species in the genus was given its common name for good reason. Its beautiful pink flowers make a stunning sight.
*Cultivation* Kolkwitzias are suitable for all except waterlogged soils in sun or light shade.

### K. amabilis

This elegant, arching deciduous shrub is normally seen in the selected form **'Pink Cloud'**, which

*Kerria japonica 'Pleniflora'*

is festooned with pink, bell-shaped flowers in late spring to early summer. H 3m (10ft), S 4m (12ft). Hardy/Z 5–9.

## LAVANDULA
### Lavender

Lavenders are well-known herb garden plants, but they have a number of other uses, principally as flowering hedging. When they are in flower, these evergreen shrubs and subshrubs will be alive with bees. They make a classic combination with old roses and can also be trained as standards.
*Cultivation* Lavenders will grow in all soil types but must have good drainage and a position in full sun. Clip hedging lightly in spring.

### L. angustifolia
(syn. *L. officinalis*)
#### Old English lavender

The species has grey-green leaves and scented blue-grey flowers all summer long. H and S 60cm (2ft). Hardy/Z 6–9. There are many selections, including **'Hidcote'** (syn. *L.* 'Hidcote Blue'), which has rich deep lavender-blue flowers; **'Munstead'**, which has soft, lilac-blue flowers; and the strong-growing **'Rosea'**, with pink flowers. H and S 60cm (2ft).

### L. stoechas
#### French lavender

Essential in any herb garden, this species has distinctive flower spikes, with bright purple, erect bracts at the top of each flower-head. It has a long flowering period. H and S 45cm (18in). Borderline hardy/Z 7–9.

## LAVATERA
### Tree mallow

A genus of evergreen, semi-evergreen and deciduous shrubs, perennials and annuals, which are highly valued for their late-season flowers. The species described is widely grown but is rather harsh in colour. The various hybrids are all improvements on the species and integrate better into mixed borders planned for late-summer interest.
*Cultivation* Grow lavateras in any well-drained soil in full sun.

### L. 'Barnsley'

One of the best-known hybrids, this semi-evergreen plant bears very pale pink mallow flowers with warm pinkish-red eyes towards the end of summer. It has a tendency to revert to type over time. H and S 2m (6ft). Hardy/Z 8.

### L. thuringiaca
#### Tree lavatera

The species bears deep pink flowers in profusion in late summer to autumn. H 2m (6ft), S 1.5m (5ft). Hardy/Z 8. The superior selection **'Ice Cool'** is similar to 'Barnsley', but the flowers do not have the red maskings. H and S 1.5m (5ft).

## × LEDODENDRON

This hybrid genus consists of a single shrub, which is a cross between *Rhododendron trichosomum* and *Ledum glandulosum* var. *columbianum*.
*Cultivation* Grow in acid, well-drained soil in partial shade.

*Kolkwitzia amabilis 'Pink Cloud'*

*Lavandula stoechas*

*Lavandula angustifolia 'Hidcote'*

× *Ledodendron* 'Arctic Tern'
(syn. *Rhododendron* 'Arctic Tern')
This compact, vigorous, evergreen
shrub bears white flowers in late
spring to early summer. H and S
60cm (2ft). Hardy/Z 8.

## LEPTOSPERMUM
Tea tree
The genus contains about 80
species of evergreen trees and
shrubs from Australia, New
Zealand and South-east Asia
grown for their foliage and small
flowers. Not for all gardens, these
plants are not reliably hardy and
have specific soil requirements,
although in the right conditions
they make charming specimens.
*Cultivation* Grow in lime-free,
reliably moist, well-drained soil in
full sun with some shelter,
particularly in cold areas.

*L. lanigerum*
Woolly tea tree
This erect species from Australia
has white flowers in early summer.
H 1.5m (5ft), S 1m (3ft).
Borderline hardy/Z 8.

*L. scoparium*
Manuka, New Zealand tea-tree
This is a variable species, which
is rarely seen in cultivation, but
there are many cultivars. The
following are half-hardy/Z 9–10.
The dwarf **'Kiwi'** has pinkish-red
flowers and reddish-purple leaves.
H and S 1m (3ft). The rarer
**'Lyndon'** has white flowers. H
and S 3m (10ft).

*Lavatera 'Barnsley'*

## LEUCOTHOE
These compact and dainty shrubs
are grown for their evergreen
foliage and flowers. They are not
reliably hardy in all situations and
have specific soil requirements.
They are good in peat beds or in
light woodland.
*Cultivation* Grow in fertile, acid
soil in sun or light shade, with
shelter from cold winds. They will
not tolerate dry conditions.

*L.* 'Scarletta'
(syn. *L. axillaris* 'Scarletta',
*L.* 'Zeblid')
This evergreen shrub bears small,
white, pitcher-shaped flowers in
late spring. The foliage reddens in
late summer, but is not shed. H
and S 60cm (2ft). Hardy/Z 5.

*L. walteri*
(syn. *L. fonanesiana*)
The form of the species most
generally seen is **'Rainbow'**, a
spreading evergreen with striking
leaves variegated with pink and
cream. The white, lily-of-the-
valley-like flowers seem incidental
when they appear in summer. H
and S 60cm (2ft). Hardy/Z 5–8.

## LEYCESTERIA
These sombre, deciduous shrubs
are grown for their late-summer
flowers and autumn fruits.
The genus, which contains six
species, is generally represented in
cultivation by the single species
described here.
*Cultivation* It is suitable for most
soils in sun or light shade.

*L. formosa*
Pheasant berry, Himalayan
honeysuckle
The first common name derives
from the appeal of the dark
purple autumn fruits to
pheasants. These follow the
drooping panicles of white and
claret-purple summer flowers.
H 2m (6ft), S 1m (3ft).
Borderline hardy/Z 7–9.

## LIGUSTRUM
Privet
An unnecessarily maligned genus,
*Ligustrum* is usually seen in
gardens as hedging, for which
purpose it is inferior to some
other plants. It is put to best use
in a mixed or shrub border as an

*Leucothoe 'Scarletta'*

unassuming backdrop to other
more flamboyant plants, but
privets are also surprisingly good
as specimens. Variegated forms
are highly effective when trained
as standards.
*Cultivation* Privets are tolerant
of any ordinary garden soil in sun
or shade.

*L. ovalifolium*
This is the privet most widely used
as hedging, when it is clipped to
keep it to size. The species, which
is usually evergreen, has plain green
leaves and white flowers in summer.
H and S 4m (13ft). Hardy/Z
6–10. The selection **'Aureum'**
(syn. 'Aureomarginatum') is
variegated with yellow and is less
vigorous. H and S 3m (10ft).

*Leptospermum scoparium 'Lyndon'*

*Leycesteria formosa*

*Ligustrum tschonoskii*

### L. tschonoskii
This handsome deciduous species is a rarity in gardens. The leaves and flowers are somewhat larger than those of most other privets. H and S 2m (6ft), but eventually tree-like. Hardy/Z 6.

## LONICERA
### Honeysuckle
Most honeysuckles are climbers, but the genus also includes the following shrubs, many of them excellent for the winter garden and extremely hardy. The deciduous species described here can be wall-trained if you choose, which can sometimes lead to more abundant flowering. *L. nitida* is useful for hedging and also for small-scale topiary.

*Cultivation* Honeysuckles will grow in any, preferably humus-rich, soil in sun or light shade. Cut back some of the oldest stems every year after flowering.

### L. fragrantissima
A good plant for winter interest, this deciduous or semi-evergreen Chinese species has small, fragrant, white and pink flowers in midwinter. Unfortunately, it is rather dull the rest of the time, unless used as a support for annual climbers, such as sweet peas. H and S 1.5m (5ft). Hardy/ Z 5–8.

### L. nitida
This dense evergreen shrub has neat, oval, dark green leaves. Both the species and the cultivar described below are ideal for hedging and may be easily controlled by pruning. H 2m (6ft), S 1.5m (5ft). Hardy/Z 7–9. The form usually seen is **'Baggesen's Gold'**, which has yellow-green leaves.

### L. × purpusii
This deciduous hybrid produces fragrant, white flowers on the bare stems in winter. Both this and the selected form described here are almost indistinguishable from *L. fragrantissima*, leading to confusion in the nursery trade. H and S 1.5m (5ft). Hardy/Z 7–9. **'Winter Beauty'** has creamy-white flowers from early winter until spring. H and S 1.2m (4ft).

*Lonicera nitida* 'Baggesen's Gold'

## MAGNOLIA
Many magnolias are trees, but there are a few shrubs in the genus that are delightful and easy to cultivate, if a little slow to get into their stride. The deciduous spring-flowerers make ideal central features in spring borders planted with dwarf narcissi, *Anemone blanda*, species tulips and crocuses.
*Cultivation* Grow in fertile, well-drained soil in sun, although in frost-prone areas early flowering magnolias benefit from some shade from morning sun at flowering times.

### M. × loebneri 'Leonard Messel'
This delightful deciduous hybrid has pale pink, spidery flowers in mid-spring. H 3m (10ft), S 2.5m (8ft). Hardy/Z 5–9.

### M. stellata
### Star magnolia
This slow-growing, deciduous species is indispensable, with masses of spidery white flowers in mid-spring. It requires a sheltered spot. H 1.2m (4ft), S 1.5m (5ft). Hardy/Z 5–9.

## MAHONIA
The genus contains about 70 species of evergreen shrubs, which are rather similar to *Berberis* – in fact, some botanists would like to unite the genera. Most have deliciously scented flowers, but their prime use is to fill inhospitable sites.

*Magnolia* × *loebneri* 'Leonard Messel'

*Cultivation* Mahonias are happy in all well-drained soils, including chalk (alkaline soil). Large-leaved species benefit from shelter from strong winds. Pruning plants when young can encourage bushiness, but some forms are naturally rangy.

### M. aquifolium
### Mountain grape holly, Oregon grape
The species has glossy green leaves and yellow flowers in late winter to early spring. H 1m (3ft), S 1.5m (5ft). Hardy/Z 6–9. There are a number of cultivars, including the vigorous and low-growing **'Apollo'**; and **'Smaragd'**, which has bronze, netted foliage. H 60cm (2ft), S 1m (3ft).

*Magnolia stellata*

*Mahonia trifolia*

*Mahonia aquifolium*

*Mahonia* × *media* 'Lionel Fortescue'

### M. japonica

This erect species produces its arching racemes of scented yellow flowers from late autumn to early spring, followed by blue-purple berries. H 2m (6ft), S 3m (10ft). Hardy/Z 7–9. The selection **'Bealei'** has more compact flower spikes.

### M. lomariifolia

This elegant species is one of the parents of *M.* × *media* (the other is *M. japonica*), which it resembles in some respects, though it is more rangy in habit and slightly less resistant to extreme cold. The racemes of flowers, which smell like lily-of-the-valley, appear from autumn to late winter and are followed by bluish, grape-like fruits. H 3m (10ft), S 2m (6ft). Hardy/Z 8–10.

### M. × media

This hybrid group includes a number of notable named garden selections, all similar and equally effective and all with long racemes of fragrant yellow flowers in winter. Leggy specimens can be pruned hard in spring. They include **'Charity'**, which has slender, upright, later-spreading spikes of very fragrant yellow flowers; **'Lionel Fortescue'**, which has upright plumes of bright yellow, slightly less fragrant flowers; and **'Winter Sun'**, which has dense clusters of yellow flowers. H 2m (6ft), S 1.2m (4ft). Hardy/Z 7–9.

### M. trifolia
(syn. *M. eutriphylla*)

This unusual species is variable, existing in both prostrate and more upright forms. The short spikes of yellow flowers appear in spring, and the leaves flush purple-red in cold weather. H and S 2m (6ft). Hardy/Z 7.

### M. × wagneri

This hybrid group contains a number of excellent garden plants. The notable **'Undulata'** (syn. *M.* 'Undulata') bears yellow flowers in spring and has hollylike leaves that, in addition to having wavy edges, turn rich plum-purple in cold weather. The rich yellow flowers appear in spring. H and S 2m (6ft). Hardy/Z 8–9.

## MYRTUS
### Myrtle

Myrtles are rich in historical associations and were traditionally used in royal wedding bouquets. In cold areas, they need to be tucked under a sheltering wall.
*Cultivation* They will grow in most soils, including chalk (alkaline), but they need a warm, sunny site. Young plants benefit from some protection in winter until they are well established.

### M. communis
#### Common myrtle

This slow-growing evergreen bushy shrub has dark green foliage and fragrant white flowers in summer, followed by purple-black berries. H and S 3m (10ft).

Borderline hardy/Z 9–10. The more compact and wind-resistant *M. communis* subsp. *tarentina* (syn. 'Jenny Reitenbach', 'Microphylla', 'Nana') has pink-flushed, white flowers and white berries. H and S 2m (6ft).

## NANDINA
### Sacred bamboo, Heavenly bamboo

The only species in the genus is this elegant evergreen or semi-evergreen shrub, which is grown for its overall appearance and summer flowers. Although related to *Berberis*, it looks nothing like it. The sacred bamboo combines well with grasses and is a good choice where a true bamboo would be too large.
*Cultivation* Grow in any well-drained but not too dry, reasonably fertile soil in sun, preferably with some shelter. Young plants may need winter protection in cold areas.

### N. domestica

The large panicles of white, starry, summer flowers are followed by red autumn berries. The leaves start purplish-red when young, turn dark green, redden again in autumn and hold their colour into winter. H 2m (6ft), S 1m (3ft). Borderline hardy/Z 7–10. **'Fire Power'** is a more compact form. H 1.2m (4ft), S 60cm (2ft). **'Richmond'** bears a mass of scarlet berries in autumn. H 2m (6ft), S 1.2m (4ft).

*Myrtus communis*

*Nandina domestica* 'Fire Power'

Nerium oleander 'Roseum Plenum'

Osmanthus delavayi

Olearia 'Waikariensis'

## NERIUM
### Oleander
This is a typical plant of the
Mediterranean (although it also
appears in China), where it is
widely planted as a kerbside
shrub. Not hardy enough to be
grown outdoors in frost-prone
climates, it makes an excellent
conservatory (porch) plant. There
is only one species, of which all
parts are poisonous.
*Cultivation* Grow in moderately
fertile, well-drained soil in full
sun. Conservatory plants can be
pruned hard to keep them compact.

### N. oleander
#### Rose bay
The evergreen species has
fragrant, pink, red, apricot, yellow

or white flowers throughout the
summer among the upright,
lance-shaped leaves. When grown
in a container it will be smaller
than the dimensions indicated. H
to 3m (10ft), S 2m (6ft).
Tender/Z 10. Selections include
**'Peach Blossom'**, which has pink
flowers; **'Roseum Plenum'**, which
has double, pink flowers; and
**'Variegatum'**, which has variegated
leaves and pink flowers. H and S
to 2m (6ft).

## OLEARIA
### Daisy bush
The daisy bushes, mainly from
Australia and New Zealand,
are fine shrubs, valued for their
daisy-like summer flowers and
evergreen foliage. They are good
in island beds and also make very
good wind-resistant shelter.
*Cultivation* Grow olearias in any
well-drained, reasonably fertile
soil in full sun.

### O. × haastii
This hybrid has clusters of
flowers in mid- to late summer
and makes a dense, rounded bush.
H 2m (6ft), S 3m (10ft).
Hardy/Z 8–10.

### O. macrodonta
#### New Zealand holly
This species is one of the most
impressive of the genus, with
large, pewter grey, holly-like leaves
and daisy-like flowers in summer.
H 6m (20ft), S 5m (16ft).
Borderline hardy/Z 9–10.

### O. 'Waikariensis'
(**syn. O. oleifolia**)
This hybrid has felted stems and
the characteristic grey leaves and
daisy-like summer flowers. H and
S 2m (6ft). Hardy/Z 8.

## OSMANTHUS
These shrubs with handsome,
evergreen leaves are related to the
olive. Plant in mixed or shrub
borders or in light woodland.
They also make an unusual hedge.
*Cultivation* Almost any soil is
tolerated in sun or shade, but
some shelter from cold winds is
desirable to avoid leaf scorch.

### O. decorus
(**syn. Phillyrea decora**)
This fine species from western

Asia is grown for its overall
appearance. The white flowers,
which appear in spring, are small
but sweetly scented. It takes
kindly to pruning. H 3m (10ft),
S 4m (13ft). Hardy/Z 6–9.

### O. delavayi
(**syn. Siphonosmanthus delavayi**)
A slow-growing species from
China, this has tiny leaves and
fragrant, white flowers in mid-
spring. H 2m (6ft), S 2.4m
(8ft). Hardy/Z 7–9.

## OZOTHAMNUS
The genus of summer-flowering,
evergreen shrubs, which look like
*Rosmarinus*, contains about 50
species. They are good in mixed
or shrub borders but are not

Olearia × haastii

Ozothamnus rosmarinifolius 'Silver Jubilee'

Paeonia suffruticosa subsp. rockii

Paeonia delavayi var. lutea

hardy enough for all gardens.
They are excellent in summer
borders.
*Cultivation* Grow in any well-
drained soil in sun. Some
protection may be necessary
in cold winters.

### O. rosmarinifolius
(syn. *Helichrysum rosmarinifolium*)
This species has an erect habit
and dark green foliage. Pinkish
buds open to heads of white
flowers in early summer. H 3m
(10ft), S 1.5m (5ft). Borderline
hardy/Z 8–9. The leaves of
'Silver Jubilee' are silvery green.
H 2m (6ft), S 1.2m (4ft).

## PAEONIA
### Peony
This is a genus primarily of
perennials, but it also includes
some magnificent deciduous
shrubs, the so-called tree peonies.
The hybrids are usually expensive,
but the outlay should not put off
the committed gardener, for these
are long-lived plants that reward
careful cultivation. All tree peonies
make splendid specimens, while
the species are probably best
grown in light woodland.
*Cultivation* Tree peonies need
rich, fertile soil in sun or light
dappled shade. Some protection
from late frost, which can damage
leaves and flowers, is desirable.

### P. delavayi
This species has rich dark red,
bowl-shaped flowers in late

spring. H 2m (6ft), S 1m (3ft).
Hardy/Z 5–8. The variety
*P. delavayi var. lutea* (syn. *P. lutea*)
has golden-yellow flowers and
deeply divided glossy foliage.

### P. suffruticosa
### Moutan
This is the species that has engen-
dered the huge range of hybrids
(many of Japanese origin). All are
hardy/Z 4–8. 'Banksii' has double,
carmine flowers; 'Reine Elizabeth'
has double, salmon-orange flowers
with ruffled margins; and 'Renkaku'
(syn. 'Flight of Cranes') has dense,
double, white flowers. *P. suffruticosa*
subsp. *rockii* (syn. 'Joseph Rock',
'Rock's Variety') is the ultimate
connoisseur's plant, with huge,
double white flowers marked with
maroon at the base. This rare
plant is not variable in cultivation.
H 2m (6ft), S 1.5m (5ft).

## PEROVSKIA
### Russian sage
A good shrub for late-summer
flowers, this tough plant comes

Perovskia 'Blue Spire'

Philadelphus 'Belle Etoile'

from Siberia. It produces a sheaf
of whitened stems covered in
small, mauve-blue flowers. It is
excellent in a Mediterranean
or gravel garden, hot sun only
enhancing its aromatic properties.
The genus is normally represented
in gardens by hybrids.
*Cultivation* Grow perovskias in
any free-draining soil in full sun.
They tolerate stony soil. Prune
hard each year in spring.

### P. 'Blue Spire'
This hybrid has silver-blue, deeply
cut leaves and spires of rich blue
flowers in late summer. H and S
to 1m (3ft). Hardy/Z 6–9.

## PHILADELPHUS
### Mock orange
The scent of the mock orange is
unmistakable and almost cloyingly
sweet when it hangs in the air in
early summer. Most of the plants
in cultivation are hybrids of
garden origin. Grow them as a
fragrant backdrop to a mixed
border. *P. coronarius* 'Aureus' can be
grown exclusively for its foliage.
*Cultivation* Mock oranges do
well in most reasonable garden
soil in sun or light shade.

### P. 'Avalanche'
This aptly named plant has masses
of scented white flowers. H and S
1.5m (5ft). Hardy/Z 5–8.

### P. 'Beauclerk'
The flowers of this distinctive,
arching shrub are characterized by

central cerise blotches. H and S
1.5m (5ft). Hardy/Z 5–8.

### P. 'Belle Etoile'
This hybrid has delicious,
fragrant single white flowers.
H 1.5m (5ft), S 1.2m (4ft).
Hardy/Z 5–8.

### P. coronarius
The species is grown less than its
lovely cultivars, which are hardy/Z
5–9. 'Aureus' has soft gold-green
leaves. It needs shelter from hot
sun, but lights up a dark corner
when the light strikes it. Pruning
just before flowering results in a
fresh crop of lime-green leaves
(at the expense of the flowers).
'Variegatus' (syn. 'Bowles'
Variety') has leaves that are edged
in cream and white flowers. H and
S 1.2m (4ft).

### P. 'Manteau d'Hermine'
One of the daintiest of the mock
oranges, this hybrid smothers
itself in double, creamy-white
flowers. H and S 45cm (18in).
Hardy/Z 5–8.

### P. microphyllus
This elegant species produces a
mass of fragrant, single, pure
white flowers. H and S to 1m
(3ft). Hardy/Z 6.

### P. 'Virginal'
This well-known and justly
popular cultivar has double, white
flowers. This is a grand plant.
Old specimens tend to become
bare at the base. H to 3m (10ft),
S 2m (6ft). Hardy/Z 5–9.

Philadelphus 'Manteau d'Hermine'

Phillyrea angustifolia

Phlomis italica

# PHILLYREA
## Jasmine box
This classy evergreen shrub was
widely grown in the 17th century
but is nowadays increasingly rare.
It is a good alternative to box
and rather faster-growing. It is
suitable for a maritime garden.
On the debit side, it is difficult
to propagate, so stocks tend to
be low.
*Cultivation* They will grow in any
fertile, well-drained soil in sun or
light shade.

### P. angustifolia
The flame-like, hard, dark green
leaves always excite comment.
The flowers, produced in spring,
are insignificant. This species
responds well to pruning. H and
S to 3m (10ft), but usually less
in gardens. Hardy/Z 7–9.

# PHLOMIS
These evergreen shrubs and
perennials have woolly grey
leaves. They are well-suited to a
Mediterranean border, grown in
association with plants such as
*Cistus* and *Halimium* and woody
herbs such as rosemary and
lavender.
*Cultivation* Phlomis need very
well-drained, only moderately
fertile soil and a position in
full sun.

### P. fruticosa
#### Jerusalem sage
The best-known species, with
whorls of sulphur-yellow flowers
appearing in summer among the
grey leaves. H and S 1.2m (4ft).
Hardy/Z 8–10.

### P. italica
Daintier than *P. fruticosa*, this
choice species has pink or pale
purple flowers. H and S 60cm
(2ft). Borderline hardy/Z 8–9.

# PHOTINIA
These excellent shrubs are grown
mainly for the brilliance of their
spring foliage. They suit a mixed
or shrub border and make a good
alternative to *Pieris* in gardens
with alkaline soil.
*Cultivation* Grow in any well-
drained soil in sun or light shade.

### P. davidiana
(**syn.** *Stranvaesia davidiana*)
This handsome shrub, semi-
evergreen in all but the coldest
areas, has as its main feature
long-lasting crimson berries,
which ripen in autumn. Some
of the leaves turn bright red at
the same time, while others
remain green. H and S 2.4m
(8ft). Hardy/Z 7–9.

### P. × fraseri
This hybrid group includes a
number of excellent selected
forms. Hardy/Z 8–9. The new
growth of the spreading form
**'Birmingham'** is deep coppery red.
**'Red Robin'** has spectacular bright
red young stems and leaves in
vivid contrast to the glossy green
older leaves. H and S 1.5m (5ft).

# PHYGELIUS
The subshrubs in this genus will
be evergreen in mild winters, but
may die back in periods of prolonged cold, although they often
reshoot from ground level. In
cold areas, they are best in the
lee of a wall.
*Cultivation* Phygelius need well-
cultivated, rich soil and a warm,
sheltered site. Cut back hard
annually in spring if the topgrowth is killed by frost.

### P. aequalis
The species, a compact shrub, has
dusky red-pink tubular flowers.
H 1m (3ft), S 60cm (2ft).
Borderline hardy/Z 7–9. The
species is less often seen than the
cultivar **'Yellow Trumpet'**, which
has light green leaves and, as the
name suggests, yellow flowers.
H 1m (3ft), S 60cm (2ft).

### P. × rectus
A group of hybrids normally
represented in gardens by one of
the several available cultivars, such
as **'African Queen'**, which has red
flowers; and **'Moonraker'**, which
has creamy yellow flowers. H 1m
(3ft), S 60cm (2ft). Borderline
hardy/Z 8–9.

Phygelius × rectus 'Moonraker'

# PIERIS
These elegant evergreen woodland
shrubs bear racemes of lily-of-the-
valley-like flowers in spring. Some
forms have eye-catching young
foliage as well.
*Cultivation* Acid soil, preferably
enriched with leaf mould, is
essential. Shelter from early
morning sun and strong winds
is also desirable. They do best
in dappled light or a site with
afternoon sun only.

### P. 'Forest Flame'
This fine hybrid is grown for its
foliage rather than for its flowers,
which are not reliably produced.
The flush of young leafy growth
in spring is brilliant red, fading to
green. H 2.2m (7ft), S 1m (3ft).
Borderline hardy/Z 7–9.

Photinia x fraseri

Phygelius × rectus 'African Queen'

Pieris 'Forest Flame'

Pieris japonica

### P. formosa
The young leaves are red, turning bronze and maturing to dark green. Sprays of white flowers are borne in spring. H and S 2m (6ft). Borderline hardy/Z 7–9. The species is normally represented in gardens in the form *P. formosa* var. *forrestii* 'Wakehurst', which has vivid red young leaves and sprays of white flowers that open from red buds.

### P. japonica
Lily-of-the-valley bush
This bushy shrub has glossy green leaves and cascading sprays of white flowers in spring. H and S 3m (10ft). Hardy/Z 6–8. Selected forms include 'Pink Delight', which has masses of pink flowers; 'Valley Rose', which has pale pink flowers; and the prolific 'Valley Valentine', which has cherry red flowers.

## PITTOSPORUM
These evergreen shrubs are grown for the interest of their leaves. Not only do some forms have coloured foliage, but the leaves also have wavy edges. Most thrive in coastal areas.
*Cultivation* These plants are suitable for most well-drained soil in sun, but they will not tolerate very cold spots.

### P. tenuifolium
This, the most popular species, is usually grown in its coloured leaf forms, which all make excellent container plants. Borderline hardy/Z 9–10. 'Irene Paterson' has very pale green leaves heavily

Potentilla fruticosa 'Medicine Wheel Mountain'

marked with white. It is slower growing than the species. H 1.2m (4ft), S 60cm (2ft). The young leaves of 'Purpureum' are green but age to purple. H 1.2m (4ft), S 60cm (2ft). The leaves of the dwarf 'Tom Thumb' turn rich purple in cold weather. H and S 1m (3ft).

## POTENTILLA
These neat, very hardy, deciduous shrubs bear masses of rose-like flowers in summer. They are a good choice for the front of a border or to mark the turn in a path. They can also be grown in rock gardens.
*Cultivation* Potentillas will grow in most well-drained soils is sun or light shade.

### P. 'Blazeaway'
This hybrid has dark green leaves and fiery orange-red flowers. H and S to 1m (3ft). Hardy/Z 5–8.

Potentilla 'Blazeaway'

Potentilla fruticosa 'Abbotswood'

### P. fruticosa
Shrubby cinquefoil
This is the best-known species, and a huge range of garden varieties have been developed from it, including 'Abbotswood', which has white flowers over a long period; 'Medicine Wheel Mountain', which has yellow flowers; 'Pretty Polly', which has pink flowers; and 'Snowbird', an unusual variety, which has double, pure white flowers. H 1m (3ft), S 1.2m (4ft). Hardy/Z 3–8.

## PRUNUS
Ornamental cherry
This genus contains over 200 species and ornamental cherries are well known, but the genus also includes a couple of fine evergreen shrubs, which are good for hedging and for clipping to formal shapes or as standards.
*Cultivation* These grow in most soils but may not do well on shallow soil over chalk (alkaline soil).

### P. laurocerasus
Cherry laurel
This useful evergreen shrub is much used for hedging, the large glossy leaves making a welcome contrast to most other hedging plants. Spikes of white flowers in spring and black autumn berries are bonuses. It can easily be kept under control by pruning. H 3m (10ft), S 2m (6ft). Hardy/Z

7–9. 'Camelliifolia' has curiously twisted leaves. H 3m (10ft), S 4m (13ft). The diseased-looking 'Marbled White' (syn. 'Castlewellan') has leaves that are heavily mottled with creamy white. H and S 5m (16ft). The well-known 'Otto Luyken' is a low-growing form with handsome, narrow leaves. H 1m (3ft), S 1.5m (5ft).

### P. lusitanica
Portugal laurel
Less familiar, but more refined than *P. laurocerasus*, this evergreen species carries glossy leaves and spikes of white flowers in early to midsummer. It makes a beautiful large standard. H 2.7m (9ft), S 2m (6ft). Borderline hardy/Z 7–9.

Prunus laurocerasus 'Marbled White'

Rhamnus alaternus 'Argenteovariegata'

## PYRACANTHA
### Firethorn
An important genus of tough, hardy, spiny, evergreen plants that tolerate exposure. The cream-coloured flowers cascading from the branches in summer are followed by equally impressive yellow, orange or red berries that last all winter. An unexpected but highly effective use for pyracanthas is as a hedge.
*Cultivation* Grow in any fertile, well-drained soil in sun or shade.

### *P. coccinea* 'Red Column'
This upright shrub has reddish shoots and vivid red berries in autumn, and shows good resistance to fireblight. H 1.5m (5ft), S 1m (3ft). Hardy/Z 7–8.

### *P.* 'Knap Hill Lemon'
An unusual variety, worth growing for its clear yellow berries in autumn. H 1.5m (5ft), S 1m (3ft). Hardy/Z 7.

### *P.* 'Soleil d'Or'
This popular hybrid has hawthorn-like white flowers in late spring succeeded by golden-yellow berries in autumn. H and S 1.5m (5ft). Hardy/Z 7.

## RHAMNUS
### Buckthorn
Fine foliage plants, sometimes evergreen, these shrubs are excellent as hedging or in a shrub border. The berries are poisonous.
*Cultivation* Grow in any reasonable garden soil in sun or light shade.

### *R. alaternus* 'Argenteovariegata' (syn. *R. alaternus* 'Variegata')
Probably the most familiar of the genus, the leaves of this evergreen are handsomely variegated with grey marbling and irregular white leaf margins. It appreciates a warm, sheltered site. H and S 1.5m (5ft). Borderline hardy/Z 7–9.

## RHODODENDRON
This large and complex genus includes plants that range from huge, tree-like shrubs to diminutive specimens for a rock garden or alpine trough. There would be a rhododendron for every garden were it not for the fact that they must have acid soil, which rules them out for some gardeners. Some are happy in containers, however, bringing them within reach for gardeners on alkaline soil. Essentially, most are wood-landers and look good in that setting, but modern varieties (especially those related to *R. yakushimanum*) are compact, dwarf plants that cope with more open situations. Rhododendrons combine well with other acid-loving shrubs, such as pieris and camellias, as well as with heathers. Deciduous rhododendrons, which are often more rangy and open in habit, are good with spring bulbs.
*Cultivation* Rhododendrons must have acid soil that is high in nutrients and well-drained. Most prefer light, dappled shade.

### Species and selected forms
### *R. augustinii* Electra Group
An evergreen shrub with funnel-shaped, violet-blue flowers in mid-spring. H 4m (13ft), S 2.5m (8ft). Hardy/Z 7–8.

Rhododendron decorum

### *R. charitopes*
This compact evergreen species, which is good in a rock garden, comes from southern Tibet. Trusses of waxy, bell-shaped, pale pink or violet flowers are borne in late spring to early summer. H and S 1m (3ft). Hardy/Z 6–8.

### *R. cinnabarinum* subsp. *cinnabarinum* Roylei Group
These evergreen hybrids have deep coppery plum to crimson, funnel-shaped flowers, which appear between mid-spring and early summer. H to 6m (20ft), S 2m (6ft). Hardy/Z 7–8.

### *R. decorum*
This tree-like evergreen species from China bears loose trusses of fragrant, white or pink flowers in early summer. It tolerates warm dry conditions. H to 6m (20ft), S 2.5m (8ft). Hardy/Z 6–8.

### *R. impeditum*
This dwarf evergreen, which is ideal for a rock garden or trough, comes from the mountains of Yunnan and Sichuan. The scaly leaves are aromatic. The blue-purple flowers open almost flat,

Rhododendron impeditum

like stars, in mid- to late spring. H and S to 60cm (2ft). Hardy/Z 6–8.

### *R. luteum*
A dazzling deciduous species, this elegant rhododendron bears highly fragrant, clear yellow flowers in late spring and early summer. It is the parent of many more compact hybrids. H and S to 4m (13ft). Hardy/Z 6–9.

### *R. hybrids*
There are a huge number of hybrid rhododendrons of garden origin of widely diverging size. The following gives an indication of the range available; all are evergreen unless otherwise stated. Hardy/Z 4–9. Plants of the **Alison Johnstone Group** have dainty, peach-pink flowers in late spring to early summer. H and S 2m (6ft). **'Bashful'** (Yakushimanum hybrid) has pink flowers aging white in spring; sun-tolerant. H and S 2m (6ft). The deciduous **'Berryrose'** has salmon-pink flowers with yellow flares in late spring; sun-tolerant. H and S 1.5m (5ft). **'Blue Peter'** has lavender-blue, frilled flowers in late spring and early summer;

Rhododendron charitopes

Rhododendron luteum

Rhododendron 'Bruce Brechtbill'

*Rhododendron* 'Cary Ann'

*Rhododendron* 'Dopey'

*Rhododendron* 'Exbury White'

*Rhododendron* 'Persil'

sun-tolerant. H and S 3m (10ft). **'Bruce Brechtbill'** has a dense habit and pale pink flowers in late spring and early summer. H 2m (6ft), S 2.5m (8ft). **Carita Group** rhododendrons have trusses of pale lemon-yellow flowers in mid-spring; they are best with some shelter. H and S 2.5m (8ft). **'Cary Ann'**, which is good for small gardens, has coral pink flowers in late spring to early summer. H and S 1.5m (5ft). The deciduous **'Cecile'** has salmon pink flowers over a long period in late spring. H and S 2m (6ft). **'Chanticleer'** has spectacular maroon-purple flowers in late spring and early summer. H and S 1.5m (5ft). The old deciduous bearing cultivar **'Corneille'** has double, creamy-pink flowers in early summer. H and S 1.5–2.5m (5–8ft). **'Curlew'** has large, pale yellow flowers in mid-spring; it does best in a cool spot. H and S 60cm (2ft). **'Cynthia'**, an old, sun-tolerant cultivar, bears huge trusses of rich crimson pink flowers in late spring. H and S 6m (20ft). The deciduous **'Daviesii'** has scented cream flowers in late spring to early summer and good autumn leaf

colour. H and S 1.5m (5ft). The compact and upright **'Dopey'** (Yakushimanum hybrid) bears rounded trusses of satiny orange-red flowers in late spring. H and S 2m (6ft). The deciduous **'Exbury White'** has large white flowers with yellow eyes in late spring and early summer and good autumn leaf colour; it makes an elegant specimen. H and S 2m (6ft). **'Fastuosum Flore Pleno'** has deep mauve flowers in late spring and early summer. H and S 4m (13ft). The free-flowering **'Golden Torch'** has pale yellow flowers fading to cream in late spring and early summer. H and S 1.5m (5ft). **'Grace Seabrook'** is a robust and vigorous form bearing conical trusses of deep pink flowers in early to mid-spring. H and S 2m (6ft). The dwarf and compact **'Hatsugiri'** bears masses of funnel-shaped, glowing crimson flowers in spring. H and S 60cm (2ft). **'Hinomayo'** has clear pink flowers in mid-spring and early summer. H and S 60cm (2ft). The deciduous **'Homebush'** has trusses of rose pink flowers in late spring. H and S 1.5m (5ft). **'Hydon Dawn'** has globular trusses of pale pink

flowers in mid-spring and early summer. H and S 1.5m (5ft). **'Hydon Hunter'** has deep pink flowers spotted with orange in mid-spring and early summer; sun-tolerant. H and S 1.5m (5ft). The robust, vigorous and sun-tolerant **'Loder's White'** gives a sumptuous display of fragrant white flowers in midsummer. H and S 3m (10ft). **'May Day'** has funnel-shaped, glowing red flowers in late spring; sun-tolerant. H and S 1.5m (5ft). **'Mrs Charles E. Pearson'** has pale mauve-pink flowers spotted with brown in late spring and early summer. H and S 2m (6ft). **'Naomi'**, which has lilac-mauve flowers in mid-spring, is the parent of **'Naomi Exbury'** (yellow-tinted flowers) and **'Naomi Pink Beauty'** (deep satin pink). H and S 5m (16ft). The deciduous **'Narcissiflorum'** has fragrant soft-yellow flowers in late spring and early summer. H and S 2.5m (8ft). **'Palestrina'**, which has pure white flowers in late spring, is an excellent choice for a small garden. H and S 1.2m (4ft). **'Penheale Blue'** has star-like, glowing deep violet flowers in early spring; sun-tolerant. H

and S 1.2m (4ft). The compact and hardy **'Percy Wiseman'** has peach-pink flowers fading to white in late spring and early summer. H and S 2.5m (8ft). The deciduous **'Persil'** has glistening white flowers with golden-orange central blotches. H and S 2m (6ft). **'Pink Pearl'** has huge trusses of soft pink flowers in mid- to late spring; sun-tolerant. H and S 4m (13ft). **'Polar Bear'** produces headily scented, lily-like, white flowers in mid- to late summer, produced freely only once the plant is mature. H and S 5m (16ft). **'Sappho'** has funnel-shaped, white flowers liberally sprinkled on the inside with dark purple-maroon in early summer. H and S 3m (10ft). The deciduous **'Strawberry Ice'** has strawberry pink flowers in mid- to late spring. H and S 2m (6ft). **'Vuyk's Rosy Red'**, which has deep rose-pink flowers in mid-spring, is excellent for a sunny rock garden. H 75cm (30in), S 1.2m (4ft). **'Wombat'**, which has small pink flowers in profusion in early summer, makes excellent groundcover, even in sun. H 25cm (10in), S 1.2m (4ft).

*Rhododendron* 'Curlew'

*Rhododendron* 'Fastuosum Flore Pleno'

*Rhododendron* 'Narcissiflorum'

*Rhododendron* 'Strawberry Ice'

*Rosmarinus officinalis*

# ROSMARINUS
## Rosemary
The evergreen, aromatic rosemary is an essential element of any herb garden, but prostrate forms make good groundcover and also work well when planted at the tops of walls. There are also some suitable for hedging, and all can be clipped to shape. Rosemaries are not long-lived but are easily raised from cuttings.
*Cultivation* Rosemary does best in free-draining, light soil in full sun. Trim hedges after flowering.

### R. officinalis
To all intents and purposes this is the only species widely cultivated. It has dark green, narrow leaves and mauve-blue flowers in summer. H and S to 1.5m (5ft). Borderline hardy/Z 7–9. There is a huge range of cultivars. **'Lady in White'** has white flowers. H and S 1m (3ft). **'Miss Jessop's Upright'** (syn.

'Fastigiatus') is an upright form with light purplish-blue flowers. H 2m (6ft), S 60cm (2ft). Plants in the **Prostratus Group** are spreading, and less hardy than the straight species. H 60cm (2ft), S 1m (3ft). **'Sissinghurst Blue'** is upright with deep blue flowers and one of the best for culinary purposes. H 1.2m (4ft), S 1m (3ft).

# RUBUS
## Bramble
In addition to a huge range of soft fruits (raspberries, black-berries and a number of hybrids), this genus also includes a few ornamental plants.
*Cultivation* Grow in well-drained, fertile soil in sun or partial shade.

### R. 'Benenden'
(syn. *R. tridel* 'Benenden')
This beautiful deciduous hybrid has masses of large, saucer-shaped, white flowers in late spring to early summer. H and S 2m (6ft). Hardy/Z 5–9.

### R. cockburnianus
Glistening white stems make this one of the finest of deciduous winter plants, an effect improved by annual hard pruning in spring. H 2m (6ft), S 1.2m (4ft). Hardy/Z 5–9.

### R. odoratus
Flowering raspberry
An erect, vigorous deciduous species with fragrant, pinkish-purple flowers in summer followed by orange-red fruits. H and S 2m (6ft). Hardy/Z 4–9.

*Ruta graveolens*

### R. thibetanus
This semi-erect species has small, purplish-red summer flowers and furry leaves, but it is grown principally for the winter interest of its stems, which are covered in a whitish bloom. Cut back hard annually for the best display. H and S to 2.4m (8ft), less with regular pruning. Hardy/Z 7–9.

# RUTA
## Rue
These subshrubs have aromatic, glaucous blue leaves. Only the species described is widely grown. Contact with the plant can cause allergic reactions in some people.
*Cultivation* Grow in well-drained soil in a sunny site. Clip plants in summer for a fresh crop of leaves.

### R. graveolens
Common rue
This evergreen species has bluish-green, much divided leaves. Yellowish flowers appear in

*Salvia officinalis* Purpurascens Group

summer. H 1m (3ft), S 75cm (30in). Hardy/Z 5–9. The form generally found in gardens is **'Jackman's Blue'**, which has leaves of a more pronounced bluish-grey and is more compact. H and S 30cm (12in).

# SALVIA
## Sage
This large genus contains annuals and perennials as well as a number of shrubby plants, which are the familiar sages, widely used as a culinary herb. They are also good enough to use in borders, with roses or in a mixed planting.
*Cultivation* Grow in any well-drained soil in full sun.

### S. officinalis
Common sage
The species has dull pewter-green leaves and blue and purple flowers. H 60cm (2ft), S 1m (3ft). Hardy/Z 6–9. Attractive selections include **'Icterina'**, which

*Rubus odoratus*

*Rubus thibetanus*

*Salvia officinalis* 'Icterina'

*Santolina chamaecyparis*

*Skimmia japonica* 'Tansley Gem'

has leaves marked with yellow and gold; **Purpurascens Group**, which has soft purple leaves; and **'Tricolor'**, with leaves marked with pink, cream and purple.

## SANTOLINA
### Curry plant

The species described is a useful evergreen, which can be used in the rock garden, as dwarf hedging or in combination with other plants, to which it offers a good foil. It is ideal for filling gaps in a border.
*Cultivation* Grow santolinas in any well-drained soil in full sun.

### S. chamaecyparis
(syn. *S. incana*)
#### Cotton lavender
This is the best-known species, a mound-forming shrub with finely dissected silvery leaves. It has lemon-yellow flowers in mid-summer, but is principally valued as a foliage plant. Clip over in

spring to neaten, if necessary, but old, straggly plants are best replaced. H and S 60cm (2ft). Borderline hardy/Z 6–9.

## SARCOCOCCA
### Christmas box, sweet box

These choice plants for the winter garden have small but highly scented flowers among the shiny evergreen leaves. Use them with snowdrops, *Arum italicum* subsp. *italicum* 'Marmoratun' and early hellebores. They make excellent groundcover under deciduous trees, and flowering stems can be cut for use in winter flower arrangements.
*Cultivation* Grow in any fertile, well-drained soil in sun or light shade. They tolerate deeper shade.

### S. confusa
This is an excellent dwarf shrub, which is useful as groundcover if planted en masse. Very fragrant, creamy white flowers are produced in midwinter. H and S 1m (3ft). Hardy/Z 6–9.

### S. hookeriana var. dignya
This naturally occurring form has deliciously scented white flowers with pink stamens in winter. H and S 1.2m (4ft). Hardy/Z 6–9.

## SKIMMIA

This small genus includes several attractive shrubs, which bear scented flowers in spring and (on female plants) crops of red berries in autumn, a fine contrast to the handsome, evergreen leaves. They are excellent in shrub or mixed borders and also work well in

containers. Young specimens of the male *S. japonica* 'Rubella' can be used in winter windowboxes.
*Cultivation* Most soils in sun or shade are suitable, but some yellowing of the older leaves can occur in alkaline conditions because of magnesium deficiency.

### S. × confusa 'Kew Green'
This male selection has fragrant, cream flowers in early spring among the narrow leaves. H and S to 1m (3ft). Hardy/Z 7.

### S. japonica
This, the most widely grown species, has distinctive narrow, glossy foliage and panicles of cream buds throughout winter that open to fragrant creamy-white flowers in spring. H and S to 1.2m (4ft). Hardy/Z 7–9. 'Rubella' is a male form with clusters of red buds through winter that open to dingy white flowers in early spring. '**Tansley**

**Gem'** is a female form, with a good crop of red berries. **'Wakehurst White'** (syn. 'Fructo-alba'), a female form, has creamy-white berries. H 50cm (20in), S 1m (3ft).

## SPIRAEA

These easy deciduous shrubs are cultivated for their flowers and leaves. Most stay reasonably compact and are suitable for small gardens. For maximum impact plant in groups of three or more, but solo plants work well with a wide range of perennials in mixed borders.
*Cultivation* These shrubs are easy to grow in most soils, in sun or light shade.

### S. japonica
The species is usually grown in one of the following forms, both of which are hardy/Z 4–9. H and S 1m (3ft). **'Anthony Waterer'** is a charming selection, with dark leaves and rich pink flowers from mid- to late summer. **'Goldflame'** has yellowish-green leaves, which are sometimes marked with red. The dull pink summer flowers make a strange combination, but pleasing when positioned next to a purple-leaved plant.

### S. nipponica 'Snowmound'
This outstanding form is smothered in creamy-white flowers in late spring or early summer. The plant tolerates hard pruning and can be kept smaller than the dimensions indicated. H and S 2m (6ft). Hardy/Z 4–9.

*Sarcococca confusa*

*Skimmia japonica* 'Rubella'

*Spiraea japonica* 'Goldflame'

*Syringa emodi*

*Syringa vulgaris 'Firmament'*

*Viburnum × bodnantense 'Dawn'*

## SYRINGA
### Lilac

Late spring can almost be defined as 'lilac time': a season easily recognized by that unmistakable scent in the air. Unfortunately, most of the hybrids, which are so impressive in flower, end up as unwieldy, rangy shrubs of small interest during the rest of the year. If you have the space, grow them in stands in a rough part of the garden. In a restricted area, choose from the species, many of which are more compact, with daintier flowers.
*Cultivation* Lilacs will grow in any well-drained soil and are especially useful on chalk (alkaline soil). They prefer sun but tolerate light shade. They can be pruned back hard.

### S. emodi
#### Himalayan lilac
This vigorous species with dark green oval leaves has very pale flowers in late spring to early summer. H 5m (15ft), S 4m (13ft). Hardy/Z 7–8.

### S. meyeri var. spontanea 'Palibin' (syn. S. palibiana, S. patula of gardens)
A most rewarding small lilac, this has very fragrant, pale lilac-coloured flowers, produced freely in late spring to early summer. H and S 1.5m (5ft). Hardy/Z 4–7.

### S. vulgaris
#### Common lilac
This is the parent of a huge range of garden forms, all heavily scented, and including **'Andenken an Ludwig Späth'**, which has wine red flowers; **'Charles Joly'**, which has double, purplish-red flowers; 'Congo', with rich pink flowers opening from darker buds; **'Firmament'**, which has pink buds opening to lilac-coloured flowers; **'Madame Lemoine'**, with double, white flowers; and **'Primrose'**, the closest to yellow, with rich cream-coloured buds opening to creamy-white flowers. H and S 3.5m (12ft). Hardy/Z 3–9.

## TEUCRIUM
### Germander

These evergreen shrubs or subshrubs have aromatic foliage. Germanders are often included in herb gardens, but are also effective as rock garden plants or in mixed borders.
*Cultivation* Grow in free-draining, light soil in full sun. Winter protection may be necessary in cold areas. Prune lightly in spring to keep plants in shape.

### T. chamaedrys
This species has glossy, holly-like leaves and purple flowers in summer. H and S 30cm (12in). Borderline hardy/Z 5.

### T. fruticans
This elegant plant has pale blue summer flowers, making a cool complement to the pewter-green leaves, which are covered in a soft silvery down. It looks beautiful billowing out at the front of a border. H 1.2m (4ft), S 4m (13ft). Borderline hardy/Z 7–10. **'Azureum'** is even more desirable, with darker blue flowers.

## VIBURNUM

This large and important genus consists of both evergreen and deciduous shrubs that, between them, provide interest throughout the year. Some are grown for their flowers (winter or spring), others for their berries, and some for both. They are essential plants. Native species are excellent in wild gardens, providing food for birds in winter. Others are good in winter gardens or mixed borders. A select few make good specimens. *V. tinus* can be trained as a standard.
*Cultivation* Grow viburnums in any reasonably fertile, well-drained soil in sun or light shade.

### V. × bodnantense 'Dawn'
One of the stars of the winter garden, this upright, deciduous, vase-shaped shrub has richly scented, pink flowers opening in mild spells from autumn to spring. H 2m (6ft), S 1.2m (4ft). Hardy/Z 7–9.

### V. carlesii
This deciduous species from Japan and Korea is almost unmatched for the scent of its white spring flowers, pink in bud and carried in rounded clusters.

*Teucrium fruticans*

*Viburnum carlesii 'Diana'*

# YUCCA

These dramatic, architectural evergreens add a touch of the exotic to any garden. They are often sold as houseplants, but the species described here are hardy enough to survive (and flower) outdoors. In their native habitat (North American desert) yuccas become trees. In gardens they are excellent when planted as focal points or sited at the corner of a border, and they make splendid permanent plantings for large containers.
*Cultivation* Grow in any well-drained soil in full sun.

Viburnum plicatum 'Mariesii'

Viburnum tinus 'Eve Price'

Weigela 'Candida'

H and S 1.5m (5ft). Hardy/Z 6–9. **'Diana'** has purplish-pink flowers that fade to white.

## V. plicatum
### Japanese snowball bush
A grand deciduous shrub with an architectural, tiered habit that makes a breathtaking specimen when in flower. Hardy/Z 5–8. **'Mariesii'** (syn. *V. mariesii*) is one of the most distinctive selections, with tabulated branches carrying flattened lacecap heads of white flowers in late spring. H 3m (10ft), S 4m (13ft). *V. plicatum* f. *tomentosum* produces blue-black berries in autumn as the leaves redden. H 3m (10ft), S 4m (13ft).

## V. tinus
### Laurustinus
An important winter shrub, this evergreen has a rounded habit and white flowers in late winter or early spring. Bluish-black berries follow the flowers. H and S 3m

Vinca minor 'Aureovariegata'

(10ft). Hardy/Z 7–9. The flowers of **'Eve Price'** open from rich eye-catching pink buds.

# VINCA
## Periwinkle
These valuable trailing evergreen subshrubs make excellent ground-cover, particularly in the dry soil under trees. They are also good in containers. A large pot planted solely with *V. major* 'Variegata' will provide material for flower arranging throughout the year.
*Cultivation* Grow in any well-drained soil in sun or shade. Mulching in dry soils will accelerate growth. Stems can root wherever they touch the ground.

## V. major
The species is not worth growing, but it has several worthy cultivars, the best of which is probably **'Variegata'** (syn. 'Elegantissima'), which has leaves with pale yellow margins. The periwinkle-blue flowers are produced mainly in early summer but never in sufficient quantities to smother the plant. H 20cm (8in), S indefinite. Hardy/Z 7–9.

## V. minor
This species, which has small leaves, is more worthwhile than *V. major* and has many more cultivars, including **'Aureovariegata'**, which has leaves edged with creamy yellow and blue summer flowers; **'Burgundy'**, which has wine-purple flowers; and **'Gertrude Jekyll'**, which has white flowers. H 15cm (6in), S indefinite. Hardy/Z 4–8.

# WEIGELA
The genus contains 12 species of deciduous shrubs with interesting leaves and trumpet-shaped flowers in early summer. They work well in a shrub border or a mixed planting, where, after flowering, they make effective backdrops to later-flowering perennials, annuals and bulbs.
*Cultivation* They do well in most soils, in sun or light shade.

## W. 'Candida'
This is an unusual garden form with pure white flowers. H and S 1.5m (5ft). Hardy/Z 5–9.

## W. florida
This is one of the less-appealing species in its wild form, but some of the selections are of great value. The following are hardy/Z 5–9. **'Aureovariegata'** is one of the prettiest. The leaves are edged with white in spring, making a fine combination with the pink flowers. The variegation deepens to yellow later on. H and S 1.2m (4ft). **'Foliis Purpureis'**, which needs careful siting, has rich purple leaves and deep pink flowers. H and S 1m (3ft).

## W. 'Looymansii Aurea'
This hybrid has yellowish-green leaves and pink flowers. It needs shelter from strong, hot sun. H and S 1.5m (5ft). Hardy/Z 5–9.

## W. middendorffiana
This superior species has sulphur-yellow flowers marked with dark orange in mid- to late spring. H and S 1.5m (5ft). Hardy/Z 5–9.

## Y. filamentosa
### Adam's needle
The species forms a rosette of stiff, upright, lance-shaped leaves. The distinguishing feature is the curly threads on the edges of the leaves. Established plants produce upright spikes, to 2m (6ft) tall, of white, tulip-shaped flowers in late summer to autumn, but not necessarily every year. H and S 1m (3ft). Hardy/Z 5–10. The leaves of **'Bright Edge'** have broad yellow edges.

## Y. gloriosa
### Spanish dagger
This plant has a thick stem topped by a rosette of hard, spiny, upright blue-green to dark-green leaves, through the middle of which the flowering spikes emerge in late summer (the flowers are similar to those of *Y. filamentosa*). Mature plants are multi-stemmed. H and S 2m (6ft) or more. Hardy/Z 7–10.

Yucca filamentosa

# Perennials

For many, a garden just would not be a garden without the contribution of perennials, often long-lived plants that provide interest year on year, usually with very little maintenance required. A herbaceous border can provide interest for many weeks in summer, but perennials also encompass many early-flowering plants (usually low-growing) that are delightful with spring bulbs, as well as plants that carry the flowering season into autumn and continue to provide colour in the garden as the days grow shorter and cooler.

Most perennials are easy to care for and provide colour for many weeks during the summer months.

# What is a perennial?

Perennials are leafy, soft-stemmed plants, distinguished from annuals and biennials in being longer lived, persisting for at least three years, usually rather longer. Most spread by sending out shoots from their roots that develop into new stems, usually soon after flowering. Over several years, the offshoots from only one plant may cover a wide area. Granted that stems (in principle at least) remain soft throughout the life of a plant, that places a restriction on how tall they can grow without falling over. Hence the majority are under 1m (3ft) in height. In some cases, the stem itself spreads sideways, usually at ground level, with the leaves and flower stems emerging from it at right angles. Such stems, which act as storage organs, are referred to as rhizomes. Many of the irises exhibit this growth pattern.

Strictly speaking, bulbs are also perennials, since they also persist from year to year, but they are treated separately in this book, as are certain other groups of plants that

Achilleas spin their heads of flowers like plates behind an exotic planting of cannas and *Crocosmia* 'Lucifer'.

have very specific cultivation requirements or garden use, such as grasses, aquatics, alpines, ferns and orchids. Some climbers are also soft-stemmed (though the majority are woody, and thus technically shrubs).

Many perennials are deciduous or herbaceous: the topgrowth dies back completely in winter, when conditions are unfavourable for growth, and the plant stays dormant underground. Fresh leafy growth reappears when the weather warms up in spring. Such popular garden perennials as bleeding hearts (*Dicentra*), columbines (*Aquilegia*), daylilies (*Hemerocallis*), delphiniums, peonies (*Paeonia*) and poppies (*Papaver*) need an annual cool season for the growth of new buds. They therefore do not grow well in tropical climates.

A precious few perennials are evergreen, and these include the splendid hellebores (*Helleborus*) and bergenias, both invaluable for winter interest, as well as some irises.

Some evergreens tend to become woody at the base with age, and are sometimes referred to as subshrubs, a characteristic that can be observed in many of the Mediterranean herbs such as the artemisias and sages (*Salvia*). Chrysanthemums and Michaelmas daisies (*Aster*) also tend to become woody, as do penstemons and pelargoniums.

Slow-growing perennials such as hellebores and peonies are best left to get on with it, but others tend to die off in the middle or form congested mats. To maintain the flower power, they should be dug up every three years or so and divided, replanting the youngest, healthiest-looking bits and composting the remainder. Those that become woody also tend to become bare at the base, but can be replaced by younger, softer-stemmed plants raised from cuttings. Rhizomatous plants can be increased by cutting up the rhizome, making sure that each section has growth buds and roots. Properly cared for, many perennials can be maintained virtually indefinitely, even as the successive generations die off over the years.

In this subtle scheme, arching, swordlike leaves are almost as important a feature as the bright blue agapanthus and orange crocosmia flowers.

A large percentage of the perennials grown in gardens today are hybrids, such as the stately peonies, phlox, chrysanthemums and delphiniums. They have often been bred to produce large flowers that are too heavy for the stems, and thus require staking. Species grown in gardens (and their forms) tend to be more modest in appearance, though of no lesser value, generally have the advantage of excellent health and do not need staking. Such plants as geraniums, thalictrums and euphorbias, which have not been extensively hybridized, are increasingly valued by gardeners for their ease of cultivation besides the charm of their flowers.

These sun-loving perennials, in a vibrant combination of reds and yellows, are basking in the summer heat reflected by the gravel path.

## Perennials in the garden

Gardeners value perennials mainly for their flowers. Nearly all flower in spring or summer, and this is when the most dramatic effects can be created. They are traditionally the star performers of the garden and in the past were often grown in dedicated borders (the so-called herbaceous border), planned for interest over a long period. Gertrude Jekyll was the progenitor of the archetypal colour border, presenting a dramatic sweep with pale pink at one end and pale blue at the other, with "hot" oranges, reds and yellows at the centre. Typically, taller plants would be placed to the back of the border, with shorter ones in front and the real ground-huggers to the fore. She also planned single colour borders, though never a white garden, a concept that skipped a generation, only emerging in the gardens of Laurence Johnstone at Hidcote and Vita Sackville-West at Sissinghurst. Breathtaking as they are, such plantings are labour-intensive, and most gardeners

nowadays favour an informal mix of perennials, grasses and shrubs.

Where there is room, the most satisfactory effects are achieved by planting in drifts or interlocking groups of three or more. A solitary large-leaved plant, such as a hosta or a rheum, can be used for impact. To avoid a spotty effect, group together plants that flower at the same time, but remember also that many perennials have interesting foliage that adds value to the border at times when they are not in flower. Peonies, hellebores and bergenias, which make satisfying clumps of foliage, are all effective partners to later-flowering plants.

Winter-flowering perennials include the essential hellebores and *Iris unguicularis*. At the other end of the year, interest focuses on the daisy tribe: chrysanthemums, Michaelmas daisies and heleniums, many continuing until the first frosts. *Schizostylis* and toad lilies (*Tricyrtis*) should on no account be overlooked for late interest.

Many of the early flowerers will flower a second time if cut back after the first flush, albeit usually less impressively. In nearly all cases, deadheading is advisable (unless you wish to gather seed for propagation). This diverts the plant's energies away from seed production and into vegetative growth instead, which will result in a larger plant for next year.

A few perennials have a very restricted use, true woodlanders such as trilliums, for instance, but most like a fairly open, sunny site in fertile, well-drained soil, and combine happily with one another. A good many provide ample material for cutting. Ground-cover plants, usually low-growing, that spread to create dense mats are useful for suppressing weeds and filling a large area of bare soil quickly. These include *Lamium* and *Alchemilla mollis*, though at times they can be almost too effective, colonizing areas of the garden to the point of becoming weeds themselves.

*Acanthus mollis*

*Achillea filipendulina* 'Gold Plate'

*Aconitum* 'Stainless Steel'

## ACANTHUS
### Bear's breeches

These stately, hardy perennials, mostly from Mediterranean countries, are of unquestioned value in the garden, in sun or shade, although they have rather sinister-looking hooded flowers. They are colonizing plants, which can be difficult to eradicate once they are established, so choose where you plant them with care. The flowers can be dried for winter arrangements.
*Cultivation* Grow in any well-drained fertile soil in sun or light shade. Flowering is best in sun.

### A. mollis
Tall spikes of hooded mauve and white flowers appear in early summer above the large, handsome, glossy green leaves. H 1.2m (4ft), S 1m (3ft). Hardy/Z 7–9.

### A. spinosus
A species that resembles *A. mollis* in all respects but for its deeply cut leaves. H 1.2m (4ft), S 60cm (2ft). Hardy/Z 6–10.

## ACHILLEA
### Yarrow

More than 80 species are included in this genus. Yarrows are tough plants, with flat heads of flowers in mid- to late summer on stout stems. The majority of them have feathery, aromatic foliage. They are indispensable for providing colour – if not vibrant – in the late summer border, working well with grasses, but some tend to be short-lived. The flowers can be dried and hold their colour well.
*Cultivation* Grow in free-draining, preferably moist, soil in full sun.

### A. filipendulina
(syn. *A. eupatorium*)
This species has flat heads of sulphur-yellow flowers in late summer. H 1.5m (5ft), S 1m (3ft). Hardy/Z 3–9. The selection 'Gold Plate', which bears slightly domed flowerheads, is more robust. H 1.2m (4ft), S 60cm (2ft).

### A. 'Moonshine'
This hybrid is grown as much for its ferny, grey-green leaves as its pale yellow flowerheads. H and S 60cm (2ft). Hardy/Z 4–8.

### A. ptarmica 'The Pearl'
A dainty plant, with heads of button-like, white flowers in summer. Plants sold under this name probably belong to The Pearl Group – in other words they have been seed-raised and thus may differ in some respects. H and S 60cm (2ft). Hardy/Z 4–9.

## ACONITUM
### Monkshood, wolf's bane
These tall plants with hooded flowers are a useful shade of rich blue. All species in the genus are poisonous.
*Cultivation* Any soil is suitable, but they do best in moisture-retentive soil in full sun, although they will also do well in shade.

### A. 'Spark's Variety'
Of all the available hybrids, this is probably the best known, with spires of rich, dark violet-blue flowers from early to midsummer. H 1.5m (5ft), S 45cm (18in). Hardy/Z 5–8.

### A. 'Stainless Steel'
This cultivar has subtly coloured, beautiful pewter grey flowers. H 1.5m (5ft), S 45cm (18in). Hardy/Z 6.

## AGAPANTHUS
### African lily
These elegant and desirable plants produce umbels of refreshing blue or white flowers in late summer. They contrast well with yellow flowers, of which there will be many at flowering time, as well as blending easily with softer tones. They also thrive in containers, in which they look very handsome. Overcrowding seems to intensify the flower power, so divide them only when absolutely necessary. They are easily raised from seed.
*Cultivation* Grow in fertile, reliably moist (but not boggy) soil in full sun.

### A. 'Ben Hope'
This hybrid has umbels of rich blue flowers from mid- to late summer. H 1.2m (4ft), S 60cm (2ft). Hardy/Z 7–10.

### A. 'Castle of Mey'
This is one of the daintier hybrids, producing rich dark blue flowers on erect stems in late summer. H 60cm (2ft), S 30cm (1ft). Hardy/Z 7.

## AJUGA
### Bugle
Useful as groundcover, these plants are grown mostly for their evergreen leaves, although the blue spring flowers make an attractive bonus. They spread by runners and will colonize any area where the conditions suit them.
*Cultivation* Grow in moisture-retentive soil in sun or light shade.

### A. reptans
This is the most widely grown bugle, although it is seldom seen in its typical form in gardens. H 10cm (5in), S 1m (3ft). Hardy/Z 3–9. Selections available include 'Atropurpurea' (syn. 'Purpurea'), which has rich burgundy-purple leaves; 'Jungle Beauty' (syn. 'Jumbo'), with large

*Agapanthus* 'Castle of Mey'

*Ajuga reptans* 'Jungle Beauty'

Alchemilla mollis

Alstroemeria 'Apollo'

Anemone × hybrida 'Königin Charlotte'

green leaves that turn warm brown in winter; and **'Variegata'** (syn. 'Argentea'), which has leaves splashed with cream and grey.

## ALCHEMILLA
### Lady's mantle
The species described, which comes from Turkey and the Caucasus, is an essential garden plant. It is an excellent filler for gaps in borders and the frothy, lime-green flowers, also good for cutting, blend with almost anything else. It makes excellent groundcover but can be invasive, and its habit of self-seeding everywhere makes it a menace in some gardens. To prevent this from happening, cut off the flowers as they fade (this will also encourage further flowers). It makes a marvellous foil to old roses and looks charming where allowed to seed in the cracks between paving.
*Cultivation* These extremely tolerant plants will grow in almost any soil in sun or light shade.

### A. mollis
The soft, almost felted, pleated, fan-like leaves emerge in early spring, followed by masses of tiny, star-like, lime green flowers throughout summer. H and S 50cm (20in). Hardy/Z 3–7.

## ALSTROEMERIA
### Peruvian lily, lily of the Incas
These exquisite plants, long associated with cottage gardens, are of undoubted distinction. The newer hybrids may be hardier and have a longer flowering season than some of the older ones, but

they have not supplanted them. Excellent in a warm, sunny border, in cold areas they need the shelter of a wall. Leave them undisturbed after planting; they may take some years to establish, but thereafter are extremely reliable plants.
*Cultivation* Peruvian lilies need reasonably fertile, well-drained soil in sun, with some shelter in cold areas. Most are best when staked, but they can be supported by neighbouring plants.

### A. 'Apollo'
This outstanding hybrid has large, white flowers marked with yellow within and flecked with brown appearing from mid-summer to autumn. H and S 60cm (2ft). Borderline hardy/Z 8.

### A. ligtu hybrids
This group of hybrids includes plants with varying flower colour, including pink, coral and salmon orange, but all are desirable. They

flower in early to midsummer. They are seed-raised, so buy plants in flower to ensure getting the desired colour. The plants can be invasive. H and S 60cm (2ft). Borderline hardy/Z 7–10.

### A. 'Morning Star'
A hybrid with rich purplish-pink flowers fading to yellow and flecked with brown from midsummer to autumn. H and S 45cm (18in). Borderline hardy/Z 8.

## ANEMONE
### Windflower
This large genus includes a few perennials of undoubted merit. Their late season and tolerance of a range of conditions make them essential plants for any garden, to say nothing of the beauty of the flowers, carried on tall, elegant, wiry stems. They are ravishing in drifts under

deciduous trees, or they can be used more formally in borders planned for late interest. They are sometimes informally referred to as Japanese anemones.
*Cultivation* These anemones do best on moisture-retentive soil in sun or shade, although they do tolerate drier, lighter soils.

### A. hupehensis
This elegant species, with white or pink, bowl-shaped flowers that seem to float at the tops of wiry stems, is rare in cultivation. H 75cm (30in), S 45cm (18in). Hardy/Z 5–8. More common is the distinguished selection **'Hadspen Abundance'**, which has rich deep pink flowers. H and S 1m (3ft).

### A. × hybrida
(syn. *A. japonica* of gardens)
This large group of hybrids are the true Japanese anemones (the plant sometimes referred to as *A. japonica* does not seem to exist). Seedlings often appear in gardens, and all are worth growing, but named forms worthy of note include **'Honorine Jobert'**, which has white flowers; **'Königin Charlotte'** (syn. 'Queen Charlotte'), which has semi-double, purplish-pink flowers with frilly petals; **'Luise Uhink'**, which has chalk-white flowers; and **'Whirlwind'**, which has semi-double, green-tinged, white flowers with twisted petals. H 1.5m (5ft), S 60cm (2ft). Hardy/Z 5–8.

Alstroemeria 'Morning Star'

Anemone × hybrida 'Luise Uhink'

*Anthemis tinctoria*

*Argyranthemum 'Mary Wootton'*

*Artemisia absinthium*

## ANTHEMIS

These cheerful plants with their daisy-like flowers are indispensable for the flower gardener because of the length of their flowering season and the freedom with which blooms are produced. Although the plants will provide endless material for cutting, they may be short-lived.
*Cultivation* Grow in well-drained soil in full sun. Regular division in spring helps maintain health.

### A. tinctoria

The species has parsley-like leaves with masses of yellow daisies in summer. H and S 60cm (2ft). Hardy/Z 4–8. The selection 'E.C. Buxton' is widely available. This essential plant has lemon-yellow flowers throughout summer that look good with blue flowers (especially campanulas) and border phlox. H and S 1m (3ft).

## AQUILEGIA
### Columbine

These short-lived perennials are notorious for seeding themselves in the garden. Unfortunately, not all seedlings develop into attractive plants, as they sometimes produce flowers of an indifferent pink or murky purple, but the best ones make elegant additions to the border, with their distinctive, spurred flowers, and usefully fill the flowering gap between spring bulbs and summer perennials. They are probably at their best when grown in informal clumps in light woodland but also blend well with irises, catmint and poppies in

cottage garden-style plantings. The genus also includes some alpines.
*Cultivation* Grow in any well-drained soil in sun or light shade.

### A. 'Lavender and White'

This hybrid has distinctive bi-coloured flowers in early summer, in lavender and creamy white, as the name suggests. H 60cm (24in), S 45cm (18in). Hardy/Z 4.

### A. vulgaris
### Granny's bonnets

This is one of the most familiar garden plants, with its dumpy purple, pink, crimson or white flowers appearing in late spring to early summer. Some of the many selections available include 'Nivea' (syn. 'Munstead's White'), which has bright white flowers; and the distinctive *A. vulgaris* var. *stellata* 'Norah Barlow', which

*Aquilegia 'Lavender and White'*

has pompon-like pink, green and white double flowers. H 60cm (24in), S 45cm (18in). Hardy/Z 4–9.

## ARGYRANTHEMUM
### Marguerite, Paris daisy

These plants are in flower for longer than any other perennial – almost throughout the growing season. They are woody plants and, as well as their obvious value in borders, they can also be grown as standards.
*Cultivation* Argyranthemums will grow in sun in most well-drained, reasonably fertile soils. Pinching out the tips of the shoots in early spring can encourage bushiness and extra flowers.

### A. gracile 'Chelsea Girl'

One of the best known cultivars, this has attractive, ferny grey leaves and an abundance of

*Artemisia absinthium 'Lambrook Silver'*

yellow-centred, white daisies from spring to autumn. H and S 60cm (2ft). Half-hardy/Z 9.

### A. 'Jamaica Primrose'

An equally valuable hybrid, this bears long-stalked, cool lemon-yellow daisies throughout the growing season. H and S 1m (3ft). Half-hardy/Z 9.

### A. 'Mary Wootton'

This fine hybrid has double, pompon-like, peach pink flowers. H and S 1m (3ft). Half-hardy/Z 9.

### A. 'Snow Storm'
### (syn. 'Jamaica Snowstorm')

This compact form has blue-green leaves and yellow-centred, white flowers. H and S 30cm (1ft). Borderline hardy/Z 9.

## ARTEMISIA
### Wormwood, mugwort

These are excellent foliage plants for borders, particularly hot, dry ones. The silvery foliage blends well with roses as well as with a range of herbaceous perennials. Artemisias, some of which are shrubby, also have aromatic foliage which has herbal applications.
*Cultivation* Grow artemisias in any well-drained, preferably gritty, soil in full sun. Prune straggly plants in spring.

### A. absinthium
### Absinthe, wormwood

This is the plant from which the spirit absinthe is distilled. In the garden it is valued chiefly for its silky-grey, divided leaves. The daisy-like flowers, produced in late summer, are insignificant. H and S 1m (3ft). Hardy/Z 5–8.

Asphodeline lutea

'Lambrook Silver' is more compact and has more finely dissected foliage. It is an excellent foil to purple-leaved plants. H and S 75cm (30in).

### A. ludoviciana
(syn. *A. palmeri*, *A. purshiana*)
**Western mugwort**
This species has dissected silver grey leaves that look as if they are lightly dusted with powder. H 1.2m (4ft), S 60cm (2ft). Hardy/Z 4–8. **A. lucoviciana var. latiloba** is shorter growing, and, like the species, looks well grown in association with pink or crimson flowering plants. H and S 60cm (2ft).

## ASPHODELINE
Jacob's rod
These stately plants, native to Mediterranean countries, are ideal for giving structure to a border.
*Cultivation* Grow in any well-drained soil in full sun.

### A. lutea
(syn. *Asphodelus luteus*)
Spires of fragrant, bright yellow flowers appear from spring to early summer above clusters of bluish-grey leaves. After flowering, the developing bead-like, green seeds continue to provide interest. H 1.2m (4ft), S 30cm (1ft). Hardy/Z 6–8.

## ASTER
This large genus includes the well-known Michaelmas daisies, essential plants for the autumn garden, many of which flower

from late summer until the first frosts. Most also last well as cut flowers. The species are as worthy of consideration as the hybrids, some of which have an annoying tendency towards mildew (although all those described are trouble-free). The genus also includes annuals.
*Cultivation* Asters will grow in any reasonably fertile soil, in sun or light shade. Some will do well in poor soil. The taller forms often benefit from staking.

### A. ericoides
The species, which is native to North America, has given rise to several garden-worthy forms. These have wiry stems that are starred with flowers, all with yellow centres, in autumn. H 75cm (30in), S 30cm (12in). Hardy/Z 5–8. **'Blue Star'** has pale blue flowers; **'Golden Spray'** has white flowers; **'Pink Cloud'** has light mauve-pink flowers.

### A. × frikartii
This group of vigorous hybrids includes some of the best of the Michaelmas daisies, all with a long flowering season. H 75cm (30in), S 38cm (15in). Hardy/Z 5–8. **'Mönch'** is an outstanding selection, which has large, lavender-blue flowers carried freely on branching stems; it is an excellent companion to shrubby lavateras. **'Wunder von Stäfa'** (syn. 'Wonder of Stafa') usually needs staking and has pinkish-blue flowers. H 1m (3ft), S 75cm (30in).

Aster × frikartii 'Mönch'

### A. laterifolius
(syn. *A. diffusus*)
The species has an unusual habit in that the erect stems produce flowering sideshoots, almost at right angles, giving a tiered effect. The flowers are white to pale lilac. H 1m (3ft), S 30cm (1ft). Hardy/Z 4–8. **'Horizontalis'**, which is rather more spreading, has pale lilac flowers. The coppery tinges acquired by its dainty leaves as the weather turns colder enhance its appeal. H 60cm (2ft), S 30cm (1ft).

### A. novae-angliae
**New England aster**
The tough, tolerant species flowers from late summer to early autumn, and is rarer in gardens than its many progeny. Hardy/Z 5–8. **'Andenken an Alma Pötschke'** (syn. 'Alma Pötschke') has rich pink flowers. H 1.2m (4ft),

S 60cm (2ft). **'Harrington's Pink'** has clear pink flowers. H 1m (3ft), S 60cm (2ft). **'Herbstschnee'** (syn. 'Autumn Snow') has white, yellow-centred flowers. H 1.2m (4ft), S 60cm (2ft).

### A. novi-belgii
**Michaelmas daisy**
Although generally applied to the whole genus, strictly the common name belongs to this species alone, the parent of a bewildering number of garden forms. It is often found growing as a weed, brightening up railway cuttings and areas of rough land with its violet-blue flowers in early autumn, which suggests a use in a wild garden or grass. The colours of the garden forms range from white, through all shades of pink, to pale and dark lavender-blue and some purples. They vary in height from dwarf forms, which are good at the edge of a border, to more substantial plants. All are hardy/Z 4–8. One of the best of the taller varieties is **'Climax'**, which has pale lavender-blue flowers in early autumn. H 1.2m (4ft), S 60cm (2ft). Among the good dwarf forms are **'Jenny'**, which has purplish-red flowers, and **'Lady in Blue'**, which has lavender-blue flowers. H 30cm (12in), S 45cm (18in).

### A. turbinellus
A refined-looking species from the United States, this has wiry stems that carry violet-blue daisies in autumn. H 1.2m (4ft), S 2ft (60cm). Hardy/Z 4–8.

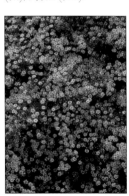

Aster ericoides 'Pink Cloud'

Aster laterifolius

Aster turbinellus

Astilbe × arendsii 'Elizabeth Bloom'

## ASTILBE

These sturdy border plants, which have striking feathery plumes of flowers in mid- to late summer, have been bred to produce a range of plants of different sizes. Since the plants appreciate damp conditions, they associate well with hostas (to which they provide a strong contrast with their attractive, ferny foliage) and *Iris sibirica*. Leave the faded flowers on the plant: they will turn a rich brown, providing continued interest through the winter months. Most of the astilbes grown in gardens are hybrids.
*Cultivation* Grow in fertile, reliably moist soil in sun or light shade. However, they will tolerate dry soil if they are grown in shade.

### A. × arendsii
This large hybrid group includes the following outstanding forms. H and S to 1m (3ft) unless otherwise indicated. All are hardy/Z 6. **'Bergkristall'** has white flowers. The late-flowering **'Elizabeth Bloom'** (syn. 'Eliblo') has pale pink flowers and bronze leaves. **'Fanal'** has long-lasting, dark crimson flowers. **'Glut'** (syn.

'Glow') is rich ruby red and flowers late. The white flowers of **'Irrlicht'** are a dramatic contrast to the dark green leaves. H and S 45cm (18in). **'Weisse Gloria'** (syn. 'White Gloria') is also white, but is bigger and early flowering. H and S 60cm (2ft).

### A. 'Bronce Elegans'
(syn. *A.* 'Bronze Elegance')
This hybrid bears plumes of pinkish-red flowers above bronze foliage. H and S 45cm (18in). Hardy/Z 6.

### A. × crispa 'Perkeo'
This is the outstanding member of this hybrid group with deep pink flowers borne in pyramidal spires. The young leaves are tinged with bronze as they emerge. H and S to 45cm (18in). Hardy/Z 4–8.

## ASTILBOIDES
Despite the name, the single species in this genus bears little resemblance to *Astilbe*. In fact, it looks more like a dwarf gunnera, for which it makes a good substitute in small gardens. It is a dramatic-looking foliage plant for a waterside location.
*Cultivation* This needs fertile, reliably moist soil in sun or light shade.

### A. tabularis
(syn. *Rodgersia tabularis*)
The large, light green leaves, which can be up to 1m (3ft) across, are held flat on upright stems. Small star-like white flowers appear in midsummer. H 1.5m (5ft), S 1.2m (4ft). Hardy/Z 5–7.

## ASTRANTIA
Hattie's pincushion, masterwort
These perennials are not especially showy in their own right, but they combine well with other more eye-catching performers. They self-seed freely, which may become a nuisance.
*Cultivation* Astrantias are easy to grow in most soils in sun or light shade, and prefer fertile, well-drained ground. The species *A. major* however tolerates drier soil.

### A. major
Greater masterwort
The species has straw-textured, green and pink, posy-like flowers in summer. Selections are worth growing with martagon lilies, which have similarly subdued flowers. H 60cm (24in), S 45cm (18in). Hardy/Z 5–7. The best forms include *A. major* subsp. *involucrata* **'Shaggy'**, which has clear pinkish-white flowers; *A. major* var. *rubra*, with purplish-red flowers; and **'Sunningdale Variegated'** (syn. 'Variegata'), which is a charming foliage plant with leaves generously splashed with green.

## BERGENIA
Elephant's ears
These tough, hardy evergreens have stout rhizomes and leathery leaves. Most flower in early spring (some as early as late winter), producing spikes of weather-resistant, bell-shaped flowers, but they can also flower intermittently at other times of year. On some, the leaves turn beetroot (beet) purple in cold weather, retaining this colour through the winter. They look best planted en masse in an informal group near woodland and are excellent with flowering cherries. They make excellent filling for 'problem' areas of the garden, providing ideal groundcover in dry, windy sites. Most are hybrids of garden origin.
*Cultivation* Any soil is suitable for bergenias, which will grow in sun or shade. For the best winter leaf colour, plant in not too fertile

Astilbe × arendsii 'Fanal'

Astrantia major

Bergenia 'Bressingham White'

soil in an open situation. Remove damaged leaves regularly to keep plants looking their best.

### B. cordifolia

This species has pink flowers among puckered leaves. H and S 30cm (12in). Hardy/Z 4–8. The selection 'Purpurea' has rich purple flowers in spring and also later in the year. The leaves flush purple in winter.

### B. hybrids

Among the best of the many forms now available are 'Baby Doll', which has pale pink flowers; 'Bressingham White', with white flowers and dark green leaves; 'Silberlicht' (syn. 'Silverlight'), which has white flowers that fade to pink; and 'Wintermärchen', with deep rose-pink flowers and leaves that turn scarlet in winter. H and S to 45cm (18in). Hardy/Z 3–8.

Bergenia 'Silberlicht'

## BIDENS

Ideal hanging basket plants (and therefore often treated as annuals), these plants produce an apparently unending succession of bright yellow flowers throughout summer. *Cultivation* Grow in any well-drained soil in full sun.

### B. aurea

A loosely branching, sprawling plant, this bears masses of bright yellow flowers. H 50cm (20in), S 40cm (16in). Half-hardy/Z 8–9.

## CAMPANULA
### Bellflower

This is a huge genus that includes choice rock plants and biennials as well as the sturdy perennials described here. Stalwarts of the border, they combine easily with a huge range of plants, especially roses. Tough and easy to grow, they are often used to introduce their refreshing blue tones to any scheme, although other colours also occur. The common name is a perfect description of the flower shape.
*Cultivation* Campanulas tolerate a range of soils, provided they are well drained, and will grow in sun or light shade.

### C. 'Burghaltii'

One of the subtlest campanulas, the smoky-lilac flowers are borne on erect stems in summer. Cutting back the stems after flowering can result in a second, albeit less impressive, crop of flowers. H 60cm (2ft), S 30cm (1ft). Hardy/Z 4–8.

Campanula lactiflora

### C. glomerata
#### Clustered bellflower

This summer-flowering species is invasive in its natural form and can be troublesome, but there are several desirable cultivars. Hardy/Z 4–8. C. glomerata var. alba 'Schneekrone' (syn. 'Crown of Snow') is a good white form. H 50cm (20in), S 60cm (2ft). 'Joan Elliott' bears large violet flowers in early summer. H 40cm (16in), S 45cm (18in). 'Purple Pixie' produces smaller, deep violet flowers late in the season. H 30cm (1ft), S 60cm (2ft). Possibly the best is 'Superba', which bears dense clusters of violet-purple flowers, ideal for adding a deeper note to plantings of red roses and peonies. H and S 60cm (2ft).

### C. lactiflora
#### Milky bellflower

There are a number of desirable forms of this Caucasian species, all flowering in summer and early autumn. The tall, sturdy stems (taller varieties will need staking in a windy location) make them excellent for giving height to a border, and they are good as companions for shrub roses and lilies. They are also tough enough to plant in rough grass. Hardy/Z 4–8. 'Loddon Anna' has soft lilac-pink flowers. H to 1m (3ft), S 45cm (18in). The dwarf form 'Pouffe' makes mounds of pale blue flowers. H and S 45cm (18in). One of the grandest cultivars is 'Prichard's Variety', which has violet-blue flowers. H 1.5m (5ft), S 60cm (2ft).

Campanula latiloba 'Percy Piper'

### C. latiloba

(syn. C. persicifolia subsp. sessiiflora) In summer this occasionally evergreen species throws up erect stems, thickly set with rich lavender-blue flowers, from the basal rosettes of leaves. H 1m (3ft), S 45cm (18in). Hardy/Z 4–8. 'Highcliffe Variety' and 'Percy Piper', both of which bear stalkless lavender-blue flowers, are similar. H 70cm (30in), S 45cm (18in).

### C. punctata

This species from Russia and Japan does best in a sandy (but fertile) soil in sun. Low-growing and somewhat spreading, it flowers in mid- to late summer. The flowers are white or mauve (usually with a pink flush) and spotted inside with red. H 30cm (12in), S 45cm (18in). Hardy/Z 5–8. C. punctata var. hondoensis has greyish-pink flowers.

Campanula punctata var. hondoensis

Chysanthemum 'Curtain Call'

Chrysanthemum 'Southway Swan'

Chysanthemum 'Taffy'

# CHRYSANTHEMUM
This large – formerly much larger – genus has been the subject of much controversy in recent years. Strictly speaking, the name is now applied only to annual species, but it is so deeply entrenched in gardening lore that it is retained here for a range of perennials that are now sometimes assigned to the genus *Dendranthema*. Many are for enthusiasts only, bred for exhibition and requiring a good deal of care under glass if they are to produce their stunning flowers. The plants described here, while of no lesser value, are reliable garden performers that, along with Michaelmas daisies, provide a welcome warmth of colour as the days grow cooler at the end of summer and into autumn (some continue into early winter). They are effective with late-flowering grasses.

*Cultivation* The plants described here do best in fertile, well-drained soil in full sun. Taller varieties need staking. Dividing plants every two years or so will help to keep them fresh.

## C. hybrids
There are a vast number of named chrysanthemums available in a range of colours to suit every possible garden scheme, and flowering in late summer into autumn. The following is just a small selection. All are hardy/Z 4–9 unless otherwise stated. '**Bronze Elegance**' has light bronze, pompon flowers. H and S 60cm (2ft). '**Curtain Call**' has anemone-centred, orange flowers. H and S 60cm (2ft). '**Emperor of China**' is an old variety, with double, silvery pink flowers; the leaves are tinged with red in autumn. H 1.2m (4ft),

S 60cm (2ft). '**George Griffiths**' is an early-flowering form, with large, deep red, fully reflexed flowers; it is often grown for exhibition. H 1.5m (5ft), S 75cm (30in). Half-hardy/Z 7–9. '**Glamour**' has warm, reddish-pink pompon flowers. H and S 1m (3ft). As the name suggests, '**Goldengreenheart**' has single, gold flowers with green centres; it is late flowering. H and S 60cm (2ft). '**Mei-kyo**' is an early-flowering plant with pink pompon flowers. H and S 60cm (2ft). '**Pennine Oriel**', an early-flowering plant, has anemone-centred, white flowers. H 1.2m (4ft), S 75cm (30in). '**Primrose Allouise**' is an early-flowering sport of 'White Allouise', with weather-resistant, incurving, soft yellow flowers. H 1.2 (4ft), S 75cm (30in). Half-hardy/Z 7–9. '**Southway Swan**'

has single flowers, with silvery pink petals surrounding yellow-green centres. H 1.2 (4ft), S 75cm (30in). '**Taffy**' has rich bronze-orange flowers. H 1.2 (4ft), S 75cm (30in).

# CIMICIFUGA
Bugbane, cohash
The imposing perennials in this genus are useful for the back of a border. The upright spikes of flowers do not need staking.
*Cultivation* Bugbanes do best when planted in reliably moist soil in a cool position.

## C. racemosa
Black snake root
This excellent plant has elegant, ferny foliage and tall bottlebrush-like spikes of white flowers throughout summer. H 2m (6ft), S 60cm (2ft). Hardy/Z 4–8.

## C. simplex
This species is similar to *C. racemosa* but is more compact and flowers rather later in the year, from late summer into autumn. H 1.2m (4ft), S 60cm (2ft). Hardy/Z 3–8. Good garden forms include **C. *simplex* var. *matsumurae* 'Elstead'**, which has purplish stems and creamy-white flowers; and '**White Pearl**', which has pure white flowers and pale green leaves. H and S 60cm (2ft).

# CLEMATIS
Most familiar in gardens are the many climbers belonging to this genus, but there are also a few perennials, worth growing for

Chysanthemum 'George Griffiths'

Chysanthemum 'Primrose Allouise'

Cimicifuga simplex

Convallaria majalis

their quiet charm. All need staking.
*Cultivation* Grow in any fertile,
preferably alkaline, soil in sun or
light shade.

### C. integrifolia

This weak-growing species has
noticeably hairy leaves and stems.
The indigo-violet flowers, borne in
midsummer, have recurving petals
like a turkscap lily. H and S 60cm
(2ft). Hardy/Z 3–9.

### C. recta

One of the best of the herbaceous
clematis, this bears masses of
scented, star-like, white flowers in
mid- to late summer, and is an
excellent foil to blue delphiniums.
H 1.2m (4ft), S 1m (3ft).
Hardy/Z 3–9. **'Purpurea'** is more
dramatic, with dark purple stems
and purple-flushed leaves, but
plants sold under this name can
vary, some being more intensely

coloured than others. H 1.2m
(4ft), S 75cm (30in).

## CONVALLARIA
### Lily-of-the-valley

With flowers of unsurpassed and
instantly recognizable fragrance,
you would think that these would
be in every garden. They can be
troublesome, however: difficult
to establish in some cases and
annoyingly rampant if they find
situations they like. The flowers
are excellent for cutting. The
plants can also be potted up and
forced under glass for early
flowers. All are toxic.
*Cultivation* Lily-of-the-valley is
best grown in fertile soil in light
shade, but it also tolerates sun.

### C. majalis

This species spreads by means of
branching underground rhizomes.
The handsome leaves emerge
in spring and are followed in late
spring by elegant sprays of bell-
shaped, fragrant, white flowers.
H 23cm (9in), S indefinite.
Hardy/Z 2–9. **'Albostriata'** is a
choice selection, with leaves striped
with silvery white. **'Fortin's Giant'**
is larger altogether and later
flowering. H and S 30cm (1ft).

## COREOPSIS
### Tickseed

The genus includes perennials and
annuals with daisy-like flowers in
summer, all excellent in borders
and ideal for cutting.
*Cultivation* Coreopsis does best in
fertile, well-drained soil in sun.
Tall varieties benefit from staking.

Coreopsis verticillata 'Moonbeam'

### C. grandiflora 'Mayfield Giant'

This selection has large, single,
yellow flowers in mid- to late
summer. H 1m (3ft), S 60cm
(2ft) Hardy/Z 4–9.

### C. verticillata

The best-known species in the
genus, with a number of selected
forms, this is a bushy plant with
star-shaped, bright yellow flowers
in early summer. H 45cm (18in),
S 30cm (12in). Hardy/Z 4–9.
**'Golden Gain'** has golden-yellow
flowers from early to midsummer.
Flowering later in the year,
**'Grandiflora'** (syn. 'Golden
Shower') has rich yellow daisies
and filigree foliage. H 60cm

(24in), S 45cm (18in). Also late-
flowering is the versatile
**'Moonbeam'**, which has pale
yellow flowers. H 40cm (16in),
S 30cm (12in).

## CRAMBE

These large, rather coarse but
undeniably dramatic plants are
excellent for giving height and
structure to borders. They are
magnificent as the dominant
feature of a white garden. After
flowering, leave the flower stem
intact and use it as a support for
a late climbing annual such as
sweet peas.
*Cultivation* Crambes will do well in
any well-drained soil in full sun.

### C. cordifolia

This species makes a mound of
rough, cabbage-like, green leaves.
In early to midsummer the flower
stem carries a gypsophila-like
cloud of scented, white flowers.
H 2.5m (8ft), S 1.2m (4ft).
Hardy/Z 6–9.

### C. maritima
### Sea kale

This tolerant species, found wild
in coastal areas, has tough,
glaucous green leaves and large
panicles of white flowers in
summer. The young stems are
edible. H 75cm (30in), S 1m
(3ft). Hardy/Z 6–9.

Clematis recta 'Purpurea'

Crambe cordifolia

*Delphinium* 'Clifford Sky'

*Delphinium* 'Fenella'

*Dianthus* 'Riccardo'

*Dianthus* 'Uncle Teddy'

# DELPHINIUM

These are grand plants but are now somewhat less popular than previously, probably because they require staking from early in the season and are susceptible to slug and snail damage, which means that a certain amount of work is necessary if they are to reach their full glory. That said, few other summer perennials can equal the colour range of these stately plants: primrose-yellow, cream, white, pale and dark blue, mauve, pink and deep purple. Recent breeding programmes (mainly in the Netherlands and the United States) have also introduced orange and red into the range, making pink strains possible. A traditional, Jekyllian-style herbaceous border would be unthinkable without them, the stronger blues associating well with *Thalictrum flavum* subsp.

*Delphinium* 'Sandpiper'

*glaucum*. The method of propagation (cuttings) has weakened the stocks of many older selections over the years, but a revival of interest in the genus has resulted in a number of vigorous plants. All parts of the plant are harmful if eaten, and the leaves can cause irritation.
*Cultivation* Delphiniums need fertile, well-drained, preferably limy soil in sun. Tall varieties need staking. Cutting back stems after flowering can result in further (though much less impressive) flowers later on.

## D. hybrids

While some of the species make good garden plants, they have not achieved the popularity of the many hybrids, only a few of which can be described here. **Elatum Group** plants have almost flat flowers in dense, upright spikes; **Belladonna Group** plants have branched stems and loose sprays of flowers. All cultivars are hardy/Z 2–7. **'Blue Nile'** (Elatum) is a classic pale blue delphinium, with flowers, each with a white eye, densely set on the spikes. H 1.5m (5ft), S 60cm (2ft). **'Casablanca'** (Belladonna), which has pure white flowers with yellow centres, is an excellent choice for a pale planting. H 1.2m (4ft), S 60cm (2ft). **'Clifford Sky'** (Elatum) has Wedgwood-blue flowers. H 1.5m (5ft), S 60cm (2ft). **'Fenella'** (Elatum) has stems densely set with semi-double, blue flowers, each with a black centre. H 1.5m

(5ft), S 60cm (2ft). **'Finsteraarhorn'** (Elatum) has cobalt-blue flowers touched with purple, each flower having a black eye. H 1.7m (5ft 6in), S 60cm (2ft). **'Langdon's Royal Flush'** (Elatum), a good choice among pink delphiniums, has conical spires of semi-double, purplish-pink flowers. H 1.5m (5ft), S 60cm (2ft). **'Mighty Atom'** (Elatum) has solidly packed spikes of semi-double, lavender-blue flowers with brown eyes. H 2m (6ft), S 1m (3ft). The charming **'Sandpiper'** (Elatum) is a compact plant, the pure white of its flowers enhanced by their dark brown eyes. H 1.2m (4ft), S 45cm (18in).

# DIANTHUS
## Carnation, pink

These appealing plants are justly popular as florist's flowers, but the genus is actually a large and complex one, simplified here as border carnations, perpetual-flowering carnations, Malmaison carnations and garden pinks. Perpetual-flowering and Malmaison carnations, which are half-hardy and can be forced into flower at any time of year, are generally grown commercially under glass.

*Dianthus* 'Spinfield Red'

The genus also includes many alpines, the biennial *D. barbatus* (sweet William) and some annuals. Many of the species are real enthusiasts' plants, and will not do well in all gardens. Where suited, however, they are splendid additions to any border, particularly in cottage garden-style plantings. The evergreen, bluish-grey leaves provide interest over a long period, making a particularly gracious picture when combined with old-fashioned roses. They are splendid edging plants, softening the lines of any path. Dianthus are not long-lived plants, but they are easily increased by cuttings or layering late in the season.

Border carnations, which are summer-flowering, are further divided by flower type as: selfs (a single colour); fancies (one colour spotted, flecked, blotched or striped with another); and picotees (one colour edged with another). They can also be clove-scented.

Garden pinks (sometimes just referred to as 'pinks') can be further divided into: old-fashioned pinks, which flower in early summer (they can be selfs; bicolours, with the central part of

*Dianthus* 'Louise's Choice'

Dianthus 'Letitia Wyatt'

Dianthus 'Dawlish Joy'

Dicentra formosa

the flower a different colour; or laced, with each petal edged in a contrasting colour); and modern pinks, which can have a longer season, from early summer to autumn (these can be selfs, bicolours, fancies or laced, and can also be clove-scented).
**Cultivation** The plants described need well-drained, neutral or alkaline soil in sun. They will tolerate some shade if it is not directly overhead.

### Border carnations

All the following border carnations are hardy/Z 4–8. H to 60cm (24in), S to 40cm (16in). Among recommended varieties are the vigorous **'Bookham Fancy'**, which has yellow flowers edged and marked with carmine-purple. **'Bookham Perfume'** has scented, deep burgundy flowers. **'Lavender Clove'** has clove-scented, lavender-pink flowers. **'Orange Maid'** has apricot flowers flecked with bronze. The flowers of **'Riccardo'** combine red and white. **'Spinfield Red'** has red flowers. **'Uncle Teddy'** is red and white.

Dianthus 'Mendlesham Maid'

### Garden pinks

All the following are hardy/Z 4–8. H to 45cm (18in), S to 30cm (12in). **'Bovey Belle'** has double purple flowers. **'Brympton Red'** has fragrant, crimson flowers with darker marbling. The scented flowers of **'Dad's Favourite'** are white laced with maroon, with dark centres. **'Dawlish Joy'** has variegated pink flowers. **'Devon Dove'** is pure white. **'Doris'**, a bicolour, has pale pink flowers with maroon centres. **'Excelsior'** has large-petalled, pink flowers; the flowers of **'Freckles'** are salmon-pink, delicately blotched with red. **'Gran's Favourite'** has clove-scented, white flowers laced with maroon; **'Joy'** has salmon-pink flowers. **'Letitia Wyatt'** has pale pink flowers. The semi-double **'London Brocade'** has pale pink flowers laced with dark red. **'Louise's Choice'** has crimson laced pink flowers; the miniature **'Mendlesham Maid'** has white flowers with frilly petal edges. The bicolour **'Monica Wyatt'** has phlox-pink flowers with ruby centres; **'Mrs Sinkins'** is fragrant, with double, white, fringed flowers; **'Musgrave's Pink'**, also fragrant, has double white flowers with green centres. **'White Ladies'** has clove-scented, double, white flowers, purer in colour than 'Mrs Sinkins'.

### DIASCIA

These interesting perennials (the genus name is pronounced with a hard 'c') bear nemesia-like flowers in a range of subtle colours, centring around coppery pink, throughout summer. They are not reliably hardy in cold areas, but, as with penstemons, cuttings are easily overwintered. They tend to

sprawl and look good at the base of a warm wall or in containers.
**Cultivation** Grow in any fertile (but not too dry) soil in full sun. Cutting the flowered stems back in summer results in further flowers in autumn.

### D. barberae 'Blackthorn Apricot'

Spires of warm apricot-pink flowers are borne from summer to autumn above the mats of dark green foliage. H 25cm (10in), S 50cm (20in). Borderline hardy/Z 8.

### D. rigescens

Of the several species, this is the best for general garden use. It is a shrubby South African native, with dense spikes of coppery-pink flowers in early and late summer. H and S 45cm (18in). Borderline hardy/Z 7–9.

### D. hybrids

There are many excellent garden forms, including **'Lilac Belle'**, which has purplish-pink flowers; **'Rupert Lambert'**, which has pink flowers; and **'Twinkle'**, which has purplish-pink flowers. H 45cm (18in), S 40cm (16in). Borderline hardy/Z 8.

## DICENTRA
### Bleeding heart

This genus contains elegant perennials with arching, glassy stems clothed with ferny foliage. The heart-shaped flowers are unique. Dicentras are excellent in shady rock gardens or light woodland, but they also tolerate more open conditions, combining

Diascia 'Rupert Lambert'

well with simple cottage garden plants, such as aquilegias, and flowering at around the same time in late spring to early summer.
**Cultivation** Grow in humus-rich, fertile soil in sun or light shade; they appreciate cool conditions.

### D. eximia

This species is similar in appearance to *D. formosa*, and there is some confusion between the two within the nursery trade, but this is daintier with typically furry foliage and tubular, pink, purple or white flowers. H 30cm (1ft), S 45cm (18in). Hardy/Z 4–8.

### D. formosa

A species with deeply divided foliage and drooping sprays of tubular, pinkish-mauve flowers. H 45cm (18in), S 60cm (24in). Hardy/Z 3–8. *D. formosa* var. *alba* is the desirable white form.

### D. spectabilis
#### Dutchman's breeches

The best-known species and deservedly popular, this produces fern-like foliage and masses of heart-shaped, rose-pink flowers that dangle appealingly from the arching stems. H 75cm (30in), S 60cm (24in). Hardy/Z 3–8. The selection **'Alba'** is if anything even more desirable, with white flowers and a slightly more compact habit. Both are good for cutting. H 60cm (24in), S 45cm (18in).

### D. 'Stuart Boothman'
(syn. *D.* 'Boothman's Variety')

This hybrid has flesh-pink flowers on arching stems amid the bluish-grey leaves. H 30cm (12in), S 40cm (16in). Hardy/Z 4–8.

Dierama pulcherrimum

Digitalis lutea

Doronicum 'Miss Mason'

## DIERAMA
**Angel's fishing rods, wandflower**
The common name is apt: these
are plants of almost unearthly
beauty, with tall, arching stems
of elegant bell-shaped flowers that
look well near water.
*Cultivation* Grow in reliably moist
soil in full sun. Winter protection
may be necessary in cold areas.

### D. pulcherrimum
**Venus' fishing rod, wandflower**
From among the grassy, evergreen
leaves, wiry stems emerge in midsummer, dangling bell-shaped
pink to lilac flowers. H 1.5m
(5ft), S 30cm (1ft). Borderline
hardy/Z 8–10. 'Blackbird' has
deep violet-mauve flowers.

## DIGITALIS
**Foxglove**
Typical woodlanders, foxgloves
also do well in more open conditions. The species described are
all subtly attractive and will seed
themselves where suited. They
suit any cottage garden-style
planting. All have spikes of characteristic, thimble-like flowers in
early summer and occasionally
produce lesser spikes later on,
even into autumn. Poisonous.
*Cultivation* Foxgloves will grow
in any fertile soil, but they do
best in humus-rich soil, in partial
shade. They will tolerate full sun.

### D. lutea
**(syn. D. eriostachya)**
This species has small, pale yellow
flowers and smooth green leaves.
H 60cm (2ft), S 30cm (1ft).
Hardy/Z 5–9.

### D. × mertonensis
The hybrid has downward-
pointing, tubular flowers the
colour of crushed strawberries,
a curious coppery, buff pink.
The leaves are greyish-green.
H 60cm (2ft), S 30cm (1ft).
Hardy/Z 5–9.

### D. purpurea
**Common foxglove**
This is the foxglove familiar
in woodlands, but it makes a
good garden plant, with mounds
of soft, grey-green leaves,
flushed purple towards the
base. It is a variable species, both
in flower colour, coming in shades
of pink, red and purple, and
height. H 1.5m (5ft), S 45cm
(18in). Hardy/Z 4–8. **D. purpurea
f. albiflora** is the delightful white-
flowered form, luminous in shade.
The leaves are unmarked green.
The form **'Suttons Apricot'** is
also desirable, with apricot-
coloured flowers.

## DORONICUM
**Leopard's bane**
These cheerful perennials have
bright yellow, daisy-like flowers in
spring. The species described is
easily pleased and can be invasive.
It is poisonous.
*Cultivation* Grow in any reasonable
soil in sun or light shade.

### D. 'Miss Mason'
This old hybrid holds its bright-
yellow daisies well above the
heart-shaped leaves in spring.
H 45cm (18in), S 60cm (2ft).
Hardy/Z 6.

### D. pardalianches
**Great leopard's bane**
A rather coarse plant, this is
suitable for colonizing light
woodland and is tough enough to
fill areas under deciduous trees and
shrubs. The yellow, daisy-like
flowers are produced in mid- to
late spring. H 1m (3ft), S 60cm
(2ft). Hardy/Z 4–8.

## ECHINACEA
**Coneflower**
Sturdy border plants, echinaceas
are essential for providing interest
from midsummer into autumn.
The prominent central boss
of stamens and the backwards
sweeping outer petals distinguish
them from all other daisy flowers.
*Cultivation* Grow in any fertile,
ideally humus-rich, well-drained
soil in sun.

### E. purpurea
This is the most widely grown
species. The flowers have rich
purple-crimson outer petals
surrounding the prominent
orange-brown centre. H 1.2m
(4ft), S 45cm (18in). Hardy/Z
3–9. 'Robert Bloom' has intense
cerise-mauve flowers. 'White
Swan' is not clear white as the
name suggests, but is touched
with fresh pale green. H 75cm
(30in), S 45cm (18in).

## ECHINOPS
**Globe thistle**
Tolerant and undemanding,
echinops are excellent in an
ecological garden, since they
attract bees and butterflies.
*Cultivation* They will grow in
any, even poor, soil in an open,
sunny situation.

### E. ritro
The jagged leaves are grey
underneath; the ball-like
flowerheads show their colour
(steely blue) before the flowers
open in late summer, giving a long
period of interest. H 60cm (2ft),
S 45cm (18in). Hardy/Z 3.

Digitalis purpurea f. albiflora

Echinacea purpurea 'White Swan'

Echinops ritro 'Veitch's Blue'

Erigeron 'Quakeress'

'Veitch's Blue' is taller, to 90cm (3ft), with darker flowerheads.

## EPILOBIUM
### Willowherb
These mainly tall plants are good for providing height in a border, and they flower over a long period.
*Cultivation* Grow in any well-drained soil that is not too rich; excessive fertility encourages leafy growth at the expense of flowers.

### E. angustifolium
#### Rosebay willowherb
The species, attractive as it is, tends to be an invasive weed in gardens so is best confined to a wild area. H 1.5m (5ft), S 1m (3ft). Hardy/Z 3–7. 'Album', with spires of pure white flowers in late summer, is less rampant.

## EREMURUS
### Foxtail lily
Stately perennials, foxtail lilies produce tall spikes of star-shaped flowers that rise above other plants in late spring to early summer. Grow them among lower plants for maximum impact. They die back after flowering, so plant near something that will cover the gap they leave, such as *Gypsophila paniculata* or late-sown annuals. The plants may need staking in windy weather.
*Cultivation* Grow in any well-drained soil in sun. They tolerate dry soil.

### E. × isabellinus Shelford hybrids
Under this name is a range of garden-worthy plants with tall spikes of yellow, orange, pink or white flowers. H 2m (6ft), S 1m (3ft). Hardy/Z 5.

### E. stenophyllus
This lovely species has slender spikes of yellow flowers, which fade to orange-brown, giving a bicolour effect. H 1.5m (5ft), S 60cm (2ft). Hardy/Z 5.

## ERIGERON
### Fleabane
Useful daisy plants, suitable for a sunny border, these suit cottage garden-style plantings. There are a large number of hybrids; only the species described is well-represented in gardens.
*Cultivation* Best in fertile, moist but well-drained soil in sun. Taller varieties may benefit from light staking.

### E. karvinskianus
#### (syn. E. muconatus)
#### Wall daisy
This spreading species has dainty white flowers from late spring to autumn. H to 30cm (1ft), S 1m (3ft). Hardy/Z 8–9.

### E. hybrids
The following hybrids flower throughout summer but can also flower intermittently at other times. They are all hardy/Z 2–7. 'Dignity' has violet-blue flowers.

H and S 45cm (18in). 'Dunkelste Aller' (syn. 'Darkest of All') has deep purple flowers with yellow eyes. H 60cm (2ft), S 45cm (18in). 'Gaiety' has mid-pink flowers. H 60cm (2ft), S 45cm (18in). The deservedly popular 'Quakeress' has white flowers flushed with pale lilac-pink. H 60cm (2ft), S 45cm (18in). 'Schneewittchen' (syn. 'Snow White') has pure white flowers, which turn pink as they age. H 60cm (2ft), S 45cm (18in).

## ERYNGIUM
### Eryngo, sea holly
Spiky, stiffly branched, architectural plants, eryngiums are perhaps best given space to make their own statement, ideally in a gravel garden, but they will also integrate into mixed borders, providing an excellent contrast to softer plants. Some are biennials.
*Cultivation* Grow in any well-drained soil in full sun. They thrive in poor, gritty soils.

### E. bourgatii
This striking plant has deeply cut, bluish-grey leaves, veined white, and spiky steel-blue cones of flowers in early to midsummer. H 60cm (2ft), S 50cm (20in). Hardy/Z 5–8.

### E. × tripartitum
This hybrid has wiry stems that branch freely, carrying many metallic-blue flowerheads throughout summer. It looks particularly striking with *Crambe maritima*. H 1m (3ft), S 50cm (20in). Hardy/Z 5–8.

Epilobium angustifolium 'Album'

Eremurus stenophyllus

Eryngium × tripartitum

*Erysimum 'Bowles' Mauve'*

# ERYSIMUM
## Wallflower

Wallflowers and tulips are a classic cottage garden combination, although bedding plants sold for this purpose are usually treated as biennials. The plants described here are all true evergreen perennials, and although they are often short-lived, they are easily increased by cuttings. All are of hybrid origin.
*Cultivation* Grow wallflowers in any well-drained, not too rich soil in sun, in a sheltered position. Dead-heading encourages further flowering.

### E. 'Bowles' Mauve'
This truly remarkable perennial belongs in every garden. Officially it produces its four-petalled, fragrant, rich mauve flowers from

*Eupatorium album 'Braunlaub'*

late winter to early summer, but it is seldom without flowers at any time of year. H 75cm (30in), S 60cm (2ft). Hardy/Z 5–9.

### E. cheiri
(syn. *Cheiranthus cheiri*)
This species is the parent of the many seed strains that are sold for raising bedding plants. The reliably perennial **'Harpur Crewe'** has double, rich yellow flowers from late spring to midsummer. H 30cm (12in), S 60cm (2ft). Hardy/Z 6–7.

### E. 'Constant Cheer'
From mid-spring to early summer this hybrid has orange-yellow flowers that fade to purple. H 60cm (2ft), S 40cm (16in). Hardy/Z 7–10.

### E. 'Parish's'
The flowers of this hybrid, produced from early spring to midsummer, open brick-red and mature to purplish-crimson. H and S 30cm (12in). Hardy/Z 7–10.

# EUPATORIUM
## Hemp agrimony

Somewhat coarse, but easily grown, these perennials are suitable for a wild garden or an informal border. They are valuable for their height and late season. Some are weeds.
*Cultivation* Any reasonable soil in sun is suitable.

### E. album
(syn. *E. rugosum* var. *album*)
This species, with hairy stems and

*Euphorbia cornigera*

leaves, has domed heads of white flowers in late summer. H 1m (3ft), S 45cm (18in). Hardy/Z 4–9. The variant **'Braunlaub'** is similar but has brownish flowers and brown-tinged young foliage. H 1m (3ft), S 45cm (18in).

### E. purpureum
## Joe Pye weed, gravel root, queen of the meadow
This imposing species has characteristically rough leaves and clusters of dull pinkish-purple flowers in late summer. H 2m (6ft), S 1m (3ft). Hardy/Z 3–8.
*E. purpureum* subsp. *maculatum* **'Atropurpureum'** is a superior form, with purple-flushed leaves and stems and light purple flowers. H 2m (6ft), S 1m (3ft).

# EUPHORBIA

A hugely significant genus, many members of which provide interest over a long period. The true flowers are insignificant, but are surrounded by showy bracts (referred to as 'flowers' below) that continue to attract attention after the true flowers have faded. The genus encompasses a vast range of perennial plants that are at home in any garden as well as shrubs, trees, exotic succulents and annuals, in addition to the popular Christmas houseplant, *E. pulcherrima*, sold as poinsettia. Euphorbias combine happily in the border with a range of other plants. The species described here are all easy to grow, but care needs to be taken when handling them: when cut or broken, the stems

exude a milky sap that can cause skin irritations.
*Cultivation* The euphorbias described below will grow in any well-drained fertile soil in sun. Any preferences of individual species are included in the relevant entry. To keep plants looking neat, cut back the flower stems of evergreen forms to ground level when the blooms have faded.

### E. amygdaloides var. robbiae
(syn. *E. robbiae*)
## Mrs Robb's bonnet
A good plant for a shady position under trees or for poor soil, this plant has rosettes of dark green leaves and dull green flowers in spring. H and S 60cm (2ft). Hardy/Z 5–9.

### E. characias
This is a variable evergreen, rather shrubby species, happy in sun or shade, but probably better in sun. It is splendid against a warm wall, when it will send out tall, billowing shoots from ground level, clothed in narrow, grey-green leaves and topped, from early spring into summer, by lime-green flowers. H and S 1.2m (4ft). Hardy/Z 7–9. Worthwhile variants include *E. characias* subsp. *wulfenii*, which has more brilliant yellow-green flowers; and subsp. *wulfenii* **'Lambrook Gold'**, which has rich golden-green flowers. H and S 1.2m (4ft).

### E. cornigera
(syn. *E. longifolia*, *E. wallichii*)
An excellent border plant, this

Euphorbia myrsinites

Euphorbia schillingii

Galega × hartlandii 'Alba'

species has dark green leaves striped centrally with paler green and, throughout summer, typical euphorbia lime-green flowers. H 50cm (20in), S 30cm (12in). Hardy/Z 7–9.

### E. dulcis

This species can be invasive but makes good groundcover in shade. It has dark green leaves, sometimes tinged with bronze, and greenish-yellow flowers in early summer. H and S 30cm (12in). Hardy/Z 6. The form 'Chameleon' is a more interesting and coveted plant than the species. It has rich purple leaves and purple-tinted flowers.

### E. griffithii

This notable early summer-flowering species is invasive but desirable as groundcover in sun or light shade, especially in one

of its named varieties. It is excellent with yellow-flowered azaleas. The species has dark green, red-ribbed leaves and colourful red, yellow and orange flowerheads. H 1m (3ft), S 60cm (2ft). Hardy/Z 5–9. Among the best cultivars are 'Dixter', which has orange flowers and red-tinged leaves; and 'Fireglow', which has tomato-red flowers. H 75cm (30in), S 1m (3ft).

### E. myrsinites
#### Myrtle euphorbia

This succulent-looking species is good in gravel gardens in full sun or in troughs, where its trailing stems are especially effective. The thick, almost triangular leaves are blue-green. The long-lasting, greenish-yellow flowers that fade to pink appear in early summer. H 15cm (6in), S 30cm (12in). Hardy/Z 6–8.

### E. polychroma
#### (syn. E. epithymoides)

A must for the spring garden, this herbaceous perennial makes a mound of foliage that in late spring becomes a mass of brilliant yellow-green as the flowers open. It is excellent with late-flowering daffodils or *Tulipa praestans*. H and S 30cm (12in). Hardy/Z 4–9.

### E. schillingii

A robust plant, this has dark green leaves and long-lasting, yellow-green flowers from midsummer to mid-autumn. It does best in light shade in reliably moist soil. H 1m (3ft), S 60cm (2ft). Hardy/Z 5–8.

## FRAGARIA
### Strawberry

Strawberries are usually grown exclusively in kitchen gardens for their edible fruit. The plant

described here has ornamental value, however, and makes an excellent edging plant as well as providing good groundcover.
*Cultivation* Grow in any moist but well-drained soil, preferably alkaline, in sun or light shade.

### F. 'Pink Panda'
#### (syn. 'Frel')

Like the edible strawberries, this plant spreads by runners and can be invasive. It has dark green leaves and, from late spring to mid-autumn, bright pink flowers but seldom fruits. H 15cm (6in), S indefinite. Hardy/Z 4.

## GALEGA
### Goat's rue

This genus of large summer-flowering perennials deserve to be better known. They resemble a giant vetch with masses of pea-like flowers and are excellent for filling gaps in large borders, associating well with a wide range of other plants.
*Cultivation* Grow in any soil, poor or fertile, in sun or shade. Tall forms may need staking.

### G. × hartlandii

This hybrid group consists of a number of worthwhile forms, usually with flowers in shades of lilac, lavender, pink or pinkish-mauve. H to 1.5m (5ft), S 1m (3ft). Hardy/Z 3–8. 'Alba' has white flowers; 'His Majesty' has pinkish-mauve and white flowers; and 'Lady Wilson' is a similar bicolour, but the flowers are a more bluish-mauve.

Euphorbia polychroma

Galega × hartlandii 'Lady Wilson'

Galium odoratum

## GALIUM
### Bedstraw
These are useful plants for filling gaps in borders, and the star-like flowers are a good foil for other, more flamboyant plants. The species described is the best known and is often included in herb gardens for its historical associations.
*Cultivation* Grow in any well-drained soil in sun or light shade. *G. odoratum* is one of the few plants that positively thrives in dry shade.

### G. odoratum
(syn. *Asperula odorata*)
**Sweet woodruff**
This species cultivated as ground cover produces masses of fragrant, star-like white flowers in late spring. H 30cm (12in), S indefinite. Hardy/Z 5–8.

## GERANIUM
### Cranesbill
It would be difficult to over-estimate the value of these plants, which have rightly gained in popularity over recent years. Easy to grow, spreading easily and combining happily with a range of other plants, they are excellent in fairly informal, cottage-garden schemes, associating particularly well with most roses. They make excellent groundcover without being invasive. Smaller types are good in rock gardens.
*Cultivation* Grow hardy geraniums in any reasonable (but not boggy) soil in sun or light shade. *G. phaeum* prefers shade.

Geranium 'Ann Folkard'

### G. 'Ann Folkard'
A fine plant, this bears a succession of magenta flowers, with blackish centres and veining, throughout summer. Early in the season the flowers are pleasingly offset by yellowish leaves, but these usually turn green by midsummer. This is a good plant for growing through small shrubs in shade. H 30cm (12in), S 60cm (2ft). Hardy/Z 5–8.

### G. clarkei
The spreading species, which is from India, has saucer-shaped flowers in shades of purplish-blue or white with purplish veining from early to late summer. H 50cm (20in), S indefinite. Hardy/Z 4–8. The species is usually represented in gardens by its selected forms, outstanding among which is **'Kashmir White'** (syn. *G. pratense* 'Rectum Album'),

Geranium 'Johnson's Blue'

whose white summer flowers are delicately veined with lilac-pink. H and S 45cm (18in).

### G. 'Johnson's Blue'
A plant for every garden, this hybrid has clear blue flowers in late spring over the mounds of copious green leaves. Cutting the plant back to ground level after flowering results in a fresh crop of leaves and (in a good year) a second flush of flowers. H 30cm (1ft), S 60cm (2ft). Hardy/Z 4–8.

### G. macrorrhizum
(syn. *G. macrorrhizum* var. *roseum*)
The species, which spreads by means of thick rhizomes, has gummy, aromatic leaves, which assume red tinges in autumn. The liverish magenta flowers are small in relation to the size of the plant and appear in late spring. H 25cm

Geranium macrorrhizum

(10in), S 50cm (20in). Hardy/Z 3–8. The flowers of the species yield in beauty to those of **'Album'**, which are not clear white, but a delicate, pale shell pink. H 30cm (1ft), S 60cm (2ft).

### G. × magnificum
This robust but sterile hybrid has handsome, slightly hairy leaves, which often redden attractively in autumn. Sticky flower stalks carry rich purple flowers, heavily pencilled with a darker shade, in late spring to early summer. H and S 60cm (2ft). Hardy/Z 4–8.

### G. phaeum
**Mourning widow, dusky cranesbill**
The common names are appropriate: the dusky purple flowers that hang from elegant, wiry stems in mid-spring have a slightly plangent air. H 60cm (2ft), S 45cm (18in). Hardy/Z 4–9. The form **'Album'** is also desirable; it has pure white flowers and golden-yellow anthers. Where grown in proximity with the species, the two will hybridize to produce plants with pleasing soft mauve flowers. **'Lily Lovell'** is a selected form with large, mauve flowers with paler centres.

## GEUM
### Avens
Simple, cottage-garden-style plants, geums provide strong colour and borders over many weeks in early summer; they are good at the front of borders.
*Cultivation* Grow geums in any reasonable soil in sun or light shade. They benefit from division every two to three years.

### G. 'Lady Stratheden'
(syn. *G.* 'Goldball')
This is one of the best known of the hybrids, with semi-double yellow flowers from late spring to midsummer. H 45cm (18in), S 30cm (12in). Hardy/Z 5–8.

### G. 'Mrs J. Bradshaw'
(syn. *G.* 'Feuerball', *G.* 'Mrs Bradshaw')
The semi-double, coppery red flowers of this hybrid can be produced at any time during the summer. H 45cm (18in), S 30cm (12in). Hardy/Z 5–9.

Geranium phaeum

*Geum 'Mrs J. Bradshaw'*

# HELENIUM
## Sneezeweed, Helen's flower
These valuable daisy-like flowers are easily grown and merit a place in any border planned for late summer and autumn interest. Together with dahlias and chrysanthemums, they bring a warm glow to the garden at the end of the season, and they look good with a range of grasses and purple-leaved plants or with the strong foliage of bergenias. Most garden forms are hybrids that have been developed in Germany.
*Cultivation* Grow in any reasonable soil in sun. Tall forms may need staking. Regular division also prevents congestion.

### H. hybrids
The following hybrids all flower from late summer to mid-autumn. All are hardy/Z 3–8. H and S 1m

(3ft). **'Gartensonne'** has light yellow flowers with dark centres; **'Indianersommer'** has rich golden-yellow flowers; **'Moerheim Beauty'**, one of the best known, has rich brownish-red flowers that age lighter brown; **'The Bishop'** has yellow flowers with dark eyes.

# HELICHRYSUM
The plants in this genus are distinguished by their daisy-like, straw-textured flowers, some of which hold their colour well when dried. Some are primarily foliage plants, useful in summer bedding schemes, or in large pots or hanging baskets.
*Cultivation* Grow in any well-drained soil in full sun. This will not tolerate wet conditions.

### H. petiolare
(syn. *H. petiolatum*)
This sprawling, evergreen subshrub is essential for hanging baskets or for trailing over the edges of a large container of seasonal plants. The typical plant has silvery, woolly leaves. H and S 1m (3ft). Half-hardy/Z 10. Selections include **'Limelight'** (syn. 'Aureum'), which has lime-green leaves; and **'Variegatum'**, which has grey-green leaves variegated with cream.

### H. 'Schweffellicht'
(syn. *H.* 'Sulphur Light')
This hybrid provides interest over a long period. The white-woolly leaves are themselves a feature before the sulphur, tawny-orange daisy-like flowers appear in mid-

*Helichrysum 'Schweffellicht'*

to late summer. H and S 35cm (14in). Hardy/Z 5–9.

# HELLEBORUS
## Hellebore
An important genus from the gardener's point of view, with many desirable plants, all with nodding flowers (some a little sinister-looking, it is true) and handsome, more or less evergreen leaves. They are indispensable in the winter garden. Hellebores thrive in the shade of deciduous trees and shrubs and will even tolerate heavy shade next to a wall. All are poisonous.
*Cultivation* Easy to grow in any fertile, well-drained (although most prefer heavy and alkaline) soil in sun or shade.

### H. argutifolius
(syn. *H. corsicus*, *H. lividus* subsp. *corsicus*)
### Corsican hellebore
This handsome species tolerates drier conditions than most other hellebores. The firm, jade-green leaves are attractive throughout the year. The clusters of apple-green, bell-shaped flowers appear in mid-spring and last until early summer. It is a splendid foil for *Iris reticulata*. H and S 1m (3ft). Hardy/Z 6–8.

### H. foetidus
### Bear's foot, stinking hellebore
A dramatic species that makes a clump of blackish-green leaves. Strong stems carrying many bell-shaped, apple-green flowers (usually edged with maroon)

appear in late winter to early spring. It looks good with snowdrops. H 75cm (30in), S 60cm (2ft). Hardy/Z 4–9. Plants of the **Wester Flisk Group** have red-tinged stems and leaf and flower stalks. H 60cm (2ft), S 45cm (18in).

### H. niger
### Christmas rose
This is one of the most desirable of the hellebores, but unfortunately it is also one of the trickiest to grow. It has dark green, leathery leaves and large glistening white flowers in mid- to late winter. It is slow to establish and needs fertile sticky soil that does not dry out. H 30cm (12in), S 45cm (18in). Hardy/Z 4–7. **'Potter's Wheel'** is a desirable selection with larger flowers.

### H. orientalis
### Lenten rose
One of the easiest hellebores to grow, this is also one of the most variable species. The flowers, which appear from late winter into spring, can be white, yellowish-cream, dusky-pink, clear glowing red or plum-purple, and can also be spotted inside with a different colour to varying degrees. All are flushed green inside and out. The leaves are also handsome: firm and with serrated edges, and of varying shades of green, paler leaves being associated with paler flower colours. Blackened leaves should be removed. H 45cm (18in), S 60cm (2ft). Hardy/Z 5–9.

*Helenium 'Indianersommer'*

*Helichrysum petiolare*

*Helleborus foetidus*

*Hemerocallis* 'Golden Chimes'

*Hemerocallis* 'Jake Russell'

*Hemerocallis* 'Joan Senior'

*Hemerocallis* 'Ruffled Apricot'

# HEMEROCALLIS
## Daylily

These almost indestructible plants, with their usually trumpet-like flowers, are of increasing value in gardens. Breeding programmes (particularly in the United States) have greatly increased the number of hybrids and the length of flowering season. The colour range is also greater, but centres around yellow and orange. They make excellent border plants, rapidly forming vigorous clumps. Although the individual flowers last only a day (hence the common name), they are freely produced over a long period, and the grassy foliage is always appealing, a refreshing sight when emerging in spring and a good foil for early bulbs. Small daylilies are excellent for edging a border; the larger kinds consort happily with hostas and peonies, as well as with roses of all kinds. The species are tough enough for a wild garden or for growing in grass.
*Cultivation* Daylilies seem to thrive in any soil but preferably one that is not too dry. Grow in sun or light shade. Lift and divide the plants every two or three years to prevent congestion.

### H. citrina
Broader leaves than average distinguish this species, whose fragrant, lemon-yellow flowers open in the evening in midsummer. H 1m (3ft), S 60cm (2ft). Hardy/Z 3–9.

### H. fulva
This species is usually grown in one of its double forms. Hardy/Z 3–9. 'Flore Pleno' has sometimes muddled, rich orange flowers in summer. H and S to 1m (3ft).

'Kwans Variegata' has similar flowers but is less robust, with leaves narrowly margined with white. H and S 75cm (30in).

### H. lilioasphodelus (syn. *H. flava*)
Late spring to early summer is the season of this semi-evergreen, evening-flowering species with scented, lemon-yellow flowers. H 75cm (30in), S 45cm (18in). Hardy/Z 3–9.

### H. hybrids
There are many named hybrids, with colours and heights to fit into every garden scheme. The following, all of which are evergreen and hardy/Z 3–9 unless otherwise indicated, are just a selection. 'Cartwheels' has freely borne, orange, nocturnal flowers in midsummer. H and S 75cm (30in). The compact 'Corky' has clear yellow flowers in midsummer. H 70cm (28in), S 40cm (16in). 'Eenie Weenie', one of the first dwarfs raised, has rounded yellow flowers in early to midsummer. H 25cm (10in), S

40cm (16in). The intriguing, semi-evergreen 'Gingerbread Man' has butterscotch-orange flowers in early summer. H 70cm (28in), S 1m (3ft). Borderline hardy/Z 8–9. 'Golden Chimes' has deep yellow flowers in early summer. H 1m (3ft), S 45cm (18in). 'Green Flutter' has light yellow flowers with green throats over a long period. H 50cm (20in), S 1m (3ft). 'Jake Russell' has golden-yellow flowers with a velvety sheen in mid- to late summer. H 1m (3ft), S 45cm (18in). The semi-evergreen 'Joan Senior', the closest to a white cultivar, has pinkish-white flowers with yellow-green throats in mid- to late summer. H 60cm (2ft), S 75cm (30in). The vigorous 'Little Grapette' has deep purple flowers in midsummer. H 30cm (12in), S 45cm (18in). 'Lusty Leland' produces an abundance of scarlet and yellow flowers over a long period in summer. H 70cm (28in), S 1m (3ft). The outstanding and prolific 'Marion Vaughn' has fragrant, lemon-yellow flowers in mid- to late

summer. H 85cm (34in), S 75cm (30in). 'Maura Loa' has brilliant orange flowers in summer. H 55cm (22in), S 1m (3ft). 'Prairie Blue Eyes' is semi-evergreen with lavender-purple flowers in midsummer. H 70cm (28in), S 75cm (30in). 'Ruffled Apricot' has characteristically crimped-edged, apricot flowers in early to midsummer. H 70cm (28in), S 1m (3ft). 'Scarlet Orbit' has bright red flowers with yellow-green throats in midsummer. H 50cm (20in), S 1m (3ft). 'Stafford', one of the best of its colour range, has rich scarlet flowers in midsummer. H 70cm (28in), S 1m (3ft). The vigorous 'Stella de Oro' is a dwarf selection, with rounded, bright yellow flowers in early summer, sometimes repeating in autumn. H 30cm (12in), S 45cm (18in).

# HEUCHERA
## Alum bell, coral bells

Invaluable plants for ground-cover, heucheras have handsome leaves, often tinted or marbled

*Hemerocallis* 'Little Grapette'

*Hemerocallis* 'Stafford'

*Heuchera* 'Pewter Moon'

with silver-grey. There are a large number of hybrids, all making excellent companions for border carnations and pinks (*Dianthus*).
**Cultivation** Grow in any reasonable soil in sun or light shade. Plants benefit from regular division.

### H. micrantha var. diversifolia 'Palace Purple'

The species is most often represented in cultivation by this form, although plants sold under this name can vary. It is a striking plant with large, purple, maple-like leaves and sprays of tiny white flowers in midsummer. H 60cm (2ft), S 45cm (18in). Hardy/Z 4–8.

### H. 'Pewter Moon'

This hybrid is grown primarily for the appeal of its heavily silver-marbled leaves rather than for its sprays of pink summer flowers. H 45cm (18in), S 30cm (12in). Hardy/Z 4.

### H. 'Strawberry Swirl'

The hybrid has ruffled green leaves, overlaid with silver, and pale pink flowers in early summer. H 45cm (18in), S 30cm (12in). Hardy/Z 4.

### × HEUCHERELLA

These dainty evergreen woodland plants, hybrids of *Heuchera* and *Tiarella*, have an old-fashioned look to them. They are clump-forming and make excellent groundcover.
**Cultivation** Grow in partial shade in any soil that does not dry out completely in summer.

Hosta nigrescens

*Hosta sieboldiana var. elegans*

### × H. tiarelloides

This beautiful evergreen ground-cover plant makes dense clusters of short leaves. The sprays of appealing, salmon-pink flowers appear in late spring. H and S 45cm (18in). Hardy/Z 4–8.

## HOSTA
### Funkia, plantain lily

This is an enormous genus, made larger by a huge number of hybrids, mostly of American origin. They are the ultimate foliage plants, combining handsomely with roses and a whole range of herbaceous perennials. They make good groundcover and look good with filigree ferns in shade gardens. They are also stylish in containers, although, being herbaceous, they do not provide year-round interest. The flowers, which are carried on tall 'scapes' in mid- to late summer, are of secondary interest, and some gardeners go as far as cutting them off.

Although of undoubted distinction, hostas are not universally popular, as many gardeners object to the slug and snail control that is necessary to guarantee perfect leaves. Apart from poisons, a good frog, toad and bird population or a hedgehog will control but not eradicate the pests. The parasitic nematode is effective on slugs only. An eco-friendly method that defies the cultivation hints given below is to restrict your choice to thick-leaved types and grow them in poor, gritty soil. This results in smaller but tougher leaves that

are less palatable to pests.
**Cultivation** Most hostas do best in fertile, humus-rich, moist soil in partial to full shade. Some will tolerate sun, but for the best leaves, the more sun, the moister the soil should be.

### H. nigrescens

This large species has broadly oval, puckered leaves that are glaucous blue when mature (the emerging shoots in spring are almost black, hence the name). The near white flowers open from pale purple buds. H and S 70cm (28in). Hardy/Z 4–9.

### H. sieboldiana

An impressive species with almost quilted, waxy, bluish-green leaves and almost white flowers. H 1m (3ft), S 1.2m (4ft). Hardy/Z 3–9. While of evident distinction, the species usually gives ground in gardens to *H. sieboldiana* var. *elegans* (syn. *H.* 'Elegans', *H. glauca*, *H.* 'Robusta'). This has even more thickly puckered and glaucous leaves.

### H. sieboldii

One of the few naturally occurring variegated species, this should not be confused with *H. sieboldiana*, which is quite different. This has oval or lance-shaped leaves with white margins and pale mauve flowers streaked with violet. H and S 60cm (2ft). Hardy/Z 4–9.

### H. ventricosa

This species has shiny green leaves with pointed tips and striking,

Hosta ventricosa

bell-shaped, deep violet flowers. H 50cm (20in), S 1m (3ft). Hardy/Z 4–9.

### H. venusta

This vigorous dwarf species is suitable for a rock garden. It has oval to lance-shaped green leaves and violet flowers, borne on scapes up to 35cm (14in) tall. H 5cm (2in), S 25cm (10in). Hardy/Z 4–9.

### H. hybrids

For convenience, the following hybrids are divided into three groups: large, measuring 64cm (25in) or more from leaf tip to opposite leaf tip; medium, 40–60cm (16–24in) from leaf tip to opposite leaf tip; and small, 38cm (15in) or less from leaf tip to opposite leaf tip. All hybrids are hardy/Z 3–9 unless otherwise stated.

Hosta sieboldii

Hosta venusta

*Hosta 'Antioch'*

## Large hybrids

'Antioch', an elegant plant, has oval leaves irregularly margined with cream or creamy white and lavender-coloured flowers. It is best in full shade. **'August Moon'** has soft yellow leaves that develop a faint greyish-blue bloom and pale greyish-lavender to white flowers. It does best in sun. **'Blue Angel'** has thick, glaucous-blue leaves (although less puckered than many of its type) and pale mauve to white flowers. **'Francee'** has leaves that are narrowly edged with white and funnel-shaped, lavender-purple flowers. **'Frances Williams'** (syn. 'Eldorado', 'Golden Circles', *H. sieboldiana* 'Frances Williams', *H. sieboldiana* 'Yellow Edge') is a famous hosta and one of the most beautiful, with deep glaucous blue leaves, margined with creamy-beige, and lavender-coloured flowers. **'Gold Standard'** has striking leaves that are generously splashed with greenish yellow, the colour becoming brighter before fading to buff beige. The flowers are greyish purple. **'Green Acres'** has

oval green, deeply ribbed leaves on tall petioles and near-white flowers. It is a striking plant when mature. **'Krossa Regal'**, a sumptuous, urn-shaped hosta, has waxy-bloomed, bluish-green leaves and lavender-coloured flowers. **'Pearl Lake'**, which has small, grey-green leaves carried on tall petioles and masses of pale lavender-coloured flowers, makes excellent groundcover. **'Piedmont Gold'** is aptly named. It has thick-textured, yellowish-green leaves with a distinct whitish bloom. The flowers are pale lavender-white. **'Sagae'** (syn. *H. fluctuans* 'Sagae', *H. fluctuans* 'Variegated') is a truly dramatic hosta with thick, blackish-green leaves margined with cream or creamy-yellow. The funnel-shaped flowers are pale lavender overlaid with purple. Sun-tolerant **'Sum and Substance'** has puckered leaves that are pointed at the tip, greenish to bright yellow in colour, depending on the amount of sun, and pale mauve flowers. **'Sun Power'** has oval to heart-shaped, yellow-green leaves and lavender flowers. **'Tall Boy'**, almost uniquely among hostas, is grown for its pale purple, funnel-shaped flowers, which are carried on unusually tall scapes. The leaves are glossy mid-green. **'Wide Brim'** has puckered, bluish-green leaves that are broadly and irregularly margined with creamy white and near-white flowers. **'Zounds'** has heavily puckered, golden-yellow leaves, which develop a metallic sheen as they mature, and pale lavender-white flowers.

## Medium hybrids

**'Blue Wedgwood'**, an elegant plant, produces heavily puckered, intense glaucous blue leaves and pale lavender to white flowers. **'Devon Green'**, a beautiful plant, has shiny dark green leaves and greyish-lavender to white flowers. **'Golden Prayers'** is a vigorous hosta, with puckered, vivid golden-yellow leaves that are held erect and almost white flowers. **'Hadspen Blue'** has substantial, glaucous-blue leaves and lavender-coloured flowers. **'Hadspen Heron'** has substantial, oval to lance-shaped, glaucous blue-green

leaves and near-white flowers. **'Halcyon'**, a good choice for a container, has intensely blue leaves and near-white flowers. **'June'**, an unusual hosta, has bluish-green leaves that have a strong yellow central splash, which darkens to greenish yellow. The flowers are pale lavender-grey. The sun-tolerant **'Midas Touch'** has, deeply puckered, heart-shaped, bright yellowish-green leaves and near white flowers. **'Shade Fanfare'** has yellowish-green leaves broadly margined with creamy white (both colours brighter in sun) and lavender flowers.

## Small hybrids

**'Blue Cadet'** has thick, rounded, puckered leaves, which are intense glaucous blue, and purple flowers. **'Blue Moon'**, which is suitable for a rock garden, has thick, puckered, dark blue leaves and pale lavender to white flowers. **'Brim Cup'** has small leaves, broadly edged with creamy white, that pucker as they age and pale lavender to white flowers. **'Ginko Craig'** has lance-shaped green leaves, crisply edged with white, and deep mauve flowers.

# INULA

These robust plants have cheerful, golden-yellow daisy flowers in summer. They are undemanding cottage garden plants.
*Cultivation* Grow in any reasonable soil in sun. Tall species may need staking.

## *I. hookeri*

Probably the best-known species, this coarse plant rapidly makes clumps that produce masses of acid yellow daisies in summer. H

*Hosta 'Shade Fanfare'*

75cm (30in), S 60cm (2ft). Hardy/Z 4–8.

## *I. magnifica*

As magnificent as its name implies, this is an ideal plant for a grand border, with masses of rich yellow daisies on stout stems in late summer. It combines superbly with orange-red roses and purple-leaved plants. H 2m (6ft), S 1m (3ft). Hardy/Z 5–8.

# IRIS

This large genus also includes bulbs. The plants described here are rhizomatous perennials – that is, they have a fleshy rootstock (actually a modified stem) at ground level – but they represent a vast number of plants that are generally divided further as described. Irises are grown for their beautiful flowers. The combination of richness and purity of colour (in all shades except red) and elegance of form is unmatched by any other garden plant. Larger border irises are magnificent, flowering at the same time as peonies. Later on, their

*Hosta 'Gold Standard'*

*Hosta 'Devon Green'*

*Hosta 'Blue Cadet'*

Inula magnifica

Iris 'Blue-Eyed Brunette'

Iris unguicularis

sword-like leaves are a good foil to other perennials and annuals. A few are best with their feet in water, in nature helping to bind the banks of streams and ponds. The winter-flowering *I. unguicularis* is unique and should be included in every garden.
**Cultivation** Bearded irises need well-drained soil, preferably neutral or alkaline, and a position in sun. The upper surface of the rhizome should be above ground level for a good summer baking, which promotes good flowering the next year. Beardless irises have varying requirements, as detailed in the individual entries below; the rhizomes are usually best planted below the soil surface. Crested irises (some of which are tender and excluded here) need fertile soil in a lightly shaded situation. All irises are of indefinite spread.

### Bearded irises

These deciduous plants have sword-like leaves arranged like a fan; the flowers have distinctive hairs (the beard) on the falls (the three petals that hang down). The

group encompasses an enormous number of hybrids, all richly coloured, of which the following are a small selection.

#### I. 'Blue-Eyed Brunette'
An iris with distinctive rich red-brown flowers with gold beards in late spring to early summer. H 1m (3ft). Hardy/Z 4–9.

#### I. 'Bold Print'
This iris has impressive flowers, basically white but heavily marked with rich purple. H 55cm (22in). Hardy/Z 4–9.

#### I. 'Chantilly'
An iris with pale lavender flowers in late spring to early summer. H 1m (3ft). Hardy/Z 4–9.

#### I. pallida
This iris, sometimes evergreen, is one of the best species for general use in the border. The warm lavender-blue flowers, good as a cut flower, open in late spring and early summer. H 1m (3ft) or more. Hardy/Z 6–9.

#### I. 'Peach Frost'
An iris with peach-pink standards and rich golden-orange falls in late spring to early summer. H to 1.2m (4ft). Hardy/Z 4–9.

### Beardless irises
These irises, some of which are evergreen, have no hairs on the falls and generally have slimmer rhizomes than those of the bearded irises.

#### I. 'Arnold Sunrise'
This early spring-flowering iris has white flowers marked with

orange. It needs neutral or slightly acid soil in sun or light shade. H 25cm (10in). Hardy/Z 5–9.

#### I. ensata
(syn. *I. kaempferi*)
**Japanese water iris**
This species is the parent of a large number of irises, all suitable for growing in moist, neutral to acid soil at the water's edge in full sun. Flowering is in midsummer. H to 1m (3ft). Hardy/Z 5–9. **'Ayasegawa'** has white flowers edged with blue; and **'Variegata'** has white markings on the leaves and deep purple flowers.

#### I. sibirica
This iris is a parent of a huge range of hybrids, referred to as Siberian irises, all good plants for sunny borders, but seeming to prefer damp soil. The species is an elegant plant, with narrow, grassy leaves and exquisite butterfly-like, rich violet-blue flowers, pencilled with white and gold, in early summer. H 1m (3ft). Hardy/Z 4–9. The following can be usefully grouped under this species, but are actually hybrids with other species and are therefore sometimes listed separately: **'Butter and Sugar'** has white and yellow flowers. H 70cm (28in). **'Ruffled Velvet'** has rich reddish-purple flowers with ruffled edges. H 55cm (22in). **'White Swirl'** is a good white variety. H 1m (3ft).

#### I. unguicularis
(syn. *I. stylosa*)
**Algerian iris**
One of the harbingers of spring, this iris is unique in the genus.

Among the copious grassy foliage, elegant lilac-mauve flowers with yellow markings unfurl from scrolled buds as early as midwinter, the main flowering being in late winter to early spring. This plant needs a hot spot in very well-drained soil: at the foot of a warm wall is ideal. For reliable flowering, the upper surface of the rhizome should be exposed to the sun and plants should be left undisturbed once established. H 23–30cm (9–12in).

### Crested irises
These resemble bearded irises except that the beard is replaced by a raised ridge.

#### I. japonica
This iris has glossy green leaves and pale lavender to white flowers in mid- to late spring that are exquisitely marked with orange and purple. H to 1m (3ft). Borderline hardy/Z 8–9. In cold gardens the reputedly hardier **'Ledger's Variety'**, similar in all other respects, is to be preferred. H to 1m (3ft).

Iris 'Chantilly'

Iris pallida

Iris sibirica

Knautia macedonica

Kniphofia 'Alcazar'

Kniphofia 'Toffee Nosed'

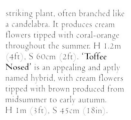

## KNAUTIA

The genus contains around 40 species of plants with scabious-like flowers, but only a few are widely grown. The flowers are attractive to bees, and the plants make excellent edging for the front of a border.
*Cultivation* Grow in any well-drained soil in sun.

### K. macedonica

The best-known species, this has crimson, pincushion-like flowers on curving stems from mid- to late summer. It makes good infill in rose gardens. H and S 60cm (2ft). Hardy/Z 5–9.

## KNIPHOFIA
**Red hot poker, torch lily**
Considered vulgar by some, there is no denying the impact that red hot pokers can have in a garden with their luminous torch-like flowers. Unfortunately, their coarse clumps of grassy foliage do not integrate well with other plants, and they tend to look best grown in isolation, for example at the foot of a warm wall. Some modern hybrids are more gently coloured and smaller, and can be grown at the front of a border. Not all kniphofias are reliably hardy, which again limits their appeal to some gardeners, but their long flowering season makes them desirable. Nearly all the plants in cultivation are hybrids of garden origin.
*Cultivation* Kniphofias need soil that does not dry out in summer and a position in full sun. Excessive winter wet is undesirable.

### K. hybrids

There are a large number of hybrids available, ranging in size, colour and flowering time. The following are all hardy/Z 6–9. **'Alcazar'**, an archetypal poker, is a substantial plant with bright red flowers in midsummer. H 1.5m (5ft), S 50cm (20in). **'Candlelight'** is an elegant plant, bearing slender spikes of clear yellow flowers in midsummer among long, narrow leaves. H to 50cm (20in), S 30cm (12in). **'Forncett Harvest'**, an autumn-flowering hybrid, has spikes of small, greenish-yellow flowers. H 1m (3ft), S 45cm (18in). One of the daintiest of recent introductions, **'Little Maid'** has soft lemon-yellow flowers in summer. H 60cm (2ft), S 45cm (18in). **'Prince Igor'** is a dramatic and vigorous plant, with large spikes of brick-red flowers that develop yellow touches at the base. It flowers from late summer to autumn. H 1.8m (6ft), S 1m (3ft). **'Samuel's Sensation'** is a striking plant, often branched like a candelabra. It produces cream flowers tipped with coral-orange throughout the summer. H 1.2m (4ft), S 60cm (2ft). **'Toffee Nosed'** is an appealing and aptly named hybrid, with cream flowers tipped with brown produced from midsummer to early autumn. H 1m (3ft), S 45cm (18in).

## LAMIUM
**Deadnettle**
Invaluable as groundcover, these plants are considered weeds by some gardeners, but some varieties are pretty and useful for filling space under trees and shrubs.
*Cultivation* Grow in any well-drained soil in sun or shade.

### L. maculatum

The species has mid-green leaves striped centrally with silver and whorls of reddish-purple, pink or white flowers in summer. H 20cm (8in), S 1m (3ft) or more. Hardy/Z 4–8. It is attractive enough but yields in appeal to the selections **'Beacon Silver'**, which has silver leaves edged in green; **'Pink Pewter'**, with grey-green leaves and pink flowers; and **'White Nancy'**, which has silver foliage and white flowers.

## LEUCANTHEMUM

These daisy flowers have been included in *Chrysanthemum*. Whatever controversy may rage over their correct names, they are superb garden plants, reliably producing a show of robust daisy flowers in summer. Undemanding, they are excellent when cut, if not the most fragrant of flowers.
*Cultivation* Most soils are suitable, although some alkalinity seems desirable. Grow in full sun.

### L. × superbum
**(syn. *Chrysanthemum maximum*)**
**Shasta daisy**
Once considered a species, this group of sturdy perennials are now known to be hybrids. All produce white flowers with yellow centres, but there are variations among the many cultivars. All are hardy/Z 5–9. **'Aglaia'** has semi-double flowers. H and S 60cm (2ft). **'Everest'** (syn. 'Mount Everest') has large, single flowers.

Kniphofia 'Candlelight'

Lamium maculatum 'White Nancy'

*Leucanthemum × superbum* 'Everest'

H to 1m (3ft), S 60cm (2ft). **'Phyllis Smith'** has charming flowers, with narrow outer petals giving a dainty, feathery appearance. H to 1m (3ft), S 60cm (2ft). **'Wirral Supreme'** has double flowers. H to 75cm (30in), S 60cm (2ft).

## LIATRIS
### Gay feather, blazing star
The feathery flowers of these perennials are unique and eye-catching, if not to all tastes. They are particularly effective as cut flowers.
*Cultivation* Grow in any soil that does not dry out and in a position in full sun.

### *L. spicata*
This is the most widely grown species, with long, upright spikes of luminous mauve flowers throughout summer. H 1m (3ft), S 30cm (1ft). Hardy/Z 4–9. **'Alba'** is an excellent white form.

## LUPINUS
### Lupin
With their tall spires of pea flowers in a range of bright colours (some being bicoloured), lupins are essential for giving height to borders in early to midsummer. Cutting them down after flowering (before they have time to set seed) can result in a second crop of (smaller) flowers in late summer, but this cannot be guaranteed so it is best to plant them behind other plants that will provide late interest. Lupins are not long-lived plants and need to be replaced regularly. They work best in groups of a single colour.
*Cultivation* Lupins need to grow in well-drained, lime-free soil and require a position in full sun.

### *L.* hybrids
There are a vast number of hybrids, all of which are hardy/Z 4–8, including the following. H 1m (3ft), S 75cm (30in). The flowers of **'Blushing Bride'** are white, flushed with pink; **'Catherine of York'** has pinkish-

orange and yellow flowers; **'Chandelier'** has pale yellow flowers; **'Deborah Woodfield'** is an unusual creamy pink. **'Esmerelder'** has lilac flowers; **'Pope John Paul'** is a good white selection; **'The Chatelaine'** has pink and white flowers; **'The Governor'** has blue and white flowers; **'The Page'** is red.

## LYCHNIS
### Catchfly
These plants, with their attractive foliage, are easily grown. They look best planted en masse and blend particularly well with old roses and all cottage-garden plants.
*Cultivation* Grow in any well-drained soil in sun or light shade.

### *L. chalcedonica*
### Maltese cross, Jerusalem cross
This cottage-garden plant has vivid scarlet flowers in midsummer. H to 1.2m (4ft), S 40cm (16in). Hardy/Z 4–8.

### *L. coronaria*
### Dusty miller, rose campion
This species has felted grey leaves, a charming foil to the magenta flowers, which appear in midsummer. H 60cm (2ft), S 45cm (18in). Hardy/Z 4–8. The white-flowered form **'Alba'** is even more desirable.

## LYSIMACHIA
### Loosestrife
Some of these plants are almost weed-like in their toughness and vigour, but all are useful as ground-cover, particularly in rough parts of the garden.

*Lysimachia nummularia* 'Aurea'

*Cultivation* Grow in sun in moist, well-drained, rich soil.

### *L. nummularia* 'Aurea'
### Golden creeping Jenny
The species is generally represented in cultivation by this selection, a spreading, mat-forming perennial with yellow leaves. The cup-shaped, yellow flowers, which appear throughout summer, are a bonus. In addition to its use as ground-cover, it is effective in hanging baskets or trailing over the edge of a large container. H 5cm (2in), S indefinite. Hardy/Z 4–8.

### *L. punctata*
### Dotted loosestrife
This invasive plant is almost a weed, particularly in the boggy soil in which it thrives. The bright yellow, cup-shaped flowers are carried in whorls on the upright stems in summer. H 1m (3ft), S 60cm (2ft). Hardy/Z 5–8.

*Liatris spicata*

*Lupinus* 'The Governor'

*Lychnis coronaria* 'Alba'

*Lysimachia punctata*

Lythrum salicaria 'Feuerkerze'

Macleaya cordata

Melianthus major

Melissa officinalis 'All Gold'

## LYTHRUM
### Loosestrife

These plants, which are suitable for a bog garden, have two seasons of interest. Not only do they attract attention when in flower in midsummer, but the whole plant often turns a vivid yellow in autumn before dying back. They self-seed prolifically unless dead-headed.
*Cultivation* Grow in reliably moist soil in sun. Staking may be necessary on windy sites.

### L. salicaria
#### Purple loosestrife

This familiar plant produces tall spikes of reddish-purple flowers in summer. H 1.2m (4ft), S 45cm (18in). Hardy/Z 4–9. It has several named forms, the best of which is **'Feuerkerze'** (syn. 'Firecandle'), whose flowers are a more intense purple. H 1m (3ft), S 45cm (18in). The similar sized **'Robert'** is bright pink.

## MACLEAYA
### Plume poppy

These are plants for a large border. Despite their size, their overall splendour suggests that they should be grown near the front of a border, where their handsome leaves can be appreciated to the full. They work well with phlox, which flowers at around the same time, as well as helping to cool down 'hot' schemes.
*Cultivation* Any fertile, well-drained soil in sun or light shade is suitable. Although tall, they never need staking.

### M. cordata
#### (syn. *Bocconia cordata*)

This is the best-known species, with plumes of cream-coloured flowers in summer. H 2m (6ft), S 60cm (2ft). Hardy/Z 4–9.

### M. microcarpa

The species is broadly similar to *M. cordata*, with plumes of creamy-white flowers, but is less desirable on account of its invasive habit. The selection **'Kelway's Coral Plume'** is worthwhile, with rich pink flowers in summer. H 2m (6ft), S 1m (3ft). Hardy/Z 4–9.

## MECONOPSIS

The genus includes annuals and biennials as well as the perennial described here, which is a useful addition to a wild garden.
*Cultivation* Grow the species described in reliably moist soil in partial shade.

### M. cambrica
#### Welsh poppy

This European species forms clumps of dissected, bright green foliage. From spring until autumn solitary poppy flowers in yellow or orange are borne on slender stems. H 45cm (18in), S 30cm (12in). Hardy/Z 6–8.

## MELIANTHUS

One of the grandest of all foliage plants, the species described becomes shrubby in warm areas where it can overwinter successfully. In cold gardens it behaves as a herbaceous perennial and is cut down by hard frosts, usually regenerating from below ground level the following spring. It is excellent for adding height to an 'exotic' planting of cannas, dahlias and half-hardy annuals.
*Cultivation* Grow in any fertile, well-drained soil in full sun. In cold areas, protect the base of the plant with a dry mulch in winter.

### M. major
#### Honey bush

Large, soft, grey divided leaves, with serrated edges, are the principal ornamental feature. In a good year plumes of brownish-red flowers can appear in summer. H 2.4m (8ft), S 2m (6ft). Half-hardy/Z 9–10.

## MELISSA
### Lemon balm, bee balm

An essential plant for the herb garden, lemon balm is also decorative enough for use as a foliage plant in mixed plantings. The leaves have a distinct citrus scent when crushed and can be used in herb teas.
*Cultivation* Grow in any well-drained soil in sun or light shade. Alkaline soil is particularly suitable.

### M. officinalis 'Aurea'
#### (syn. *M. officinalis* 'Variegata')

The straight species bears pale yellow flowers in summer, but is of limited ornamental value. More interesting are **'All gold'**, with golden yellow leaves and lilac-tinged white flowers; and **'Aurea'** (syn *M. officinalis* 'Variegata'), with green leaves splashed with gold. H 60cm (2ft), S 45cm (18in). Hardy/Z 4–9.

## MENTHA
### Mint

Most mints are grown for their culinary rather than for their ornamental use, and they are indispensable in the herb garden, although they can be invasive. The flowers are of scant interest.
*Cultivation* Unlike most other herbs, mints prefer moist soil, but they will grow in almost any garden soil, in sun or shade. Some

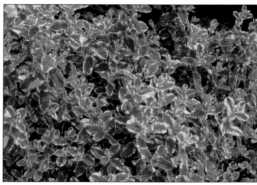

Mentha suaveolens 'Variegata'

Monarda didyma

means of restraining the roots is advisable (for instance by growing them in pots sunk in the ground).

### M. × gracilis
(syn. M. × gentilis)
**Ginger mint, red mint**
Apart from its culinary use, this hybrid, with upright, red-tinged stems and lilac-pink flowers, is of little ornamental value. Hardy/Z 4–9. More interesting is the selection **'Variegata'** (syn. 'Aurea'), which has bright green leaves speckled and striped with yellow. The best leaf colour is produced in sun. H and S 60cm (2ft).

### M. suaveolens
**Apple mint**
This invasive mint, sometimes wrongly known as M. rotundifolia, has apple-scented leaves and pink to white flowers. H 1m (3ft), S indefinite. Hardy/Z 5–9.

**'Variegata'** (apple mint, pineapple mint) is a more attractive form. The leaves are marked with creamy-white, and it has a sharper fragrance (of apples) than the species. It sometimes produces plain cream leaves.

## MONARDA
### Bergamot
These excellent border plants bear showy heads of hooded flowers from mid- to late summer in a range of clear colours. The leaves are similar to those of mint. The stems are square in cross-section. They are ideal for a mixed or herbaceous border. Most of the plants in cultivation are hybrids.
*Cultivation* Monardas, particularly those with purplish flowers, prefer reliably moist soils in sun, but they will grow in most soils if improved with organic matter.

Morina longifolia

### M. didyma
**Oswego tea, sweet bergamot**
This species, which is often in-cluded in herb gardens, has dense heads of pinkish-red flowers in mid- to late summer. H 1m (3ft), S 45cm (18in). Hardy/Z 4–9. **'Alba'** has white flowers.

### M. hybrids
The garden hybrids, all flowering from midsummer to early autumn, and all hardy/Z 4–9, include the following. **'Beauty of Cobham'** has pale pink flowers held in purple calyces and leaves that are flushed purple. H 1m (3ft), S 45cm (18in). **'Cambridge Scarlet'**, the most widely grown cultivar, has rich red flowers held in plum red calyces. H 1m (3ft), S 45cm (18in). **'Croftway Pink'** has rose-pink flowers. H 1m (3ft), S 45cm (18in). **'Mahogany'** has purplish-red flowers. H 1m (3ft), S 45cm (18in). The tall **'Mohawk'** has light mauve flowers with paler bracts. H 1.2m (4ft), S 45cm (18in). **'Prärienacht'** (syn. 'Prairie Night') has dark lilac flowers. H 1m (3ft), S 45cm (18in). **'Snow Queen'** has pale pinkish-white flowers. H 1m (3ft), S 45cm (18in). The vigorous **'Squaw'** has scarlet flowers. H 1m (3ft), S 45cm (18in).

## MORINA
### Whorlflower
Elegant rather than showy, these plants need a fairly prominent position in borders among low-growing plants for their distinction to be apparent. Only the species

described is generally grown.
*Cultivation* Grow in fertile, well-drained but moist soil in sun. Although hardy, cold, wet conditions in winter can kill it.

### M. longifolia
The species forms a rosette of thistle-like leaves, from which the flower spikes emerge in summer. These carry whorls of tubular flowers set in thorny collars that open white, turn to clear rose pink, then darken to crimson after they have been fertilized. H 1m (3ft), S 30cm (1ft). Hardy/Z 5–8.

## MUSA
### Banana
These exotic-looking plants are grown for their lush, tropical leaves – in cold climates, fruit is hardly likely to appear, let alone ripen. They can be used as bedding plants with cannas, dahlias and tender perennials and also look dramatic in containers. The species described is more or less hardy and can survive cold winters if given adequate protection.
*Cultivation* Grow in any fertile soil in full sun. Protect plants over winter with a mulch of straw or other dry material.

### M. basjoo
(syn. M. japonica)
**Japanese banana**
This species has huge, simple, bright green leaves that tend to split horizontally and fold over. H and S 1.5m (5ft) (more in favourable conditions). Borderline hardy/Z 9–10.

Monarda 'Snow Queen'

Musa basjoo

*Myrrhis odorata*

*Oenothera fruticosa* subsp. *glauca*

# MYRRHIS
## Sweet cicely
A genus of one species, this is a fragrant cow-parsley-like plant that seeds itself willingly throughout the garden. It is especially effective near water or in a wild garden, and the flowers will light up any dark corner. It makes a delicate contrast to more dramatic plants such as rheums.
**Cultivation** Grow in any reasonable soil in sun or light shade. It prefers cool, damp situations.

### M. odorata
The ferny leaves are aniseed-(anise seed-) scented and can be used in salads when young. The fluffy heads of flowers appear in early summer. H and S 1m (3ft). Hardy/Z 4–8.

# NEPETA
## Catmint
The catmints are essential in any garden, especially cottage gardens. They make excellent edging plants, effectively softening the hard edges of paths with their billowing habit, and are an excellent foil to herbaceous perennials and old roses. Plants become woody with age.
**Cultivation** Grow in any well-drained soil in full sun.

### N. × faassenii
(syn. N. mussinii)
This hybrid is the commonly grown catmint, making mounds of aromatic, soft sage green leaves. The lavender-coloured flowers will

appear in succession throughout the summer if regularly cut back as they fade. H and S 45cm (18in). Hardy/Z 4–9.

### N. racemosa
A spreading catmint with soft grey-green leaves and lavender-coloured summer flowers. H 30cm (1ft), S 60cm (2ft). Hardy/Z 4–9. There are several cultivars, including **'Snowflake'**, which has white flowers; and **'Walker's Low'**, which has an arching habit and is somewhat taller. H 30–45cm (12–18in), S 60cm (2ft).

### N. 'Six Hills Giant'
Generally considered the most distinguished of the catmints, this hybrid is bigger than the species

in all its parts. It has the typical soft grey-green leaves and masses of lavender-coloured flowers on upright stems in summer. It can be used as a low – albeit floppy – hedge. H and S to 1m (3ft). Hardy/Z 4–9.

# OENOTHERA
## Evening primrose
Plants of unique charm, evening primroses have large, cool lemon-yellow flowers that open in the evening – hence the common name. They are excellent for adding dots of colour among lower-growing plants, and, because they are attractive to butterflies, are ideal for a wild garden.
**Cultivation** Grow in any well-drained soil in sun. Tall plants may need staking.

### O. fruticosa
(syn. O. linearis)
Sundrops
This species is sometimes grown as a biennial and is distinct in that the flowers are open during the day. H 60cm (2ft), S 40cm (16in). Hardy/Z 4–8. On 'Fyrverkeri' (syn. 'Fireworks') the stems and leaves are flushed with brown, and the yellow flowers open from red buds. H 45cm (18in), S 30cm (12in). *O. fruticosa* subsp. *glauca* (syn. *O. tetragona*, *O. tetragona* var. *fraseri*) has greyish-green leaves and pale yellow flowers. H 60cm (2ft), S 40cm (16in).

### O. macrocarpa
(syn. O missouriensis)
Ozark sundrops
This prostrate species produces a

*Nepeta racemosa* 'Walker's Low'

*Ophiopogon planiscapus* 'Nigrescens'

Origanum vulgare 'Aureum'

Osteospermum 'Lady Leitrim'

long succession of bright yellow flowers that open from red calyces throughout summer and into autumn. It is an ideal plant for the front of a sunny border. H 23cm (9in), S 60cm (2ft). Hardy/Z 4–8.

## OPHIOPOGON
### Lilyturf

A genus normally represented in gardens by the form described here, which is more a conversation piece as a 'black' plant than a thing of beauty. For the most impact, grow it in gravel. It is especially effective in a Japanese-style planting.
*Cultivation* Grow in fertile, preferably lime-free or slightly acid soil in sun or light shade.

### O. planiscapus

The straight species, an evergreen, grass-like plant with deep green leaves and small, bell-shaped pale pinkish-purple flowers, is of small distinction. Hardy/Z 6–9. Of greater interest are its cultivars, especially **'Nigrescens'** (syn. *O.* 'Arabiscus'; 'Black Dragon'; 'Ebony Knight'), with black-purple leaves and small, purplish, bell-shaped flowers. The plant spreads slowly by stolons. H and S 20cm (8in).

## ORIGANUM
### Oregano, marjoram

Apart from their value as culinary herbs, marjorams are of great value in the ornamental garden. In many cases the small flowers

are carried in coloured bracts that persist for several weeks, making these plants of long-lasting appeal.
*Cultivation* Grow in any well-drained soil in sun.

### O. laevigatum

This species has dark green leaves that are less aromatic than those of some other marjorams. Its principal interest lies in its late-summer, purplish-pink flowers. It looks good with grey-leaved plants. H and S 45cm (18in). Hardy/Z 5–8.

### O. vulgare
#### Oregano, wild marjoram

This is the species most widely grown in herb gardens, but its tiny mauve flowers in late summer are also appealing in a modest way.

Origanum vulgare

H and S 60cm (2ft). Hardy/Z 6–9. **'Aureum'** is more compact, and grown mainly for its golden-yellow leaves, which become progressively greener during the season. It flowers only sparsely. H and S 30cm (12in).

## OSTEOSPERMUM

These attractive, evergreen daisies, scarcely without a flower throughout the growing season, are of borderline hardiness and are thus often treated as summer bedding, in borders, containers and hanging baskets. However, they are reliably perennial given some shelter or can easily be overwintered as cuttings. Most of the plants sold commercially are hybrids.
*Cultivation* Grow in well-drained soil in full sun. To ensure winter survival in cold areas, grow them in the shelter of a warm wall. Protecting them with a dry mulch during the cold months will further increase their chances of overwintering safely.

### O. hybrids

In recent years many new cultivars have been developed, extending the colour range and style of the petals. All have daisy-like flowers. **'Buttermilk'** is upright, with primrose yellow flowers. H and S 60cm (2ft). Borderline hardy/Z 9–10. **'Lady Leitrim'** has white flowers that age to pink. H and S 35cm (14in). Half-hardy/Z 9. **'Whirligig'** (syn. 'Tauranga') has flowers with distinctive, spoon-

shaped, white petals, which are mauve on the reverse, and with white centres. H and S 60cm (2ft). Half-hardy/Z 9–10. **'White Pim'** (syn. *O. ecklonis* var. *prostratum*) is low-growing. The flowers have white petals and purplish-blue centres. H 10cm (4in), S 30cm (12in). Half-hardy/Z 9.

## PAEONIA
### Peony

Gorgeous flowers and lustrous foliage characterize this genus. The hybrids – of which there are many – are sumptuous, but the species are equally beautiful in a different way, with simple, bowl-shaped flowers. The fact that the hybrids need staking is unlikely to deter many gardeners, for peonies are essential garden plants, either as soloists, perhaps offset by hostas or other plants with bold, simple leaves, or, where there is room, in grand groups. The species work well in light woodland. Plant spring bulbs around them, which will flower as the red peony buds appear from ground level. Peonies are usually slow to establish, but reward patience and are generally long-lived and trouble-free. The genus also includes a number of highly desirable shrubs.
*Cultivation* Peonies need fertile, humus-rich, well-drained soil, ideally in sun. Peonies will grow in light shade, but the flowering will be delayed and possibly impaired. They do not like being transplanted.

*Paeonia lactiflora* 'Alice Harding'

***P. cambessedesii***
**Majorcan peony**
This beautiful species has single, poppy-like, deep rose-pink flowers in spring, a glowing complement to the striking foliage, which is deep green suffused with crimson-purple. Unfortunately, it is not reliably hardy in cold gardens. H and S 45cm (18in). Borderline hardy/Z 7–8.

***P. lactiflora***
**(syn. *P. albiflora, P. japonica* of gardens)**
The species, from Russia, China and Tibet, has handsome, dark green leaves and fragrant, single, white to pale pink flowers. It has given rise to many fine cultivars. Hardy/Z 3–7. **'Adolphe Rousseau'** has rich red, double flowers. H and S 60cm (2ft). **'Alice Harding'** has creamy-white, double flowers. H and S to 1m (3ft). **'Bowl of Beauty'**, an aptly named plant, has glowing satin-pink petals, which open to reveal a central boss of cream-coloured petaloids in mid- to late spring. H and S 1m (3ft). **'Duchesse de Nemours'** (syn. 'Mrs Gwyn Lewis') has globe-shaped, double flowers in early to mid-spring. The outer petals are white, the inner creamy-yellow. H and S 60cm (2ft). **'Félix Crousse'** produces a profusion of silky, clear cerise pink flowers over a long period in mid-spring. H and S 75cm (30in). The pleasingly scented **'Laura Dessert'** is a ravishing plant, if rather slow to establish. It has cream or pale lemon-yellow flowers that open from pink-tinged buds to reveal a central mass of creamy-yellow inner petals. H and S 1m (3ft). **'Président Poincaré'** is a tall, vigorous variety, with dark, red-veined leaves and semi-double, garnet-red flowers in mid-spring. H and S 1m (3ft). A deservedly popular cultivar with a good track record, **'Sarah Bernhardt'** has large, double, soft silvery pink flowers in late spring. Strong flower stems make this a good peony for cutting. H and S 1m (3ft). **'White Wings'**, a cultivar flowering in late spring, has deliciously fragrant single flowers with glistening white petals surrounding golden-yellow stamens. H and S 75cm (30in).

***P. mlokosewitschii***
**Caucasian peony**
This is one of the most desirable of all the species, even if its moment of glory is all too brief. The pewter green foliage is attractive throughout the season, a splendid foil to its cool lemon-yellow flowers, which are open for no more than a week in spring.

*Papaver orientale* 'Effendi'

*Papaver orientale* 'Khedive'

A massed planting creates a breathtaking sight. H and S 60cm (2ft). Hardy/Z 5–8.

***P. officinalis***
The true species has single pink or red flowers and is seldom seen in cultivation. Unnamed hybrids with fully double, white, red or pink flowers are often sold under this name, all fragrant and flowering in mid- to late spring. H and S 60cm (2ft). Hardy/Z 4–8.

## PAPAVER
**Poppy**
Simple, beautiful plants for late spring, the flowers have silk-textured petals of unique appeal. In borders, poppies are superb curtain-raisers to the rose season. Most will have died back by midsummer, but it is possible to cover their traces with a planting of *Gypsophila paniculata* or late-flowering annuals. Many have attractive seedheads, which are good for drying for indoor decoration. Some poppies are annuals and self-seed generously. ***Cultivation*** Poppies do best in poor, dry soil in sun.

***P. orientale***
Most of the perennial poppies grown in gardens are descended from this species, although some are manifestly hybrids involving other species. They are usually grouped under *P. orientale* for practical reasons; they all produce their large, bowl-shaped flowers in late spring. All are hardy/Z 3–7. **'Beauty of Livermore'** has scarlet flowers, each petal blotched with black at the base. H and S 1m (3ft). **'Black and White'** has white petals blotched with black at the base. H and S 1m (3ft). **'Cedric Morris'** (syn. 'Cedric's Pink') has subtly coloured greyish-pink flowers. H and S 1m (3ft). **'Effendi'** has orange-red flowers. H and S 1m (3ft). **'Karine'** has pale pink, flat flowers with maroon centres. H and S 80cm (32in). **'Khedive'** has pale pink flowers. H and S 1m (3ft). **'Picotee'** has frilly-edged flowers that are white flushed with salmon pink. H and S 1m (3ft).

## PELARGONIUM
With a seemingly endless succession of cheerful flowers, in shades of white, pink and crimson, pelargoniums are the archetypal summer plant. These (usually) evergreen perennials are infinitely versatile: whether they are grown in hanging baskets, containers, windowboxes or as bedding, they belong in every

*Paeonia lactiflora* 'Bowl of Beauty'

*Paeonia lactiflora* 'Adolphe Rousseau'

Pelargonium inquinans

Pelargonium triste

Pelargonium 'Schōne Helena'

Pelargonium 'Ashley Stephenson'

summer planting, either on their own or with other bedding plants such as lobelias, alyssums and *Helichrysum petiolare*.

The genus is huge. The large number of species (native mainly to South Africa) and the sheer quantities of named varieties can seem bewildering. Breeders have devised various categories for subdividing them, as described. **Cultivation** All the plants described here are tender and are best grown in containers. Most potting composts (soil mixes) are suitable, though it is wise to add grit or perlite to the mixture to improve the drainage. Feed with a high-potassium feed when in growth to prolong flowering. Most are best in full sun, but will also tolerate light shade. Plants can be overwintered in bright, frost-free conditions. Keep the compost barely moist.

### P. betulinum
This decorative plant is probably a parent to both the regal and

unique pelargoniums. It has large, pink or purplish-pink (occasionally white) flowers that are heavily veined with purple-red. H and S 30–60cm (1–2ft). Tender/Z 10.

### P. inquinans
This branching species has red-hairy stems, soft, almost circular leaves and scarlet, pink or white flowers. H to 1m (3ft), S 50cm (20in). Tender/Z 10.

### P. triste
This appealing species has hairy, carrot-like leaves on short stems. The flowers are brownish-purple or (sometimes) yellow or brown and are remarkable in releasing a strong freesia-like scent at night. H 15cm (6in), S 45cm (18in). Tender/Z 10.

### Zonal pelargoniums
The leaves are banded (or 'zoned') with a darker colour, and for most gardeners these are the typical pelargonium. This very large group is sometimes further sub-

divided. All are tender/Z 10. **'Appleblossom Rosebud'** has tightly clustered, double, pale pink flowers that are flushed deeper pink. H and S 35cm (14in). **'Happy Thought'** has rounded leaves, with pale cream or yellow-green centres, a pale brown zone, and a broad, bright green margin. The small flowers are crimson. H and S 40–45cm (16–18in). **'Irene'** has generous clusters of crimson, semi-double flowers. H and S 45cm (18in). **'Joan Fontaine'**, a good bedding plant, is branching and bushy, with dark green leaves and pale salmon pink flowers with small white eyes. H and S 25–30cm (10–12in). **'Lass o' Gowrie'** has tri-coloured leaves, green margined with silver-green overlaid with a dark, reddish band, and bright scarlet flowers. H and S 25–30cm (10–12in). **'Mr Everaarts'** is a neat, bushy plant that is ideal for windowboxes, with double, rose pink flowers. H and S to 20cm (8in). **'Mr Henry Cox'** has strongly tri-coloured foliage, with a brilliant golden margin surrounding a green centre, overlaid by a deep red-black zone, and single, salmon-pink flowers. H and S 30cm (12in). **'Plum Rambler'** has unusual, double, plum-red flowers. H and S 40cm (16in). **'Red Black Vesuvius'** (syn. 'Black Vesuvius') has blackish-green leaves with an even darker zone and an abundance of rich scarlet flowers. H and S 13cm (5in). **'Scarlet Rambler'** has clusters of eye-catching, double, brilliant scarlet flowers. H and S 40cm (16in). **'Schöne Helena'** is erect

and stocky, with semi-double, large, clear salmon flowers carried in large heads. H and S 40cm (16in). **'Silver Kewense'** has leaves variegated silver and green and crimson flowers. H and S 13cm (5in). **'Wallis Friesdorf'** has dark, blackish-green leaves and narrow-petalled, semi-double, deep rose pink to scarlet flowers. H and S to 20cm (8in).

### Regal pelargoniums
These have large, richly coloured flowers. All are tender/Z 10. **'Ashley Stephenson'** is compact, with creamy-pink flowers blotched and pencilled with mahogany red. H and S to 35cm (14in). **'Black Magic'** produces rich blackish-red, velvety flowers. H and S to 35cm (14in). **'Fleur d'Amour'** has pale leaves and soft pink and white frilly-edged flowers. H and S to 35cm (14in). **'Sunrise'** has large, salmon-orange flowers that have white throats and are strikingly blazed with magenta. H and S to 40cm (16in).

Pelargonium betulinum

Pelargonium 'Irene'

Pelargonium 'Black Magic'

Pelargonium 'Moon Maiden'

### Angel pelargoniums
These pelargoniums are derived from regals and are similar to them but smaller. All are tender/ Z 10. **'Catford Belle'** is compact, producing an abundance of small, mauve-purple flowers that are frilled and marked with purple. H and S 30cm (12in). **'Jer'Rey'** has masses of deep red-purple flowers edged with crimson over an extended period. H and S to 35cm (14in). **'Moon Maiden'** has almost circular, pale pink flowers, which are marked with rich deep pink, and neat, dark green leaves. H and S 45–50cm (18–20in).

### Decorative pelargoniums
Similar to regal pelargoniums, these have smaller leaves and flowers. All are tender/Z 10. **'Black Knight'** has masses of small, purple-black flowers that are edged with lavender. H and S 40cm (16in). **'Madame Layal'** has bicoloured flowers: deep plum-purple upper petals edged

white and white lower petals marked dark purple. H and S 45cm (18in). **'Sancho Panza'**, which does well in light shade, has deep purple flowers with paler, lavender-coloured borders that are attractive to bees. H and S to 45cm (18in).

### Scented-leaf pelargoniums
As the name suggests, these have aromatic leaves, and it is for these that they are grown: the flowers are small and simple, like those of the species. They are popular as houseplants. All are tender/Z 10. Members of the **Fragrans Group** make lax, open plants with pine-scented, grey-green leaves and small white flowers on trailing stems. H and S to 20–25cm (8–10in). **'Lady Scarborough'** makes a loose mound of lemon-scented foliage, above which appear small, pale pink flowers with dark purple veining. H and S to 50cm (20in). **'Little Gem'** has soft leaves that release a warm rose-lemon scent and an abundance of small mauve flowers. H and S to 45cm (18in).

### Unique pelargoniums
These make large, shrubby plants with soft, aromatic leaves; the flowers usually bear some mauve coloration. All are tender/Z 10. **'Pink Aurore'** has warm pink flowers, the upper petals strongly marked with a burgundy blaze. H and S to 50cm (20in). **'Rollisson's Unique'**, a lax variety, has magenta-purple flowers marked darker purple, and rose-scented leaves. H and S 40–45cm (16–18in).

Pelargonium 'Pink Aurore'

### Stellar pelargoniums
Both the flowers and leaves are roughly star shaped. All are tender/ Z 10. **'Bird Dancer'**, a neat plant, has spidery, narrow-petalled, pale pink flowers. H and S to 20cm (8in). **'Fandango'** (syn. 'Stellar Fandango') has flowers in a clear shade of salmon-pink. H and S to 18cm (7in). **'Meadowside Midnight'** has blackish-green leaves edged with paler green and orange-red flowers. H and S 18cm (7in). **'Rads Star'** has clear rose pink flowers with white eyes. H and S to 20cm (8in). **'Strawberry Fayre'** produces single to double, coral-red flowers with white eyes reliably throughout the summer. H and S to 25cm (10in).

### Ivy-leaved pelargoniums
Thick, shield-like leaves are borne on trailing stems; these are ideal for hanging baskets. All are tender/Z 10. **'Eclipse'** produces large, open heads of salmon-pink flowers. S 60cm (2ft). **'Giro Fly'**

Pelargonium 'Strawberry Fayre'

has rosebud-like, double, bright purple-red flowers that are crowded together in balls. S 60cm (2ft). **'Golden Lilac Gem'** is very ornamental, with golden-green leaves and double lilac flowers. S 60cm (2ft). **'Harvard'** has semi-double, deep wine red flowers on long-jointed stems. S 60cm (2ft). **'Rigi'** is strong-growing, with semi-double, cerise pink flowers, which are feathered with burgundy red. S 60cm (2ft). **'Rio Grande'** has double, blackish-maroon flowers and shiny green leaves. S 60cm (2ft).

## PENSTEMON
Penstemons are becoming increasingly popular, both for their spikes of foxglove-like flowers that appear throughout the summer and for their ease of cultivation. They make excellent border plants, but need a sheltered spot in cold areas. As a rule, the larger the flowers and leaves, the more tender the plant. Taking cuttings in late summer to autumn will ensure continuing stocks, although plants cut back by frost often regenerate from ground level. Smaller types are good in rock gardens.
*Cultivation* Grow in fertile, well-drained soil in full sun.

### P. hybrids
The following hybrids are suitable for borders. **'Andenken an Friedrich Hahn'** (syn. 'Garnet') is useful in borders for providing the elusive clear claret red over a long period. H 75cm (30in), S 60cm (2ft). Borderline hardy/Z 7-9. **'Apple Blossom'** has soft

Pelargonium 'Black Knight'

Pelargonium 'Little Gem'

Penstemon 'Sour Grapes'

Penstemon 'Pennington Gem'

Penstemon 'Russian River'

Persicaria bistorta 'Superba'

pink flowers from midsummer until autumn. H and S 45cm (18in). Borderline hardy/Z 5–8. **'Evelyn'** is a neat-growing penstemon with slim, warm rose pink flowers striped inside with paler pink. H 45cm (18in), S 30cm (12in). Hardy/Z 6–9. **'Pennington Gem'** is a popular hybrid with large, soft pink flowers from midsummer to mid-autumn. H 75cm (30in), S 45cm (18in). Borderline hardy/Z 5–8. At its dramatic best when grown en masse, **'Russian River'** has small, dark purple flowers over a long period. H 45cm (18in), S 30cm (12in). Borderline hardy/Z 6–9. A well-known penstemon, **'Sour Grapes'** has large flowers of a rich violet-purple hue, with the characteristic white insides, striped with purple. H 60cm (2ft), S 45cm (18in). Borderline hardy/Z 6–9. An appealing plant, **'Stapleford Gem'** produces flowers that combine two colours: lilac-blue and cream. H 60cm (2ft), S 45cm (18in). Hardy/ Z 6–9. **'White Bedder'** (syn. 'Snow Storm') is a beautiful plant, which is essential in a white garden. It has pure white flowers that acquire pink tints as they age. H 60cm (2ft), S 45cm (18in). Borderline hardy/Z 6–9.

# PERSICARIA
## Knotweed
A genus of rampant plants that includes annuals as well as perennials, which are good for mass planting in damp soil. Most have a long flowering season.
*Cultivation* Grow in reliably moist soil in full sun or light shade.

### P. affinis
(syn. *Polygonum affine*)
The species is seldom grown in its typical form, being represented in cultivation usually by the excellent **'Darjeeling Red'**, which has drumstick-like heads of pinkish-red flowers in summer and autumn. H 25cm (10in), S 50cm (20in). **'Dimity'** is shorter with light pink flowers. H 10cm (4in), S 48cm (18in). **'Superba'**, a vigorous plant, has pale pink flowers. H 25cm (10in), S 50cm (20in). Hardy/Z 3–9. All turn rich reddish-brown in autumn, and are effective for a long time in winter.

### P. amplexicaulis
(syn. *Bistorta amplexicaulis*, *Polygonum amplexicaule*)
Bistort
This semi-evergreen species has erect, lavender-like spires of pink flowers from summer to autumn. It is particularly effective with Michaelmas daisies. H and S 1.2m (4ft). Hardy/Z 5. The robust **'Firetail'** is bright red.

### P. bistorta
(syn. *Polygonum bistorta*)
Bistort
The semi-evergreen species is almost always encountered in the form **'Superba'**, in some ways similar to *P. affinis* 'Superba' but not to be confused with it. It forms strong clumps that produce bottlebrush-like spikes of cool pink flowers on stiff stems in late spring to early summer. The damper the soil, the longer the flowering period. H and S 60cm (2ft). Hardy/Z 4.

### P. virginiana
(syn. *Polygonum virginianum*, *Tovara virginiana*)
The species is seldom grown, but the following selection is a beautiful foliage plant. **'Painter's Palette'** has green-and-cream marbled leaves generously blotched with brown and touched with pink. H and S 60cm (2ft). Hardy/Z 5.

# PHLOX
This is a large genus of popular evergreen and herbaceous perennials, which give an air of grandeur to borders from midsummer onwards with their pyramid-shaped heads of flowers. They are useful for providing soft colours at a time when orange and yellow are predominant in the garden, as well as being richly scented. There is a huge number of cultivars, mostly developed from *P. maculata* and *P. paniculata*, plants belonging to the former species being generally slighter and more elegant. The genus includes alpines.

*Cultivation* The phlox described here need humus-rich soil and a position in sun.

### P. maculata
Meadow phlox
The species is characterized by hairy, often red-spotted stems. The cultivars, hardy/Z 4–8, all have flowers in the white–pink–lilac range and include **'Alpha'** with soft pink flowers; the excellent **'Omega'**, which has white flowers with violet eyes; and **'Schneelawine'** (syn. 'Avalanche') with white flowers. H 1m (3ft), S 45cm (18in).

### P. paniculata
Perennial phlox
The species has smaller flowers than the many cultivars developed from it. The fragrant flowers are white or lilac. It is excellent in a wild garden. H 1.2m (4ft), S 60cm (2ft). Hardy/Z 4–8. More garden forms have been derived from this species than from *P. maculata*, all making slightly more imposing plants. **'Blue Ice'** has white flowers opening from pink buds. H 75cm (30in), S 60cm (2ft). The free-flowering **'Eve Cullum'** has rich pink flowers with deeper pink eyes. H 1.2m (4ft), S 60cm (2ft). **'Fujiyama'** has white flowers. H 75cm (30in), S 60cm (2ft). **'Little Laura'** is a compact selection with purple flowers. H 65cm (26in), S 45cm (18in). **'Mother of Pearl'** has white, pink-tinted flowers. H 1.2m (4ft), S 60cm (2ft). **'Prince of Orange'** has orange-red flowers. H 80cm (32in), S 45cm (18in).

Persicaria virginiana 'Painter's Palette'

Phlox paniculata 'Mother of Pearl'

Phormium cookianum 'Cream Delight'

# PHORMIUM
## Flax lily, New Zealand flax

These architectural foliage plants form imposing clumps of stiff, upright leaves, giving style and substance to borders and making an effective contrast to rounded shrubs and any plant with soft or filigree leaves. They are equally effective in containers. Be careful when handling them: the leaf tips are sharply pointed and can cause injuries. There are many selected forms with dramatically coloured leaves. The robust flowering spikes, which appear in summer, are also eye-catching.
*Cultivation* Grow phormiums in any, preferably reliably moist, soil in full sun or light shade. A winter mulch of straw or other dry material may be necessary in cold districts. Remove damaged leaves regularly.

### P. 'Bronze Baby'
This dramatic hybrid (sometimes listed as a form of *P. tenax*) has bronze-purple, arching leaves and is useful where there is not

enough room for larger forms. H and S 60cm (2ft). Borderline hardy/Z 8–10.

### P. cookianum
### Mountain flax
This distinguished species has plain, light green leaves and is effective where a dramatic stroke is needed. H 2m (6ft), S 1.2m (4ft). Borderline hardy/Z 8–10. *P. cookianum* **'Cream Delight'** is less vigorous. The leaves have a broad cream band along the centre. H and S 1.2m (4ft).

### P. 'Sundowner'
This handsome plant has erect bronze-green leaves with deep pink edges. H and S to 2m (6ft). Borderline hardy/Z 8–10.

### P. tenax
### New Zealand flax
The species has smooth, grey-green, sword-shaped leaves. H 4m (13ft), S 2m (6ft). Borderline hardy/Z 8–10. Plants in the **Purpureum Group** have leaves overlaid with various shades of bronze-purple. H 2.4m (8ft), S 2m (6ft).

# PHYSOSTEGIA
## Obedient plant

This small genus of perennials exhibits a unique characteristic: the stems can be moved to any position, hence the common name. The species described makes a good border plant but can be invasive.
*Cultivation* Grow in reliably moist, humus-rich soil in sun or light shade.

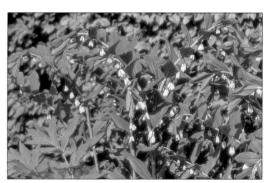

Polygonatum × hybridum

### P. virginiana
### (syn. *P. speciosa*)
The species has spikes of white, red or pink flowers in late summer. H 1m (3ft), S 60cm (2ft). Hardy/Z 3–9. *P. virginiana* subsp. *speciosa* **'Variegata'** is a neater-growing form, with white-edged leaves and deep pink flowers. **'Summer Snow'** (syn. 'Snow Queen') is a good white variety. H and S 60cm (2ft).

# POLYGONATUM
## Solomon's seal

These quietly elegant plants are related to lily-of-the-valley and enjoy similar conditions. Their arching stems and beautiful leaves make them ideal companions for hostas and ferns, especially in woodland gardens. Sawfly caterpillars often decimate the leaves after flowering, but without affecting the plant's longevity.
*Cultivation* They are best in

humus-rich, heavy, moisture retentive soil in shade but will tolerate most other conditions, apart from hot and dry situations.

### P. × hybridum
### (syn. *P. multiflorum* of gardens)
This, the best-known member of the genus, is a hybrid of *P. multiflorum* and *P. odoratum*. The arching stems appear in spring and bear small, lightly fragrant, bell-shaped flowers, which are white tipped with green, in late spring. H 1m (3ft), S 30cm (1ft). Hardy/Z 4–8. **'Striatum'** (syn. 'Variegatum') is a less vigorous form with cream-edged leaves. H 60cm (2ft), S 30cm (1ft).

# PRIMULA
## Primrose

This large and complex genus contains about 400 species of perennials, some suitable for mixed plantings, others for bedding, while a few are happiest in a rock garden. Charming though they are, they are not for all gardens, many having highly specific cultivation needs, and some particularly choice species (excluded here) are definitely best grown under glass. The plants described below do well in cool, damp atmospheres and may even seed themselves to the point of becoming a nuisance where suited. All have characteristic rosettes of spoon-shaped leaves from which the flowering stems arise. Another characteristic (but not of all) is 'farina', a flour-like bloom on the stems and leaves, which can provoke an allergic reaction.

Phormium tenax Purpureum Group

Physostegia virginiana

Physostegia virginiana 'Summer Snow'

Primula beesiana

Shorter growing primulas are delightful with dwarf spring bulbs and are good in windowboxes; primroses and polyanthus are archetypal cottage-garden plants; moisture-lovers are effective near water (preferably running water); and they are among the few plants that combine happily with rhododendrons as well as being good companions for the smaller hostas. So-called candelabra types are distinctive and graceful plants, with flowers carried in whorls up the stems.

*Cultivation* The plants described here are best in moisture-retentive, preferably neutral soil in sun or light shade (the more sun, the damper the soil should be). Candelabra types need moist soil.

### P. beesiana

This candelabra primula, which is deciduous or semi-evergreen, produces whorls of magenta flowers from late spring to early summer. H 45cm (18in), S 30cm (12in). Hardy/Z 5–8.

### P. bulleyana

The semi-evergreen species, a candelabra primula, is valued for its sharp orange flowers, which are produced throughout summer. H and S 60cm (2ft). Hardy/Z 6–8.

### P. denticulata
#### Drumstick primula

This distinctive species has golfball-like heads of purple flowers on stout stems in spring. H and S 30cm (1ft). Hardy/ Z 4–7. *P. denticulata* var. *alba* is a desirable form with white flowers. 'Rubra' is one of many selections with reddish-purple flowers.

### P. florindae
#### Giant cowslip

One of the largest species, this candelabra primula will produce satisfying mounds of foliage in damp soil, above which the erect stems carry mealy, deliciously fragrant, soft yellow flowers in early summer. It looks best planted en masse. H 1.2m (4ft), S 1m (3ft). Hardy/Z 5–8.

### P. 'Inverewe'

A well-known candelabra hybrid, this has bright red flowers in summer. H 75cm (30in), S 60cm (2ft). Hardy/Z 6–8.

### P. Polyanthus Group

This large hybrid group is understood here to include primroses (with flowers carried singly) and polyanthus (with clusters of flowers on upright

Primula Polyanthus Group

stems). The so-called 'hose-in-hose' polyanthus apparently have one flower emerging from the inside of another and are much sought after. Seed mixtures are available, and seed-raised plants in a range of jewel-like colours (some appealingly combining two or more) are often sold unnamed for use in bedding schemes. Depending on how they have been raised, they can flower from late winter to mid-spring in their first year. Most lose vigour the season after planting, but the following are reliably perennial and will flower in spring once established. They will grow in most garden soils that have been improved with organic matter. All are hardy/Z 6–8. Flowers of the evergreen plants in the **Gold-laced Group** (polyanthus) have an old-fashioned look, with purple-brown flowers margined with golden-yellow. H 25cm (10in), S 30cm (12in). **'Guinevere'** (syn. 'Garryarde Guinevere'; polyanthus) is distinctive, with pink flowers on red stalks and evergreen leaves suffused with bronze. H 13cm (5in), S 25cm (10in). The evergreen or semi-evergreen **'Lady Greer'** (polyanthus) has small, pale yellow flowers. H 15cm (6in), S 30cm (12in). The evergreen **'Schneekissen'** (syn. 'Snow Cushion'; primrose) has white flowers. H 10cm (4in), S 20cm (8in). Plants in the **Wanda Group** (primrose) are evergreen or semi-evergreen and have warm bluish-purple flowers. H to 15cm (6in), S 30cm (12in).

### P. pulverulenta

A vigorous species, this candelabra primula has very mealy stems carrying rich pinkish-red flowers with darker eyes over a long period in summer. H 1m (3ft), S 60cm (2ft). Hardy/Z 6–8. Plants grouped as **Bartley Hybrids** vary in colour from pink to pinkish-purple and have contrasting eyes. H 1m (3ft), S 60cm (2ft).

### P. veris
#### Cowslip

A familiar sight in damp meadows, this dainty species can be established in grass, as long as the ground is damp. The small, fragrant, yellow flowers hang from the stems in late spring. H and S 25cm (10in). Hardy/Z 6–8.

Primula denticulata

Primula pulverulenta

Primula veris

Pulmonaria saccharata

Rheum palmatum

# PULMONARIA
## Lungwort

Pretty plants for the spring garden, pulmonarias provide a long season of interest as the rough-textured, grey-spotted leaves expand in size. Some are more or less evergreen. Plant them with dwarf bulbs in areas around deciduous trees or shrubs. They make a good alternative to hostas for those gardeners reluctant to use slug pellets, and they are worth trying in conditions inhospitable to most other plants.
*Cultivation* Grow these easily pleased plants in any reasonably fertile, well-drained soil in light (or even full) shade.

### P. angustifolia
Blue cowslip
This species differs from most other pulmonarias in having small, unspotted, deciduous leaves. The flowers, which open in spring, are rich blue, an effective contrast to yellow forsythias. H 23cm (9in), S 45cm (18in). Hardy/Z 4–8. Selections include 'Munstead Blue', which has violet flowers that age to blue. H 23cm (9in), S 45cm (18in).

### P. officinalis
Jerusalem cowslip, spotted dog
This evergreen species has pink flowers, which age to violet-blue. The mid-green leaves are spotted with white. H 30cm (12in), S 45cm (18in). Hardy/Z 4–8.

### P. rubra
This evergreen species, which makes excellent groundcover, has coral-red flowers that hold their colour, opening in late winter in a good year. The leaves are plain green. H 40cm (16in), S 60cm (2ft). Hardy/Z 4–8.

### P. saccharata
Jerusalem sage
This species has the most heavily marked leaves – sometimes the whole leaf is silver. The spring flowers are pink, aging to blue. H 30cm (1ft), S 60cm (2ft). Hardy/Z 3–7. Plants of the **Argentea Group** have narrow leaves that are almost all silver. The flowers are red, aging to violet.

### P. 'Sissinghurst White'
This outstanding hybrid, developed from *P. officinalis*, has white flowers and leaves spotted with silver. H 25cm (10in), S 45cm (18in). Essential in a white garden. Hardy/Z 4–8.

# RHEUM

These are fine plants for the water's edge or for a large border. The genus includes the edible rhubarb, a handsome foliage plant in its own right. The plants described below are strictly ornamental and are especially effective as 'accent' plants in a large border but will lend an exotic touch to any garden.
*Cultivation* Rheums need fertile, reliably moist soil in sun or light shade.

### R. 'Ace of Hearts'
(syn. *R.* 'Ace of Spades')
This hybrid is especially effective if placed where the crimson undersides of its large, heart-shaped, dark green leaves will be lit up by the sun. The plumes of tiny, pinkish-white flowers that rise up in summer are an added – if not the principal – attraction. H 1.2m (4ft), S 1m (3ft). Hardy/Z 6.

### R. alexandrae
Unlike other members of the genus, this species is grown less for its glossy dark green leaves (smaller than on other species) than for its flowers, which are hooded by conspicuous cream bracts and carried on tall stems in early summer – a ghostly apparition in the twilight. It does not do well in all gardens, seeming to prefer cool, moist climates. H 1.2m (4ft), S 60cm (2ft). Hardy/Z 6–8.

### R. palmatum
Chinese rhubarb
Probably the grandest rheum, this plant will command any planting. Above its mound of large, deeply cut, red-veined leaves, spires of starry, greenish flowers arise in early summer. H and S 2m (6ft). Hardy/Z 5–9. The leaves of 'Atrosanguineum' (syn. 'Atropurpureum') are vivid red on emergence in spring, retaining that colour until the deep pinkish-red flowers appear.

# ROMNEYA
Californian tree poppy, matilija poppy
The tree poppy is both beautiful and maddening in equal measure.

Pulmonaria 'Sissinghurst White'

Rudbeckia fulgida

Their deeply divided, grey foliage and huge, glistening white flowers make these plants highly desirable, but they are difficult to establish and, once at home, become aggressively rampant rapidly. Grow them in large borders and keep them well away from paths and house walls: they have been known to penetrate bricks and mortar.
Cultivation These plants do best in sun in deep, fertile, slightly heavy soil, although most types of soil are tolerated as long as it is not boggy.

### R. coulteri
This striking species has large, fragrant, poppy-like flowers with crumpled white petals surrounding a central boss of deep yellow stamens. H 2.1m (7ft), S 1m (3ft). Borderline hardy/Z 6–9.

## RUDBECKIA
### Coneflower
Essential plants for borders in late summer, rudbeckias are sturdy and easy to grow. The petals of the daisy-like flowers droop away from the contrasting centres in a most appealing way. They combine well with grasses.
Cultivation Grow in any reasonable soil in sun. Tall varieties may need staking.

### R. fulgida
**Black-eyed Susan**
This species makes for an excellent garden plant. The vivid yellow flowerheads with striking black centres appear from summer to autumn. H 75cm (30in), S 30cm (12in). Hardy/Z 3–9. **R. fulgida** var. **sullivantii** 'Goldsturm' has large, richer yellow flowerheads. H 60cm (2ft), S 30cm (12in).

### R. 'Goldquelle'
This hybrid has double flowers with yellow petals surrounding greenish centres. It associates well with *Artemisia lactiflora*. H 1m (3ft), S 60cm (2ft). Hardy/Z 4–9.

## SALVIA
### Sage
In addition to important shrubby plants for the herb garden, this genus includes a number of fascinating perennials (as well as some annuals). These are becoming better known and exert a subtle attraction.
Cultivation Grow in any well-drained soil in full sun. *S. uliginosa* needs damp soil.

### S. candelabrum
This woody based, almost shrubby species is rare in cultivation but of undoubted garden merit. It has wrinkled, somewhat hairy leaves and blue to violet flowers, flecked with white, in summer. H and S 1m (3ft). Borderline hardy/Z 7.

### S. uliginosa
**Bog sage**
This full, graceful species, which sometimes needs staking, has sprays of clear blue flowers from late summer to mid-autumn. It makes a fine companion to cannas. H 1.5m (5ft), S 45cm (18in). Borderline hardy/Z 6–10.

## SCHIZOSTYLIS
### Kaffir lily
These plants will brighten up the autumn (and winter) garden with

Schizostylis coccinea 'Major'

their elegant spikes of fresh-looking flowers. Kaffir lilies spread rapidly, so regular division is advisable. Although there is only one species, there are a number of desirable selections.
Cultivation Grow in any but dry soil in sun. Plants will not thrive in soil that dries out in summer.

### S. coccinea
The whole plant looks like a miniature gladiolus, with slender, grassy leaves and spikes of cup-shaped, bright red flowers. H 60cm (2ft), S 23cm (9in). Borderline hardy/Z 6–9. Among the many cultivars are '**Major**' (syn. 'Grandiflora'), which has bright clear red flowers; '**Sunrise**' (syn. 'Sunset'), which has salmon pink flowers; and '**Viscountess Byng**', one of the last to flower, with pale pink flowers. H 60cm (2ft), S 23cm (9in).

Romneya coulteri

Salvia candelabrum

Schizostylis coccinea

*Sedum aizoon*

# SEDUM
## Stonecrop

These tough, hardy plants are not immediately appealing, but their merits slowly become obvious: fleshy, healthy leaves that tolerate drought and late flowers that attract bees and butterflies. They are good plants for 'problem' areas of the garden. The genus also includes small species for the rock garden and tender species, which are usually grown as houseplants.
*Cultivation* Sedums thrive in any well-drained, even poor, soil in full sun.

### S. aizoon
(syn. *S. maximowiczii*)
One of the first sedums to flower, the star-shaped yellow flowers, held in flat heads, begin to open

*Sedum* 'Herbstfreude'

in midsummer. The leaves are green and toothed at the edges. H and S 45cm (18in). Hardy/Z 4–9. **'Euphorbioides'** (syn. 'Aurantiacum') is more dramatic, with red stems, darker leaves and richer yellow flowers. H 35cm (14in), S 30cm (12in).

### S. 'Herbstfreude'
(syn. *S.* 'Autumn Joy')
This robust hybrid is probably the best known of all sedums. It has large, fleshy grey-green leaves and heads of scented flowers in autumn, deep pink at first, turning to salmon-pink and aging to a rich brick-red. H and S 60cm (2ft). Hardy/Z 3–9.

### S. spectabile
Iceplant
Probably one of the parents of 'Herbstfreude', this species is roughly similar to the hybrid but is smaller and has pinkish-mauve flowers. H and S 45cm (18in). Hardy/Z 4–9. Among the many cultivars are **'Brilliant'**, which has bright pink flowers; and **'Iceberg'**, which is a good white.

### S. 'Vera Jameson'
One of the most dramatic of the sedums, this hybrid has glaucous, purple leaves and heads of dusky-pink flowers in late summer. H 30cm (12in), S 45cm (18in). Hardy/Z 4–9.

# SIDALCEA
## False mallow, prairie mallow

Mallow-like flowers, like miniature hollyhocks, characterize this genus, which, from the gardener's point of view, consists mainly of hybrids. They are excellent additions to the mixed or herbaceous border and work well in cottage gardens.
*Cultivation* Grow in any reasonable soil in sun or light shade. Tall varieties may need staking. Cutting down the stems after flowering can result in further flowers.

### S. hybrids
There are several fine hybrids, mostly developed from *S. malviflora* (checkerbloom) and flowering in early to midsummer. **'Elsie Heugh'**, one of the palest, has spikes of fringed, pink flowers. H 1m (3ft), S 45cm (18in).

*Sidalcea* 'Elsie Heugh'

**'Oberon'** has clear pink flowers. H 1m (3ft), S 45cm (18in). **'Puck'**, which is more compact and robust, has deep pink flowers. H 40cm (16in), S 30cm (12in). Hardy/Z 5–7.

# SISYRINCHIUM

These plants, which have iris-like leaves, have a happy knack of seeding themselves around – generally to good effect. They are excellent in gravel gardens, their stiffly upright habit providing effective contrast to mat-forming plants. They can also be grown in borders. The genus includes annuals as well as the perennials described here.
*Cultivation* Grow in sun in any well-drained soil that is not too fertile and preferably gritty and alkaline.

*Sisyrinchium striatum*

### S. striatum
(syn. *Phaiophleps nigricans*)
The best-known species, this has compact tufts of sword-shaped, grey-green leaves and, in summer, slender spikes of straw yellow flowers, striped purple on the reverse of the petals. H 75cm (30in), S 23cm (9in). Hardy/Z 6–9. **'Aunt May'** (syn. 'Variegatum') has leaves edged creamy-yellow. H 50cm (20in), S 20cm (8in).

# STACHYS
## Betony, hedge nettle

A group of charming edging plants for a border or for a Mediterranean scheme – the hotter and drier it is, the more they like it.
*Cultivation* Grow in any well-drained soil in full sun. *S. macrantha* will take some shade.

### S. byzantina
(syn. *S. lanata*)
Lamb's ears, bunny's ears
Softly furry, silvery leaves, enhanced by hot sun, characterize the plants of this low-growing species. The flower spikes appear in summer and are also furry, swaddling the tiny pinkish-purple flowers. H 45cm (18in), S indefinite. Hardy/Z 4–8. There are a large number of selections, all of which make good edging plants to rose beds, including **'Cotton Boll'** (syn. 'Sheila McQueen'), which has flowers that look like balls of cotton wool; **'Primrose Heron'**, which

*Stachys byzantina* 'Silver Carpet'

*Tradescantia* Andersonia Group 'Innocence'

*Thalictrum flavum* subsp. *glaucum*

*Tradescantia* Andersoniana Group 'Isis'

has leaves with a pronounced soft yellow flush; and **'Silver Carpet'**, a valuable non-flowering form, which is useful where a low mat of foliage is required.

### S. macrantha
(**syn. S. grandiflora**)
This slightly coarse plant has corrugated, dark green, hairy leaves and rich rose-mauve flowers in summer, which combine in a particularly pleasing fashion with old-fashioned roses. H 60cm (2ft), S 23cm (9in). Hardy/Z 4–8.

## THALICTRUM
Meadow rue
Still all too rare in gardens, these are plants of considerable style. They combine delicacy with stature and bring a touch of freshness to borders with their frothy flowers at the height of summer. Use them as a contrast to plants that have bolder, showier flowers or combine them with the foaming *Gypsophila paniculata* for a romantic billowing cloud of blossom.
*Cultivation* Grow in any fertile, well-drained soil in sun or light shade.

### T. aquilegiifolium
This species is distinguished by its aquilegia-like foliage, although it is much taller and the flowers are far from similar. Appearing in early summer, these are a fluffy mass of warm pinkish-lilac. H 1m (3ft), S 60cm (2ft). Hardy/Z

5–8. Also worth growing are *T. aquilegiifolium* var. *album*, which has white flowers, and **'Thunder-cloud'**, which has dramatic dark purple flowers.

### T. flavum
Yellow meadow rue
The species has glaucous grey leaves and masses of fluffy yellow flowers in summer. H 1m (3ft), S 45cm (18in). Hardy/Z 5–9. The leaves of *T. flavum* **subsp.** *glaucum* (syn. *T. speciosissimum*) are more pronouncedly glaucous.

## TIARELLA
Foam flower
Dainty woodland plants, tiarellas are useful as groundcover in shady areas of the garden. They are grown primarily for the appeal of their leaves; the pretty flowers are an attractive bonus.

*Tiarella cordifolia*

*Cultivation* Tiarellas do best in humus-rich, fertile soil in shade; they prefer cool conditions.

### T. cordifolia
The heart-shaped leaves of this species take on bronze tints in cold weather. Upright spikes of creamy white flowers appear in summer. H and S to 30cm (12in). Hardy/Z 3–8.

### T. wherryi
(syn. *T. cordifolia* var. *collina*)
Although it is broadly similar to *T. cordifolia*, this is more compact and has white or pink flowers. H and S 20cm (8in). Hardy/Z 3–8. **'Bronze Beauty'** has bronze-tinged leaves and pink flowers. H and S 20cm (8in). Hardy/Z 3–8.

## TRADESCANTIA
The flowers are unusual in having only three petals, which gives them a distinctive appearance. Tradescantias are easy to grow and look good towards the front of mixed or herbaceous borders, providing thick cover and flowering reliably. The genus also includes some well-known house-plants, grown mainly for their variegated leaves.
*Cultivation* Grow in any well-drained soil in sun.

### T. Andersoniana Group
This hybrid group includes a number of worthy garden plants, all of which are hardy/Z 4–9, including **'Innocence'**, which has

pure white flowers; **'Isis'**, with rich indigo-blue flowers; and **'J.C. Weguelin'**, with pale blue flowers. H and S 45cm (18in).

## TRICYRTIS
Toad lily
These are gracious little flowers for the end of the season. They need a prominent position in borders, where their unique appeal can be appreciated. They are also effective in light woodland.
*Cultivation* Grow in any fertile soil in light shade.

### T. formosana
This species sends up tall, thin, branching flower stems with glossy oval leaves in early autumn. The small, lily-like flowers are mauve, heavily spotted with darker mauve. H to 1m (3ft), S 45cm (18in). Hardy/Z 7.

*Tricyrtis formosana*

Trifolium repens 'Purpurascens Quadrifolium'

# TRIFOLIUM
## Clover
With the exception of the plant described, most clovers are generally considered to be weeds. Nevertheless, selected forms are effective at the front of a border and are essential in wildflower gardens, the flowers being especially attractive to bees.
*Cultivation* Grow clover in moist, neutral soil in sun.

### T. repens
#### Dutch clover, shamrock
The species is normally encountered as a lawn weed but the form **'Purpurascens Quadrifolium'** has attractive maroon-purple leaves edged with green and typical white clover flowers in summer. H 10cm (4in), S indefinite. Hardy/Z 4–7.

# TRILLIUM
## Trinity flower, wood lily
These dramatic woodlanders are among the most desirable of spring-flowering plants, but unfortunately they are not always easy to please. Where they are happy, a massed planting can be breathtaking (although isolated clumps are also effective), but they are best appreciated when kept away from daintier flowers.
*Cultivation* Grow in fertile soil, preferably enriched with leaf mould, in shade, ideally beneath overhanging deciduous trees.

### T. grandiflorum
#### Wake robin
One of the grandest of the genus, this is also the best-known species. The flowers, which have three curving, pure white petals, open in spring above the large, simple leaves. H 38cm (15in), S 30cm (12in). Hardy/Z 4–9.
**'Flore Pleno'**, which has double white flowers, is if anything even more sumptuous.

# TROLLIUS
## Globe flower
Pleasing perennials for the spring garden, globe flowers are good in borders with tulips, although they really prefer damp conditions and are ideal for a streamside planting or bog garden. They are also good companions to rhododendrons.
*Cultivation* Grow in reliably moist soil in sun or light shade. Also worth trying in ordinary soils provided they are not in full sun.

Trillium grandiflorum 'Flore Pleno'

### T. × cultorum
The hybrid group contains a large number of selections, all of which are hardy/Z 3–7, flowering from mid-spring to midsummer. The unique **'Alabaster'** has pleasing soft ivory-yellow flowers, but is none too vigorous. H 60cm (2ft), S 40cm (16in). The early-flowering **'Earliest of All'** has yellow flowers. H 50cm (20in), S 40cm (16in). **'Orange Princess'** is vigorous and has orange-yellow flowers. H to 60cm (2ft), S 45cm (18in).

# VERBASCUM
## Mullein
A genus of stately plants, many of which are grown as biennials, but including a number of perennials. They are excellent for giving height to summer borders.

*Cultivation* Grow in any well-drained soil in sun. Tall plants may need staking.

### V. chaixii
#### Nettle-leaved mullein
This sturdy semi-evergreen species has woolly, upright stems, which are densely set with buttercup-like yellow flowers in summer. H 1m (3ft), S 45cm (18in). Hardy/Z 5–9. The selected form **'Album'** has white flowers.

### V. 'Helen Johnson'
A very desirable hybrid, this is difficult to propagate – hence the high price of plants in the nursery trade. The spikes of pinkish-brown flowers bring a unique colour into the garden. H 1m (3ft), S 45cm (18in). Hardy/Z 5–8.

### V. 'Mont Blanc'
This hybrid has pure white flowers, so has an honoured place in white gardens, the grey-green leaves adding to its value. H 1m (3ft), S 30cm (1ft). Hardy/Z 6.

# VERBENA
Not all verbenas are reliably hardy, and that has probably kept them out of many gardens, but the ones described here are all worth taking a chance on. They provide a long season of colour and for that reason deserve their place, even if they behave as annuals and succumb to winter frost (the

Trollius × cultorum 'Earliest of All'

Verbascum chaixii 'Album'

*Verbena bonariensis*

*Viola 'Jackanapes'*

genus also includes true annuals). Verbenas are delightful in borders, popular as bedding, and short varieties also work well in containers (including window-boxes) and hanging baskets.
*Cultivation* Grow in any well-drained soil in full sun. In cold areas a dry mulch can help them overwinter.

### V. bonariensis
This is a plant that should be in every garden. The tall stems (square in cross-section) are much-branched and have a profusion of heads of small, luminous violet flowers from summer until well into autumn. It combines happily with almost every other plant in the garden, as well as adding an airy charm all of its own. Even where not hardy, it

tends to seed itself freely. For the best effect, plant in groups. H to 1.5m (5ft), S 30cm (1ft). Borderline hardy/Z 7–10.

### V. 'Sissinghurst' (syn. V. 'Saint Paul')
This is one of a number of hybrids with a low, spreading habit, and it is, therefore, ideal for the front of a border. It has heads of glowing magenta flowers throughout the growing season. H 20cm (8in), S 60cm (2ft). Borderline hardy/Z 5–9.

## VERONICA
### Speedwell
These easy-to-grow plants are excellent in mixed and herbaceous borders, and the spikes of flowers are produced over a long season. Mostly in the violet-blue-lilac range, they provide an excellent contrast to orange and yellow daylilies. Small species are good in rock gardens.
*Cultivation* Grow in any ordinary garden soil in sun or light shade.

### V. longifolia
This species has hebe-like spikes of lavender-blue flowers in late summer and autumn. H 1m (3ft), S 30cm (1ft). Hardy/Z 4–8. **'Blauer Sommer'** is more compact and has clear blue flowers. H 50cm (20in), S 30cm (12in).

## VIOLA
### Violet
This huge genus containing about 500 species includes annuals

(pansies), biennials and alpines as well as a number of perennials. They are excellent for carpeting large areas, especially under trees and shrubs. There are also a huge number of hybrids, omitted here, developed for exhibiting.
*Cultivation* Grow in any well-drained soil in sun or light shade.

### V. biflora
### Twin flowered violet
This dwarf rhizomatous species is found in Europe to Northern Asia and North America. Kidney- to heart-shaped pale green leaves are borne on thin stems and lemon-yellow flowers, veined dark purple-brown on the lower petals, appear either solitary or in pairs in late spring to summer. H 5-15cm (2-6in), S 15cm (6in). Hardy/Z 4-8.

### V. 'Jackanapes'
A delightful hybrid with a cheeky look to its yellow and brown flowers, the yellow petals streaked with purple. It tends to be short-lived. H 12cm (5in), S 30cm (12in). Hardy/Z 5–7.

### V. labradorica
### Labrador violet
This species is a prolific self-seeder in conditions that suit it, and charming where allowed to naturalize beneath shrubs. Its dainty, apple purple flowers appear above the bronze-tinged leaves in spring. H to 8cm (3in), S indefinite. Hardy/Z 4–8.

## ZAUSCHNERIA
### Californian fuchsia
This genus of sun-loving perennials provides brilliant material for the front of a border, the funnel-shaped flowers being a vivid scarlet in most cases.
*Cultivation* Good drainage is essential, as is a position in full sun. They are best with the shelter of a warm wall in cold areas, where they are not reliably hardy.

### Z. californica
This, the best-known species, has attractive, lance-shaped, grey-green leaves, the perfect foil to the luminous scarlet flowers, produced from late summer to early autumn. H and S 45cm (18in). Hardy/Z 6–9. **'Dublin'** has slightly longer, bright orange-red flowers. H 25cm (10in), S 30cm (12in).

*Veronica longifolia*

*Zauschneria californica*

# Annuals

Annuals are unrivalled for bringing
colour into the garden throughout
the warmer months. They bring any
border to vivid life within a matter of
weeks, and give an established air to
even a new garden. Besides their use
in the larger garden, they are also
excellent in tubs, hanging baskets and
all manner of containers. Many bring
other rewards, being deliciously
scented or attractive to beneficial
insects, or providing cut flowers for
the house.

Few plants provide the gardener with such a wide range of colour and
form as the annuals.

# What is an annual?

An annual is a plant that completes its life cycle within one growing season: the seed germinates, grows, flowers, sets seed and dies all within the space of a year. The seed is dormant until the return of conditions favourable to germination, usually the next spring. In the case of biennials, the seed usually germinates as soon as it is set, in summer or autumn, and the young plantlet overwinters to flower the following year (but the entire process is still completed within the twelve months).

As with the rest of gardening, these definitions are by no means hard and fast. Many annuals can be treated as biennials, and vice versa. Some supposed annuals often survive the winter to flower again the following year, but, since their powers are greatly reduced, are best weeded out and replaced with new stock. There are also a number of plants that are usually described as "short-lived perennials": in other words, they can overwinter and survive a number of years, but since their health and strength cannot be relied on, they too are best replaced annually.

Another group of plants (which includes the popular tobacco plant *Nicotiana*) are truly perennial in their country of origin, but, since they will flower in the same year that they are sown, can be treated as annuals in cold areas where they cannot be expected to overwinter. Theoretically, of course, it is possible to overwinter them under glass, though it is hardly worth it, considering the high heating costs involved against the cheapness of a packet of seeds.

Bearing in mind that seed-raised plants always carry the potential for variation, the seed of most annuals is

This traditional annuals border consists of begonias and ageratum planted to provide strong blocks of colour for interest.

sold as mixtures or strains. The basic charateristics of the plants raised will be the same but some aspect (usually flower colour) will vary. Occasionally it is possible to isolate an individual colour through careful selection.

## Annuals in the garden

There are countless uses for annuals, and they are particularly valuable in a new garden to create an impact quickly or to fill in the gaps before more permanent plants such as trees, shrubs and perennials have grown to fill their allotted space. Few gardeners these days embark on the elaborate bedding schemes still to be seen in public parks and gardens – such plantings are labour-intensive – but it is nevertheless possible to indulge in such fantasies on a smaller scale, in large tubs, window-boxes or hanging baskets planted for seasonal appeal. You can also use annuals in the open garden to try out a particular colour scheme before investing in longer-lived plants, but some gardeners are quite happy to ring the changes annually, and areas of the garden are left

unplanted specifically for growing a different selection of annuals each year.

The key to their appeal is that they provide such solid blocks of colour over a long period. Many cover themselves in flower to the extent that the leaves are completely hidden, and these are the plants that are traditionally chosen for jazzy schemes designed to make an impact at flower shows. Some annuals, such as *Eschscholzia*, can be used more informally: simply scatter the seed over a gappy border in late spring, and by summer you will be enjoying a sea of colour.

With their length of flowering season, annuals are also unmatched for attracting a range of beneficial insects into the garden. French marigolds (*Tagetes*) and nasturtiums (*Tropaeolum*) are often planted in vegetable plots, since they attract hoverflies, which feed on aphids. It is worth including a few of these among your roses (or among any other ornamental plants prone to aphid attack).

All annuals thrive in containers. For hanging baskets or to cascade down the sides of a large container, those with trailing stems are the most suitable. Certain strains of *Petunia* and *Lobelia* have been specially developed for this very purpose. Compact annuals on the other hand, such as *Lobularia* and *Ageratum*, are ideal for windowboxes.

## Growing annuals from seed

For the widest choice, order seed from a seed merchant: their catalogues are often very extensive and also provide useful growing tips. Otherwise, buy seed from a garden centre, nursery or hardware store.

Easiest to raise from seed are those with large seeds (such as nasturtiums) that can be sown in situ where they are to flower. Others are also suitable for sowing in situ, but if the seed is very fine and has to be scattered, it may be necessary to thin seedlings later on. Some hardies are best sown in containers (either pots or seed trays). These should be kept outdoors in a cold frame and covered in cold weather (keep the covers on during the day if the temperature is below freezing). All seedlings in containers should be

This very modern style of planting relies on a wide range of annuals that flower simultaneously to create a beautifully informal border.

pricked out as they grow and potted on to prevent overcrowding.

Half-hardy annuals need to be started off in the protected environment of a propagator. Bottom heat will speed up germination, but is by no means essential, especially as the days lengthen and warm up in spring. Seedlings should be hardened off before being planted outdoors (when there is no longer any danger of frost). Remove the cover from the propagator for increasingly long

periods during the day over a number of weeks until you can leave it off entirely. As the temperature warms up from mid-spring, place the seedlings outdoors during the day, again for increasingly long periods. By late spring they should be ready for planting out in their flowering positions.

With a few notable exceptions (principally sweet peas), little is to be gained by sowing early – later sowings will catch up. For an extended display, it is often worth staggering sowings. Some hardy annuals can be sown in autumn for flowers the following spring. When the plants are exhausted, replace them with spring sowings. Conversely, it is possible to make late sowings of half-hardies (up to early summer) for a late summer to early autumn display, replacing a spring sowing. For this reason, precise flowering times are not given in the descriptions to follow.

If you do not have time to raise your own seedlings, buy young plants from garden centres in spring – though you may not have as wide a choice as you would like.

Annuals come in a wide variety of flower forms and colours, which many gardeners make use of for interesting combinations each year.

Ageratum houstonianum 'Blue Danube'

## AGERATUM
Floss flower
These fluffy half-hardy annuals, mostly in shades of blue, are ideal for edging a border. They are also excellent in windowboxes.
Cultivation Grow in any soil in full sun. Sow from late winter onwards in a propagator.

A. houstonianum
Most seed and hybrid strains are listed under this species, although they may result from crosses with other species. 'Blue Danube' forms compact hummocks of rich lavender-blue flowers; 'Blue Mink' has powder-blue flowers; 'North Star' has warm purplish-blue flowers; 'Pinky Improved' is an unusual dusky pink variety; and 'Summer Snow' is a good white form. H and S 15cm (6in) or more. Half-hardy/Z 8.

## ALCEA
Hollyhock
Hollyhocks are quintessential cottage-garden plants, such that most gardeners are prepared to put up with their tendency to develop rust for the sake of their spires of mallow-like flowers. Although they can be perennial, their propensity to disease makes it advisable to treat them as biennials and discard plants that have flowered. Plant them towards the back or middle of a border. The flowers attract butterflies.
Cultivation Grow in any soil in sun. Sow in summer for flowering the following year and transplant in autumn, if necessary.

Ageratum houstonianum 'North Star'

A. rosea
(syn. Althaea rosea)
The papery-textured flowers, carried the length of tall, felted stems, are characteristic of this Turkish species. Named forms and strains include plants in Chater's Double Group, which have peony-like, double flowers in a range of colours; and the impressive 'Nigra', which has dramatic, rich chocolate-maroon flowers. H 2m (6ft), S 60cm (2ft). Hardy/Z 6–9.

## AMARANTHUS
Love-lies-bleeding
The unusual tassel-like flowers of these half-hardy annuals are not to all tastes, although they are indispensable in a 'hot' scheme of reds, oranges and purples.
Cultivation Grow in any soil in sun or light shade. Sow in containers in early spring.

A. caudatus
The species produces pale green leaves and dangles its tassels of

Amaranthus caudatus

Antirrhinum majus 'Double Madam Butterfly Mixed'

tiny blood-red flowers from mid- to late summer. H and S to 1.2m (4ft). Half-hardy. 'Viridis' has electric green flowers that fade to cream. H and S 60cm (2ft). 'Pygmy Torch' has purple-flushed leaves and red flowers. H and S 45cm (18in).

## ANGELICA
These stately biennials are well known in herb gardens, but they can also be effectively deployed in ornamental mixed borders, where they will add height and structure.
Cultivation Grow in any fertile soil in sun or light shade. Sow the seed as soon as it is ripe.

A. archangelica
(syn. A. officinalis)
Archangel
In its first year this species produces fresh green leaves with

Angelica archangelica

serrated edges. In the second year tall, ribbed stems carry domed heads of tiny greenish flowers. H 2m (6ft), S 1m (3ft). Hardy/Z 4–9.

## ANTIRRHINUM
Snapdragon
The unique "snapping" lips of the flowers of snapdragon gives them a certain appeal to children. These half-hardy annuals provide strong blocks of colour – white, yellow, orange, pink and red (some flowers being bicoloured) – in beds and borders.
Cultivation Any soil in full sun is suitable. Sow in a propagator from midwinter.

A. majus
The many hybrids are often ascribed to this species. They are characterized by upright spikes of richly coloured flowers over a long period from summer to the first frosts. All are half-hardy. 'Black Prince' has deep crimson flowers and bronze foliage. H 45cm (18in). 'Brazilian Carnival' has bicoloured flowers in a combination of colours. H 60–90cm (2–3ft). 'Double Madam Butterfly Mixed' has rather muddled, double flowers in a range of colours. The flowers are excellent for cutting. H 60–90cm (2–3ft). 'Kim Orange Bicolor' has dazzling flowers, combining brilliant orange and yellow. H 25–30cm (10–12in). Plants from the Royal Carpet Series are vigorous and ideal for bedding, with flowers in a range

Antirrhinum majus 'Black Prince'

*Bellis perennis* 'Dresden China'

*Begonia semperflorens* Cocktail Series

of colours. H 25–30cm
(10–12in). Plants raised from the
**Sonnet Series**, which are also in
mixed colours, show good weather
resistance. H 45cm (18in).

## BEGONIA

In addition to the tuberous
species and houseplants, this large
genus includes a number of
tender annuals, which are useful
for bedding or for growing in
hanging baskets.
*Cultivation* Grow in any soil in
sun or light shade. Sow in a
propagator from midwinter (this
is not always successful and it can
be advisable to buy in young
plants as plugs for growing on).

### B. semperflorens

These versatile plants, with pink,
red, white or bicoloured flowers,
can also be used as summer houseplants. All are tender/Z 10.
The single flowers in the **Cocktail
Series** are set off by round, bronze
leaves. H 20–30cm (8–12in),
S 30cm (12in). Flowers in the
**Coco Mixed Series** are also offset
by rich bronze leaves. H 20–30cm
(8–12in), S 30cm (12in).
Plants in the **Options Mixed**
series can have green or bronze
leaves. H 20–30cm (8–12in),
S 30cm (12in).

## BELLIS

The genus includes the attractive
lawn daisies that generally appear
unannounced in all gardens, but
the hardy biennials described here
are appealing bedding plants for
early in the season. They are also

delightful in windowboxes.
*Cultivation* Grow in any soil in
full sun. Sow in summer for
planting out in autumn.

### B. perennis

This species, which is native to
Europe, is the parent of a number
of seed strains, all producing
rosettes of leaves and flowers in
shades of red, pink or white. All
are hardy/Z 4–8. **'Dresden
China'**, a dwarf form, has small,
pink, double flowers with quilled
petals. H and S to 10cm (4in).
Plants in the **Habanera Series**
have flowers with long petals,
each flower to 5cm (2in) across.
H and S to 20cm (8in). The
**Pomponette Series** produces
double, tightly quilled, pompon
flowers, each to 4cm (1½in)
across. H and S 15cm (6in).

## BIDENS

These plants are actually perennial
in frost-free conditions but are
usually treated as annuals. Their
trailing habit and dainty, fern-like
foliage make them ideal for
hanging baskets or to soften the
edge of a large container.
*Cultivation* Grow in any soil in
sun or light shade. Sow in a
propagator in early spring.

### B. aurea 'Sunshine'

This form is the one most
commonly seen. It has bright
yellow flowers over a long period
from early summer until the first
frosts. H 50cm (20in). S 40cm
(16in). Half-hardy/Z 8.

## BRACTEANTHA

These Australian annuals have
daisy-like flowers with distinctive
papery petals. They are excellent
for filling gaps in summer
borders, holding their colour
well in hot sun.
*Cultivation* Grow in any well-
drained soil in sun. Sow in a
propagator in spring.

### B. bracteata
(syn. *Helichrysum bracteatum*)
**Golden everlasting, strawflower**
Most of the seed strains and
cultivars are included within this
species. Tender/Z 9–10. **Bright
Bikinis Series** is a dwarf strain
with double, pompon-like flowers
in white or shades of red, pink
and yellow. H 30–45cm
(12–18in), S to 30cm (12in).
**'Coco'** (syn. *Helichrysum* 'Coco')
has straw white flowers with
yellow centres. H 1m (3ft), S
30cm (12in). **'Silvery Rose'** has
clear pink flowers with yellow
centres. H to 75cm (30in), S
30cm (12in).

## CALCEOLARIA
### Slipper flower

This is a large genus containing
about 300 species, although only
a few are widely available. Selected
forms are grown as half-hardy
annuals for summer bedding.
The common name refers to the
shape of the inflated flowers.
*Cultivation* Grow in well-drained
soil in sun. Sow in a propagator
in spring or, for earlier flowers
the following year, in summer.

*Bracteantha bracteata* 'Coco'

**C. Herbeohybrida Group**
Most of the strains grown in
gardens belong to this complex
hybrid group, which involves a
number of species. Besides their
garden use, they can also be
grown as flowering pot plants for
conservatories. Half-hardy/Z 9.
The **Anytime Series** produces
dwarf plants in a range of colours
that are good for growing in
containers under glass. H and S
to 20cm (8in). **'Bright Bikinis'**
has dense heads of yellow, orange
or red flowers. H and S 20cm
(8in). **'Kentish Hero'** has vivid
yellow flowers marked with
orange-red to maroon. H and S
to 30cm (12in). **'Sunset Mixed'**
is a strain of bushy plants that
produce clustered flowers in
shades of red, including some
bicoloured with yellow or orange.
H and S to 30cm (12in).

*Bellis perennis* Pomponette Series

*Calceolaria* 'Kentish Hero'

*Calendula officinalis* 'Fiesta Gitana'

*Cerinthe major*

*Cleome hassleriana* 'Helen Campbell'

*Cleome hassleriana* 'Pink Queen'

## CALENDULA
### Pot marigold

The common name refers to the culinary use of these hardy annuals, not to their suitability for containers. They are rather coarse plants of easy cultivation (often seeding themselves indiscriminately), but valued for their cheery flowers.
*Cultivation* Grow in any soil in full sun. Sow in situ from autumn onwards.

### C. officinalis
The straight species has single orange flowers and aromatic, light green leaves. H and S to 60cm (2ft). Hardy/Z 6. There are several named selections. Plants in the **Art Shades Mixed Series** have flowers in shades of orange, apricot or cream. H and S 60cm (2ft). **'Fiesta Gitana'** is a more compact form, which has orange or yellow (sometimes bicoloured) flowers. H and S 30cm (1ft). The flowers of **'Pacific Apricot'** have pale apricot petals, tipped in a deeper shade. H and S to 30cm (12in).

## CENTAUREA
### Knapweed, hardheads

The genus contains about 450 species of annuals and perennials, of which the species described is an indispensable plant for a wild-flower meadow, attracting bees and butterflies into the garden. Selected forms are good for cutting.
*Cultivation* Grow in any well-drained soil in sun. Sow in containers in late winter to early spring.

### C. cyanus
### Cornflower
The species can have blue, pink, purple or white flowers through-out summer and into autumn. H to 1m (3ft), S 30cm (1ft). Hardy/Z 7. **'Blue Diadem'** has double, rich blue flowers and is more compact. H 75cm (30in), S 30cm (12in).

## CERINTHE
### Honeywort

Until recently, these hardy annuals were little known, but gardeners have slowly become more aware of their subtle charms. They are grown for their coloured bracts, of interest over a long period in summer, rather than the true flowers, which are insignificant.
*Cultivation* Grow in any well-drained soil in sun. Sow in spring in containers or in situ.

### C. major
The species, from southern Europe, has sea-green bracts tinged with yellow and purple.

H to 60cm (2ft), S 30cm (1ft). Hardy/Z 5. The flowers of the more compact **'Kiwi Blue'** are shaded more blue-purple. H 45cm (18in), S 30cm (12in). **'Purpurascens'** has rich purple-blue flowers with cream insides. H to 45cm (18in), S 30cm (12in).

## CLEOME
### Spider flower

These beautiful plants, with airy domed heads of scented flowers, lend elegance to any planting. They are among the tallest of the half-hardy annuals.
*Cultivation* Grow in any well-drained soil in sun. Sow in a propagator from late winter.

### C. hassleriana
### (syn. C. pungens, C. spinosa of gardens)
Most of the garden forms are grouped under this species. H 1.2m (4ft), S 45cm (18in). Half-hardy/Z 1–11. **'Colour Fountain'**, has flowers in shades of pink, lilac, purple and white. Single-

colour selections include **'Cherry Queen'**, with reddish flowers; **'Helen Campbell'** (syn. 'White Queen'), with pure white flowers; **'Pink Queen'**, with pinkish-white flowers; and **'Violet Queen'**, with mauve flowers.

## COBAEA
### Cathedral bell,
### cup-and-saucer vine

The common name is descriptive: the large flowers really are like cups and saucers. This tender annual (a perennial in its native Mexico) is an ideal plant for adding seasonal interest to a pergola or can be grown on a tripod to give height to a border.
*Cultivation* Grow in any moderately fertile soil in sun, preferably with some shelter. Sow in a propagator in spring.

### C. scandens
Where grown as an annual this species, which climbs by means of tendrils, will produce large, fragrant, velvety-purple and green

*Cerinthe major* 'Kiwi Blue'

*Cerinthe major* 'Purpurascens'

*Cobaea scandens*

Convolvulus tricolor 'Royal Ensign'

Coreopsis grandiflora 'Early Sunrise'

Cosmos bipinnatus 'Versailles Tetra'

flowers from summer to autumn. H to 3m (10ft), more in favourable conditions. Tender/Z 9–10. The attractive **C. scandens f. alba** has white flowers aging to yellowish-cream.

# CONVOLVULUS

In addition to the pernicious bindweed, this genus includes some highly desirable hardy annuals that, with their spreading habit, make excellent hanging basket plants.
*Cultivation* Grow in any well-drained soil in sun. Sow in situ in spring or in summer for flowers the following year.

## C. tricolor
(syn. *C. minor*)
This species is actually a short-lived perennial, but is best treated as an annual. It has short-lived, blue, funnel-shaped flowers, borne in succession all summer long. H 40cm (16in), S 30cm (12in). Hardy/Z 8. Strains in single colour and mixtures are also available, of which one of the best is **'Royal Ensign'**. It has rich, deep blue, trumpet-shaped flowers with yellow and white centres. H and S 35–50cm (14–20in).

# COREOPSIS
### Tickseed
These plants produce cheerful, usually bright yellow daisy flowers over a long period in summer.
*Cultivation* Grow in any well-drained soil in sun or light shade. Sow in situ from late winter, or from midsummer to autumn for early flowers the following season.

## C. californica
This erect annual produces a vivid show of yellow daisies over grassy foliage. H to 45cm (18in), S to 30cm (12in). Hardy/Z 1–11.

## C. grandiflora
This perennial species is parent to a number of strains that are invariably grown as annuals. All are hardy/Z 4–9. **'Early Sunrise'** bears masses of semi-double, yellow flowers, which are excellent for cutting. H 45cm (18in), S 38cm (15in). **'Mayfield Giant'** has large, single, bright yellow flowers. H 1m (3ft), S 45cm (18in).

# COSMOS

With one of the longest flowering seasons of any annual, these half-hardies are of unquestioned value, quite apart from the distinction of the glistening flowers and feathery foliage. They are also excellent for cutting.
*Cultivation* Grow in any soil in sun. Sow in situ after all danger of frost has passed.

## C. bipinnatus
Most of the available seed strains are ascribed to this species. All are half-hardy/Z 1–11. **'Sea Shells'** has distinctive flowers, with rolled, almost tubular florets in shades of crimson, pink and white, some being bicolours. H to 1m (3ft), S 45cm (18in). The compact plants in the **Sonata Series** produce carmine, pink or white, bowl-shaped flowers. Single-colour selections include **'Sonata White'**, which has pure white flowers and grows to 60cm (2ft), and **'Sonata Pink'**, which has all-pink flowers. H 45cm (18in), S 30cm (12in). **'Versailles Tetra'** has greyish-pink flowers with a darker area towards the golden-yellow centres. H 1m (3ft), S 45cm (18in).

# DIANTHUS
### Pink
Most dianthus are perennials or rock garden plants, but there are also a few annuals and the appealing biennial, sweet William, a plant of old-fashioned charm that is essential for any cottage-style planting.
*Cultivation* Grow in any well-drained soil in sun. Sow sweet Williams in midwinter, in containers, for flowers in late summer, or in summer, in situ, for flowers the following spring. Sow annuals in containers in early spring.

## D. barbatus
### Sweet William
Uniquely in the genus, this biennial produces flowers in dense rounded heads. The deliciously scented flowers can be red, pink or white; some are bicoloured. H to 70cm (28in), S 30cm (12in). Hardy/Z 4. **Indian Carpet Mixed** is a dwarf strain. H and S 15cm (6in).

## D. chinensis
(syn. *D. sinensis*)
### Chinese pink, Indian pink
The annual pinks are usually grouped under this species. They are all excellent in containers or for edging borders. Hardy/Z 7. Plants in the **Carpet Series** have flowers in a range of colours and are good in exposed situations. H and S to 20cm (8in). **'Fire Carpet'** is bright red. The **Heddewigii Group** includes **'Black and White Minstrels'**, an eye-catching strain, with flowers in various colours, highlighted with white. H 30–38cm (12–15in), S to 30cm (12in). Plants in the compact **Princess Series** have masses of scarlet, white, crimson or salmon-pink flowers, and usually bloom early. H and S 20cm (8in).

Cosmos bipinnatus 'Sonata Pink'

Dianthus barbatus

*Echium vulgare*

## ECHIUM
The genus includes perennials and shrubs as well as the hardy annuals described here. They are easy to grow and the upward-facing flowers will attract bees and butterflies into the garden, making them a good choice for a wildlife border. They can also be treated as biennials. The plants contain a skin irritant.
*Cultivation* Grow in any soil in full sun. Sow in spring for flowers the same year, or in late summer for flowering the following spring.

### E. vulgare
Viper's bugloss
This annual or biennial produces tall spikes of bell-shaped, blue, pink or white flowers over a long period. H to 1m (3ft), S 30cm (12in). Selected forms are more compact. H to 30cm (12in). **'Blue Bedder'** has blue flowers; those of the **Dwarf Hybrids** can be blue, lavender, pink or white. Hardy/Z 1–11.

*Echium vulgare* 'Blue Bedder'

*Eschscholzia californica*

## ESCHSCHOLZIA
California poppy
These hardy annuals are gratifyingly easy to grow, and it is possible to develop your own strains by weeding out unwanted colours as the flowers appear and letting the remainder self-seed.
*Cultivation* Any well-drained soil in full sun is suitable. Sow in situ from spring onwards. Late sowings will flower the following year.

### E. californica
The species typically produces satiny, yellow-orange flowers (although they can also be red, yellow or white). H to 30cm (12in), S 15cm (6in). Hardy/Z 6. Plants in the **Thai Silk Series** have fluted petals (giving a double appearance) in scarlet, orange, pink-orange, yellow, cream and white, while the **Thai Lemon Silk Series** has yellow flowers only. H to 20cm (8in), S 10cm (4in).

## FELICIA
Kingfisher daisy
The delightful plants described are actually tender perennials, which are ideal for use in summer hanging baskets or at the edges of large containers.
*Cultivation* Grow in any soil in sun. Sow in a propagator in spring; named forms are best increased by cuttings.

### F. amelloides
This species has lax stems with an abundance of vivid blue, yellow-centred, daisy flowers throughout summer. H and S 30cm (12in). Tender/Z 10. **'Santa Anita'** has large, deep blue flowers.

## GAZANIA
Treasure flower
These half-hardy annuals would be perennials in a warm climate. Needing heat, they are ideal candidates for growing along the foot of a wall. The flowers open fully only in sunshine.
*Cultivation* Most soils in full sun are suitable, but a sheltered spot is desirable in cool areas. Sow in a propagator from late winter.

### G. varieties
**Chansonette Series**, a prolific strain, produces exotic-looking flowers in shades of lemon-yellow, rich golden-yellow, apricot, orange, bronze, lavender-pink or carmine red, all zoned with a contrasting colour. H and S 23–30cm (9–12in). Plants in the **Daybreak Series** produce bronze, orange, pink, yellow or white flowers, usually with a contrasting central zone. **'Daybreak Orange'**, a perennial grown as an annual, has orange flowers only, which stay open longer than other varieties. H to 20cm (8in), S to 25cm (10in). Half-hardy/Z 8–10.

## GLAUCIUM
Horned poppy
The species described here is a short-lived perennial best treated as a biennial. Thriving in dry spots, it is ideal for sowing in the cracks in paving or in a gravel garden. The common name refers to the curved, horn-shaped seedcases.
*Cultivation* Grow in well-drained, preferably dry and not too fertile soil in sun. Sow in situ in spring or autumn.

*Gazania* 'Daybreak Orange'

*Glaucium flavum*

### G. flavum
Yellow horned poppy
The species forms a rosette of blue-green leaves from which arise hairy stems carrying clear yellow, poppy-like flowers in summer. H 60cm (2ft), S 30cm (1ft). Hardy/Z 7.

## HELIANTHUS
Sunflower
Most sunflowers are coarse plants, although they can be very effective in splendid isolation. The seeds are a valuable food source for birds in winter, suggesting use in an ecological garden, and the temptation to cut the plants down after the flowers have faded should be resisted if possible. Shorter types are good in mixed borders. The genus includes some useful perennials, as well as the hardy annuals described here.
*Cultivation* Most soils are suitable (although heavy, lime clays seem to be preferred) in sun. Sow in situ in spring. Tall plants may need staking.

### H. annuus
This species sends up a stout stem at the top of which is a solitary, although huge, daisy-like yellow flower with a brown or purple centre. H 2.5m (8ft), S 60cm (2ft). Hardy/Z 4–7. There are many selections. **'Moonwalker'** has lemon-yellow petals surrounding chocolate brown centres. H 1.2m–1.5m (4–5ft), S 60cm (2ft). **'Music Box'**, a good dwarf, has a mixture of cream, yellow to dark red flowers, some being bicolours. H to 70cm (28in), S 45cm (18in).

*Helianthus annuus*

'**Teddy Bear**', very dwarf, has rounded, very double, powder-puff flowers in golden-yellow. H 45cm (18in), S 30cm (12in).

## HELIOTROPIUM
### Heliotrope
The species described is actually an evergreen shrub in its native Peru but is treated as a half-hardy annual in colder climates. The wrinkled leaves and fragrant, richly coloured flowers make it a distinctive bedding plant. It is also suitable for windowboxes and other containers.
*Cultivation* Grow in most soils in full sun. Sow in a propagator in spring. Named varieties are best raised from cuttings, although 'Marine' and its variants, such as 'Mini Marine', can be raised from seed.

### H. arborescens
(syn. *H. peruvianum*)
### Cherry pie
The species has rich green leaves and domed heads of violet, purple or white flowers throughout summer. H and S to 45cm (18in). Half-hardy/Z 10. Many cultivars

have been developed, including the strongly growing '**Chatsworth**', which has purple flowers; '**Marine**', which is a dramatic and highly desirable form with very dark green leaves and deep purple flowers; and '**Mini Marine**', which is roughly similar but more compact. H and S 35cm (14in).

## HESPERIS
### Dame's violet, sweet rocket
This cottage-garden favourite produces phlox-like flowers, which are fragrant in the evening. Perennial in favourable conditions, this is best treated as a biennial in most gardens and is indispensable in a border planned for scent.
*Cultivation* Grow these plants in any well-drained soil (preferably neutral to alkaline) in sun or light shade. Sow in situ in spring.

### H. matronalis
The species, a good butterfly plant, produces domed heads of flowers in shades of purple (usually pale, but darker and white flowers are also possible) from late spring to midsummer. H 60cm (2ft), S 30cm (1ft). Hardy/Z 4–9. *H. matronalis* var. *albiflora* has white flowers only.

## IMPATIENS
### Busy Lizzie
These annuals are invaluable for providing colour in shady borders. Use them in borders, containers, windowboxes or – especially – hanging baskets for a long period of interest. Packed tightly, they will produce a ball of flowers.
*Cultivation* Grow in any soil in

*Ipomoea tricolor* 'Purpurea'

light to full shade. Sow in a propagator in late winter. Seed can be tricky to germinate and it may be more practical to buy in young plants as seedlings or plugs.

### I. New Guinea Group
These striking plants have the added attraction of exotic-looking red, bronze or rich green leaves, sometimes marked with yellow and pink. The flowers can be pink, red, purple, orange or white. H 45cm (18in), S 40cm (16in). Tender/Z 10. '**Tango**' is a superb selection, with deep orange flowers offset by rich bronze leaves. H 35cm (14in), S 30cm (12in).

### I. walleriana
Most of the seed strains are grouped under this species. **Double Carousel Mixed** produces well-branched plants with double, rose-like flowers in orange, pink, red and white, with some bicolours. H and S 23–30cm (9–12in). Plants of the **Super Elfin Series** are free-flowering and compact, with flowers in a range of dazzling colours. H and S 15cm (6in). '**Tempo Peach Frost**' has pink flowers edged scarlet. H and S to 25cm (10in). '**Victoria Rose**' has pink flowers. H and S 23–30cm (9–12in). Tender/Z 10.

*Ipomoea lobata*

## IPOMOEA
### Morning glory
With their trumpet-shaped, convolvulus-like flowers, these tender plants are true glories of the garden, with a shade of blue probably unmatched by any other summer flowers. The species described here are twining climbers, which look charming when they are allowed to wander through other plants, but they can also be more formally trained on vertical wires or other supports.
*Cultivation* Morning glories need well-drained soil in sun, preferably in a sheltered site. Sow in a propagator from late winter.

### I. lobata
(syn. *Mina lobata*)
### Spanish flag
This climber is grown for its variety of beak-like flowers. Initially scarlet, they age to orange, yellow and finally white, all colours appearing simultaneously. H and S 1.2–2m (4–6ft) or more. Tender/Z 10.

### I. tricolor
The straight species is well worth growing, for the joy of its clear blue, white-throated flowers. H to 4m (13ft), but probably less in cool gardens. Tender/Z 8. Selected forms include '**Flying Saucers**', which has larger flowers striped blue and white; and '**Heavenly Blue**', which has richer blue flowers with white throats and '**Purpurea**', with rich purple, white-throated flowers.

*Heliotropium arborescens* 'Marine'

*Hesperis matronalis* var. *albiflora*

*Impatiens walleriana* 'Victoria Rose'

*Lathyrus odoratus 'White Supreme'*

# LATHYRUS

For many gardeners, summer would not be summer without the delicious scent of these tendril climbers. Cutting the flowers for arrangements is actually to the benefit of the plant, since it will greatly extend the flowering season. Some gardeners like to grow them for this purpose alone and relegate them to the vegetable plot trained on cordons, which seems a pity, because their flower colours blend so happily with other plants. In borders they have great charm if allowed to climb over wigwams of peasticks or trellis obelisks.
*Cultivation* Grow in any soil in full sun. Sweet peas need a long growing season, so sow from late autumn in special sweet pea tubes, which will minimize disturbance to the roots on planting out.

### *L. odoratus*
Sweet pea
Both the specific name and common name are slightly misleading. Not all strains are scented, and some are distinctly more fragrant than others (the sweet peas described are all richly scented unless otherwise indicated). H to 2m (6ft) unless otherwise stated. Hardy/Z 1–11. **'Cream Southborne'** produces large, frilled, cream flowers. The prolific **'Firecrest'** has unusual bicoloured flowers of fiery red and orange. **'King Size Navy Blue'**, one of the darkest blues, has wavy-edged flowers on long slender stems. **'Orange Dragon'**

has startling orange (only lightly scented) flowers, which hold their colour best in a position that is sheltered from hot sun. Plants of the **Snoopea Group** are compact and have no tendrils. The flowers can be white, pink, red or purple. H to 60cm (2ft). One of the best white varieties available is **'White Supreme'** with outstandingly fragrant flowers produced on long, strong stems.

# LAVATERA

Among the 25 species in the genus are a number of perennials. The annuals are easy and resilient hardy plants, which are ideal for plugging summer gaps in borders.
*Cultivation* Any soil in full sun is suitable. Sow in containers from late winter or in situ in mid-spring.

### *L. trimestris*
Most of the annual lavateras are listed under this species. They make bushy plants with mallow flowers. Selections include **'Mont Blanc'**, which has dark leaves and glistening white flowers; and **'Silver Cup'**, a very weather-resistant form, which has glowing silvery pink flowers with darker veins. H to 1m (3ft), S 45cm (18in). Hardy/Z 5–9.

# LIMNANTHES
Poached egg plant
These hardy annuals, with their simple white and yellow flowers, will attract a wide range of beneficial insects (especially bees) into the garden. They seed themselves readily, particularly in gravel.

*Limnanthes douglasii*

*Cultivation* Most well-drained soils in full sun are suitable. Sow in situ in spring or in early autumn for early flowers the following year.

### *L. douglasii*
This easily grown species has gleaming yellow, buttercup-like flowers, with white edges to the petals, throughout summer. H 15cm (6in), S 20cm (8in). Hardy/Z 8.

# LOBELIA
Given the chance, these half-hardy annuals would be perennial, but they are usually raised annually from seed. Compact forms are the mainstay of park bedding schemes, while a hanging basket would be virtually unthinkable without the trailing kinds. Lobelias are among the precious few shade-tolerant annuals. Most are blue, although there are also selections in other

*Lobelia erinus 'Cambridge Blue'*

colours. The genus also includes true perennials and shrubs.
*Cultivation* Grow in any soil in sun or light shade. Sow in a propagator from late winter.

### *L. erinus*
The annuals are usually usefully grouped under this species. All are hardy/Z 5–8. The compact **'Cambridge Blue'**, which is suitable for bedding, has clear sky-blue flowers. H and S 10cm (4in). Trailing varieties suitable for hanging baskets include those in the **Cascade Series**. Individual colour selections are **'Blue Cascade'**, **'Crimson Cascade'**, **'Lilac Cascade'**, **'Red Cascade'** and **'White Cascade'**. H 15cm (6in), S 30cm (12in). **'Crystal Palace'**, a compact form suitable for bedding, has dark blue flowers. H and S 10cm (4in). **'Sapphire'** has rich blue flowers with white eyes. H and S 15cm (6in).

# LOBULARIA
Sweet alyssum
These tough little hardy annuals are very useful. They will seed themselves in various nooks and crannies around the garden, generally to good effect. Easy to grow, they are excellent for edging a path or border and are especially tolerant of coastal conditions. They also work well in containers and windowboxes. The flowers are scented.
*Cultivation* Alyssums will grow in any well-drained soil in sun. Sow in containers in late winter or in situ in spring.

*Lavatera trimestris 'Mont Blanc'*

Lobularia maritima 'Carpet of Snow'

## L. maritima
(syn. *Alyssum maritimum*)
This species, native to the Canary Islands, has a huge range of selections. Most make compact hummocks. All are hardy/Z 1–11. 'Carpet of Snow', which is neat-growing and ground-hugging, has white flowers. H 10cm (4in), S 30cm (12in). 'Oriental Night' has rich purple flowers. H 10cm (4in), S 30cm (12in). The flowers of 'Sweet White' are white and smell of honey. H 10cm (4in), S 30cm (12in). 'Trailing Rosy Red', which has pinkish-purple flowers, is less compact than the others; its trailing habit makes it ideal for hanging baskets. H 10cm (4in), S 40cm (16in).

## LUNARIA
### Honesty, satin flower
These modest biennials (some-times persisting a bit longer) have two seasons of interest. The pretty spring flowers are followed by distinctive, papery, oval seedheads, which are excellent in dried arrangements. Honesty often appears unbidden in gardens and once established is unlikely to die out.
*Cultivation* Honesty tolerates most soil, in sun or light shade. Sow in situ from late spring to early summer.

## L. annua
(syn. *L. biennis*)
This European species has usually purple, sometimes white, flowers in spring followed by translucent white seedheads in autumn. H 1m (3ft), S 30cm (1ft). Hardy. For white flowers only, sow seeds of *L. annua* var. *albiflora*. 'Alba Variegata' is a desirable garden form with white variegated leaves and white flowers. 'Variegata' has similar leaves but flowers in shades of purple.

## MATTHIOLA
### Stock, gillyflower
Among the most fragrant of all flowers, these beautiful, hardy biennials (which can also be treated as annuals) can be sown in succession for an extended season. The flowers, which are white, pink, lavender, lilac or crimson, blend well with virtually all others. Night-scented stock, the most fragrant of all, has rather insignificant looking flowers of light mauve. Seed can usefully be scattered among showier but scentless plants.

*Cultivation* Any soil in sun is suitable. Sow seed from summer onwards for flowers the following year and from late winter for flowers the same year.

## M. incana
Most strains are usefully gathered within this species and include Brompton stocks and Ten Week stocks. So-called Brompton stocks, which are biennials, are available in a wide colour range. H 50cm (20in), S 30cm (12in). There are many dwarf strains including the **Cinderella Series**, plants of which produce multiple spikes of double flowers. H 30cm (12in), S 10cm (4in). 'Cinderella Antique Pink' is a selection with flowers in a unique shade of bronze-pink. **Ten Week Mixed** are annuals, with branching spikes of usually double flowers in a range of colours. H 30cm (12in), S 20cm (8in). Hardy/Z 6.

## M. longipetala subsp. bicornis
(syn. *M. bicornis*)
### Night-scented stock
This annual species is grown for the power of its scent alone. The lilac-mauve flowers open, modest in appearance and sparsely scattered up the stems, in the evening. H 30cm (1ft), S 23cm (9in). Hardy/Z 5.

## MYOSOTIS
### Forget-me-not
Although they will seed on their own freely, it is worth sowing these biennials afresh every season – the named forms always have flowers of a more intense colour than their natural progeny. Indispensable for most spring bedding schemes, forget-me-nots make a classic cottage-garden combination with pink tulips.
*Cultivation* Forget-me-nots will grow in most well-drained soils in sun or, preferably, light shade. Sow outdoors in early summer.

## M. sylvatica
The straight species has mid-blue, yellow-eyed flowers in spring and early summer and grey-green leaves. H 30cm (12in), S 15cm, (6in). All forms are hardy/Z 5–8. 'Blue Ball' is a more compact form with indigo flowers. H and

S 15–20cm (6–8in). The flowers of 'Compindi', another dwarf form, are even darker. H and S 15–20cm (6–8in). 'Rosylva' is something of a novelty, with large flowers of clear pink. H 30cm (12in), S 15cm (6in).

## NEMOPHILA
These hardy annuals have delightfully marked, cup-shaped flowers. They should be planted near the edge of a border or in a container or windowbox where this feature can be fully appreciated best.
*Cultivation* Most soils are suitable, although it should ideally be re-liably moist. Plant in sun or light shade. Sow in situ in spring, or in autumn for larger plants that will flower earlier the following year.

## N. maculata
### Five spot
The common name is descriptive. Each pale blue petal is marked at the edge with a dark blue spot. This is a charming plant for a hanging basket. H and S to 30cm (12in). Hardy/Z 1–11.

## N. menziesii
### Baby blue eyes
In summer, this carpeting species is smothered in sky-blue flowers with paler centres. It is excellent for adding late colour to a rock garden. H 15cm (6in), S 30cm (12in). Hardy/Z 1–11. 'Pennie Black' has blackish-purple flowers with scalloped, silvery edges and is more ground hugging. H 10cm (4in), S 30cm (12in).

Lunaria annua

Matthiola longipetala subsp. bicornis

Nemophila menziesii

Nicotiana 'Lime Green'

# NICOTIANA
## Tobacco plant
These sticky, half-hardy annuals (actually tender perennials) bear flowers that remain closed at daytime but perk up at dusk and give off an incense-like fragrance. Modern selections are more compact and floriferous, but have not displaced older varieties.
*Cultivation* Grow in any soil in full sun or light shade. Sow in a propagator in spring.

### N. langsdorfii
This distinctive annual is one of few species grown in its straight form. The branching stems carry drooping, pale, lime-green flowers. It combines well with a wide variety of border plants. H 1.5m (5ft), S 35cm (14in). Half-hardy/Z 7.

Nicotiana langsdorfii

### N. 'Lime Green'
Blending with all other flowers, this popular selection produces lime sherbet flowers throughout the summer. H 60cm (2ft), S 20cm (8in). Half-hardy/Z 7.

### N. × sanderae
Most of the annual strains are considered to belong to this hybrid group. All are half-hardy/Z 7. Plants of the **Domino Series** are branching and bushy, with red, white, pink or green flowers. Domino Series **'Salmon Pink'** is only lightly scented but produces unique salmon-pink flowers. H 30–45cm (12–18in), S 25cm (10in). Plants in the **Havana Series** are compact. The selection **'Apple Blossom'** has unusually coloured flowers: pale pink with darker pink reverses, giving a two-tone effect. H 30cm (12in), S 20cm (8in). Plants in the **Merlin Series** are compact and bushy, ideal for containers or the front of a border. The flowers can be purple, crimson, lime green or white (bicolours being a possibility). Seed is also often sold as single colour selections; the white-flowered ones are usually the most potently scented. H and S 23–25cm (9–10in).

### N. sylvestris
This beautiful Argentinean species, which is actually a short-lived perennial, sometimes behaves as a biennial, surviving winter cold and flowering only in its second year. The fragrant, white flowers

are carried in a candelabra-like arrangement on tall plants in summer, making this an excellent 'dot' plant. H 1–1.2m (3–4ft), S 60cm (2ft). Half-hardy/Z 9–10.

# NIGELLA
## Love-in-a-mist
These charming and elegant annuals are dainty cottage-garden stalwarts, almost as attractive when the seedheads develop as when they are in flower; the feathery foliage is a definite bonus. They are easy to grow.
*Cultivation* Grow in any soil in sun. Sow in situ from spring onwards.

### N. damascena
The species is the parent of the garden strains, all of which are hardy/Z 1–11. **'Dwarf Moody Blue'** is a compact form, which can be used to make a temporary low hedge at the margin of a border. The flowers are sky blue. H 15–20cm (6–8in), S 10cm (4in). The popular and widely grown **'Miss Jekyll'** has bright blue, semi-double flowers. H 45cm (18in), S 15cm (6in). The rarer and desirable **'Miss Jekyll Alba'** is white. H 45cm (18in), S 15cm (6in). Plants in the **Persian Jewel Series** have flowers in a range of colours: pink, blue, violet and white. H 38cm (15in), S 15cm (6in).

# OENOTHERA
## Evening primrose
These stately annuals and biennials produce a succession of

Nigella damascena 'Miss Jekyll'

Oenothera biennis

flowers over the summer months that are valuable for attracting butterflies and other beneficial insects into the garden. Some open only in the evening – hence the plant's common name. All have a cool beauty. The genus includes some perennials.
*Cultivation* Evening primroses will grow in any well-drained soil in sun. Sow in situ in autumn; annuals can also be sown in containers in spring.

### O. biennis
This species can be treated as an annual or a biennial and will usually seed itself. From basal rosettes of leaves emerge tall stems carrying shorter leaves and the large, cup-shaped, scented yellow flowers. H 1m (3ft), S 40cm (16in). Hardy/Z 4.

Papaver rhoeas

Papaver somniferum

# PAPAVER
Poppy

Annual and biennial poppies, all hardy and easy to grow, are as valuable in gardens as their perennial cousins. Some will seed themselves, often to good effect, but sometimes to the point of becoming weeds. All have characteristically silky-textured flowers and are excellent in wildflower gardens as well as in borders.

*Cultivation* Any soil in sun is suitable. Sow annuals in situ in early spring, or in autumn for earlier flowers the following season. Biennials can be sown in situ in summer.

### P. croceum
(syn. *P. nudicaule* of gardens)
Arctic poppy, Icelandic poppy

The species, usually grown as a biennial, has blue-grey leaves and fragrant, yellow, white or pale orange flowers. H to 30cm (12in), S 15cm (6in). Hardy/Z 4–8. Some ravishing strains, all with glistening flowers, including some doubles, have been developed. **Meadow Pastels** is a mixture that produces large, single flowers in shades of white, pink, rose pink, yellow and orange on sturdy stems. Early sowings can flower the same year. They are excellent for cutting. H to 30cm (12in), S 15cm (6in). **Oregon Rainbows** produces smaller plants, with flower colours including apricot, pink, soft cream and lemon-yellow. H to 25cm (10in), S 10cm (4in).

### P. rhoeas
Corn poppy, field poppy

This is the annual species that appears on arable land that has been recently cultivated, the soil disturbance effectively breaking the seed's dormancy. The typically red flowers are a familiar sight, blanketing entire fields in summer. H to 1m (3ft), S to 30cm (1ft). Hardy/Z 5. Selected strains include the well-known **Shirley Series**, which produces semi-double or double flowers in red, pink, lilac and white, some flowers uniting two colours. Self-sown seedlings that revert to type should be weeded out if the characteristics of the strain are to be maintained. H 60cm (2ft), S 30cm (1ft).

### P. somniferum
Opium poppy

The species, which has blue-green leaves, produces pink, purplish, red or white flowers, followed by striking seedheads. H 1m (3ft), S 30cm (1ft). Hardy/Z 7. Double forms have distinctive ruffled petals. **'Hen and Chickens'** has pink flowers, but is really grown for its larger than average seedheads, which can he dried for winter decoration. H 30cm (12in), S 20cm (4in). Plants raised from the **Peony Flowered** group live up to their name and have double flowers in red, purplish-pink, pink or white. H 1m (3ft), S 30cm (1ft). **'White Cloud'** has large, double white flowers. H 1m (3ft), S 30cm (1ft).

# PETUNIA

The trumpet flowers of these sticky, half-hardy annuals have an immediate appeal. Most are ideal bedding plants, but recent introductions with trailing stems are best in hanging baskets. Blue-flowered plants are often heavily scented. All petunias grown in gardens are hybrids (sometimes lumped under the catch-all name *P. × hybrida*). According to flower size, they are usually divided among the three groups specified below (some seed merchants have created other divisions).

*Cultivation* Petunias need well-drained soil in sun. Sow in a propagator from late winter.

Petunia 'Blue Daddy'

### P. Grandiflora Group

Plants in this group produce the largest flowers. The **Aladdin Series** has wavy-edged flowers in an impressive colour range, including blue, red, burgundy, pink, lilac and white. H to 30cm (12in), S to 1m (3ft). The **Daddy Series** has flowers in unique shades of plum burgundy, orchid lavender, pink, blue and red, all with a velvety texture and darker veins. **'Blue Daddy'** has silver-blue flowers with darker veins and is early-flowering. H to 35cm (14in), S 1m (3ft). The well-known **Surfinia Series** produces vigorous plants of trailing habit that makes them ideal for hanging baskets. Flower colours include pink, red and blue. H 40cm (16in), S 1m (3ft). Half-hardy/Z 7.

### P. Milliflora Group

Plants in this group produce quantities of small flowers. H and S to 30cm (12in). **Fantasy Series** plants are smothered with flowers in a range of colours throughout summer. They are ideal for containers and hanging baskets. H 15cm (6in), S to 30cm (12in). Half-hardy/Z 7.

### P. Multiflora Group

This, the largest group, is characterized by medium-sized flowers on bushy plants. Plants in this group are the most weather resistant. **Carpet Mixed** produce low-growing, spreading plants that flower early in shades of pink, red, plum purple, rich blue and white. **'Carpet Buttercream'** is a selection that has creamy-yellow flowers only. H to 25cm (10in), S to 1m (3ft). Petunias belonging to the **Duo Series** have double flowers in a range of colours, including some strongly veined flowers and some bicolours. H to 30cm (1ft), S to 1m (3ft). The **Mirage Series** has plants with red, pink, blue and lavender flowers, all attractively veined with darker shades. H to 30cm (1ft), S to 1m (3ft). **Storm Mixed** petunias produce rain-resistant flowers in shades of salmon, white, pink and lavender. Single colour selections are available. **'Lavender Storm'** is vigorous, with pale yellow-throated lavender flowers. H 20–30cm (8–12in), S to 1m (3ft). Half-hardy/Z 7.

Petunia 'Lavender Storm'

Salvia fulgens

## SALVIA
### Sage

In addition to the well-known culinary herb, this large genus includes several annuals, as well as some perennials and subshrubs that can be treated as annuals or biennials in cool climates. Most have spikes of vivid flowers, while some are grown more for the appeal of the conspicuous bracts that surround them.
*Cultivation* Salvias prefer light, well-drained soil and a position in sun. Sow even hardy varieties in a propagator in mid-spring, or in situ once all danger of frost has passed; late sowings flower later.

### S. fulgens
### (syn. S. cardinalis)
A woody-based perennial or sub-shrub in its native Mexico, this upright plant produces spikes of vivid red flowers in summer. It is electric with *Verbena bonariensis*. H 1.2m (4ft), S 75cm (30in). Half-hardy/Z 9–10.

### S. patens
This species is of borderline hardiness, but most gardeners are prepared to persevere with it for the sake of the very vivid blue flowers produced from summer to autumn. H 60cm (2ft), S 45cm (18in). It sometimes survives as a perennial. Borderline hardy/Z 7–9. Among the cultivars are **'Cambridge Blue'**, which has paler blue flowers; and **'White Trophy'**, which has white flowers.

### S. sclarea var. turkestanica
The species is most often seen in this naturally occurring form. It is a hardy perennial best treated as a biennial. The plant is branching, with erect, pink stems and pink-flecked white flowers held in purple bracts. A choice plant for the border. H to 1m (3ft), S 30cm (1ft). Hardy/Z 4–7.

### S. splendens
### Scarlet sage
This species includes the vivid red cultivars familiar in park bedding schemes, although other colours also occur. **'Blaze of Fire'** is a compact and early-flowering form. H 30cm (12in), S 20cm (8in). Plants belonging to the **Phoenix Series** can have pink, purple, white, red or lilac flowers. H 25–30cm (10–12in), S 20cm (8in). **'Red Arrows'** has the advantage of deep green leaves to set off the scarlet flowers. H 30cm (12in), S 20cm (8in). The flowers of **'Sizzler Burgundy'**, also red, are long-lasting. H 30cm (12in), S 20cm (8in).

### S. viridis
### (syn. S. horminum)
### Annual clary
This species is grown for its pink, purple or white bracts. The stems can be dried for winter decoration. H to 50cm (20in), S 23cm (9in). Hardy/Z 4–7. **'Claryssa'** is a dwarf form with somewhat more brightly coloured bracts. H to 40cm (16in), S 20cm (8in).

Salvia sclarea var. turkestanica

Tagetes erecta Jubilee Series 'Golden'

## TAGETES
### Marigold

These are among the easiest of half-hardy annuals to grow, and provide a reliable, long-lasting display throughout summer. There are two large groups, African marigolds and French marigolds, African marigolds tending to be taller and less spreading than the French. Hybrids between the two groups also exist, as well as a range deriving from *T. tenuifolia*. Single-flowered French marigolds make good companions for plants that are attacked by aphids: they attract hoverflies, which will help control the pests.
*Cultivation* Any fertile soil in sun is suitable. Sow in a propagator in spring.

### T. erecta
### African marigold
These plants have fully double, daisy-like flowers, in shades of cream, yellow and orange. Half-hardy/Z 9. **Crackerjack Mixed** plants have bold, double flowers in orange, golden-yellow and lemon-yellow. H 60cm (2ft), S 30cm (1ft). The **Gold 'n' Vanilla Series** includes creamy white flowers. H 50–75cm (20–30in), S 30cm (1ft). **Jubilee Series 'Golden'** is a single

Tagetes erecta Gold 'n' Vanilla Series

colour selection with golden-yellow flowers. H 50cm (20in), S 30cm (1ft).

### T. patula
### French marigold
The flowers of these marigolds can include more than one colour. Plants of the **Boy O' Boy Series** are neat and compact, making them very suitable for window-boxes. The double flowers, with crested centres, can be yellow, orange or rich brownish-red. H and S 15cm (6in). **'Gypsy Sunshine'** bears a heavy crop of double butter-yellow flowers. H and S 15–20cm (6–8in). **'Naughty Marietta'** has single deep yellow flowers marked with maroon. H 30–40cm (12–16in), S 25cm (10in). Half-hardy/Z 9.

### T. tenuifolia
These marigolds are bushy and produce domes of flowers. Half-hardy/Z 9. Plants of the **Gem Series** have single flowers in shades of yellow or orange, marked with darker colours. **'Golden Gem'** is a selection with golden-yellow flowers. H and S 15–23cm (6–9in). **Starfire Mixed** has red and yellow flowers, some dramatically bicoloured. H and S 15–23cm (6–9in).

Tagetes tenuifolia 'Golden Gem'

*Tropaeolum majus* Alaska Series

*Zinnia haageana* 'Profusion White'

## TROPAEOLUM
**Nasturtium**
These half-hardy annuals, which are perennials in warm climates, are gratifyingly easy to grow. Some strains make large plants with trailing stems, which are useful for providing quick cover, although the large leaves tend to mask the flowers. The more compact forms are good for bedding or, more informally, for slipping into the cracks in paving. The young leaves and the flowers are edible. The genus also includes some hardy perennials.
*Cultivation* Grow in any, but not too fertile, soil in sun. Sow in situ from mid-spring onwards.

### T. majus
This is the species to which the annual strains are most usually ascribed. All are half-hardy/Z 8–9. The **Alaska Series** produces plants with leaves that are attractively marbled with cream and pink; the flowers can be brilliant orange, red or yellow. H 20–30cm (8–12in), S 45cm (18in). '**Empress of India**' is a compact form, with rich purplish-green leaves and bright scarlet flowers. H to 30cm (12in), S 45cm (18in). Plants raised from seed of the **Gleam Series** are trailing, with semi-double flowers in yellow, red or orange. H to 40cm (16in), S to 60cm (2ft). Plants in the **Whirlybird Series** make low mounds, with upward-facing yellow or red flowers. H to 25cm (10in), S to 40cm (16in).

## VIOLA
**Pansy**
An endearing genus that includes perennials and rock garden plants as well as the charming hardy annuals and biennials described here. Attractive as the self-coloured strains are, most gardeners find the bicolours more appealing: the mask-like markings make the flowers look like faces. So-called winter pansies will flower intermittently from late autumn onwards, reaching their peak in spring. With successive sowings it is possible to produce flowering plants throughout the year. All pansies make ideal bedding and container plants; a winter windowbox is virtually unthinkable without them.
*Cultivation* Any soil in sun or light shade is suitable. Seed germinates best at low temperatures (maximum 10°C/50°F). Summer pansies are best treated as biennials and sown in containers in summer for flowering from the following spring, although they can also be sown from late winter for flowers the same year. Winter pansies should be sown in summer. Take care to keep summer sowings cool.

### V. × wittrockiana
Seed strains are usually ascribed to this complex hybrid group, which has emerged from cross-breeding a number of species. All are hardy/Z 4–9.

**Summer pansies**
'Jolly Joker' has intense orange and purple flowers. H and S 15–23cm (6–9in). 'Lilac Frost' has glistening lilac flowers that are blotched centrally with rich purple. H and S 15–20cm (6–8in). **Majestic Giants Mixed** plants produce huge bicoloured flowers in a range of iridescent colours; early-flowering, they show greater tolerance to extremes of weather than other strains. H and S 15cm (6in). 'Padparadja' has intense, solid orange flowers. H and S 15cm (6in). 'Velour Purple Wings' makes compact mounds that are smothered with miniature flowers with purple and cream petals. The cream petals are edged with mauve and shade to yellow at the centre. H and S 18cm (7in).

**Winter pansies**
Plants belonging to the **Floral Dance Series** are reliable and produce flowers in a range of colours. Selections in single colours are available. H and S 15–23cm (6–9in). **Universal Mixed** plants are compact, producing both self-coloured and bicoloured flowers in a colour range including red, purple, yellow, apricot and white. H and S 15–20cm (6–8in).

## ZINNIA
These half-hardy annuals, with their dahlia-like flowers, bring an exotic touch to the garden.

Unusually among half-hardy annuals, they are best sown where they are to flower, since they resent root disturbance.
*Cultivation* Grow in any soil in sun. Seed can be sown in containers in spring, but it is better to sow them in situ from late spring.

### Z. elegans
This Mexican species encompasses a number of seed strains. Tender/10–11. Plants of the **Cactus-flowered Group** have large double flowers, similar to those of a cactus-flowered dahlia, in a range of colours. H to 1m (3ft), S 30cm (1ft). The **Desert Sun Series** produces large, pleated flowers in primrose yellow, ivory white and golden-yellow, which are excellent for cutting. H 1m (3ft), S 30cm (1ft). 'Double Dwarf Mixed' is a compact strain, with fully double flowers in white, salmon, pink, yellow and scarlet. H 20cm (8in), S 15cm (6in). 'Envy' has semi-double, chartreuse green flowers. H 75cm (30in), S 30cm (12in). 'Envy Double' is fully double.

### Z. haageana
(syn. *Z. angustifolia*)
**Mexican zinnia**
Strains allotted to this species are somewhat more compact than those of *Z. elegans*. Half-hardy/Z 9–10. Plants raised from **Persian Carpet Mixed** produce double, bicoloured flowers in shades of golden yellow, maroon, purple, chocolate, pink and cream. They are seemingly impervious to weather extremes. H 38cm (15in), S 30cm (12in). 'Profusion White' has white flowers. H 30cm (12in), S 10cm (4in).

*Tropaeolum majus* 'Whirlybird Gold'

*Viola* 'Padparadja'

# Climbers

Climbers are among the most dramatic and rewarding garden plants, lifting your eyes skywards as they reach towards the sun. They are ideal for beautifying walls, fences and ugly outbuildings and can also be draped over pergolas to provide welcome shade in summer or used to carpet banks. Some have spectacular flowers that can be deliciously scented. Others are grown for their leaves, while the evergreens provide year-round interest, a good foil to other flowering plants in summer and supplying welcome greenery in winter.

Allowed to ramble through roses and perennials, this clematis lifts its flowers to the sun.

# What is a climber?

Climbers are a fascinating group of plants. Typically, a climber is a woodland dweller, with its feet in the cool, leafy soil on the forest floor. Its long, flexible stems scamper up tree trunks and into their branches, usually with considerable vigour. On reaching the canopy, it spreads sideways and produces flowers that turn to face the sun. This natural habit is one that most gardeners spend considerable efforts on circumventing.

Most climbers have woody stems, and thus are essentially shrubs, but others are soft-stemmed perennials, and some are herbaceous, dying back completely in winter. There are also some annual climbers, sweet peas (*Lathyrus odoratus*) being the best-known.

Climbers have evolved various methods of attaching themselves to their host plant in the wild. Some have special suckering pads that adhere to the host, ivies (*Hedera*), Virginia creeper (*Vitis*) and the climbing hydrangea being notable

examples. Other climbers, such as honeysuckles (*Lonicera*), have twining stems that twist themselves around the host plant. A third group have specialized tendrils – for instance, passion flowers (*Passiflora*) – or twining leaf stalks (clematis being the best example), which cling to narrow stems. A fourth group, which includes most of the roses (dealt with in their own section of this book) and bougainvillea, have thorns that allow the plant to hook itself into tree bark as it ramps upwards.

A further group should not be overlooked. This comprises so-called scandent climbers, woody plants with long, flexible stems that have no means of supporting themselves. Some clematis come into this category, as well as the popular winter jasmine (*Jasminum nudiflorum*) and the beautiful potato vines (*Solanum*). Such plants can be treated like other climbers but have to be tied to their supports as they grow.

## Climbers in the garden

While most plants present their flowers at eye level or below, climbers raise your gaze skywards, and thus bring a dynamism to the garden that is unmatched by any other group. They are high-value plants in that they can fill a large amount of space above ground, while actually only occupying a small area of soil.

In the artificial environment of a garden, climbers do not need to be grown into a host plant, but can be used to clothe a wall or fence, or to cover a pergola or trellis screen. In all these cases, you have to be careful to match the vigour of the plant to the structure that will support it. Many a climber has pulled down a fence, but it is an old wives' tale that suckering climbers will damage the

mortar on house walls: only if the mortar is unsound to begin with are you likely to experience problems. Perennial climbers and some of the less vigorous clematis are effective grown on trellis obelisks or pyramids in borders. A related, but highly effective, method is to train such plants on trellis panels set horizontally in the border on posts, to create a table of flowers that you can look down on.

You can imitate the way climbing plants behave in the wild by siting them near a suitable host plant and treating this as the support. You can plan for the two plants to flower simultaneously, in complementary, toning or even clashing colours, or for the one to follow the other, thus providing for a long season of interest. The summer-flowering perennial pea (*Lathyrus*) makes a good companion for a shrub rose such as 'Nevada' or 'Canary Bird', whose moment of glory comes earlier in season. The flame creeper (*Tropaeolum speciosum*) looks

Bougainvillea and *Trachelospermum jasminoides* make an entrancing combination in this Californian garden.

A tripod supports the vigorous hybrid clematis 'Jackmanii'. Once fully grown it will cover the support completely so it cannot be seen.

spectacular when its luminous crimson flowers light up a sombre yew hedge, and many clematis are suitable for growing into flowering shrubs. Such combinations are a matter of taste: an extreme example would be to grow *Clematis montana* into a mature conifer, a striking if bizarre sight, but honeysuckles and wisterias always strike a romantic note when allowed to ramble through mature deciduous trees.

Another use is as ground cover, a method of cultivation that is particularly effective on a bank or in a wild garden. Many climbers will actually root where the stems touch the ground (especially self-clingers such as ivy), thus creating a weed-suppressing carpet.

Many of the less rampant climbers can be grown in containers, provided these are deep enough to accommodate the root system. They can be trained on trellis panels in the same way as climbers in the open garden, or can simply be allowed to trail over the sides of the container. Ivies are very effective when grown in this way, as are some of the weaker-growing clematis.

## Pruning and training climbers

Most climbers are vigorous plants that benefit from pruning occasionally to keep them under control. That said, it is generally impractical to prune climbers grown informally into trees and shrubs, and these can be given their head – hence the importance of choosing climbers that will not swamp the host.

On planting, cut out any dead, diseased or damaged stems and lightly trim back the remainder. Fan them out and tie them loosely to the support. If they are not long enough to reach the support, attach them to canes tied to the support. As the plant grows, train in the

The dainty *Clematis viticella* 'Purpurea Plena Elegans' supported by the pergola dangles its flowers in among the hanging basket's traditional mix of fuchsias and trailing annuals.

stems as near to the horizontal as possible to encourage even flowering. Thorny and scandent climbers will need to be tied in. If you are training the climber up a post (for instance, the upright of a pergola), wrap the stems around the support rather than tying them in vertically.

As a general rule, prune early-flowering climbers immediately after flowering, and late-flowering ones at the start of the growing season. Once the climber has filled

its allotted space, shorten overlong shoots and remove any crossing stems. Cut back thick, old stems to ground level. You can then shorten side shoots, if necessary. A plant that has really got out of hand can be given a new lease of life by renovative pruning. In late winter, cut back all the stems to near ground level. Feed the plant well, and new growth should be vigorous.

For pruning clematis and wisteria, see their own entries in this chapter.

*Actinidia kolomikta*

*Akebia quinata*

The plants listed are all deciduous unless otherwise indicated.

## ACTINIDIA

In addition to the ornamental species described here, this genus of twining climbers also includes *A. deliciosa* (kiwi fruit, Chinese gooseberry).
*Cultivation* Grow actinidias in any reasonably fertile soil in sun or light shade.

### *A. kolomikta*

This climber from eastern Asia is grown for its leaves, which look as if they have been splashed with cream and pink paint. The leaves show different colours each year (although they are always plain green on emergence, and will remain so in a very shaded site). The plant is not to everyone's taste, but it is attractive grown into the branches of a tree. H and S 3m (10ft). Hardy/Z 4–9.

## AKEBIA
### Chocolate vine

An interesting genus of five species of twining climbers, with several members that deserve wider recognition than they currently receive. Few are showy, but the plants have a subtle appeal.
*Cultivation* Grow in any fertile, well-drained soil in sun or light shade.

### *A. quinata*

The dark purple-brown flowers that appear in mid-spring are not particularly conspicuous and can be lost among the compound, evergreen leaves, only the vanilla scent indicating their presence.

Where two plants are grown in proximity, sausage-shaped, purple fruits can develop in autumn. H and S 4m (13ft). Hardy/Z 4–9.

## BOUGAINVILLEA

These half-hardy evergreen climbers are grown not for their flowers, which are inconspicuous, but for the brightly coloured bracts that surround them. The spiny stems have to be tied to a trellis. In a conservatory, plant with caution, because if the conditions are favourable they will be rampant. In warm climates they are impressive over large pergolas or allowed to cascade down banks. Combining them with *Trachelospermum jasminoides* will provide the scent they lack.
*Cultivation* In a conservatory use a loam-based compost and water freely when in active growth. A potash-based fertilizer, applied from spring to early summer, will boost flowering. Keep in full light and allow the temperature to drop no lower than 10°C (50°F).

*Bougainvillea* 'Miss Manila'

### *B.* × *buttiana*

This large hybrid group contains a number of desirable plants, including **'Killie Campbell'**, which has large, coppery-orange bracts with ruffled edges. H and S to 10m (33ft) or more. Half-hardy/Z 10.

### *B.* 'Miss Manila'
(syn. *B.* 'Tango')

The bracts, to 5cm (2in) long, are reddish-pink. H and S to 10m (33ft) or more. Half-hardy/Z 10.

### *B.* 'San Diego Red'
(syn. *B.* 'Hawaiian Scarlet', 'Scarlett O'Hara')

The bracts are bright red shading to orange. H and S to 10m (33ft) or more. Half-hardy/Z 9–10.

## CAMPSIS
### Trumpet vine, trumpet creeper

These climbers with aerial roots are not as widely planted as you might expect, given the attraction of the trumpet-shaped flowers, which are produced from late summer to early autumn. Their lack of popularity is, perhaps, because the blooms are rarely produced in quantity.
*Cultivation* These climbers need any reasonably fertile, well-drained soil and a position in sun.

### *C. radicans*
(syn. *Bignonia radicans*, *Tecoma radicans*)
### Common trumpet creeper

This species from the south-eastern United States has trumpet-shaped, orange-red flowers, which are borne in clusters in late summer. H and S to 10m (33ft). Borderline hardy/Z 5–9.

*Campsis radicans*

### *C.* × *tagliabuana* 'Madame Galen'

A hybrid of considerable vigour, with deep apricot flowers, veined with salmon pink, and lightly hairy leaves. H and S to 10m (33ft). Borderline hardy/Z 4–10.

## CELASTRUS
### Bittersweet, staff vine

Unusually, this twining climber is grown for its colourful berries rather than for the flowers.
*Cultivation* Grow these climbers in fertile, well-drained soil in sun or light shade.

### *C. orbiculatus*
(syn. *C. articulatus*)
### Oriental bittersweet

The starry, greenish summer flowers of this species from eastern Asia are succeeded by yellow berries, which split to reveal vivid red seeds. Both male and female plants are required to ensure good fruiting. **'Diana'** is female, **'Hercules'** is male, but if you have room for only one plant, look for one from the **Hermaphrodite Group**. H and S to 10m (33ft) or more. Hardy/Z 5–8.

## CLEMATIS

This huge genus of leaf-stalk climbers includes a few herbaceous perennials, and there are also a few non-climbing, sprawling types. There is a clematis for virtually every season of the year. Both species and hybrids are usually divided into three groups, depending on the flowering season. Group 1 clematis flower from the start of the year to late spring on growth made during the previous season. Group 2 clematis flower twice: first in late spring on the previous season's growth and later, in mid- to late summer, on the current season's growth. This group includes some double-flowered hybrids, although only the flowers borne in the first flush are double. Group 3 clematis flower from midsummer to early autumn on the current season's growth.

Best known are the large-flowered hybrids, which are excellent for growing against walls and fences. Some have plate-like flowers, but the viticella hybrids have smaller flowers, and the texensis types are like miniature tulips. There are a number of hybrids that make an even daintier effect. The species are all effective over pergolas and when allowed to romp through trees. The non-climbing clematis described below do not twine but have long, flexible, sprawling stems. They can be used to flop into other plants, or they can be fan-trained against walls and fences. When planting clematis, always bury the stems to a depth of up to 15cm (6in) to encourage stem rooting, which will enhance the plant's overall vigour.
*Cultivation* Grow clematis in any well-drained soil (although they seem to do best in alkaline conditions) in sun or light shade, with shade at the roots.

Prune as follows. Group 1 clematis require no regular pruning, but congested plants can, if necessary, be thinned after flowering. Harder pruning is tolerated, but the next year's flowering will be impaired. On Group 2 clematis thin congested growth in late winter, cutting back old stems to the base and shortening others as necessary, bearing in mind that these will carry the current season's flowers. Deadhead after the first flush of flowers. For a single flush of late flowers, treat as for Group 3 (although double cultivars will produce single flowers only). Prune Group 3 clematis in late winter (early spring for texensis and viticella types), cutting back all stems to near ground level. Species and very vigorous hybrids can be also be left unpruned, depending on the effect required.

*Clematis florida* 'Sieboldii'

### C. alpina (Group 1)
### Alpine clematis
This dainty species has nodding, bell-shaped, blue flowers from spring to early summer. Selections include 'Frances Rivis', which has white-centred, mid-blue flowers with slightly twisted petals; and 'Helsinborg', which has deep purple-blue flowers. H 3m (10ft), S 1.5m (5ft). Hardy/Z 7–9.

### C. armandii (Group 1)
This species, one of the few ever-green clematis, has long, leathery, dark green leaves and clusters of scented, white flowers in spring. A vigorous plant, it is best trained against a warm wall in cold areas. Selections include 'Apple Blossom', which has flowers that are initially pale pink; and 'Snowdrift', with pure white flowers that are larger than the type. H and S to 9m (30ft). Borderline hardy/Z 7–9.

### C. cirrhosa (Group 1)
### Fern-leaved clematis
This is usually the first of the

*Clematis armandii* 'Snowdrift'

clematis to flower: according to most books it begins to bloom in midwinter, but occasional flowers can be produced as early as autumn. These are bell-shaped, with a papery texture, and are creamy-white in colour, sometimes speckled with brownish-red inside. H 3m (10ft), S 1.5m (5ft). Hardy/Z 7–9, but best in a warm, sheltered position.

### C. flammula (Group 3)
Masses of fragrant, star-like, white flowers cover the plant in late summer and early autumn. This is tolerant of poor soil and is excellent for growing through a tree. H 6m (20ft), S 3m (10ft). Borderline hardy/Z 7–9.

### C. florida (Group 2)
This elegant species has two outstanding selections, both producing two flushes of passionflower-like flowers. 'Flore Pleno' has double, greenish-white flowers; 'Sieboldii' has creamy-white flowers with a central boss

of rich purple stamens. Both are weak-growing and need a warm, sheltered spot and fertile soil. H 2m (6ft), S 1m (3ft). Borderline hardy/Z 6–9.

### C. macropetala (Group 1)
The bell-shaped flowers of this species, which appear in mid- to late spring, have only four petals, but appear to be double because some of the stamens are petal-like. They are blue or violet-blue. H 3m (10ft), S 1.5m (5ft). 'Blue Bird' has semi-double, clear blue flowers. The charming 'White Moth' (syn. *C. alpina* 'White Moth') has pure white flowers. Hardy/Z 6–9.

### C. montana (Group 1)
The most vigorous of the early clematis, this is the last to flower, with white flowers appearing in late spring. H 5–8m (15–25ft), S 3m (10ft). Hardy/Z 6–9. Selections include the long flowering 'Continuity' – hence the name – with creamy-white, pink-tinged flowers; 'Elizabeth', which has pale pink, richly scented flowers; and the vigorous *C. montana* f. *grandiflora*, which bears many white flowers.

### C. rehderiana (Group 3)
This vigorous species produces a mass of bell-shaped, creamy yellow, cowslip-scented flowers in late summer. This is an excellent choice for growing into a sturdy tree. H 6m (20ft), S 3m (10ft). Hardy/Z 6–9.

### C. tangutica (Group 3)
This species produces bright yellow, lantern-like flowers with pointed sepals and a prominent central boss of stamens, which are borne from midsummer to autumn and are followed by silky, silvery grey seedheads. There is much confusion between this species and the roughly similar *C. tibetana*, which will hybridize with it freely. H 6m (20ft), S 3m (10ft). Hardy/Z 6–9.

### Hybrids
The following are large-flowered clematis, H and S around 2.4m (8ft) unless otherwise indicated. All are hardy/Z 4–9.

*Clematis montana* 'Continuity'

*Clematis montana* 'Elizabeth'

Clematis 'Allanah'

## Group 2 clematis

'Barbara Dibley' has bright cerise-pink flowers with darker barring; 'Bees' Jubilee' is deep mauve-pink, aging lighter, and is best in shade; 'Duchess of Edinburgh' is weak-growing with double, dahlia-like, white flowers; the spectacular 'Fireworks' has luminous violet flowers with mauve-carmine bars; 'Gillian Blades' has large white flowers; 'Lasurstern' has mauve-blue flowers, fading to silvery mauve; 'John Warren' has pale greyish-pink flowers, which are veined and edged with deeper pink; 'Marie Boisselot' (syn. 'Mme le Coultre') is a free-flowering plant with pure white flowers with overlapping sepals; 'Mrs Cholmondeley' produces pale lavender-blue flowers over a long period; 'Mrs George Jackman' has creamy-white flowers, the first flush of which are semi-double; the well-known 'Nelly Moser' has pinkish-mauve flowers with carmine bars; 'Silver Moon' has

Clematis 'Gravetye Beauty'

gleaming lavender-white flowers; 'Royalty' has purplish-mauve flowers, the first flush of which are semi-double; 'Vyvyan Pennell' has rich lilac-blue flowers, the first flush of which are double.

## Group 3 clematis

The sepals of the bright ruby red 'Allanah' do not overlap; the non-climbing *C.* × *aromatica* has small, fragrant, deep-violet flowers; 'Bill Mackenzie' has bright yellow, thick-textured, lantern-like flowers, which are followed by fluffy seedheads, H 7m (23ft), S 3m (10ft); 'Duchess of Albany' (texensis) has warm pink flowers banded with red; 'Gravetye Beauty' (texensis) produces red flowers with pink reverses to the sepals; the dainty 'Huldine' (viticella) has pearly white flowers with recurving sepals; 'Jackmanii', one of the most popular of all the hybrids, has purple flowers; the rich purple flowers of 'Jackmanii Superba' are darker than those of 'Jackmanii'; the non-climbing *C.* × *jouiana* 'Praecox' has small, pale purplish-blue flowers overlaid with silver; 'Kermesina' (viticella) has deep crimson flowers; 'Pagoda' (texensis) has warm pinkish-red flowers; the fully double, very distinctive flowers of 'Purpurea Plena Elegans' (viticella) are deep purplish-pink; 'Rouge Cardinal' has dusky red flowers; the flowers of 'Royal Velours' (viticella) are a deep velvety purplish-red; the young shoots of *C.* × *triternata* 'Rubromarginata', which has small, fragrant, pink flowers, are often decimated by slugs and snails; 'Victoria' has rose-purple flowers, fading to mauve; the flowers of 'Ville de Lyon' (viticella) are deep pinkish red.

## CLIANTHUS

Hardy in only the most favoured spots, clianthus have intriguing, claw-like flowers. Though not strictly climbers, these plants have arching stems that are easily and effectively, if the flowers are to be enjoyed to the full, trained in a fan shape. They can also be grown in cool conservatories (porches).
*Cultivation* Grow in well-drained soil in sun, siting against a warm wall in cold areas.

Eccremocarpus scaber

### C. puniceus
Lobster claw, parrot's bill, glory pea
This species, the commonest in cultivation, produces its flowers in late spring to early summer, usually in shades of gleaming red. Selections include 'Albus', which has exquisite ivory white flowers touched with green; and 'Roseus' (syn. 'Flamingo'), which has deep rose red flowers. H 4m (13ft), S 3m (10ft). Borderline hardy/Z 8.

## ECCREMOCARPUS
Chilean glory vine
The species described is often grown as an annual, but it is a truly perennial plant, albeit not evergreen in cold winters, when it dies back to ground level. It looks effective when allowed to wander through a hedge.
*Cultivation* Grow in well-drained soil in sun. This species can also be grown in a container in an unheated conservatory.

### E. scaber
The tubular orange flowers appear over a long period from summer right until the first frosts of autumn. H 3m (10ft), S 1m (3ft). Borderline hardy/Z 7–9.

## FALLOPIA
The species described is one of the most rampant of all garden plants. Known as the mile-a-minute plant, it is recommended with caution. Nevertheless, it is unmatched for covering an unsightly outbuilding in record time, but any attempt to restrain its vigour is futile – it is a bottom-of-the-garden plant.

Hedera canariensis 'Gloire de Marengo'

*Cultivation* This will grow in any reasonable garden soil, in sun or light shade.

### F. baldschuanicum
(syn. *Bilderdykia aubertii*, *Fallopia aubertii*, *Polygonum baldschuanicum*)
Russian vine, mile-a-minute plant
This species' chief claim to ornamental value lies in its generous sprays of tiny white flowers, borne in late summer. H and S 15m (50ft). Hardy/Z 5–9.

## HEDERA
Ivy
These self-clinging climbers are among the most useful of garden plants, but their positive virtues are easily overlooked. *H. helix* is virtually a weed in some gardens, which should not blind you to the beauties of some of its cultivars. All ivies provide excellent evergreen cover for walls and fences, and can also do well as groundcover in the dry soil under trees where little else will grow. Another attractive use is trailing over banks with other plants, such as groundcover roses.
*Cultivation* Most ivies do well in any reasonable (preferably alkaline) soil in shade. Variegated ivies tend to produce plain green shoots in acid soil; large-leaved forms do best in sun.

### H. canariensis
Canary Island ivy, North African ivy
Some confusion surrounds the naming of this species, which is variously listed as *H. algeriensis*, *H. canariensis* var. *algeriensis* or *H. canariensis* of gardens. No matter

what it is called, the plain green species is hardly a true garden plant, and it is usually represented by one of the following selections. **'Gloire de Marengo'** has green leaves irregularly margined with cream. H and S to 4m (13ft). **'Marginomaculata'** is a dramatic plant, if none too hardy, with leaves marbled and spotted with cream and green. It is sometimes grown as a houseplant. H and S to 4m (13ft). **'Ravensholt'** has very large, shiny, green leaves on red stems. H and S to 5m (16ft). Borderline hardy/Z 8.

### H. colchica
#### Persian ivy
The species from northern Iran and the Caucasus is usually encountered in the form of one of the following. **'Dentata'** has enormous, dull green leaves, occasionally notched at the edges. H and S 5m (16ft) or more. The leaves of **'Sulphur Heart'** (syn. 'Paddy's Pride') are irregularly marked with yellowish-green at the centre. H and S 5m (16ft). Hardy/Z 6–9.

### H. helix
#### Common ivy, English ivy
The species is common in hedgerows and on waste ground but is seldom cultivated as a garden plant. It has a huge number of cultivars. These ivies are easily controlled by pruning. All are hardy/Z 5–9 unless otherwise stated. **'Ambrosia'** has small, slightly curled and twisted leaves, lightly variegated with cream. H and S 1.2m (4ft). Hardy/Z 5. The young leaves of **'Angularis**

*Hedera helix* 'Buttercup'

Aurea'** are bright golden yellow, becoming mottled with green as they age. H and S 4m (13ft). The leaves of **'Boskoop'**, a good houseplant, are claw-like. H and S 1m (3ft). Borderline hardy/Z 6. **'Bruder Ingobert'**, also good as a houseplant or in a hanging basket, has variably shaped leaves that are deep grey-green edged with creamy white. H and S 1m (3ft). Borderline hardy/Z 6. **'Buttercup'** produces its best leaf colour, a rich golden yellow, where it is in sun for at least half the day. H and S 2m (6ft). The mid-green leaves of **'Chicago Variegated'** are variegated with pale yellow. H and S 3m (10ft). The aptly named **'Curvaceous'** is a variegated sport of 'Manda's Crested', with wavy-edged, mid-green-grey leaves with cream margins. H and S 2m (6ft). **'Duckfoot'** has a bushy habit and is good for edging a border. H and S 1m (3ft). Among the variegated forms, **'Eva'** is outstanding, with leaves margined

with creamy yellow. It is good for hanging baskets and as a houseplant. H and S 1.2m (4ft). Borderline hardy/Z 8–9. The young leaves of **'Fantasia'** are cream, heavily speckled with green, turning plain green as they age. H and S 1.2m (4ft). Borderline hardy/Z 8. **'Glacier'** has grey-green leaves edged creamy white. H and S 2m (6ft). **'Green Ripple'** is a vigorous form suitable for groundcover. H and S 2m (6ft). The leaves of **'Jersey Doris'** emerge creamy white, developing green speckling before turning solid green. It is best grown in full light. H and S 1.2m (4ft). Hardy/Z 6. **'Little Luzii'** is excellent in flower arrangements and at the edge of a windowbox. The creamy gold leaves are mottled with green and hold their colour well. H and S 1m (3ft). Borderline hardy/Z 6. **'Manda's Crested'** was the first of the curly ivies. It has forked plain green leaves that turn bronze in winter. H and S 2m (6ft). The slow-growing **'Midas Touch'** has heart-shaped leaves that are basically dark green with patches of lighter green and irregularly blotched with yellow. It can scorch in an exposed site. H and S 1m (3ft). **'Oro di Bogliasco'** (syn. 'Goldheart') is very hardy, and the leaves retain their generous central golden-yellow blotch even in shade. H and S 2.2m (7ft) or more. **'Parsley Crested'** is an attractive ivy with rounded leaves that are crested at the edges and turn bronze in cold weather. It is good in a hanging basket. H and S 2m (6ft). **'Pedata'** (syn. 'Caenwoodiana') has distinctive, narrowly lobed, dark green leaves veined with greyish white. It is best against a wall. H and S 4m (13ft). **'Perkeo'** has unusual puckered leaves that are light green and turn red in cold weather. H and S 45cm (18in). Borderline hardy/Z 6–9. The leaves of **'Sagittifolia Variegata'** are variegated with golden yellow. This is a good ivy for the front of a windowbox, and it needs good light. H and S 1m (3ft). **'Spetchley'** is the smallest ivy available, with densely packed leaves that turn wine red in cold

*Hedera colchica*

weather. It is good as groundcover. H and S 30cm (1ft). Borderline hardy/Z 5. **'Triton'** (syn. 'Green Feather'), an eye-catching ivy, is a sprawling plant with deeply cut leaves. The three central lobes are elongated and twisted. H and S 45cm (18in).

## HUMULUS
### Hop
This is a commercially important genus, because hops are used to make beer, so providing one plant of interest to gardeners for its glowing foliage.
*Cultivation* Grow in any reasonably fertile, well-drained soil. The form described needs full sun for the best leaf colour.

### H. lupulus
The straight species, a herbaceous twining climber, is not worth growing, but the selection **'Aureus'** is an outstanding plant wherever a curtain of foliage is needed. H and S to 6m (20ft). Hardy/Z 6–9.

*Hedera helix* 'Bruder Ingobert'

*Hedera helix* 'Pedata'

*Humulus lupulus* 'Aureus'

Jasminum officinale 'Aureum'

Lapageria rosea

Lonicera periclymenum 'Graham Thomas'

# HYDRANGEA

This genus of shrubs also includes the outstanding climber described below, its single drawback being its reluctance to put on growth when young. Mature specimens are spectacular, grown either against walls or into trees.
*Cultivation* Hydrangeas tolerate a range of soil types, but the climbing species described does best in humus-rich, reliably moist soil in light shade.

### H. anomala subsp. petiolaris
This self-clinging climber has creamy white 'lacecap' flowers in early summer. H and S 4m (13ft). Hardy/Z 4–9.

# JASMINUM
### Jasmine
For many gardeners, the heady scent of jasmine epitomizes summer; indeed, it can become almost overpowering. The winter jasmine has no scent, although the brilliant yellow flowers are undoubtedly welcome in the depths of winter.

*Cultivation* Grow in any well-drained soil in sun or light shade.

### J. nudiflorum
### Winter jasmine
Not strictly climbing, the stems of this Chinese species are lax and trailing. It can be trained against a wall or allowed to cascade down a bank. The cheery bright yellow flowers open during warm spells on the bare branches from late autumn to early spring. H and S 2m (6ft) or more. Hardy/Z 6–9.

### J. officinale
### Common white jasmine
This, the best-known species, is a twining climber with deliciously scented white flowers from midsummer to early autumn. 'Aureum' has leaves splashed with golden yellow. H and S to 5m (16ft). Borderline hardy/Z 9–10.

# LAPAGERIA
A beautiful plant for a cool conservatory (porch) named after Empress Josephine, whose original name was Josephine de la Pagerie. There is only one species.
*Cultivation* Lapagerias need lime-free soil or potting compost (soil mix) in a lightly shaded position.

### L. rosea
### Chilean bellflower
This evergreen, twining climber has elongated bell-like, rich pinkish-red flowers that hang from the stems in late summer and autumn. H and S 3m (10ft), often less in a container. Half-hardy/Z 9–11. *L. rosea* var. *albiflora*, with white flowers, is possibly lovelier. H and S 3m (10ft). Borderline hardy/Z 10.

# LATHYRUS
A large genus that includes many deliciously scented annuals and shrubs, as well as the delightful and easy-to-grow herbaceous tendril climbers described here. They are charming if allowed to wander through a hedge, but they can also be used more formally on tripods to give height to mixed borders. The flowers resemble those of the annual sweet peas.
*Cultivation* Grow in any well-drained soil in sun or light shade.

### L. grandiflorus
### Everlasting pea
This suckering species has glowing pinkish-purple flowers in summer and is good in a wild garden. H and S 2m (6ft). Hardy/Z 6–9.

### L. latifolius
### Everlasting pea
The species has vivid magenta flowers. Selections include the vigorous 'Rosa Pearl', which has pink flowers, and 'White Pearl', which has pure white flowers. H and S 3m (10ft). Hardy/Z 8–9.

# LONICERA
### Honeysuckle, woodbine
The scent of the honeysuckle is unmistakable, and fortunately can be enjoyed twice a year, since there are both early- and late-flowering varieties. These twining plants can make mounds and become congested with time. Although they can be used to cover walls and fences, they are at their best when grown more informally in a woodland or wild garden.
*Cultivation* Honeysuckles will do well in any soil that is not too dry, in a position where the roots are in shade.

### L. periclymenum
### Woodbine
This is a common woodlander throughout Europe and has deliciously scented, creamy-white flowers in summer. H and S 3m (10ft) or more. Hardy/Z 5–9. 'Belgica' (early Dutch honey-suckle) has pink and red flowers in midsummer, followed by red berries. 'Graham Thomas' bears

Hydrangea anomala subsp. petiolaris

Lathyrus latifolius 'White Pearl'

Lathyrus grandiflorus

Monstera deliciosa

copper-tinted, creamy flowers all summer long. 'Serotina' (late Dutch honeysuckle) has purple and red flowers from midsummer to autumn. Hardy/Z 5–9.

*L. × tellmanniana*
This hybrid would no doubt be more widely appreciated were it not for the lack of the characteristic honeysuckle scent – a drawback in the eyes of some. This is more than compensated for by the large, rich amber-orange flowers that appear in early summer, lighting up shady areas of the garden. H and S 3m (10ft). Hardy/Z 7–9.

## MONSTERA
**Swiss cheese plant**
Popular as a houseplant, the species described here is rarely given sufficient headroom to show what it is really made of. Although tolerant enough to withstand the central heating of most living rooms, it is at its superb best in a large conservatory or greenhouse and can be used to shade orchids.
*Cultivation* Grow in large pots of preferably loam-based compost in light shade and mist daily to simulate rainforest conditions.

*M. deliciosa*
**Swiss cheese plant**
The common name refers to the holes that develop in the large glossy leaves as they mature. This is a scrambling plant that needs tying to its support. As it climbs higher it develops aerial roots, which can trail down to the ground. It seldom flowers in

cultivation. H 3m (10ft), S 2m (6ft), but can be considerably more. 'Variegata' is a desirable selection, the leaves of which are splashed with creamy white. Tender/Z 10.

## MUTISIA
These tendril climbers are not reliably hardy in cold areas, but they can be grown in an unheated conservatory.
*Cultivation* Grow in almost any well-drained soil in a sunny, sheltered site. In cold areas, train against a warm wall or grow under glass.

*M. decurrens*
A real connoisseur's plant, this has brilliant orange, daisy flowers in summer. H 3m (10ft), S 2m (6ft). Borderline hardy/Z 9–10.

## PARTHENOCISSUS
These foliage plants are grown mainly for their spectacular autumn colour. All the species described here cling by means of suckering pads and are excellent on walls.
*Cultivation* Grow in fertile, well-drained soil in sun or light shade.

*P. henryana*
**(syn. *Vitis henryana*)**
**Chinese Virginia creeper**
This species has dark green leaves that are distinctively marked with central silvery white veins; they turn red in autumn. H and S to 10m (30ft). Borderline hardy/Z 7–9.

*P. quinquefolia*
**(syn. *Vitis quinquefolia*)**
**Virginia creeper**
This species is well known by its common name, its claim to garden merit lying in its vivid red autumn leaf colour. Eye-catching as cover for a large wall, it can also be dramatic weaving through the branches of a large tree, such as a silver birch. H and S 15m (50ft). Hardy/Z 4–9.

*P. tricuspidata*
**Boston ivy**
This vigorous species has maple-like green leaves that turn rich orange-red in autumn. H and S 15m (50ft). 'Beverley Brook' is less vigorous and has smaller

Parthenocissus quinquefolia

leaves. The leaves of 'Lowii' are tinged with purple when they emerge. The leaves of 'Veitchii' open purple, mature to green, then turn red-purple in autumn. Hardy/Z 5–9.

## PASSIFLORA
**Passionflower**
The range of these tendril climbers has increased considerably over the past few years, and a number of new forms, mostly conservatory plants, have been introduced. The flowers are highly distinctive: ten outer petals surround a crown of central filaments, inside which are the prominent stamens and styles.
*Cultivation* The hardy *P. caerulea* can be grown in any well-drained soil in sun in a sheltered position. Conservatory plants need to be in large pots of fertile compost with some protection from hot sun.

*P. caerulea*
This species can be evergreen, but if cut down by frosts will usually

Passiflora caerulea 'Constance Elliot'

Passiflora caerulea

regenerate from ground level. The summer flowers are white, with filaments banded blue, white and purple. H and S to 10m (30ft), but generally much less in cool climates. 'Constance Elliot' has fragrant, creamy white flowers with red stigmas. Borderline hardy/Z 7–9.

*P. quadrangularis*
**Giant granadilla**
This South American species produces large, fragrant flowers in summer, with striking, twisted, violet and white filaments. H and S 10m (30ft), less in a container. Tender/Z 10.

## PHILODENDRON
Well known as houseplants, the two root-climbing, evergreen species described here are fine foliage plants, which look good trained up moss poles.
*Cultivation* Use standard potting compost and keep sheltered from direct bright sunlight. Winter temperatures should not fall below 15°C (59°F).

*P. melanochrysum*
**(syn. *P. andreasum*)**
**Black-gold philodendron, velour philodendron**
This Colombian species has velvety textured, heart-shaped leaves, with a pronounced coppery tint when young. They can be up to 1m (3ft) long and 30cm (1ft) across. H 3m (10ft), generally much less as a container plant. Tender/Z 10.

*P. scandens*
**Sweetheart vine, heart leaf**
This well-known houseplant has shiny, mid-green, heart-shaped leaves with pointed tips. H and S 3m (10ft), but easily restrained. Tender/Z 10.

Pileostegia viburnoides

Schisandra rubrifolia

Solanum crispum 'Glasnevin'

## PILEOSTEGIA

The evergreen species described is a dramatic root climber related to *Hydrangea*. The fact that it is not reliably hardy has probably kept it out of most gardens, but it is well worth trying in a sheltered situation, either growing up a tree trunk or across a wall.
*Cultivation* Grow in any reasonably fertile soil in sun or light shade with some shelter from severe cold.

### P. viburnoides

This self-clinging climber from China and India has glossy, leathery leaves and clusters of small creamy-white flowers in late summer and autumn. H and S to 6m (20ft). Borderline hardy/Z 7–10.

## PLUMBAGO
### Leadwort

These South African climbers are grown for their flowers, which are mostly an appealing clear blue, although there are also white forms. The plants do not climb unaided but need to be tied to some form of support.
*Cultivation* Grow in pots of high-fertility compost such as John Innes No. 3 (loam-based soil mix) and keep in a sunny or lightly shaded spot.

### P. auriculata
(syn. *P. capensis*)
**Cape leadwort**
The clusters of pale sky-blue flowers are produced from summer to early winter. H and S 1.5m (5ft) or more in a favourable site. Tender/Z 9–10.

## SCHISANDRA

These twining climbers are hardy but seem to do best in sheltered gardens. They are delightful when grown so that they can climb into trees in light woodland or against walls, but the species described has one drawback for owners of small gardens: for reliable fruiting, plants of both sexes must be grown in proximity.
*Cultivation* Grow in sun or light shade in fertile soil that does not dry out excessively.

### S. rubrifolia

This twining species produces scarlet to dark red flowers in early summer, followed, on female plants, by red berries. H and S 10m (30ft). Hardy/Z 8–10.

## SOLANUM

These delightful climbers deserve to be better known. They produce an abundance of potato flowers over a long period and are generally easy in cultivation. Both the species described are lax

Plumbago auriculata

climbers, which need to be tied to their supports.
*Cultivation* Grow solanums in any well-drained soil in full sun.

### S. crispum
**Chilean potato tree**
This species, which can be evergreen, is usually represented in cultivation by the form 'Glasnevin', which is reputedly hardier. The deep blue flowers, with prominent central yellow 'beaks', are carried in clusters over many weeks in summer. H and S to 5m (16ft). Borderline hardy/Z 8–9.

### S. jasminoides
**Potato vine**
The straight species has grubby, grey flowers, but the selection 'Album' is a real beauty, with yellow-centred, white flowers. In cold areas, this is best trained against a warm wall. A harsh winter may kill the topgrowth, but it should recover if the base of the plant is protected with a dry mulch. H and S 3m (10ft). Half-hardy/Z 8–10.

## STEPHANOTIS

A lovely plant for a conservatory (porch) or as a houseplant, the species described has richly scented, waxy white flowers.
*Cultivation* Use standard potting compost and keep in good light, but not direct sunlight. In winter, the temperature should not drop below 13°C (55°F).

### S. floribunda
**Bridal wreath, floradora**
This twining evergreen has thick,

glossy, pointed leaves and can flower at any time when in growth. H and S to 3m (10ft), but usually much less when container-grown. Tender/Z 10.

## THUNBERGIA
### Clock vine

These climbers are too tender to grow outdoors in any but frost-free gardens, but the twining species described can be treated as an annual. In addition to providing temporary cover against a small trellis, it is also effective on tripods in borders or containers or allowed to trail without support from a hanging basket or large trough.
*Cultivation* Thunbergias will grow in any reasonable garden soil – or standard potting compost (soil mix) for container-grown plants – in a warm, sunny spot.

### T. alata
**Black-eyed Susan**
The simple yellow or orange flowers, produced over a long period during summer and into autumn, have pronounced dark purple-brown throats – hence the common name. H to 2m (6ft), S 25cm (10in) or more if grown as a perennial. Tender/Z 10.

## TRACHELOSPERMUM

The genus contains about 20 species, and the one described is among the most worthwhile of all climbers, with attractive, evergreen leaves and a long succession of small but incomparably scented flowers from summer until autumn. It deserves a prime spot in any garden and makes an excellent companion to *Bougainvillea* in a frost-free climate.
*Cultivation* Grow in sun or light shade in any well-drained soil. In a cold climate, train against a warm wall.

### T. jasminoides
**Star jasmine, confederate jasmine**
This species from China and Japan has leathery, pointed, glossy green leaves on twining stems, although these need tying to their support initially. The white flowers are curiously twisted. H to 9m (30ft), but usually much less in cold climates. Borderline hardy/Z 8–10.

Trachelospermum jasminoides

Tropaeolum speciosum

Vitis vinifera 'Purpurea'

## TROPAEOLUM

As well as the highly desirable climber described here, the genus includes the popular annual nasturtiums. A yew hedge festooned with this plant is an eye-catching sight in late summer, but it does not always prove easy to establish in gardens, a cool, damp climate appearing to suit it best.
*Cultivation* Grow in reliably moist, lime-free soil in sun or light shade. It does not like hot, dry conditions.

### T. speciosum
#### Scottish flame flower, flame creeper
The common names of this herbaceous perennial make appropriate reference to the colour of the brilliant red flowers, which appear throughout the summer. H and S to 3m (10ft). Borderline hardy/ Z 7–9.

## VITIS

This genus of tendril climbers is important commercially for the production of grapes, both for the table and for wine-making. The plants described here are principally of ornamental value and are good for covering walls or clothing pergolas.
*Cultivation* Grow in poor soil in sun.

### V. 'Brant'
This vigorous and attractive hybrid is a value-added plant in that its bloomy purple-black grapes are edible; these ripen in autumn as the leaves, which are veined yellow-green, turn dark purple-red. H and S to 12m (40ft) or more. Hardy/Z 5–9.

### V. coignetiae
#### Crimson glory vine
This species from Japan and Korea is really valued for its spectacular autumn leaf colour – yellow, orange and deep scarlet – although it also produces crops of inedible, bloom-covered black grapes. H and S 15m (50ft). Hardy/Z 5–9.

### V. vinifera
#### Tenturier grape
The species is the parent of the many varieties grown for edible crops and also of a number of purely ornamental selections. 'Purpurea' is one of the most widely grown. The leaves mature to purple, then develop even richer hues in autumn as the blackish, unpalatable fruits ripen. H and S 9m (30ft). Hardy/Z 6–9.

## WISTERIA

Possibly the most desirable of all flowering climbers, wisterias bear dramatic racemes of scented pea flowers in late spring to early summer. Old specimens trained against house walls are breathtaking, as are those trained to embrace arching bridges over water. They are also spectacular trained over arches, pergolas or – in a less formal garden – allowed to ramp into sturdy host trees. When shopping for wisterias, look for named varieties grafted on to vigorous rootstocks, expensive though these are. Seed-raised wisterias often have poor flowers, and plants raised from cuttings can lack vigour.
*Cultivation* Grow in any deep, fertile, well-drained soil in sun or light shade. Although fully hardy, they flower best when trained hard against a warm wall to ripen the stems. Prune young plants each year in late summer, cutting back any of the current year's growth that exceeds the allotted space and tying in suitably placed new stems to fill in the framework. Once the framework is established, in late summer cut back all stems that exceed the framework. Shorten laterals to five or six leaves. In midwinter, cut these back further to two or three buds from the base of the stem. These are the spurs that will carry the flowers.

### W. floribunda
#### Japanese wisteria
The species has hanging racemes, up to 30cm (12in) long, of fragrant, violet-blue flowers in early summer. Selections include 'Alba' (syn. 'Snow Showers', *W. multijuga* 'Alba'), a desirable white-flowered form; 'Kuchi-beni' (syn. 'Lipstick', 'Peaches and Cream'), which has lilac-pink and white flowers; and 'Multijuga' (syn. 'Longissima', 'Macrobotrys'), which bears purple flowers in racemes to 60cm (2ft)long. H and S to 9m (30ft). Hardy/ Z 4–10.

### W. × formosa
This hybrid group includes one of the most dramatic of all wisterias, 'Yae-kokuryû' (syn. 'Black Dragon', 'Kokuryû'), which produces long, hanging racemes of rich purple, double flowers. H and S to 9m (30ft). Hardy/ Z 6–9.

### W. sinensis
#### Chinese wisteria
This wisteria is somewhat more vigorous than the Japanese species. In its typical form, it has faintly-scented violet-blue flowers in late spring; 'Alba' has white flowers; and 'Caroline' has fragrant, deep blue-purple flowers. H 15m (50ft)or more, S 9m (30ft). Hardy/Z 5–9.

Vitis 'Brant'

Wisteria floribunda 'Kuchi-beni'

Wisteria sinensis

# Roses

As a garden plant, the rose is unrivalled. Few other plants have attracted so much attention from breeders and down the ages they have epitomized the summer garden. From the uncomplicated charm of the species to the sophistication of the hybrid teas, there is a rose for virtually every purpose, as hedging, to give weight and substance to borders, as specimens or to provide cut flowers. The climbers provide magnificent cover for walls and pergolas, while nowadays the range has been extended to include tough, compact, disease-resistant plants that are excellent as ground cover or for growing in containers.

Elegant hybrid tea roses are esssential plants for any cottage garden scheme, here combining well with phlox and other border perennials.

# What is a rose?

Roses are a breed apart. No other plant genus has been so extensively hybridized to produce the wide range of plants that we enjoy in gardens today.

Roses are shrubs, mainly deciduous ones. In the wild, some make huge plants, colonizing vast areas and finding their way into trees, hooking themselves into the bark by means of their thorns.

## Rose classification

The classification of roses represents an attempt to bring some order to a vast and diverse range of plants. However, in many cases, the distinctions are far from clear cut. Roses are generally classified as follows:

### Wild roses

These comprise the species, their selections and certain hybrids. They usually have one flush of single flowers in early summer, often followed by decorative hips in autumn.

### Old roses

● *Bourbon roses* are vigorous, and are usually repeat-flowering. They are often suitable for training as short climbers. *Portland roses* are similar, but repeat more reliably and generally make smaller plants.
● *Centifolia roses* (sometimes also called cabbage, Provence or Holland roses) make lax shrubs with large, many-petalled flowers that weigh down the arching canes. *Moss roses* are a closely allied group, distinguished by the characteristic mossy growth on their stems and calyces.
● *China roses* are dainty, repeat-flowering shrubs with small flowers and leaves. *Tea roses*, also repeat-flowering, are thin-stemmed with slender, pointed flower buds. Few are hardy enough to be grown outdoors in cold areas.

Correctly supported, many a climbing rose will reach the eaves of a house and be smothered in flowers in summer.

● *Damask roses* are lax, spreading shrubs, usually with fragrant flowers in clear colours. The leaves are typically greyish green and are downy underneath.

## Flower shapes

*Flat flowers* are single (five petals) or semi-double (ten petals) and open flat.
*Cupped flowers* are single to fully double, with curving petals.
*Rounded flowers* have a rounded outline formed by overlapping petals.
*Rosette flowers* are low-centred and flat, with many short, crowded petals.
*Quartered rosette flowers* are similar to rosettes, but the petals are arranged in distinctive quarters.
*Pointed and urn-shaped flowers*, characteristic of Chinas, teas and hybrid teas, are high-centred and open from slender, elegant buds.
*Pompon flowers* are small and ball-like with many short petals, and are usually carried in clusters.

● *Gallica roses* are usually upright, compact shrubs with coarse leaves and flowers in shades of pink, rich crimson and purple. The group includes some striped roses.
● *Hybrid perpetuals* are vigorous and usually repeat-flowering. They tend to be leggy but this is a problem that can be overcome by pegging down the lax shoots.
● *Scotch roses* are dense shrubs with *R. pimpinellifolia* in their make-up.

## Modern roses

● *Climbing roses* usually have long, stiff stems that make them suitable for training. The flowers, similar to those of hybrid teas and floribundas in appearance, are produced in one or – more usually – two flushes.
● *Floribunda* or *cluster-flowered roses* are repeat-flowering, with single to fully double flowers in clusters.
● *Ground-cover roses* have a lax, trailing habit, rather like miniature climbers. They typically have clusters of small flowers, produced over a long period.
● *Hybrid tea* or *large-flowered roses* are characterized by large, high-centred flowers carried singly (but sometimes in small clusters) that open from pointed buds. They are repeat-flowering. Some are of stiff, ungainly habit.
● *Miniature roses* are compact plants, usually under 30cm (12in) high, with sprays of tiny, usually scentless flowers. They are repeat-flowering.
● *Patio* or *dwarf cluster-flowered bush roses* are similar to floribundas but are much smaller, making them ideal container plants.
● *Polyanthas* are now more or less obsolete. Tough and repeat-flowering, with trusses of small flowers, they are the forebears of the modern floribundas.
● *Rambler roses* are large shrubs of exceptional vigour, with long flexible,

often trailing stems. Typically they flower early in the season on the previous season's wood.

● *Rugosa roses* are tough, hardy shrubs with characteristically wrinkled leaves and single to double flowers in succession throughout summer and autumn. Some have showy autumn hips.

● *Shrub roses* comprise a vast group of plants that do not fit into any of the above categories. They are usually larger than other modern roses and thus less suitable for bedding. Flowers can be single to double and can appear in one or two flushes. This group includes the so-called *English roses*, bred by David Austin, which combine the flower shape of the old roses with the repeat-flowering habit of modern roses.

## Roses in the garden

Many people associate roses with bedding, and while it is true that many of the floribundas and hybrid teas are outstanding in a massed planting, the genus as a whole is much more versatile than that.

Many of the shrub roses are stylish plants that can be planted either as specimens or as elements of a mixed planting, combining happily with a range of other shrubs and perennials. The old roses earn their place in the garden largely on the merits of their sumptuous, usually deliciously scented flowers, as well as the romantic associations of their names – 'Cardinal de Richelieu', 'Duchesse de Montebello', 'Souvenir de la Malmaison', to mention just three.

A surprising number of roses are also excellent for hedging (though not providing an evergreen screen), thorny types making good barrier or boundary hedges. The rugosas are well suited for this purpose.

'Albertine' is an enduring favourite for its incomparable scent, trained here to allow the fragrance to waft through open windows.

The obvious way to grow the climbers and ramblers is by training them against a house wall, fence or over a pergola, but they can also be trained against trellis panels to screen one part of the garden from another. Shorter types can be grown over trellis obelisks or pillars to give height to a border. One of the most dramatic ways of growing climbers and ramblers is into the arms of a tree, but here you must make sure that the host is sturdy enough to bear the weight of the rose – some are vigorous plants that can swamp the tree. Among the most effective are those that bear a close resemblance to the species, such as 'Albéric Barbier' and 'Rambling Rector'.

Many of the more recent introductions make splendid ground cover, not just those defined as "groundcover roses". They are tough plants, handsome even when out of flower. Having been bred to be compact, to suit the modern garden, which tends to be smaller, they are also ideal plants for containers. Excellent health and length of flowering season only add to their merits.

Training the fragrant and long-flowering 'Dublin Bay' to climb up the wooden trellis is an effective and attractive way of screening one part of the garden from another.

### 'Agnes'

An upright, healthy rugosa of undoubted distinction, this bears double, scented, pale yellow flowers in summer, with only a few following in autumn. It combines the toughness of the rugosas with an old-rose look to the flowers. H 2m (6ft), S 1.2m (4ft). Hardy/Z 2–9.

### R. × alba 'Alba Maxima' (syn. R. × alba 'Maxima')

This alba rose dates from the 15th century, or even earlier, and is sometimes assumed to be the white rose of York. It is also a beauty, with untidy, double, very fragrant flowers that are tinged pink on opening in summer, then fade to creamy white. Red hips follow. It is also known as the great white rose, the Jacobite rose or the Cheshire rose. H 2.1m (7ft), S 1.5m (5ft). Hardy/Z 4–9.

### R. × alba 'Alba Semiplena' (syn. 'Semiplena')

An alba rose, this has been grown in gardens since the 16th century or before. It is a graceful shrub with clusters of semi-double, very fragrant, milky white flowers in summer. These open flat to display prominent golden stamens, with red hips making a second display in autumn. 'Alba Semiplena' is usually held to be the white rose of York, competing for that title with R. × alba 'Alba Maxima'. H 2.1m (7ft), S 1.5m (5ft). Hardy/Z 4–9.

### 'Alba Meidiland' (syn. 'Meiflopan')

This is a groundcover rose, and unusually for a rose in this group, the pure white, fully double flowers are good for cutting. H 1m (3ft), S 1.2m (4ft). Hardy/Z 4–9.

### 'Albéric Barbier'

This vigorous rambling rose is a good choice for brightening up a shady wall or a dull tree. In early to midsummer, masses of double, rosette, creamy white, scented flowers cover the plant. To compensate for the lack of further flowers, the glossy leaves often hang on through the winter. H 5m (16ft), S 3m (10ft). Hardy/Z 4–9.

### 'Albertine'

A vigorous rambling rose, this has fully double, light pink flowers, which appear in a single flush in midsummer, opening from copper-tinted buds; they become untidy as they age. The rich, distinctive scent of this rose has assured its continuing popularity, despite its all too obvious drawbacks: its talon-like thorns and propensity to mildew. Thinning the growth after flowering to improve air circulation can help the latter problem. H 5m (16ft), S 4m (12ft). Hardy/Z 4–9.

### 'Alec's Red' (syn. 'Cored')

This is a bushy hybrid tea with fully double, heavily scented, rich red flowers that open from pointed buds throughout summer and into autumn. A versatile rose, it is suitable for cutting, bedding and as a hedge, but blackspot can be a problem. H 1m (3ft), S 60cm (2ft). Hardy/Z 4–9.

### 'Alexander' (syn. 'Harlex')

An upright hybrid tea, this has double, luminous red flowers opening from pointed buds from summer to autumn. The leaves are glossy dark green and show good resistance to disease. The flowers are produced on long stems, which means that this is a good rose for cutting as well as for planting as a tight hedge with little sideways spread. H to 2m (6ft), S 75cm (2ft 6in). Hardy/Z 4–9.

### 'Allgold'

A compact floribunda and an ideal bedding rose, this bears a succession of double, lightly scented, bright yellow flowers from summer to autumn. H 75cm (2ft 6in), S 50cm (20in). Hardy/Z 5–9.

### 'Aloha'

This climbing rose bears a succession of cupped, fully double, sweetly scented, light pink flowers from summer to autumn. The leaves are dark green, leathery and healthy. This is a rain-resistant variety, which is also good in a container. H 3m (10ft), S 2.5m (8ft). Hardy/Z 4–9.

*Rosa* 'Alec's Red'

*Rosa* × *alba* 'Alba Semiplena'

*Rosa* 'Albertine'

Rosa 'Anna Ford'

Rosa 'Apricot Nectar'

Rosa 'Avon'

Rosa 'Baby Masquerade'

## 'Amber Queen'
### (syn. 'Harroony', 'Prinz Eugen van Savoyen')
A neat-growing floribunda, this rose bears clusters of fully double, heavily scented, rich amber-yellow flowers, which open from rounded buds. Its compact habit makes it a good choice for bedding, hedges and containers. H and S 50cm (20in). Hardy/Z 4–9.

## 'Anna Ford'
### (syn. 'Harpiccolo')
This is a dense, low-growing patio rose. The warm orange-red flowers, produced freely from summer to autumn, open flat from pointed buds to reveal yellow centres. One of the earliest of its type, this remains a popular bedding or container rose. H 45cm (18in), S 38cm (15in). Hardy/Z 4–9.

## 'Anne Harkness'
### (syn. 'Harkaramel')
An upright, branching floribunda, this bears large clusters of pointed, urn-shaped, double, soft buff-yellow flowers from late summer to autumn. Spectacular when in full flower, This is a disease-resistant rose that is suitable for bedding, hedging and cutting. H 1.2m (4ft), S 60cm (2ft). Hardy/Z 4–9.

## 'Apricot Nectar'
This bushy floribunda bears tight clusters of large, fully double, sweetly scented, pinkish-buff-apricot flowers from summer to autumn. It is a good hedging rose, but it can be susceptible to mildew from midsummer. H 80cm (32in), S 65cm (26in). Hardy/Z 4–9.

## 'Arthur Bell'
An upright, branching floribunda, this bears clusters of semi-double to double, bright yellow flowers that pale as they age. The scent is outstanding for a rose of this type. This is a versatile rose, suitable for bedding, hedging and containers; the autumn flowering is especially good, making it a good companion for annuals and late-flowering perennials and bulbs. H to 1m (3ft), S 60cm (2ft). Hardy/Z 4–9.

## 'Avon'
### (syn. 'Fairy Lights', 'Poulmulti', 'Sunnyside')
From summer to autumn this compact, spreading groundcover rose bears clusters of small, semi-double, fragrant, pinkish-white flowers, which open flat to reveal golden stamens. Besides its obvious uses for massed planting and as a low hedge, this rose can also be grown successfully in containers. H 30cm (1ft), S 1m (3ft). Hardy/Z 4–9.

## 'Baby Masquerade'
### (syn. 'Baby Carnival', 'Tanba', 'Tanbakede')
Many people believe that this miniature rose is more attractive than its full-sized equivalent. From summer to autumn it carries clusters of tiny, double, rosette-shaped flowers, which open yellow and fade to pink then to deeper red, so that all the colours are present at any one time. The rose is probably seen at its best when grown as a miniature standard. H and S 40cm (16in). Hardy/Z 4–9.

Rosa 'Anne Harkness'

Rosa 'Arthur Bell'

**'Belle de Crécy'**
The quartered-rosette, sweetly scented flowers of this gallica rose are produced in abundance in midsummer. They open rich purple-pink then fade to a greyish pale pink. It has a laxer habit than most other gallicas and its arching stems may require some support; alternatively, simply allow them to trail into neighbouring shrubs. It does not flower as well in poor, light soil. H 1.2m (4ft), S 1m (3ft). Hardy/Z 5.

**'Blairii Number Two'**
In midsummer, this strangely named bourbon, first raised in 1845, carries an abundance of large, cupped, fully double, sweetly scented flowers, which are pale silvery pink with deeper pink centres. However, unlike some other bourbon roses, it produces only a few further blooms in autumn, if any. Untrained, it will grow into an arching shrub about 2.1m (7ft) high and across. Its vigour and flexible canes make it suitable for growing as a pyramid, on a pergola or against a wall, where it can reach 5m (16ft). H 4m (12ft), S 2m (6ft). Hardy/Z 4–9.

**'Blue Moon'**
(syn. 'Blue Monday', 'Mainzer Fastnacht', 'Sissi', 'Tannacht')
An intriguing hybrid tea, this is not one of the best overall, but is worth growing for the individual

*Rosa* 'Belle de Crécy'

flowers. Borne in summer and autumn, they are not blue, as the name implies, but silvery lilac, a colour associated with the old roses. However, the flower form is modern: high-centred and shapely. It is also one of the most sweetly scented of modern roses. 'Blue Moon' needs careful placing in the garden because of its curious colouring; it is perhaps best grown in isolation under glass. H 1m (3ft), S 60cm (2ft). Hardy/Z 4–9. The climbing form is also worth considering, but it needs good cultivation and a site where the flowers will not be bleached by too much sun.

**'Bobbie James'**
One of the most vigorous of ramblers, this rose looks like its wild antecedents. In summer it is covered with clusters of small, white, semi-double flowers that are also sweetly scented. It is a

*Rosa* 'Blue Moon'

good choice for growing into a large tree, and although it would be just as dramatic over a large pergola, its vigour could cause problems. H 10m (33ft), S 6m (20ft). Hardy/Z 5–9.

**'Buff Beauty'**
This is an excellent modern shrub rose or hybrid musk. The name refers to the colour of the cupped, fully double, sweetly scented flowers, which are pale buff-apricot, fading to creamy white in hot sun. They are carried in clusters in two distinct flushes, the autumn flowering being less profuse than the summer. 'Buff Beauty' can be used for hedging but needs the support of horizontal wires, since the canes are often bent down low by the weight of the flowers. Mildew may be a problem in late summer but need not deter you from growing this rose. H and S 1.5m (5ft). Hardy/Z 6–9.

**'Cardinal de Richelieu'**
This grandly named gallica – and one of the most sumptuous – was produced in 1840. It makes a

*Rosa* 'Buff Beauty'

compact bush and will exceed its usual size if the flexible stems are supported. The clusters of scented, dark maroon flowers appear in midsummer; the petals are velvety in texture and reflex as the flowers age to form a ball shape. The stems are well-covered with healthy, dark green leaves. This rose needs fertile, well-drained soil and regular thinning of the old wood to give of its best. H 1m (3ft), S 1.2m (4ft). Hardy/Z 4–9.

**'Cécile Brünner'**
Sometimes identified as the sweetheart rose or Maltese rose, this is a dainty, airy cultivar, which is classified as either a China rose or a polyantha. It flowers over a long period from early summer to mid-autumn, when clusters of elegant, pointed buds open to urn-shaped, delicately scented, pale pink flowers, which become more untidy as as they age. H and S 1m (3ft). Hardy/Z 5–9. A climbing form is available, which is less restrained and easily reaches 6m (20ft) in all

*Rosa* 'Blairii Number Two'

*Rosa* 'Cardinal de Richelieu'

*Rosa* 'Cécile Brünner'

Rosa 'Céleste'

Rosa 'Charles de Mills'

Rosa 'Chinatown'

Rosa 'Complicata'

directions; it is ideal for growing into a tree. The white-flowered bush form 'White Cécile Brünner' is rare.

### 'Céleste'
### (syn. *R. × alba* 'Celestial')
The date of the introduction of this Alba rose is unrecorded, but it is certainly a very old cultivar, perhaps dating back to ancient times. The semi-double, sweetly scented, shell-pink flowers, with petals that seem almost transparent, are borne in summer and open flat to reveal prominent golden stamens. Red hips succeed them in autumn. H and S 2m (6ft). Hardy/Z 4–9.

### *R. × centifolia* 'Cristata'
### (syn. 'Chapeau de Napoléon', 'Crested Moss')
This distinguished centifolia rose is sometimes included among the moss roses, though incorrectly, since only the calyces and not the stems are mossed. It makes a graceful, slender-stemmed shrub. In summer it produces drooping, cupped, fully double, richly scented, deep silvery-pink flowers that open flat and are sometimes quartered. The alternative name, 'Chapeau de Napoléon' (Napoleon's hat), refers to the unopened buds, which look like a tricorn hat. H 1.5m (5ft), S 1.2m (4ft). Hardy/Z 4–9.

### 'Charles de Mills'
### (syn. 'Bizarre Triomphant')
This is a gallica rose of unknown origin. The fully double, quartered-rosette, moderately scented, rich crimson flowers, which appear in summer, fade with grey and purple tones as they mature. The

abundant foliage is matt dark green. It makes a compact shrub, but the slender stems may need staking to support the large flowers as they open. H 1.2m (4ft), S 1m (3ft). Hardy/Z 4–9.

### 'Chinatown'
### (syn. 'Ville de Chine')
A floribunda rose, this is probably unmatched for size and overall vigour; indeed, it is sometimes justifiably classified as a shrub rose. The fragrant clusters of fully double, bright golden-yellow flowers are freely produced throughout summer and into autumn among glossy dark green leaves. It is ideal grown at the back of a border as a backdrop for smaller plants, as a hedge or as a specimen plant. H 1.5m (5ft), S 1m (3ft). Hardy/Z 5–9.

### 'City of London'
### (syn. 'Harukfore')
A spreading floribunda, this shows some of the characteristics of one of its parents, 'New Dawn', notably its continuity (it flowers from summer to autumn), its scent and its appealing soft pink colour. More versatile than some other members of this group, if it is pruned fairly hard it can be used for bedding, but with minimum pruning it can also be treated as a specimen or trained as a short climber. It also associates well with old roses. H to 2m (6ft), S to 1.2m (4ft). Hardy/Z 4–9.

### 'Compassion'
From summer to autumn this climbing rose produces shapely, rounded, fully double, sweetly scented, warm apricot-pink flowers. It is an excellent choice

for a pillar or a sturdy garden fruit tree. H 3m (10ft), S 2.5m (8ft). Hardy/Z 4–9.

### 'Complicata'
### (syn. *R. gallica* 'Complicata')
Although this is a gallica rose, it has few of the characteristics normally associated with the group and is of uncertain origin, its pedigree possibly including the vigorous species *R. canina*. Its name also implies double flowers; in fact, they are single but are produced in abundance all along the arching canes in summer. Bright porcelain pink, they are sweetly scented and open wide to reveal white centres and golden stamens. Unusually for a gallica, the matt greyish-green leaves are rather pointed. 'Complicata' tolerates light, sandy soils and can be used as a rambler among trees and shrubs in a wild garden

or it can be trained on a pillar; H and S 2.5m (8ft) if supported, probably more as a climber. Hardy/Z 4–9.

### 'Constance Spry'
### (syn. 'Autance')
This was one of the first of David Austin's 'English' roses, and it is still one of the best, although it flowers once only, in midsummer. The large, cupped, fully double, peony-like flowers of this shrub rose are rich pink and heavily scented. It can also be grown as a climber on a pillar or against a wall, where it will tolerate some shade. Even as a shrub it is best given some support or pruned hard to keep it compact. Untrained, it will grow into a large, lax shrub. H and S to 2m (6ft), though the spread can sometimes exceed the height. Hardy/Z 4–9.

Rosa 'Constance Spry'

Rosa 'Duc de Guiche'

**'Danse du Feu'**
A stiffly branched climbing rose that, as far as the flower colour – luminous red – is concerned has not been surpassed, and it has retained its place in catalogues in spite of its tendency towards blackspot. The rounded, double flowers appear from summer to autumn, but the scent is not strong. H and S 2.5m (8ft). Hardy/Z 4–9.

**'Desprez à Fleurs Jaunes'**
**(syn. 'Jaune Desprez')**
This exquisite, vigorous climbing rose, introduced in 1830, should be planted more widely. The double flowers, borne throughout summer, are an unusual creamy buff-yellow and are also sweetly scented. The lax, flexible canes make this an excellent choice for training against a wall, preferably a sunny one. H and S 5m (16ft). Hardy/Z 6–9.

**'Du Maître d'Ecole'**
The date of origin of this gallica rose is in dispute, but some authorities say it was introduced in 1840. It makes a compact plant, and in summer the weight of blossom makes the stems arch over. The fragrant, fully double, quartered-rosette, carmine-pink flowers open flat and fade to lilac-pink and grey. H and S 1m (3ft). Hardy/Z 4–9.

**'Dublin Bay'**
**(syn. 'Macdub')**
A valuable red climber, this has almost fluorescent flowers. Double and lightly scented, they are carried in clusters from summer to autumn among glossy, healthy leaves. It is a good choice if space is limited, in a border on a tripod, for instance, since the growth tends to be upright. H and S 2.2m (7ft). Hardy/Z 4–9.

**'Duc de Guiche'**
The fully double, highly scented flowers of this outstanding gallica change colour as they age. Rich crimson initially, they develop purple veining before finally flushing purple. H and S 1.2m (4ft). Hardy/Z 4–8.

**'Duchesse de Montebello'**
This spreading gallica was bred before 1829. The open-cupped, fully double, sweetly fragrant flowers are soft blush pink. The foliage is light green. It is one of the daintiest and neatest growing of the gallicas. H and S 1.2m (4ft). Hardy/Z 4–8.

**'Elina'**
**(syn. 'Dicjana', 'Peaudouce')**
A bushy hybrid tea, this has fully double, lightly scented, creamy white flowers, which open to reveal lemon-yellow flushed centres. The flowering season lasts from summer to autumn. A versatile rose and easy to grow, it is generally healthy and can be used for bedding and cutting. H 1m (3ft), S 75cm (2ft 6in). Hardy/Z 4–9.

**'Escapade'**
**(syn. 'Harpade')**
This elegant floribunda has a freely branching habit, and it is also something of a novelty in being an outstanding garden plant. The semi-double, sweetly scented flowers, which are borne in clusters throughout summer into autumn, are of unusual coloration: they are soft lilac-pink, opening flat to reveal white centres and golden stamens. Unlike some other roses, it blends easily with other plants; it occasionally produces pure white flowers within the cluster, which adds to its charm. Shiny, light green foliage is borne in abundance. H to 1.2m (4ft), S 60cm (2ft). Hardy/Z 4–9.

Rosa 'Fantin-Latour'

**'Fantin-Latour'**
A centifolia rose, this makes a handsome, vase-shaped shrub, which is ideal as a specimen. The many-petalled, cup-shaped flowers are delicately scented. They are blush-pink and are borne in profusion over a long period in summer, their petals reflexing to reveal a green button eye. 'Fantin-Latour' was named in honour of the French painter, admired for his flower pieces, some of which include roses. Spraying against mildew may be necessary in summer. H and S to 2.2m (7ft). Hardy/Z 4–9.

**'Félicité Parmentier'**
This compact Alba rose bears a single crop of cup-shaped, highly scented, quartered, pale blush-pink flowers, which open from primrose yellow buds in midsummer. The densely packed petals fade to almost white in hot sun and reflex to form a ball

Rosa 'Du Maître d'Ecole'

Rosa 'Duchesse de Montebello'

Rosa 'Escapade'

Rosa 'Félicité Parmentier'

Rosa 'Graham Thomas'

shape. The leaves are healthy and grey-green. One of the daintiest of its type, this is suitable for the smallest garden. H and S 1.2m (4ft). Hardy/Z 4–9.

### 'Fred Loads'
A strongly upright floribunda, this rose is ideal for the back of a border. Its generous clusters of semi-double, pleasantly scented, soft orange-vermilion flowers are produced from summer to autumn, making it invaluable for a long display in a mixed planting. Hard pruning can keep it in bounds, or it can be used for hedging. The flowers last well in water. H 2m (6ft), S 1m (3ft). Hardy/Z 5–9.

### 'Fru Dagmar Hastrup'
(syn. 'Frau Dagmar Hartopp')
This compact, spreading rugosa rose bears single, pale pink

summer flowers, which open almost flat to reveal prominent golden stamens; large, tomato-red hips develop in autumn as a second, sparser flush appears. This makes an excellent low hedge and can also be used for ground cover, possibly in light woodland. H 1m (3ft), S 1.2m (4ft). Hardy/Z 3–9.

### 'Frühlingsgold'
A Scotch hybrid rose, sometimes classified as a modern shrub rose, this makes a vigorous shrub, each arching cane reaching up to 2.2m (7ft) in length. The large, cupped, semi-double, fragrant, primrose-yellow flowers cover the stems in late spring to early summer, opening flat from long, pointed buds to display golden stamens. Its toughness and thorniness suggest that it might be used as a barrier plant at the end of the garden rather than in the border. H 2.5m (8ft), S 2.2m (7ft). Hardy/Z 4–8.

### *R. gallica* var. *officinalis*
(syn. *R. officinalis*)
This is a bushy gallica rose, which has been recorded in gardens since the 13th century. In summer it produces an abundance of large, semi-double, sweetly fragrant, light crimson flowers, which open flat and reveal golden stamens. Rich in historical association both as the red rose of Lancaster and the medieval apothecary's rose, this remains a superb garden plant in its own right. H and S 1.2m (4ft). Hardy/Z 5–9.

### *R. gallica* 'Versicolor'
An eye-catching gallica rose, this old rose was first recorded in the 16th century but is probably much older. The lightly scented flowers, produced in midsummer, are semi-double, opening flat to reveal golden stamens. The pale pink petals are dramatically splashed and striped with red and crimson. The common name, Rosa Mundi, reputedly commemorates Fair Rosamund, the mistress of Henry II of England. H and S 1.2m (4ft). Hardy/Z 5–9.

### 'Gentle Touch'
(syn. 'Diclulu')
Neat and upright, this patio rose bears clusters of double, slightly fragrant, pale salmon-pink flowers, opening from urn-shaped buds, from summer to autumn. In addition to its suitability for containers and as groundcover, 'Gentle Touch' is excellent as a cut flower. H and S 40cm (16in). Hardy/Z 4–9.

### 'Gloire de Dijon'
One of the oldest climbing roses still in cultivation, this was introduced in 1853 and is usually one of the first climbers to flower. The striking, fully double, fragrant, quartered-rosette, buff-apricot flowers are produced over a long period from late spring to late summer. Its early flowering makes it susceptible to frosts, so grow it against a warm wall in cold areas. H 5m (16ft), S 4m (13ft). Hardy/Z 5–9.

### 'Golden Showers'
This climbing rose is a perennial favourite for many gardeners. It produces clusters of double, lightly scented, yellow flowers from summer to autumn. The flowers lack distinction, having few petals, but the reliability of this rose in a variety of situations, including light shade, has ensured its longevity. H 3m (10ft), S 2m (6ft). Hardy/Z 4–9.

### 'Graham Thomas'
A vigorous modern shrub or 'English' rose, this is one of the best of its type, combining the flower form of the old roses with a decidedly modern colour – rich orange-yellow – and a long season that lasts from summer to autumn. The rose is named in honour of the great rosarian, Graham Stuart Thomas. H and S 1.2m (4ft). Hardy/Z 4–9.

Rosa 'Frühlingsgold'

Rosa gallica var. officinalis

*Rosa* 'Gruss an Aachen'

*Rosa* 'Ingrid Bergman'

*Rosa* 'Just Joey'

### 'Gruss an Aachen'

Bred around 1909, this rose is variously described as a floribunda or a polyantha, but it has the air of an old rose. The shapely, deeply cupped, fully double, delicately scented flowers, which are carried in clusters from early summer to autumn, are tinged with pink on opening then fade to creamy white. A long flowering season and low habit of growth make 'Gruss an Aachen' an outstanding bedding rose. H and S 1m (3ft). Hardy/Z 4–9.

### 'Handel'

A vigorous climber, branching stiffly from the base, this bears double, urn-shaped, only lightly scented flowers from midsummer to autumn. These have cream petals, which are edged with pink, creating an unusual effect. With hard pruning it can be grown as a shrub; in any case its stiff canes make it a reluctant climber. Fan the stems against a wall or spiral them up a pillar. Blackspot may be a problem. H 3m (10ft), S 2.2m (7ft). Hardy/Z 4–9.

### 'Iceberg'
### (syn. 'Fée des Neiges', 'Korbin', 'Schneewittchen')

One of the most successful roses ever produced, this deservedly popular floribunda has retained its place in the catalogues ever since its introduction in 1958. The double, ivory-white, lightly scented flowers open from tapering, pink-flushed buds and are produced in two very distinct flushes, with, unusually, the later, autumn display surpassing the summer one. An outstanding rose of its type, it can be used for bedding, hedging or cutting, but is best, with minimum pruning, as a specimen. H to 1.5m (5ft), S 1m (3ft). Hardy/Z 4–9. The climbing form, **'Climbing Iceberg'**, is equally valuable in the garden, suited to fences or trees.

### 'Ingrid Bergman'
### (syn. 'Poulman')

This upright, branching hybrid tea bears fully double, only lightly scented, deep red flowers from summer to autumn. Good for cutting, bedding and in containers, this is one of the best roses in its colour range. H 75cm (2ft 6in), spread 60cm (2ft). Hardy/Z 4–9.

### 'Ispahan'

A compact damask rose, this was first recorded in 1832 but is quite probably much older and is possibly Persian in origin. Large clusters of cupped, loosely double, reflexing, richly scented, pink flowers appear throughout summer. The grey-green foliage is attractive. 'Ispahan' has a longer flowering season than most other damasks and is in bloom for up to six weeks. H 1.2–1.5m (4–5ft), S 1–1.2m (3–4ft). Hardy/Z 4–9.

### 'Just Joey'

The charm of the individual flowers makes this upright hybrid tea rose worth growing. Opening from long, shapely buds, throughout summer, the flowers are a warm coppery orange-pink with slightly ruffled petals, developing creamy buff tints as they age. Disease-resistance is another virtue. H 75cm (2ft 6in), S 60cm (2ft). Hardy/Z 4–9.

### 'Königin von Dänemark'
### (syn. 'Queen of Denmark', 'Belle Courtisane')

This tall, elegant alba is thought by many to be one of the loveliest of all old roses. The luminous pink, fully double, quartered-rosette and richly scented flowers are borne in summer, and fade to rose-pink as they mature,. It also has one of the longest flowering seasons, up to six weeks, and the flowers have good resistance to wet weather. H to 1.5m (5ft), S 1.2m (4ft). Hardy/Z 4–9.

### 'Korresia'
### (syn. 'Friesia', 'Sunsprite')

A neat, upright floribunda, this bears clusters of shapely buds, opening to fragrant, bright golden-yellow flowers, from summer to autumn. It can be used for bedding and for cut flowers; it is similar to 'Allgold' but has bigger flowers. H 75cm (30in), S 60cm (2ft). Hardy/Z 4–9.

### 'Laura Ford'

This miniature climber is unusual in that its dainty yellow double flowers are also scented. Borne from summer to autumn, they appear in clusters among small, shiny, dark green leaves. A good choice for a small garden, this rose is also suitable for growing in a container. H to 2.2m (7ft), S 1.2m (4ft). Hardy/Z 4–9.

### 'Madame Alfred Carrière'

This reliable, free-flowering, climbing rose was introduced

*Rosa* 'Iceberg'

*Rosa* 'Ispahan'

*Rosa* 'Königin von Dänemark'

Rosa 'Korresia'

Rosa 'Madame Hardy'

Rosa 'Madame Isaac Pereire'

in 1879. It bears creamy white, double, cupped, fragrant flowers from summer to autumn on almost thornless stems. Although the flowers are not of individual beauty, its many virtues – length of season, health, tolerance of shade – make this one of the best choices for growing against a house wall. H 5m (16ft), S 3m (10ft). Hardy/Z 5–9.

### 'Madame Grégoire Staechelin' (syn. 'Spanish Beauty')

The sight of this vigorous climbing rose in full flower in early summer is unforgettable. The fully double, sweetly scented, warm pink flowers hang in clusters on arching stems. There is no repeat flowering. The large, showy hips redden in autumn, but not reliably. H 6m (20ft), S 4m (13ft). Hardy/Z 4–9.

### 'Madame Hardy'

An undoubted queen among roses, this damask dates from 1867. The fully double, quartered-rosette, strongly scented, white flowers are borne in profusion in summer, the petals reflexing to reveal a green button eye. It is generally considered to be one of the most sumptuous of old roses, though the flowers may be spoilt by rain. H and S 1.5m (5ft). Hardy/Z 4–9.

### 'Madame Isaac Pereire'

A bourbon rose, introduced in 1881, this retains its place in the catalogues on account of its strong scent, which is all but unsurpassed in a genus noted for exactly that attribute. The flower colour is also of note: a luminous, deep cerise pink. Produced throughout summer and into autumn, the flowers open as quartered-rosettes but become muddled as they mature, especially those of the first flush. A tendency towards mildew is its only drawback. H 2.5m (8ft), S 2m (6ft), possibly more if grown as a climber. Hardy/Z 4–9.

### 'Margaret Merril' (syn. 'Harkuly')

An upright floribunda, this bears clusters of large, shapely, double, sweetly scented, pure white flowers from summer to autumn. In addition to its versatility in the garden, it can also be grown in containers and is useful as a cut flower. Blackspot can be a problem, but the rose is worth persevering with for its delicious scent. H 1m (3ft), S 60cm (2ft). Hardy/Z 4–9.

### 'Marguerite Hilling' (syn. 'Pink Nevada')

A sport of the popular 'Nevada', this shrub rose is similar in all respects apart from the colour of its semi-double flowers, which are pale pink and smother the arching canes in early summer. Healthy and vigorous, it makes an excellent specimen. H and S to 2.2m (7ft). Hardy/Z 4–9.

### 'Mermaid'

This beautiful climber is vigorous once established, but it can take some years to do this. The flowers are produced spasmodically from midsummer until autumn, with a handful later. The elegant, pointed buds open to reveal single, pale yellow, fragrant saucers with prominent golden stamens that persist after the petals have dropped. The leaves are glossy and can be evergreen; the stems are viciously thorny. Tolerant of some shade, 'Mermaid' may be cut back by hard frost, so appreciates some shelter. H and S 6m (20ft). Hardy/Z 4–9.

### 'Mountbatten' (syn. 'Harmantelle')

The clusters of mimosa yellow flowers are beautifully set off by the glossy dark green leaves on this shrub rose. With minimum pruning this makes an excellent specimen. H to 1.5m (5ft), S to 1m (3ft). Hardy/Z 4–9.

### 'Mrs Oakley Fisher'

This rather spindly hybrid tea has claims to attention on account of its unusual flowers. Not only are they subtle in colour – soft apricot-yellow flowers fading to pale buff yellow – but they are deliciously fragrant and, unusually for a rose in this group, single. H and S 1m (3ft). Hardy/Z 6–9.

Rosa 'Laura Ford'

Rosa 'Margaret Merril'

Rosa 'Mountbatten'

*Rosa* 'Orange Sunblaze'

### 'Nevada'
This vigorous shrub rose, which tolerates some shade, puts on a great show in early summer, when its arching, blackish canes are smothered in semi-double, creamy white flowers; their elusive fragrance seems to hang on the air. A few flowers are occasionally produced later in the season. It is best with light pruning. H and S to 3m (10ft). Hardy/Z 4–9.

### 'New Dawn'
This vigorous, healthy rambler is valued for its late flowering. From midsummer there is a great profusion of deliciously fragrant, silvery pink, semi-double flowers, which continue until well into autumn. Its thorny stems and occasional stiffness of habit need to be taken into consideration when planting. H and S to 5m (16ft). Hardy/Z 4–9.

### 'Nozomi'
This was one of the first ground-cover roses to be bred and is still one of the best, producing clusters

*Rosa* 'Pascali'

of single, only lightly scented, very pale pink to white flowers in midsummer. The trailing stems, which are covered in glossy dark green leaves, will root where they touch the ground. To maintain the creeping habit, cut back upward-growing shoots in winter. It can also be treated as a miniature climber. H 45cm (18in), S to 1.5m (5ft). Hardy/Z 4–9.

### *R.* × *odorata* 'Mutabilis' (syn. *R. chinensis* 'Mutabilis')
A China rose, of uncertain age and parentage, this was evidently grown in China for many years before its introduction to Europe in 1894. The single flowers, produced over a long period from mid-spring to autumn, are unusual: flame orange in bud, they open to coppery yellow then fade to pink, the pink deepening to purple as they age. None too hardy, this rose is best grown in the shelter of a warm wall, where it can reach a height of 3m (10ft) with a spread of 2m (6ft). In the border it can also be trained on a tripod. H 1.2m (4ft), S 1m (3ft). Borderline hardy/Z 7–9.

### *R.* × *odorata* 'Pallida'
Introduced to Europe around 1752 but undoubtedly much older, this China rose has one of the longest flowering seasons of all roses. From summer until the first winter frosts it produces double, cupped, sweetly fragrant, clear pink flowers amid elegant, pointed leaves. None too hardy, in some areas it will need growing against a warm wall to give of its best. It can also be trained as a climber. It is sometimes known as the old blush China rose or Parsons' pink China rose. H 1–3m (3–10ft), S 2m (6ft). Borderline hardy/Z 7–9.

### 'Orange Sunblaze' (syn. 'Meijikatar', 'Orange Meillandina', 'Sunblaze')
A neat and dainty miniature rose, this bears fully double, only lightly scented, bright vermilion-orange flowers from summer to autumn. It is an excellent choice where space is limited or for a container. H and S 30cm (12in). Hardy/Z 4–9. There is also a

*Rosa* 'Queen Mother'

climbing form, 'Climbing Orange Sunblaze' (syn. 'Meiji Katarsar'), which produces a dazzling display when grown on a sunny wall.

### 'Pascali'
This is one of the few pure white hybrid teas (albeit lightly touched with creamy buff). Shapely double, only lightly scented flowers are displayed from early summer into autumn. The rain-resistance of the flowers is unsurpassed in this colour range; they are also exceptionally long-lasting when cut. H 1m (3ft), S 75cm (2ft

6in). Hardy/Z 4–9. **'Climbing Pascali'**, a climbing form, shares the same qualities.

### 'Peace' (syn. 'Gioia', 'Gloria Dei', 'Madame A. Meilland')
One of the most popular hybrid teas ever produced, this rose is surely worthy of revival. The large, fully double, only lightly scented flowers are pale yellow with pink flushes, and they appear from midsummer to autumn. Its present lack of popularity is due to its supposed coarseness – that

*Rosa* 'Peace'

*Rosa* 'Président de Sèze'

*Rosa* 'Roseraie de l'Haÿ'

is, it is a vigorous, spreading, bushy rose that makes a fine specimen with light pruning. H 1.5m (5ft), S 1m (3ft). Hardy/Z 4–9.

### 'Président de Sèze'
Richly scented, large, quartered flowers appear on this sturdy gallica rose in summer. The centre petals are rich magenta-purple, the colour fading across the flower to soft lilac-pink, almost white, at the edges. The leaves are larger than is usual for a gallica rose. A well-grown specimen is a stunning sight when in full bloom. H 1.2m (4ft), S 1m (3ft). Hardy/Z 4–9.

### 'Queen Mother'
(syn. 'Korquemu')
This spreading patio rose deserves its popularity. The dainty buds open to semi-double, clear pink flowers from summer to autumn. It does well in a container and is sometimes available as a weeping standard. H 45cm (18in), S 60cm (2ft). Hardy/Z 4–9.

*Rosa* 'Royal William'

### 'Rambling Rector'
A vigorous rambling rose, this is covered with clusters of small, semi-double, fragrant, white flowers in summer. Small red hips follow in autumn. It is suitable for growing into a large tree, and a mature rose in full flower is an impressive sight, but it is not a rose suited to every garden. H and S 6m (20ft). Hardy/Z 5–9.

### 'Roseraie de l'Haÿ'
Despite its reluctance to produce the characteristic autumn hips, this is one of the best of the rugosa roses. Its value rests on its strongly scented, velvety, wine-red flowers, which open to reveal creamy stamens. The blooms are produced in abundance from summer to autumn. The wrinkled leaves redden in autumn. Dense and spreading, 'Roseraie de l'Haÿ' makes an excellent hedge and can also be planted in light woodland. H 2m (6ft), S 1.2m (4ft). Hardy/Z 4–9.

### 'Royal William'
(syn. 'Duftzauber '84', 'Fragrant Charm '84', 'Korzaun')
An upright hybrid tea, this rose is valued for its succession of large, fully double, fragrant, deep crimson flowers. The graceful blooms are carried on long stems from summer to autumn. This rose is excellent planted en masse for a stunning effect, or it can be grown to provide flowers for cutting. H 1m (3ft) S 75cm (2ft 6in). Hardy/Z 4–9.

### 'Savoy Hotel'
(syn. 'Harvintage', 'Integrity')
This bushy hybrid tea has strong stems that carry large, shapely, fully double, fragrant, light clear pink flowers from summer to autumn and with good repeat-flowering. It is a versatile rose, which provides excellent material for cutting, as long as you keep it well fed. H 1m (3ft), S 60cm (2ft). Hardy/Z 4–8.

### 'Schneezwerg'
(syn. 'Snow Dwarf')
A rugosa rose introduced in 1912, this has a dense, spreading habit. The anemone-like, semi-double, white flowers open flat to

*Rosa* 'Savoy Hotel'

reveal golden stamens. They are followed by small, orange-red, tomato-shaped hips. Although its flowers are unremarkable, this rose is perhaps at its best in autumn; the foliage does not change colour, but the flowers continue to appear alongside the reddening hips. In order to get the best of both worlds, therefore, deadhead selectively in summer. H 1.2m (4ft), S 1.5m (5ft). Hardy/Z 3–9.

### 'Sexy Rexy'
(syn. 'Heckenzauber', 'Macrexy')
This is an outstanding floribunda, of upright habit. It produces clusters of shapely, fully double, palest coral-pink flowers throughout summer and autumn. These are shown off by plentiful

*Rosa* 'Schneezwerg'

dark, glossy leaves. It is a versatile rose good for general garden use, growing in containers and for providing cut flowers. H and S 60cm (2ft). Hardy/Z 4–9.

### 'Sombreuil'
A distinctive and unusual rose, this is generally classified as a climbing tea, although it is not particularly vigorous, nor are its flowers tea-like, lacking a high centre. Borne from summer to autumn, the sweetly scented blooms are flat, quartered rosettes, creamy white in colour and acquiring pink tinges as they age. Wet weather will ruin them. H and S to 2.4m (8ft) when grown as a climber with support, but smaller if allowed to grow as a lax shrub. Hardy/Z 5–9.

*Rosa* 'Sexy Rexy'

*Rosa* 'Stanwell Perpetual'

*Rosa* 'The Queen Elizabeth'

**'Southampton'**
**(syn. 'Susan Ann')**
This is an excellent floribunda, with an upright, branching habit and shiny, dark green leaves. Clusters of large, double, soft apricot-orange flowers, which are flushed with scarlet, are carried from early summer into autumn; the petals are wavy-edged. The scent is not especially strong. H 1m (3ft), S 60cm (2ft). Hardy/Z 4–9.

**'Souvenir de la Malmaison'**
This beautiful, dense, spreading bourbon rose, produced in 1843, commemorates the famous garden created by Empress Josephine at Malmaison, although it is not clear whether it was actually grown there. Repeat-flowering throughout the summer, it bears very fragrant, fully double, soft pink flowers, which open to a quartered-rosette shape as they fade to blush-white. One major drawback is that the silk-textured

flowers may be spoilt by wet weather. H and S 1.5m (5ft). Hardy/Z 4–9.

**'Stanwell Perpetual'**
This Scotch rose, raised in 1838, forms a dense, prickly shrub. The double, sweetly scented, attractive blush pink to white flowers open flat and are produced almost continuously throughout summer among the grey-green leaves. Tolerant of poor soil and some shade, this rose is ideal for growing in light woodland; it also makes a good hedge. H and S 1.5m (5ft). Hardy/Z 5–9.

**'Sweet Dream'**
**(syn. 'Fryminicot')**
One of the best of the patio roses, this produces an abundance of fully double, lightly scented, soft apricot-orange flowers from midsummer to autumn. It is usually well covered with glossy, healthy foliage. A good edging plant, 'Sweet Dream' is also

suitable for growing in a container. H 40cm (16in), S 35cm (14in). Hardy/Z 4–9.

**'Tango'**
**(syn. 'Macfirwal', 'Rock 'n' Roll', 'Stretch Johnson')**
This upright floribunda is chiefly of interest to flower arrangers. From summer to autumn it produces clusters of semi-double flowers of some distinction: the petals, frilled at the edges, are orange-red with white rims, yellow at the base and on the reverse. H 75cm (2ft 6in), spread 60cm (2ft). Hardy/Z 4–8.

**'The Fairy'**
A dainty floribunda or polyantha, this has a dense, mounding habit and is well worth considering if you are planning an autumn border. It flowers later than almost any other rose, the clusters of small, double, light pink flowers appearing only from midsummer, but then continuing in profusion until the onset of winter. H and S 60cm (2ft). Hardy/Z 4–9.

**'The Queen Elizabeth'**
**(syn. 'Queen Elizabeth', 'The Queen Elizabeth Rose')**
This is one of the best of all the floribundas, but not especially characteristic of the group. Its vigour and strongly vertical habit really make it unsuitable for most of the purposes for which the floribundas were developed. It is best used at the back of a border or as a tall, informal hedge. Its fully double, china pink flowers, which are freely carried from summer to autumn, last well when cut. H 2.2m (7ft), S 1m (3ft);

with minimal pruning it will easily top 3m (10ft). Hardy/Z 4–9. The climbing form, **'Climbing the Queen Elizabeth'**, is also well worth growing.

**'Troika'**
**(syn. 'Royal Dane')**
An outstanding hybrid tea, this has an upright, branching habit. The display of large, shapely, double, lightly scented, copper-orange flowers, sometimes veined scarlet, continues throughout summer and into autumn. Disease- and weather-resistant, this is a good choice for a massed planting and also provides good cut flowers. H 1m (3ft), S 75cm (2ft 6in). Hardy/Z 4–9.

**'Tuscany Superb'**
**(syn. 'Double Velvet')**
This erect gallica rose was raised before 1837. The large, semi-double, lightly scented, deep crimson flowers are produced in midsummer. They open flat, showing golden stamens, then fade to purple. Tolerant of poor

*Rosa* 'Souvenir de la Malmaison'

*Rosa* 'Sweet Dream'

*Rosa* 'The Fairy'

*Rosa* 'Tuscany Superb'

*Rosa* 'Veilchenblau'

*Rosa* 'Whisky Mac'

*Rosa* 'William Lobb'

soil, this is one of the few old roses that is suitable for hedging. It is not too thorny. H 1.5m (5ft), S 1m (3ft). Hardy/Z 4–9.

### 'Veilchenblau' (syn. 'Blue Rambler', 'Violet Blue')

A vigorous rambling rose, this was introduced in 1909. In midsummer it bears clusters of sweetly scented, semi-double, violet-pink flowers with yellow stamens; the flowers fade to an unusual purplish grey as they mature. The leaves are glossy and light green. More modest than most ramblers, this rose is suitable for a small garden and is best grown with some shelter from the midday sun. H and S 4m (13ft). Hardy/Z 4–9.

### 'Whisky Mac' (syn. 'Tanky', 'Whisky')

This famous hybrid tea has retained its popularity despite its propensity to die-back and fungal diseases. Its appeal lies in the unusual colouring of its sumptuous double flowers, which are a rich golden-orange of unrivalled intensity, and with a fragrance to match. Since it needs almost constant attention, this is really a plant for dedicated rose-growers only. H 75cm (2ft 6in), S 60cm (2ft). Hardy/Z 4–9.

### 'White Bells'

A dense, spreading groundcover rose, this bears a single, but abundant, crop of small, fully double, white flowers in summer. It is shade-tolerant, and thus useful for difficult areas of the

garden, but overall perhaps not as good as some other groundcover roses. H 60cm (2ft), S 1.2m (4ft). Hardy/Z 5–9.

### 'White Cockade'

This is one of the few white climbing roses. The perfectly shaped, fully double flowers appear almost continuously from summer to autumn, and the absence of a strong scent in no way detracts from its overall merit. Slow-growing, it is a good choice for growing in a container or on a short pillar. H 2.2m (7ft), S 1.5m (5ft). Hardy/Z 4–9.

### 'White Grootendorst'

A vigorous rugosa rose, with a dense, spreading habit, this produces clusters of small, double, scentless, white flowers, particularly notable for the frilly edges of the petals, which look like carnations. Like most of the rugosas, it tolerates some shade and poor soil, making it ideal for a wild garden. H 1.2m (4ft), S 1m (3ft). Hardy/Z 3–8.

### 'William Lobb' (syn. 'Duchesse d'Istrie')

This rather sprawling moss rose is worth growing for its sumptuous rosette flowers. Richly scented, they open magenta-purple in midsummer from heavily mossed buds, then pass through a remarkable range of tones before fading to a subtle violet-grey. The ungainly habit makes it unsuitable as a specimen. Instead, try it wrapped around a tripod or as a short climber on a pillar or against a wall. H and S 2m (6ft). Hardy/Z 4–9.

### *R. xanthina* 'Canary Bird'

This wild rose is usually one of the first to flower in the garden, offering a burst of welcome colour in late spring. The single, cupped, scented, canary yellow flowers have prominent stamens. In a good year there will be a second, though lesser, flush of flowers in autumn. It makes an attractive arching shrub, although it is sometimes available as a grafted standard, when it makes a fine specimen. H and S 2.2m (7ft). Hardy/Z 5–9.

### 'Yellow Doll'

This spreading miniature rose has double, slightly scented, bright yellow flowers, which are produced singly or in clusters from summer to autumn. Rather unusually for a miniature, it is good for cutting; it can also be forced under glass for early flowers. It will tolerate harsh weather conditions. H and S to 30cm (12in). Hardy/Z 3–8.

### 'Yesterday' (syn. 'Tapis d'Orient')

A floribunda or polyantha rose, this has an elegant, open, spreading habit and a long flowering season, from summer to autumn. The clusters of semi-

double, fragrant, deep lilac-pink flowers open flat to reveal paler centres and golden stamens. It is good for cutting and, given lighter pruning than usual, makes an attractive specimen. H and S 1m (3ft). Hardy/Z 4–9.

### 'Zéphirine Drouhin'

This climbing rose is notable for its thornless stems, making it a good choice for an archway or pergola or for framing a doorway. In summer and autumn it produces clusters of double, cupped to flat, fragrant, magenta flowers. It can be prone to mildew. H 3m (10ft), S 2m (6ft). Hardy/Z 4–9. **'Kathleen Harrop'** is a pale pink sport.

*Rosa* 'Yesterday'

# Bulbs

Few groups of plants provide the gardener with such a range of brilliant colours as the bulbs, and nearly all are easy to grow. There is scarcely a moment in the year when they do not make a contribution, from the diminutive harbingers of spring that brighten up the garden from late winter, the bold tulips and daffodils that epitomize spring, to the exotic, slightly tender dahlias and gladioli that carry on the interest into autumn, with a host of others in between. Hyacinths and hippeastrums can be forced to flower in the dead of winter indoors, ensuring that you need never be without flowers.

Easy and reliable, these alliums raise their heads of almost geometric precision above the lower-growing perennials.

# What is a bulb?

Bulbs are perennials that have evolved a specialized mechanism, which allows them to survive periods of extreme heat or extreme cold, sometimes both. Essentially, a bulb is an energy store that enables the plant to return to a state of dormancy at times when conditions are unfavourable for growth. The bulb itself is an underground structure that is made up of scales fixed to a basal plate. The scales – actually modified leaves – surround a small piece of stem tissue, which produces a large bud near the centre of the bulb. In some cases, for instance daffodils (*Narcissus*) and tulips (*Tulipa*), the scales are tightly packed and are encased in a papery outer covering (the tunic). Lilies (*Lilium*), however, have fleshy, rather open scales. Roots grow from the bottom of the basal plate.

During the growing season, the plant builds a food supply through its leaves. As the winter or dry season approaches, the exposed parts of the plant die, but the bulb with its stored food remains alive underground. At the beginning of the next growing season, the bulb's central bud sends out a shoot, which produces a stem, leaves and flowers above the ground. Food stored in the bulb fuels the young shoot's rapid growth.

Typically (though not invariably) a bulb reproduces itself vegetatively by producing a number of bulblets around the basal plate. Eventually these split from the parent bulb, which then dies.

Corms and tubers are usually considered alongside bulbs, since their growth patterns are similar, and they have comparable garden uses. A corm is a modified stem with a bud on top, which produces shoots. After flowering, a new corm, formed at the

A wonderful matching display of spring-flowering tulips rising above lower-growing annual pansies in similar shades.

base of the old stem, grows on top of the old corm, which then dies. Smaller corms also develop around the base of the old corm. Gladioli, crocosmias and crocuses are corms.

Here, tulips are used more informally and interplanted with bedding wallflowers to edge a path.

Tubers are thickened fleshy roots or stems. They can be covered with scaly leaves or with fibrous roots. Growth buds develop on the top of the tuber, which gets larger with age and can persist for several years. Dahlias, begonias and cyclamen are good examples.

In the discussion to follow, all bulbs, corms and tubers are loosely referred to as bulbs.

## Bulbs in the garden

Being mostly trouble-free and easy to grow, bulbs are essential garden plants. They are excellent for creating short bursts of colour, whether as a massed planting in beds or woodland, in drifts in grass, combined with other border plants or in containers.

In the dictionary section that follows, spreads are not given for those bulbs that have only a single growing point, for instance lilies and daffodils.

Nearly all bulbs need well-drained soil, either in full sun or light shade. None is adapted to deep shade. Bulbs from hot countries such as South Africa – this group includes many of the summer- and autumn-flowering bulbs – need baking conditions if the bulb is to survive and flower from year to year. At the foot of a wall that faces the midday or afternoon sun is often ideal. Woodland bulbs thrive in fertile, leafy soil, ideally in the dappled shade cast by deciduous trees.

Early bulbs are the delight of the spring garden, providing vivid colour before the perennials have begun to wake up. They are ideal additions to any mixed border. In a fairly informal, cottage-style planting, taller bulbs such as tulips, alliums and lilies can be planted to rise above lower-growing perennials. Bulbs can also be used more formally: tulips and hyacinths that grow to a uniform height are often effective where planted in blocks. The hyacinths have the advantage of an inimitable scent. Many of the later-flowering bulbs, such as dahlias and cannas, that are on the tender side, are best treated as bedding plants in colder areas, and these work well with annuals and other late-flowering tender perennials to bring the gardening season to a close with a blaze of colour.

Spring bulbs are excellent for naturalizing, a gardening principle that allows plants to build up colonies. Drifts of anemones in woodland are a breathtaking sight in spring, but many more are suitable for growing in more open situations in grass: a lawn studded with dwarf bulbs is a delight. It is important to choose robust selections that can compete with the grass, however, or the effect will be short-lived. *Crocus*

*tommasinianus* is very useful for early flowers, and most of the so-called chrysanthus hybrids will be able to hold their own. Many of the daffodils can also be used. However, if the bulbs are to persist from year to year, they must be allowed to complete their growth cycle and die down completely before you mow the lawn, so early-flowering varieties are usually the ones recommended for this purpose. It is perfectly possible to use later-flowering types and mow around the clumps, but the grass will grow tall amid the clumps, resulting in a less tailored look. Snake's head fritillaries (*Fritiallaria meleagris*) are excellent in a meadow garden where the ground is reliably moist, but here you do have to let the grass grow under your feet, as they are relatively late flowering. In a woodland garden, consider camassias, erythroniums and some of the lilies. Cyclamen are particularly valued, not

only for their late season and ease of cultivation but also because they will thrive in the dry ground beneath deciduous trees and shrubs, a situation inhospitable to most other plants.

Although none is a true alpine, dwarf bulbs are excellent in the rock garden, relishing the superior drainage and the reflected heat from the rocks. Several of the species crocuses and tulips can be grown in this way, and look charming pushing through creeping or cushion plants, but again you have to be careful to match their vigour if one is not to put paid to the other.

Nearly all bulbs thrive in containers, especially those that benefit from a summer roasting. For the best effect, pack the bulbs in tightly. Include a few trailing ivies at the edge and a few bedding plants to cover the surface of the container for the best display.

Dahlias, such as this richly orange variety 'David Howard', are an ideal choice for bringing the summer to a colourful end.

Achimenes 'Prima Donna'

# ACHIMENES
## Hot water plant, cupid's bower
These tender plants are usually grown as houseplants. Nearly all plants sold commercially are hybrids, and they have short, trumpet-shaped flowers in shades of blue, peach, pink, red and orange and shiny, velvety leaves. The common name is misleading. When they are in growth the plants should be watered with barely tepid water, never hot water, which would kill them. The lax stems make them an excellent choice for hanging baskets. After they have died down the stunning bulbs, which look like miniature white pine cones, should be dried and stored over winter.
*Cultivation* These plants do best in containers in a light place but out of direct sun. Water them freely when in growth but keep them dry in winter at a temperature of 10°C (50°F).

### A. hybrids
Hot water plants flower over a long period from early summer to autumn. There are many named varieties, including **'Blue Gown'**, which has blue flowers; **'Harry Williams'**, which has red flowers; **'Prima Donna'**, which has pink flowers; and **'Snow Princess'** with white flowers. H and S 30cm (12in) or more. Tender/Z 10.

# ALLIUM
## Ornamental onion
Only a few species of this large and important genus are grown in the flower garden. Some have the distinctive pungent, onion smell, making them unsuitable for mass plantings. They combine well with old roses, and some, if grown in large quantities, will protect against aphids and fungal disease. Their bold, spherical heads of flowers make a strong statement, and they are the perfect foil for more flamboyant flowers. They look good dotted among lower growing perennials such as geraniums. The seedheads (which can be dried for winter decoration) are almost as attractive as the flowerheads. Small species can also be grown in rock gardens.
*Cultivation* Any well-drained soil in a sunny spot is suitable for alliums, although they will also tolerate semi-shade. Dead-head to prevent self-seeding.

### A. cristophii
### (syn. A. albopilosum, A. christophii)
### Star of Persia
This species, originally from Turkey, has large flowerheads, up to 20cm (8in) across, of silver-purple, star-like flowers in late spring to early summer. These are attractive even after the flowers have faded. H 60cm (2ft), S 18cm (7in). Borderline hardy/ Z 7–10.

### A. giganteum
### Giant onion
One of the tallest alliums, this dramatic plant, which is native to central Asia, has large purple flowerheads, up to 20cm (8in) across, carried at the top of the erect stems in late spring to early

Allium karataviense

Amaryllis belladonna

summer. H to 170cm (70in), S 15cm (6in). Hardy/Z 6–10.

### A. hollandicum
### (syn. A. aflatunense of gardens)
The species is native to central Asia. It bears globular heads, to 10cm (4in) across, of lilac-purple flowers from mid- to late spring. The blue-green leaves are also attractive. Plant in groups for the best display. H 1.2m (4ft), S 10cm (4in). **'Purple Sensation'** is a selection with deep purple flowers. H 1m (3ft), S 10cm (4in). Hardy/Z 4–10.

### A. karataviense
This low-growing species from central Asia works well in containers as well as near the front a mixed border. It would be worth growing for its leaves alone, which are pewter-grey edged with maroon. The dull lilac-pink

Allium moly

flowers – interesting rather than beautiful – appear in late spring to early summer. H to 25cm (10in), S 10cm (4in). Hardy/ Z 4–9.

### A. moly
### Golden garlic, lily leek
A species from southern Europe, suitable for a rock garden. It bears a profusion of yellow flowers in late spring to early summer. The grey-green leaves remain attractive over a long period. It is good for naturalizing in light shade and reliably damp soil. H to 30cm (12in), S 5cm (2in). Hardy/Z 3–9.

### A. roseum
### Rosy garlic
One of the most appealing alliums, the species is native to southern Europe and northern Africa. It has loose heads of scented pink flowers borne on sturdy stems in late spring to early summer. H 60cm (2ft), S 5cm (2in). Hardy/Z 8.

### A. sphaerocepahlon
### Round-headed leek
A good allium for a massed planting, this species, native to Europe, northern Africa and western Asia, bears almost pear-shaped heads of reddish-purple flowers in late spring and early summer. It combines especially well with hostas, *Alchemilla mollis* and ornamental grasses. H 1m (3ft), S 8cm (3in). Hardy/Z 6–10.

Allium roseum

Anemone blanda

## AMARYLLIS

There is only one species in this South African genus, which is related to *Hippeastrum* and is usually sold as 'amaryllis'. The true amaryllis can be a star of the autumn garden, with its trumpet-like flowers, which are rather small in relation to the size of the overall plant. They look best grown in isolation, revelling in the comfort of a sheltered spot at the base of a warm wall, with nothing to compete with their beauty.
*Cultivation* Full sun is essential for these plants, which should be grown in a sheltered spot in fertile, well-drained soil. Plant with the neck of the bulb just above soil level. The flower stems may need staking. In cold areas, cover with a dry mulch of straw or similar material in winter.

### A. belladonna
**Belladonna lily, Jersey lily**
The leaves appear in spring, then die down in early summer. About two months later stems appear, carrying fragrant, bright pink, trumpet-like flowers. H 75cm (30in), S 10cm (4in). Borderline hardy/Z 7–10.

## ANEMONE
**Windflower**
The genus contains both spring-flowering corms as well as some valuable autumn perennials. A major claim to distinction is that the corms include some with red flowers, a colour in short supply in the garden until the tulips make their mark.
*Cultivation* Different species have different light requirements, but any soil type is acceptable, as long as it is well drained. *A. apennina* prefers dappled shade, ideally beneath deciduous trees. *A. blanda* prefers full sun, but will also grow (although it will flower less freely) in light shade. *A. coronaria* needs sun.

### A. apennina
**Blue anemone**
This species from southern Europe bears starry blue flowers, sometimes tinged with pink, in early spring. H 15cm (6in), S 30cm (12in). Hardy/Z 6–9.

### A. blanda
One of the most worthwhile species, this plant is found in south-eastern Europe. It has daisy-like flowers in white or shades of pink, blue and mauve in mid-spring. It is an excellent choice for carpeting large areas under deciduous trees. H and S 15cm (6in). Selections include 'Blue Shades', which has light to dark blue flowers; 'Pink Star', which has pink flowers; 'Radar', with deep mauve-pink flowers, shading to white towards the centre; and 'White Splendour', which has white flowers.

### A. coronaria
This species, seldom grown in its typical form, has two main hybrid groups, De Caen (with single flowers) and St Brigid (with double flowers). They flower from late spring to late summer, depending on when they were planted. They are often sold in mixtures, but there are also several selected forms, including 'Die Braut' (syn. 'The Bride'; De Caen Group), which has green-centred, white flowers; 'Hollandia' (syn. 'His Excellency'; De Caen Group), which has white-centred, red flowers; 'Lord Lieutenant' (St Brigid Group), which has dark blue flowers; 'Mister Fokker' (De Caen Group), which has violet-blue flowers; 'Mount Everest' (St Brigid Group), which has white flowers; 'The Admiral' (St Brigid Group), which has purple-pink flowers; and 'The Governor' (De Caen Group), which has red flowers. H 30–40cm (12–15in), S 15cm (6in). Hardy/Z 8–10.

### A. nemorosa
**Wood anemone**
A graceful plant, which is native to Europe, this is ideal for naturalizing beneath shrubs and trees, where it benefits from the shade. The white, cup-shaped flowers are borne in spring. H 15cm (6in), S 20cm (8in). Hardy/Z 4–8.

## ARUM
**Lords and ladies, cuckoo pint**
These tuberous perennials are quiet but handsome plants for a woodland garden. Lords and ladies is a common hedgerow plant in northern Europe; the plant described is a treasured garden form. It has two seasons of interest: the leaves emerge in late autumn and are at their best by late winter, when they make a splendid foil for snowdrops. The plant then dies down to ground level, when spikes of juicy-looking (but poisonous) red berries appear in late summer.
*Cultivation* Arums will grow in any, preferably fairly moisture-retentive soil in partial shade.

### A. italicum
As its name suggests, this is an Italian species, but it also found elsewhere in the Mediterranean. The dark green leaves have white veins. A greenish-white spathe encloses the spike of orange-red berries. H 40cm (16in), S 20cm (8in). The leaves of *A. italicum* subsp. *italicum* 'Marmoratum' (syn. 'Pictum') are beautifully marbled with cream and pink, appearing in autumn and lasting through the winter, dying back the following spring. Spikes of poisonous orange-red berries poke through the soil in autumn. Although frost flattens the leaves, they do stand up again as they thaw. It combines well with snowdrops. H to 45cm (18in), S 20cm (8in). Hardy/Z 7–9.

Anemone coronaria 'Die Braut'

Anemone nemorosa

Arum italicum subs. italicum 'Marmoratum'

Begonia × tuberhybrida 'Illumination Orange'

# BEGONIA

This large genus contains about 900 species, including several annuals and a range of perennials that are usually grown as foliage houseplants. None of these plants are hardy, so in frost-prone climates they need to be lifted for overwintering or treated as annuals. Dwarf varieties make excellent bedding material for colour borders and are equally good in containers. Pendulous varieties are ideal subjects for a hanging basket. Some hybrid begonias have huge flowers and have been bred for enthusiasts. These, omitted here, must be grown in containers in controlled conditions under glass in order to give of their best.
*Cultivation* Tuberous begonias do best in a neutral soil or compost

Begonia × tuberhybrida 'Giant Flowered Pendula Yellow'

(soil mix) in light shade. Plants grown in containers should be lifted after the topgrowth has died back and stored dry in a frost-free place over winter. To coax them out of dormancy the following spring, repot the tubers into fresh compost, water and keep at a temperature of 16–18°C (61–64°F).

## B. sutherlandii
This elegant, spreading species from South Africa is an ideal subject for a hanging basket and is perhaps best grown on its own with no competition from other plants. Its clear orange flowers are produced in succession throughout the summer. H 15–30cm (6–12in), S 30cm (12in). Half-hardy/Z 10.

## B. × tuberhybrida
This vast hybrid group encompasses a range of different types and cultivars. They can be broadly divided into the Multiflora group (which are suitable for summer bedding) and the Pendula group (which have trailing stems and are suitable for hanging baskets). All are tender/Z 10. Flowers of the **Cascade Series** (Pendula) can be orange, pink, red or yellow. H and S to 30cm (12in). **'Giant Flowered Pendula Yellow'** (Pendula) has double yellow flowers. H and S to 20cm (8in). **'Helene Harms'** (Multiflora) has double yellow flowers. H and S to 45cm (18in). Flowers of the **Illumination Series** (Pendula) are pink or orange, **'Illumination Orange'** being a selected form. H 60cm (2ft), S 30cm (1ft). **'Madame Richard Galle'** (Multiflora) has double copper flowers. H and S 45cm (18in). Plants of the **Non Stop Series** (Multiflora) have double flowers in shades of orange, apricot, pink, yellow and red, and have a slightly more extended flowering period than the others. H and S 20cm (8in).

# CAMASSIA
## Quamash
This North American genus has not crossed the Atlantic very successfully, probably because it flowers at around the same time

Camassia leichtlinii

as bluebells, which most British gardeners seem to prefer. While nothing can match the blue of an English bluebell, camassias have a comparable distinction and should be more widely grown. They are best in drifts in light woodland or, as a prairie plant, in grass, but they can also be grown in borders.
*Cultivation* Any reliably moist garden soil is suitable, but these plants prefer humus-rich soil in sun that is not waterlogged in winter. They tolerate dappled shade but may flower less freely.

## C. cusickii
This species flowers in late spring, its spikes of blue flowers combining well with *Dicentra spectabilis*. H 60–80cm (24–32in), S 10cm (4in). Borderline hardy/Z 3–8.

## C. leichtlinii
This quamash readily forms compact groups. The star-like greyish-white or bluish purple flowers appear in late spring in tapering spikes. H 1m (3ft), S 10cm (4in). Borderline hardy/ Z 5–9. Among selected forms are **'Alba'**, which has white flowers, and plants in the **Caerulea Group**, with flowers in shades of blue.

# CANNA
## Indian shot plant, Indian reed flower
These are exotic plants for the autumn garden. Even if they did not flower, they would be worth

Canna 'President'

growing for their large, smooth leaves, which often have a bronze cast. Use them with grasses, brilliant annuals and dahlias to bring the season to a close with a flourish. They are also excellent in large containers.
*Cultivation* Grow cannas in fertile soil in full sun. In cold climates cannas need to be bedded out. Bring the rhizomes into growth in containers in late winter or early spring and keep them in a frost-free greenhouse or conservatory. When there is no further risk of frost plant them out just deep enough to cover with soil. In autumn, cut back the topgrowth, dig up the rhizomes and store them dry in a frost-free place over winter.

## C. hybrids
The cannas grown in gardens are hybrids, of which there are many. All the following have green leaves unless otherwise indicated. All are half-hardy/Z 7–10. **'Black Knight'** has dark red flowers and bronze leaves. H 1.8m (6ft), S 50cm (20in). **'City of Portland'** has yellow-edged, rose pink flowers. H 1m (3ft), S 50cm (20in). **'Ingeborg'** has salmon pink flowers and bronze leaves. H 60cm (2ft), S 50cm (20in). The free-flowering **'Lucifer'** has yellow-edged crimson flowers. H 60cm (2ft), S 50cm (20in). **'Orchid'** has pink flowers. H 60cm (2ft), S 50cm (20in). **'President'** has bright red flowers. H 1m (3ft), S 50cm (20in). The

*Canna 'Roi Humbert'*

flowers of **'Primrose Yellow'** are pale yellow. H 60cm (2ft), S 50cm (20in). **'Richard Wallace'** has canary yellow flowers. H 80cm (32in), S 50cm (20in). **'Roi Humbert'** has orange-red flowers and bronze leaves. H 80cm (32in), S 50cm (20in). **'Rosemond Coles'** has yellow-edged, bright red flowers. H 1.5m (5ft), S 50cm (20in). The orange flowers of **'Wyoming'** are frilled and have darker orange edges; the leaves are bronze. H 1.8m (6ft), S 50cm (20in).

## CARDIOCRINUM
### Giant lily
The name giant lily is well deserved from the point of view of the flowers, which certainly are lily-like, but the plant itself is unlike any lily, having rounded

*Cardiocrinum giganteum*

leaves and a pyramidal habit. They are not plants for the average garden. They need to stand in splendid isolation, or in small groups, in woodland clearings, where their scale and majesty can be best appreciated. Patience is needed: they take up to seven years to reach flowering size, when they die off, leaving seedlings behind. For a regular display you need to build up a colony of various ages.
*Cultivation* Cardiocrinums need fertile soil (ideally enriched with leaf mould) in light, dappled shade.

### C. giganteum
This imposing plant produces stout stalks clothed with immense leaves that are smaller towards the top, giving a narrowly pyramidal outline. The trumpet-shaped summer flowers are greenish-white with maroon red throats. H to 3m (10ft), S 1m (3ft). Hardy/Z 7–9.

## CHIONODOXA
### Glory of the snow
This small genus provides some delightful plants for early spring, typically with starry blue flowers. Grow them in a rock garden or in a border, or under deciduous trees and shrubs.
*Cultivation* Chionodoxas will grow in any but waterlogged soil in sun or light shade.

### C. forbesii
(syn. *C. luciliae* of gardens)
The lavender-blue flowers, with white centres, appear in early spring – sometimes earlier, after a

*Chionodoxa forbesii 'Pink Giant'*

*Colchicum 'The Giant'*

mild winter. It is an excellent subject for naturalizing. H 15cm (6in), S 3cm (1in). Hardy/Z 3–9. There are several cultivars, including **'Alba'**, which has white flowers; and **'Pink Giant'**, which has slightly larger white-centred, pink flowers.

### C. sardensis
This species is dwarfer than *C. forbesii*, but the deep blue flowers are more numerous. H 10cm (4in), S 4cm (1½in). Hardy/Z 5–9.

## COLCHICUM
### Autumn crocus, naked ladies
The flowers of colchicums are always a surprise when they appear in autumn – it is easy to forget that the corms are in the garden. The leaves, large and glossy, do not appear until the following spring (the best time to transplant them, if this is necessary). They are excellent in light woodland or planted around shrubs. In borders the leaves can be a nuisance in spring. Robust types are also excellent for naturalizing in grass.
*Cultivation* Grow in any good garden soil, ideally in light shade.

### C. speciosum
This, the most widely grown member of the genus, produces

goblet-shaped, pink flowers in early autumn. H 25cm (10in), S 10cm (4in). Hardy/Z 4–9. **'Album'** has pure white flowers that are green at the base.

### C. 'The Giant'
This is one of many hybrids, with the typical large, lilac-pink flowers. H to 20cm (8in), S 10cm (4in). Hardy/Z 4–9.

### C. 'Waterlily'
This is a popular double form, with pinkish-purple flowers that, unfortunately, are not very weather-resistant. H 12cm (5in), S 10cm (4in). Hardy/Z 4–9.

*Colchicum speciosum 'Album'*

*Crinum × powellii 'Album'*

# CRINUM
## Swamp lily
This South African genus is similar to *Amaryllis*, and the plants enjoy similar conditions. In cold gardens, crinums need the hottest spot available, which will usually be at the base of a warm wall. They are best in splendid isolation, when the handsome, strap-shaped leaves and impressive trumpet-like flowers can be seen to advantage. Crinums take some years to adapt after planting, and by the time they are ready to flower, the bulbs will be almost as big as footballs. Left undisturbed, the display will improve year on year. They also do well in containers.
**Cultivation** Plant in fertile, humus-rich soil in full sun, with shelter from wind. In cold areas a dry mulch of straw in winter can help to protect the dormant bulbs from frost.

### C. × powellii
This hybrid (of *C. bulbispermum* and *C. moorei*) is the plant most frequently offered for sale. In late summer to early autumn

*Crocosmia 'Lucifer'*

(sometimes earlier in favourable climates), it produces robust stems, topped with trumpet-like, pink flowers. H 1.2m (4ft), S 60cm (2ft). Borderline hardy/Z 7–10. **'Album'**, a distinguished selection, has white flowers. H 1m (3ft), S 60cm (2ft).

# CROCOSMIA
## Montbretia
This South African genus was not highly rated until Alan Bloom and others began to develop a range of hybrids, all with larger flowers than the plants previously seen in gardens, the most impressive of which, 'Lucifer', is an essential addition in any planting scheme. Excellent as they are as border plants, combining well with roses and annuals, they also look effective when grown in isolation in large groups, almost as a specimen.
**Cultivation** Crocosmias are tolerant of most garden soils in sun or light shade, but avoid sites that are too hot and dry.

### C. × crocosmiiflora
The hybrid group includes many garden-worthy forms. **'Emily McKenzie'** has orange flowers with brown throats from midsummer to autumn. H 45cm (18in), S 8cm (3in). Also flowering from midsummer to autumn, **'Solfatare'**, which is sometimes sold as *C.* 'Solfaterre', produces a succession of apricot-yellow flowers among its grassy, bronze-tinged leaves. H 60cm (2ft), S 8cm (3in).

### C. 'Lucifer'
This superb plant produces brilliant tomato red flowers in late summer and pleated, fan-shaped leaves. H 1.2m (4ft), S 8cm (3in). Borderline hardy/Z 7–9.

# CROCUS
Essential as they are in the spring garden, it is worth remembering that this large genus also includes some autumn-flowering forms – although confusingly colchicums are often sold under the common name 'autumn crocus'. Their bowl-shaped flowers are distinctive, as are their narrow,

*Crocus chrysanthus 'Blue Pearl'*

striped leaves. Almost every flower colour but pink is available, and some are attractively striped. A few have stamens in a contrasting colour. Robust hybrids are splendid for naturalizing in lawns, and can create a stunning effect, either in the traditional mixture of colours, or with a more subtle selection of just one or two shades. They can also be grown in shallow pans, bowls and alpine troughs, which is perhaps the best way of displaying some of the more choice and delicate species. Established bulbs tend to flower earlier than new plantings.
**Cultivation** Grow the larger species and hybrids in a position in full sun in any garden soil (as long as it is not waterlogged). If crocuses are naturalized in lawns, wait until six weeks after flowering before mowing to allow time for the new cormlets to reach flowering size. Dwarf species are best in very free-draining soil or in shallow pans of gritty compost in an alpine house or bulb frame.

### Early-flowering crocuses
#### C. ancyrensis
Each corm of this Turkish species produces three golden-yellow flowers in late winter. H 8cm (3in), S 5cm (2in). Hardy/Z 5–8. The selection **'Golden Bunch'** is more robust, with up to five flowers per corm. H 5cm (2in), S 4cm (1in).

#### C. chrysanthus
This species, from Greece and Turkey, is seldom grown in its straight form but is usually

represented in cultivation by its many selections, all flowering in late winter to early spring and including **'Advance'**, yellow, with violet outer petals; **'Blue Pearl'**, which has silver-blue flowers; **'E.A. Bowles'**, which has golden-yellow flowers; **'Ladykiller'**, which has slender, pure white flowers marked with purple; **'Snow Bunting'**, pure white; and one of the most spectacular cultivars, **'Zwanenburg Bronze'**, which has rich yellow flowers marked with purple-brown. H 8cm (3in), S 5cm (2in). Hardy/Z 3–8.

#### C. sieberi
Flowering in late winter to early spring, this species from the Balkans and Crete has yellow-centred, light blue flowers with striking bright orange pistils. H 8cm (3in), S 5cm (2in). Among the worthwhile forms are the golden-throated, white **'Albus'** (syn. 'Bowles' White'), which flowers in early spring; **'Firefly'**, which has unusual violet-red flowers; and the eye-catching *C. sieberi* subsp. *sublimis* **'Tricolor'**, which has flowers banded in the centre with purple, white and yellow. Hardy/Z 3–8.

#### C. tommasinianus
One of the best-loved species, this crocus, from the Balkans, Bulgaria, Hungary and Siberia, is also one of the best for naturalizing, producing gleaming lavender flowers in late winter. H 10cm (4in), S 2.5cm (1in). The different selections, which are

*Crocus tommasinianus*

*Crocus sieberi* subsp. *sublimis* 'Tricolor'

among the earliest crocuses to flower, are the cause of some confusion within the nursery trade. 'Ruby Giant' has large, rich purplish-red flowers; 'Whitewell Purple' also has purplish-red flowers, but with silvery mauve lining inside and more slender than those of 'Ruby Giant'. Hardy/Z 3–8.

### C. vernus

The species, as found in Italy, Austria and Eastern Europe, is usually represented in gardens by its many selections, all of which are excellent for naturalizing and flower in late winter to early spring. These include 'Jeanne d'Arc', which has pure white flowers; 'Pickwick', which has greyish-white flowers, striped with violet; and 'Remembrance', which has violet flowers with a silvery sheen. H 10cm (4in), S 8cm (3in). Hardy/Z 3–8.

*Crocus vernus* 'Remembrance'

### Autumn-flowering crocuses
### C. banaticus

An unusual crocus from Central Europe, this has lilac flowers in early autumn, which look effective in drifts near the front of a border. It needs soil that stays moist in summer. H 10cm (4in), S 5cm (2in). Hardy/Z 3–8.

### C. ochroleucus

This species from the Middle East has slender, creamy white flowers. It is excellent for naturalizing in grass or under deciduous shrubs and is one of the easiest of the late species to grow. H 5cm (2in), S 2.5cm (1in). Hardy/Z 3–8.

### C. pulchellus

A species native to the Balkans and Turkey with pale lilac-blue flowers. A vigorous crocus that likes dry soil in full sun. H 12cm (5in), S 4cm (1½in). 'Zephyr' has larger flowers. Hardy/Z 3–8.

## CYCLAMEN
### Sowbread

This delightful genus is native to the Mediterranean. The flowers are unique and distinctive, with their swept-back petals. Some cyclamen are not hardy and have been used to produce a range of houseplants with larger flowers. The hardy species are invaluable in the garden, as they belong to a select group of plants that thrive in dry shade and are therefore excellent for planting beneath trees, where in time they will build up large colonies. The leaves are usually beautifully marked. Make sure that any plants you buy are seed raised; wild populations have been decimated through over-collection.

*Cultivation* Hardy cyclamen prefer moderately fertile, moist but well-drained soil in partial shade, but they will tolerate drier soils. An annual mulch of leaf mould is beneficial. *C. persicum* hybrids grown as houseplants should be kept out of direct sunlight when in full growth. When watering, avoid wetting the upper surface of the tuber, which can collect water and rot. In winter keep the plants dry and place the pots in full light.

### C. coum

This species flowers from late winter to mid-spring, in a variety of colours, from purple-violet to pink and white. H 8cm (3in), S 10cm (4in). Hardy/Z 5–9.

### C. hederifolium
(syn. *C. neapolitanum*)
The name indicates that the leaves are ivy-like. The fact that they remain green when many other plants are below ground makes this a valuable plant for winter interest. The flowers, which may be deep pink, pale pink or pinkish-white, appear in late summer to mid-autumn. H 10cm (4in), S 15cm (6in). Hardy/Z 5–9.

### C. persicum

This species is the parent of a large number of hybrids that are often sold unnamed. The scented flowers range in colour from white to a glowing cerise red and appear in winter and spring. Some combine two colours on the frilly petals. H and S to 15cm (6in). Tender/Z 9–10.

## DAHLIA

These exotic-looking flowers are now enjoying something of a revival. They are the ideal plant for adding a splash of colour to the autumn garden, with their perfectly formed, almost geometric flowers. Flower colours include white, all shades of pink, red, orange, yellow and a warm rosy purple. Some combine more than one colour. For maximum impact,

*Cyclamen coum*

*Dahlia* 'Small World'

plant dahlias in groups. Tall varieties are excellent for the back of a border.

Dahlias have been extensively hybridized, resulting in a range of flower shapes classified as described below.

*Cultivation* Dahlias need rich soil (although they do reasonably well in any ordinary, well-drained soil) in full sun. Pinch out the growing tips for bushiness and deadhead to keep the flowers coming. Tall varieties, particularly those with very large flowers, need staking. In cold areas the tubers should be lifted after the topgrowth has been blackened by frost, then dried off and stored over winter for planting out again the following spring. Alternatively, treat them as annuals and plant fresh tubers each year. For earlier flowers, start them into growth in containers under glass six weeks before planting out.

*Cyclamen hederifolium*

*Dahlia* 'Ellen Huston'

All the following dahlias are half-hardy/all zones.

## Single-flowered dahlias (Division 1)
One or two rows of petals surround a central disc. Mostly dwarf, these dahlias are suitable for bedding. **'Ellen Huston'** has orange-red flowers and contrasting purple-tinged foliage. H and S 30cm (12in). **'Moonfire'** has single, deep gold flowers with vermilion centres and dark bronze-green foliage. H 75cm (30in), S 30cm (12in). **'Tally Ho'** has red flowers with yellow centres and dark copper foliage. H and S 60cm (2ft).

## Anemone-flowered dahlias (Division 2)
The flowers are double, with one or more rings of outer petals surrounding a central group of tubular florets. Those of **'Paso Doble'** have white outer petals and yellow centres. H 1m (3ft), S 60cm (2ft). **'Scarlet Comet'** has vivid red flowers with upright central petals. H 1.2m (4ft), S 60cm (2ft).

## Collerette dahlias (Division 3)
The flowers have two rings of outer florets around a central group of disc florets.

*Dahlia* 'Hillcrest Regal'

**'Chimborazo'** has flowers with a yellow-tipped collar. H 1.2m (4ft), S 60cm (2ft). **'Hillcrest Regal'** has maroon flowers with a white-tipped collar. H 1.2m (4ft), S 60cm (2ft).

## Waterlily dahlias (Division 4)
The flowers classified large, medium, small or miniature, are fully double and flattened. **'Figurine'** has small, pink and white flowers. H 1.2m (4ft), S 60cm (2ft). **'Glorie van Heemstede'** has small, orange-yellow flowers. H 1.2m (4ft or more, S 60cm (2ft). **'Lismore Willie'** has small, pale gold flowers. H 1.2m (4ft), S 60cm (2ft). **'Porcelain'** has small, white flowers flushed with lilac-pink. H 1.2m (4ft), S 60cm (2ft).

## Decorative dahlias (Division 5)
The flowers, classified as giant, large, medium, small or miniature, are fully double, and the tips of the petals are bluntly pointed. **'Alva's Supreme'** has giant, soft yellow flowers. H 1.2m (4ft) or more, S 60cm (2ft). **'Charlie Two'** has medium, light yellow flowers. H 1.2m (4ft), S 60cm (2ft). **'David Howard'** has miniature, rich orange flowers and copper-tinged foliage. H 1m (3ft) or more, S 60cm (2ft). **'Fire Mountain'** has miniature, bright red flowers and very dark green foliage. H 1.2m (4ft) or more, S 60cm (2ft). **'Hamari Gold'** has giant, golden-bronze flowers. H 1.2m (4ft), S 60cm (2ft). **'Karenglen'** has miniature, orange-red flowers. H 1m (3ft), S 60cm (2ft). **'Kenora Valentine'** has large, brilliant red flowers. H 1.2m (4ft), S 60cm (2ft). **'Kidd's Climax'** has giant, yellow-flushed pink flowers. H 1m (3ft) or more, S 60cm (2ft). **'Phill's Pink'** has small, warm orange-pink flowers, the petals yellow at the base. H 1m (3ft), S 60cm (2ft). **'Skipley Spot'** has small, red flowers with white-tipped petals. H 1m (3ft), S 60cm (2ft).

## Ball dahlias (Division 6)
The flowers, small or miniature, are fully double and globe-shaped. **'Cornel'** has small, rich red

*Dahlia* 'Figurine'

flowers. H 1.2m (4ft), S 60cm (2ft). **'Jomanda'** has miniature, terracotta-red flowers. H 1m (3ft) or more, S 60cm (2ft).

## Pompon dahlias (Division 7)
The flowers are fully double and globe-shaped with petals that are round or blunt at the tips. **'Minley Carol'** has orange flowers with a hint of red at the tips of the petals. H 1m (3ft) or more, S 60cm (2ft). **'Small World'** (syn. 'Bowen') is one of the best white dahlias. The flowers are sometimes flecked with purple. H 1m (3ft) or more, S 60cm (2ft). **'Willo's Surprise'** has wine red flowers. H 1m (3ft) or more, S 60cm (2ft).

## Cactus dahlias (Division 8)
The flowers, classified as giant, large, medium, small or miniature, are fully double and have rolled, pointed petals. **'Doris Day'** has small, cardinal red flowers. H 1m (3ft) or more, S 60cm (2ft). **'Kiwi Gloria'** has small, lilac-pink and white flowers. H 1m (3ft) or more, S 60cm (2ft).

## Semi-cactus dahlias (Division 9)
As for cactus dahlias, but the petals are rolled to only half their length. **'Belle of the Ball'** has large, lavender-pink flowers. H 1.2m (4ft), S 60cm (2ft). **'Eastwood Moonlight'** has medium, pale yellow flowers. H 1m (3ft) or more, S 60cm (2ft). **'Fidalgo Climax'** has large, bright yellow flowers. H 1.2m (4ft), S 60cm (2ft). **'Hamari Accord'** has large, clear yellow flowers. H 1.2m (4ft), S 60cm (2ft). **'Hayley Jane'** has small, white flowers, the petals tipped with purple. H 1.2m (4ft) or more, S 60cm (2ft). **'Kenora Challenger'**

*Dahlia* 'Alva's Supreme'

has large, pure white flowers. H 1.2m (4ft), S 60cm (2ft). **'Kenora Sunset'** has medium, orange-red flowers with yellow centres. H 1.2m (4ft), S 60cm (2ft). **'Lemon Elegans'** has small, pure yellow flowers. H 1.2m (4ft), S 60cm (2ft). **'Match'** has small, white flowers, the petals tipped with purple. H 1.2m (4ft), S 60cm (2ft). **'Nargold'** has medium orange and gold flowers, with ragged petals. H 1.2m (4ft), S 60cm (2ft). **'Pink Pastelle'** has medium, bright pink flowers, with white centres. H 1.2m (4ft), S 60cm (2ft). **'Piper's Pink'** has small, glowing pink flowers. H and S 60cm (2ft). **'So Dainty'** has miniature, orange-bronze flowers. H 1m (3ft) or more, S 60cm (2ft). **'Tahiti Sunrise'** has medium, yellow flowers, the petals tipped with red. H 1.2m (4ft), S 60cm (2ft). **'Weston Pirate'** has miniature, dark red flowers. H 1m (3ft), S 60cm (2ft). **'White Moonlight'** has medium, white flowers. H 1.2m (4ft), S 60cm (2ft).

## Miscellaneous (Division 10)
This designation covers a wide range of hybrids that are sometimes defined further as peony-flowered, orchid-flowered, mignon, gallery and so on, not all

*Dahlia* 'Jomanda'

Dahlia 'Art Deco'

Eranthis hyemalis

Erythronium dens-canis

Eucomis bicolor

of which are universally accepted. **'Art Deco'** (dwarf bedding) has orange flowers. H and S 25–30cm (10–12in). **'Bishop of Llandaff'** has semi-double bright red flowers with yellow centres and blackish-red foliage. H 60cm (2ft) or more, S 45cm (18in). **'Fascination'** (dwarf bedding) has pinkish-purple flowers and dark bronze foliage. H 60cm (2ft), S 45cm (18in). **'Rembrandt'** (dwarf bedding) has pink flowers, the petals tipped with darker pink. H and S 25–30cm (10–12in). **'Renoir'** (dwarf bedding) has deep pink flowers, more open than those of 'Rembrandt'. H and S 25–30cm (10–12in).

## ERANTHIS
### Winter aconite

These are one of the earliest bulbs to come into flower. They are robust enough to penetrate a light covering of snow, which is a charming effect when it occurs. Like snowdrops, they transplant best when putting on growth after flowering, so when buying them, look for plants 'in the green' rather than dormant tubers. They are excellent when planted to

Dahlia 'Hayley Jane'

carpet large areas beneath deciduous trees. The flowers, surrounded by a characteristic 'ruff' of green leaves, open only when the sun is shining. *Cultivation* Grow in any well-drained soil, ideally humus-rich, in sun or light shade.

### E. hyemalis
(syn. *Aconitum hyemale*)
The species has bright green leaves, forming a ruff beneath the lemon-yellow flowers. H 8cm (3in), S 5cm (2in). Hardy/ Z 4–9. Plants in the **Cilica Group** (syn. *Aconitum cylicum*) have rather larger flowers thatn those of the species, and the leaves of the ruff are smaller. H 10cm (4in), S 5cm (2in).

## ERYTHRONIUM
### Dog's tooth violet

To those who grow them, these are one of the delights of the spring garden, although their presence is fleeting. The flowers, with their upswept petals, are of unique charm, and the leaves of some forms are attractively mottled. Grow them in clumps around deciduous trees and shrubs or on lightly shaded rock gardens. *Cultivation* They will grow in most soils enriched with organic matter, and moisture retentive without being boggy. They prefer a cool spot, out of sun in summer: in the shade of deciduous trees is ideal. They must not be allowed to dry out. Plant them as soon after you buy them as possible and cover them with a mulch in dry summers.

### E. californicum
The species is usually represented in cultivation by **'White Beauty'** (syn. *E. revolutum* 'White Beauty'),

which has large white flowers with brownish-yellow throats in mid- to late spring. The leaves are flecked with brown. H 20–25cm (8–10in). S 25cm (10in). Hardy/Z 3–9.

### E. dens-canis
European dog's tooth violet
The beautiful species produces one flower, which may be white, pink or lilac, on each stem in early to mid-spring. H and S 25cm (10in). Hardy/Z 3–9. **'Rose Queen'** has pink flowers. H and S 25cm (10in).

### E. 'Pagoda'
Probably the most popular of all the dog's tooth violets, 'Pagoda' has nodding, yellow flowers in late spring. The glossy, faintly mottled leaves are green. H 40cm (16in), S 15cm (6in). Hardy/Z 4–9.

## EUCOMIS
### Pineapple plant

So-called because of the pineapple-like flowers, which have a characteristic tuft of green leaves at the

top of the spike, these South African species do best in a sheltered spot (such as by a warm wall) and also thrive in containers. The flowers are attractive to bees. *Cultivation* Grow in full sun in moderately fertile, well-drained soil. Protect in winter with a mulch of straw or other similar dry material.

### E. bicolor
This species produces spikes of green flowers from mid- to late summer among the strap-shaped leaves. H 30–60cm (1–2ft), S 20cm (8in). **'Alba'** has white flowers. Borderline hardy/Z 8–10.

### E. comosa
(syn. *E. punctata*)
A species with tall, narrow spikes of white flowers that are edged with purple. H 75cm (30in), S 20cm (8in). Borderline hardy/Z 8–10.

Erythronium 'Pagoda'

*Fritillaria imperialis* 'The Premier'

*Fritillaria meleagris*

# FRITILLARIA
## Fritillary

This is a variable genus, containing species that provide garden plants fit for a number of purposes. The imposing crown imperial is good for adding height to spring borders, while the snake's head fritillary is excellent for naturalizing in meadows or by the streamside. Others are connoisseurs' plants, needing special conditions but providing ample reward with their subtly coloured flowers. Only a few of the nearly 100 species are widely grown, all with pendent, bell-like flowers.
*Cultivation* Most fritillaries do well in any well-drained soil in sun. *F. meleagris* does best in heavier, moisture-retentive soil in sun or light shade but will tolerate ordinary soil. Bulbs of *F. imperialis* are prone to rotting. Planting them on their sides will help to prevent water collecting on the hollow upper surface.

## F. imperialis
### Crown imperial

These majestic plants are unmistakable. The yellow, orange-red or red flowers hang down from the tops of erect, sturdy stems in late spring. Plant the bare bulbs (which are unpleasantly scented) as soon after purchase as possible. H 1.2m (4ft) or more, S 30cm (1ft). Selections include **'Lutea'**, which has yellow flowers; **'Rubra'**, vermilion-red; and **'The Premier'**, which has orange-red flowers. Hardy/Z 5–9.

## F. meleagris
### Snake's head fritillary

This species is often found growing wild in damp European meadows. The flowers, which come in late spring, are appealingly chequered with dull purple. In the right conditions this species will self-seed. H 30cm (12in), S 5cm (2in). *F. meleagris* var. *unicolor* subvar. *alba* has white flowers that are delicately touched with green. Hardy/Z 3–8.

## F. michailovskyi

Also flowering in late spring, this species has fascinating bell-like flowers that are a dusky reddish-purple edged with yellow. Grow in a shady rock garden or an alpine trough. H 20cm (8in), S 5cm (2in). Hardy/Z 5–8.

# GALANTHUS
## Snowdrop

Few plants have the charm of the snowdrop or are as welcome. They are usually among the first flowers to appear in the gardening year. Each flower has six petals, the outer three longer than the inner ones. Unusually among bulbs, snowdrops seem to prefer slightly damp soil. They are delightful in drifts in light woodland, or pushing through ivy.
*Cultivation* Most snowdrops do best in reliably moist soil, in a spot where they are in sun when in growth but lightly shaded when dormant; beneath deciduous trees and shrubs is usually an ideal spot.

## G. elwesii

This species from Turkey and the Balkans is less well known than *G. nivalis* but possibly superior. It is a larger plant, with bright green, strap-shaped leaves and flowers with large green spots on the inner petals. H to 25cm (10in), S 8cm (3in). Hardy/Z 3–9.

## G. nivalis

The best-known of the snowdrops and one that will naturalize very easily. The bell-shaped, pure white flowers hang downwards, the outer petals flaring outwards to reveal the green markings on the inner ones. H and S 10cm (4in). **'Flore Pleno'**, the double form, is no less charming. Hardy/Z 3–9.

# GALTONIA
## Cape hyacinth, summer hyacinth

These elegant plants, valued for their late season, provide a welcome freshness to summer borders where they are allowed to rise above annuals or late-flowering perennials. The flowers open in succession on the flower spike, from bottom to top, providing interest over a number of weeks.
*Cultivation* Galtonias need fertile, well-drained soil in a sunny spot.

## G. candicans

The most popular species, this bears spikes of fragrant white flowers in late summer to early autumn. H 1–1.2m (3–4ft), S 10cm (4in). Hardy/Z 7–10.

## G. viridiflora

The species is similar to *G. candicans* but has green flowers. H 1m (3ft), S 10cm (4in). Half-hardy/Z 7–9.

# GLADIOLUS

Nowadays a less popular flower with gardeners than formerly, the gladiolus is still an excellent florist's flower. The ease with which it hybridizes has led to a huge number of selected forms.

The spikes can be picked while still in bud, and the flowers will open indoors. They do not combine well with other plants but can be used in a colour border in large groups. Otherwise, grow them in a picking border exclusively to provide flowers for the house. Shorter-growing forms are also effective in containers.
*Cultivation* Hardy gladioli will grow in any well-drained soil in full sun. The large-flowered hybrids need fertile soil that does not dry out in summer. Where these will not survive the winter, lift the corms in autumn and dry them off. Snap off the old corm and store the new one in a dry, frost-free place over winter for planting out again the following spring. Tall varieties need staking.

## G. communis subsp. byzantinus (syn. G. byzantinus)

The exception to all other gladioli, this elegant species flowers in late spring. The rich magenta flowers (typical of gladioli but much smaller) are produced in long spikes. A superb plant for naturalizing, it is also effective in borders and large rock gardens. H 1m (3ft), S 8cm (3in). Borderline hardy/Z 7–10.

## G. hybrids

Gladiolus hybrids, of which there are a vast number, are usually classified according to flower size: giant, large, medium, small and miniature. Butterfly gladioli are small-flowered, often with a contrasting patch of colour on the lower petals. Primulinus gladioli have funnel-shaped

*Galtonia candicans*

*Gladiolus communis* subsp. *byzantinus*

*Gladiolus* 'Seraphin'

*Hippeastrum* 'Christmas Star'

## HYACINTHOIDES
### Bluebell
This genus includes the well-known English bluebell, as well as the rather coarse Spanish species. Bluebells are excellent for colonizing areas beneath deciduous trees. *Cultivation* Grow in any reasonable garden soil in light shade.

### H. hispanica
### (syn. *Scilla campanulata*)
### Spanish bluebell
A rather more robust species than the English bluebell (with which it will hybridize), this sends up erect stems with blue, bell-shaped flowers in spring. H 60cm (2ft), S 10cm (4in). Hardy/Z 4–9.

### H. non-scripta
### English bluebell
Broadly similar to the Spanish bluebell, this species has daintier, somewhat darker blue flowers, which are also more tubular. They are borne in late spring. There are a number of pink and white forms. H to 60cm (2ft), S 8cm (3in). Hardy/Z 6–9.

## HYACINTHUS
### Hyacinth
Nothing can match the scent of hyacinths. In addition, they have one of the widest colour ranges of all the bulb genera, including the elusive blue. Only the hybrids are cultivated. Planted in blocks in beds, they are a little stiff and formal, and they do not integrate well with other plants. It is better to tuck them into odd corners and allow the scent to hit you as you wander around the garden. Otherwise, they are good in bowls and can be grown as houseplants. 'Forced' bulbs are sold from autumn onwards, and these will flower in the middle of winter, but all can be grown indoors initially. Planted out in the garden after flowering, they will take a season or two to recover. The more compact forms are best for growing outdoors; larger ones are top-heavy and are best kept inside. *Cultivation* Outdoors, grow in any well-drained soil in full sun. If treated as annuals, they can be planted in light shade. Indoors, grow in bowls of special bulb fibre. Bulbs for forcing should be

*Hyacinthus* 'Amethyst'

planted up and placed in a cool, dark place (such as a dry cellar or garage) for 8–10 weeks, then brought into a light, warm room for flowering 3–4 weeks later. Alternatively, they can be grown in special glass hyacinth vases that allow the roots to be in water while keeping the actual bulb dry.

### H. hybrids
The following flower naturally in mid-spring but can be forced to flower at other times. All are hardy/Z 6–9. 'Amethyst' has lilac-blue flowers; 'Anna Marie' is bright pink; 'Blue Jacket' is an arresting deep blue; 'Carnegie' has pure white flowers; 'City of Haarlem' is bright yellow; 'Gipsy Queen' is a subtle salmon orange; the double flowers of 'Hollyhock' are deep red; 'Jan Bos' is carmine red; the well known 'L'Innocence' is pure white; 'Ostara' has deep violet-blue flowers; and 'Pink Pearl' has pink flowers. H 20– 30cm (8–12in), S 8cm (3in).

*Hyacinthus* 'City of Haarlem'

flowers that are less densely packed on the spike than with the other types. All flower from midsummer to early autumn and are half-hardy/Z 7–10. 'Aristocrat' (medium) is late, with purple flowers. H 1m (3ft), S 10cm (4in). 'Bluebird' (small) is early, with rich violet-blue flowers. H 1m (3ft), S 10cm (4in). The greenish-yellow flowers of 'Green Woodpecker' (butterfly) are blotched with red. H 1.5m (5ft), S 12cm (5in). 'Lady Godiva' (primulinus) is white. H 60cm (2ft), S 10cm (4in). 'Leonore' (primulinus) has bright yellow flowers. H 1m (3ft), S 10cm (4in). The salmon pink and yellow flowers of 'Mykonos' (butterfly) are marked with red. H 1m (3ft), S 10cm (4in). 'Peter Pears' (large) is soft apricot-orange. H 1.2m (4ft), S 18cm (7in). 'Seraphin' (butterfly) has muffled pink flowers with white throats. H 70cm (28in), S 10cm (4in). 'The Bride' (miniature) is pure white. H 1m (3ft), S 10cm (4in). 'Trader Horn' (giant) has deep, rich scarlet flowers. H 1.2m (4ft), S 18 cm (7in).

## HIPPEASTRUM
Confusingly, these are usually sold under the name 'amaryllis'. Few of the species are grown, but there are a growing number of hybrids, all with huge, showy flowers, intended for growing exclusively as houseplants. They are often sold in packs with pots and compost (soil mix) for the Christmas gift market. Large bulbs produce more flowers (up to five) on each stem than smaller ones.

*Cultivation* Use any proprietary compost, with added grit (both for drainage and weight because these plants can be top-heavy). Plant with the neck of the bulb above the surface of the compost. Keep them well-watered and stand them in full light, but not directly next to a window. Stake the flower stem if necessary.

### H. hybrids
There are many cultivars, with a wide range of flower forms and colours. All are tender/Z 10. 'Apple Blossom' has white flowers with pink-edged petals. H 50cm (20in), S 30cm (12in). 'Christmas Star' is an attractive, compact form with white flowers that are edged and striped with bright red. H to 45cm (18in), S 30cm (12in). 'Florida' has bright red flowers. H to 60cm (2ft), S 30cm (12in). 'Snow Queen' is one of several white-flowered amaryllis, others being 'White Dazzler' and 'White Lady'. H to 60cm (2ft), S 30cm (12in).

*Hippeastrum* 'Florida'

*Iris reticulata 'George'*

# IRIS

Irises form a large genus that includes true bulbs (in the generally accepted sense of the term) as well as perennials (so-called rhizomatous irises are treated as perennials in this book). Some have very specific cultivation needs. Early-flowering species seldom last long in the garden and are best treated as annuals. So-called 'Dutch irises' are grown commercially for the cut flower market. Bulbous irises are excellent in borders, rock gardens and containers.
*Cultivation* Bulbous irises need a preferably well-drained, alkaline soil, in full sun.

## I. bucharica

This species, native to central Asia, has fragrant, golden-yellow and white flowers in mid-spring, blotched with either green, brown or violet. It needs protection from winter wet and is probably best grown in an alpine house. H 40cm (16in). Hardy/Z 4–9.

## I. danfordiae

This delightful dwarf species from Turkey, valued for its bright yellow flowers, blooms in late winter. It will tolerate some shade. H 10cm (4in). Hardy/Z 6–9.

## I. reticulata

This dainty species from the Caucasus is one of the first bulbous plants to flower in the gardening calendar, producing its rich violet-blue, yellow-splashed flowers in late winter. It is excellent in rock gardens and shallow pans but unfortunately is not reliably perennial, so it is advisable to plant fresh stocks annually. H 15cm (6in). Hardy/Z 6–9. Selections include **'George'**,

which has deep purple flowers; **'Harmony'**, with deep blue flowers; **'Joyce'**, which has sky blue and orange flowers; and **'J.S. Dijt'**, with purple-violet flowers.

## Xiphium irises

This large group, consisting mainly of robust hybrids that are easy to grow, includes irises sometimes referred to as 'Dutch irises', 'English irises' and 'Spanish irises'. They make excellent border plants that flower in late spring or early summer, but they are forced to flower at any time for the cut flower market. They are often sold as mixed colours, but there are several named selections, including **'Apollo'**, with yellow and white flowers; **'Casablanca'**, with white flowers; **'Imperator'**, which have blue and orange flowers; **'Professor Blaauw'**, deep blue; **'Symphony'**, with yellow and white flowers; and **'Telstar'**, deep blue. H 60–65cm (24–26in). Hardy/Z 5–8.

# LEUCOJUM
## Snowflake

These neglected bulbs look like large snowdrops, but differ in having six white petals of equal length, each one spotted with yellow-green at the tip. These plants appreciate damp soil and are at their most attractive when planted on the banks of a natural stream. They can also be grown in borders and rock gardens.
*Cultivation* The snowflakes described here need fertile soil that does not dry out and a position in full sun or light shade.

## L. aestivum
### Summer snowflake

This is the most commonly grown species. Despite the name,

it flowers in mid-spring, producing green-tipped white flowers and glossy green leaves. H 40cm (16in), S 8cm (3in). Hardy/Z 4–9.

## L. vernum
### Spring snowflake

The flowering period of this often coincides with the snowdrops (late winter to early spring). They need a fertile soil and are best left undisturbed after planting. H 35cm (14in). Hardy/Z 4–8.

# LILIUM
## Lily

This huge genus is also one of the most varied in terms of cultivation: there are lilies for sun, for shade, acid or alkaline soils. Lilies work well in mixed summer borders, appreciating the shade at their roots that the neighbouring plants provide. They are also excellent in pots. A few are delightful in woodland, but building up colonies of good size can take several years.
*Cultivation* All the lilies described here need well-drained soil and are better off where their flowers will be in sun while their roots are shaded. A few will tolerate light overhead shade. Most prefer acid to neutral soil, although some tolerate alkaline soil, with a few even preferring it. Many modern hybrids have been bred to thrive whatever the pH. Individual requirements are specified in the entries below.

## Asiatic hybrids (Division 1)

Derived from Asiatic species and hybrids, these are sturdy stem-rooting lilies. There are three subdivisions: 1a, with upward-facing flowers; 1b, with outward-facing flowers; and 1c, with

*Lilium 'Concorde'*

pendent flowers. All are hardy/Z 4–8. **'Admiration'** (1a) has large, unscented, creamy yellow flowers spotted with maroon in early to midsummer. H to 40cm (16in). **'Bronwen North'** (1c) is striking with slightly scented, pale mauve-pink flowers heavily spotted and lined with purple in early summer. H to 1m (3ft). **'Concorde'** (1a), an excellent border plant, has unscented, lemon-yellow flowers, greenish at the base, that open from early to midsummer. H to 1m (3ft). **'Connecticut King'** (1a) is a popular hybrid, with unscented, rich deep yellow flowers in early summer. H to 1m (3ft). **'Côte d'Azur'** (1a) produces unscented, rich pink flowers in early to midsummer. H to 1m (3ft). **'Eros'** (1c) has nodding, fragrant, turkscap flowers in midsummer. The sepals are pinkish orange spotted with maroon. H to 1.2m (4ft). **'Karen North'** (1c) bears lightly scented turkscap flowers in midsummer. The sepals are orange-pink, lightly spotted with darker pink. H to 1.4m (55in). **'Mont Blanc'** (1a) produces unscented, brown-spotted, white flowers in early to midsummer. H to 70cm (28in). **'Orange Pixie'** (1a) has unscented, bright orange flowers in summer that are spotted with

*Leucojum aestivum*

*Lilium 'Bronwen North'*

*Lilium 'Orange Pixie'*

*Lilium* 'Roma'

chocolate-maroon. H to 40cm
(16in). **'Peggy North'** (1c) is a
good border lily, with lightly
scented turkscap flowers in midsummer. The sepals are glowing
orange spotted with dark brown.
H to 1.5m (5ft). **'Roma'** (1a)
has fragrant creamy white flowers,
lightly spotted with maroon,
which open in early to
midsummer. H to 1.2m (4ft).

## Martagon hybrids (Division 2)
Derived mainly from *L. martagon*
and *L. hansonii*, these are hardy,
mainly stem-rooting lilies with
turkscap flowers, suitable for light
shade or woodland. All are hardy/
Z 4–8. **'Mrs R.O. Backhouse'**, a
famous lily, is one of the oldest
still in cultivation. It has
unscented, turkscap flowers that
hang from the stems in early to
midsummer. The sepals are
orange-yellow with maroon
spotting and are flushed pink on
the outside. H 1.3m (52in).

## Candidum hybrids (Division 3)
Derived from *L. chalcedonicum*,
*L. candidum* and other European
species (excluding *L. martagon*),
this is a small group of lilies with
sometimes scented, turkscap
flowers. They are usually not
stem-rooting. **L. × testaceum**
(Nankeen lily) is a lime-tolerant

*Lilium* Bellingham Group

hybrid bearing fragrant, turkscap
flowers in early to midsummer.
The sepals are pale apricot-pink
lightly spotted with red. H 1.2m
(4ft). Hardy/Z 5–8.

## American hybrids (Division 4)
Derived from American species,
these are rhizomatous lilies, with
sometimes scented, usually
turkscap flowers. They are not
stem-rooting. **Bellingham Group**
have occasionally fragrant turkscap
flowers that can vary in colour
from yellow to orange and orange-
red, all spotted deep brown and
appearing in early and midsummer.
They are excellent for naturalizing
in light shade and need acid soil,
preferably reliably moist. H to
1.5m (5ft). **'Shuksan'** is a
selected form, with lightly
scented, tangerine-yellow flowers
tipped with red and spotted with
black or reddish-brown. H to
1.2m (4ft). Hardy/Z 4–8.

## Longiflorum hybrids (Division 5)
Derived from *L. formosanum* and *L.
longiflorum*, this is a small but
growing group of lilies with
fragrant, trumpet- or funnel-
shaped flowers, usually grown for
the cut flower market.

## Trumpet and Aurelian hybrids (Division 6)
Derived from Asiatic species
(excluding *L. auratum, L. japonicum,
L. rubellum* and *L. speciosum*), these
are mostly hardy, fragrant, stem-
rooting lilies. There are four
subdivisions: 6a, with trumpet-
shaped flowers; 6b, with usually
outward-facing, bowl-shaped
flowers; 6c, with shallowly bowl-
shaped flowers that often open
flat; and 6d, with sepals that are
distinctly recurved. The lilies
described are borderline hardy/
Z 4–8. In mid- and late summer
the beautiful lilies in the **African
Queen Group** (6a) have heavily
scented, tangerine-apricot flowers
that are veined with deep purple
on the outside. H 2m (6ft).
**'White Henryi'** (6d) has large,
fragrant flowers in midsummer
that open flat. The sepals are
white, flushed deep orange at the
base and with rust-red papillae. H
to 1.5m (5ft).

*Lilium* African Queen Group

## Oriental hybrids (Division 7)
Derived from species from the
Far East, these are late-flowering
lilies, often with scented flowers.
Most are lime-hating and need
sun or partial shade. There are
four subdivisions: 7a, with
trumpet-shaped flowers; 7b, with
bowl-shaped flowers; 7c, with flat
flowers; and 7d, with sepals that
are distinctly recurved. All are
hardy/Z 4–8. **'Acapulco'** (7d) has
fragrant, rich pink flowers with
recurving sepals. H to 1m (3ft).
**'Belle Epoque'** (7b), which
flowers from midsummer to early
autumn, has white to soft pink
flowers, each sepal centrally
banded with cream. H to 1m
(3ft). **'Casa Blanca'** (7b) has
heavily scented, pure white flowers
in mid- to late summer. H to
1.2m (4ft). **'Little Joy'** (7d),
bred for container growing, is a
sturdy dwarf, with unscented
flowers with recurved, pink to
soft red sepals, spotted with dark
maroon. H to 35cm (14in). From
midsummer to early autumn
**'Royal Class'** (7b) produces
fragrant flowers, the sepals
varying in colour from white to
soft pink, with a central yellow
band and prominent papillae. H
to 1m (3ft). **'Star Gazer'** (7c) is
a popular lily, albeit lime-hating.
From midsummer it produces rich

*Lilium* 'Acapulco'

*Lilium* 'Royal Class'

crimson-pink, unscented flowers
that are spotted with darker pink.
H to 1.5m (5ft).

## Other hybrids (Division 8)
This group includes all hybrids
not accommodated by the other
groups. **'Moneymaker'** produces
up to six, sweetly scented, clear
pink flowers in midsummer. H to
1m (3ft). Hardy/Z 4–8.

## Species (Division 9)
This group includes all true
species and their forms.

### *L. auratum*
### Golden-rayed lily
This species from Japan has the
largest flowers of any lily. The
heavily scented flowers open in
late summer to autumn; the
sepals are white, usually spotted
with crimson, and banded with
yellow and with fleshy papillae. It
needs acid soil. H to 1.5m (5ft).
Hardy/Z 5–8.

### *L. candidum*
### Madonna lily
This is a species from the Balkans
and eastern Mediterranean with
fragrant, trumpet-shaped, pure
white flowers in summer. Grow in
neutral to alkaline soil and plant
the bulbs shallowly. H to 2m
(6ft). Hardy/Z 4–9.

*Lilium* 'Moneymaker'

Lilium regale

Lilium speciosum var. album

Muscari armeniacum 'Blue Spike'

### L. formosanum

This elegant but slightly tender species is native to Taiwan. In late summer and early autumn fragrant, trumpet-shaped, white flowers open from buds that are strongly flushed with wine purple. It needs moist, acid soil. H to 1.5m (5ft). Borderline hardy/ Z 5. The naturally occurring variant **L. formosanum var. pricei** is hardier and much smaller. H to 30cm (12in).

### L. henryi

This Chinese species is clump-forming and easy to grow. In late summer elegant stems carry hanging, lightly scented, orange, turkscap flowers, spotted darker. It is best in neutral to alkaline soil in light shade. H to 3m (10ft). Hardy/Z 4–9.

### L. martagon
### Martagon lily, common turkscap lily

This species occurs in a range from northwest Europe to northwest Asia. The turkscap flowers, slightly unpleasant to smell, hang from the stems in early to midsummer. They are dull pink, spotted with maroon. It does well in almost any well-drained soil in sun or light shade. H to 2m (6ft). The naturally occurring **L. martagon var. album** is a desirable white form. Hardy/Z 4–8.

### L. regale
### Regal lily

An essential plant in any garden, this species is found growing wild in western China. Opening in midsummer, its richly scented,

white flowers have yellow bases and are heavily stained purple on the outside. It tolerates most well-drained soils. H to 2m (6ft). Hardy/Z 4–9. **L. regale var. album** has pure white flowers with golden yellow anthers.

### L. speciosum

This attractive species from China, Japan and Taiwan needs moist, acid soil, preferably in light shade. The pale pink or white, fragrant, turkscap flowers are produced in late summer. H to 2m (6ft). There are a number of selected forms, including **L. speciosum var. album**, which has white flowers with prominent papillae; **'Krätzeri'**, which has white sepals striped green on the back; and **'Uchida'**, which has brilliant crimson flowers, spotted with green or darker red and tipped with white. Hardy/Z 5–8.

## MUSCARI
### Grape hyacinth

These flowers do indeed resemble miniature hyacinths, and their shape and deep purple-blue colour are also evocative of tiny grape bunches. They self-seed freely, making them a weed in some gardens, but can be of of value for their unassuming charm. They are seen at their best when planted in large, river-like drifts among shrubs and trees.

*Cultivation* Grow in any well-drained soil in sun or light shade.

### M. armeniacum

This is the most commonly grown species, with clusters of dull blue, bell-like flowers in spring. Try it in conjunction with

the yellow-flowered *Doronicum orientale*. H to 20cm (8in), S 5cm (2in). Hardy/Z 2–9. Selected forms include **'Blue Spike'**, which has double flowers; and **'Fantasy Creation'**, which has flowers that fade to green. H to 20cm (8in), S 5cm (2in).

### M. botryoides

The straight species is rarely cultivated, but the selection **'Album'** is becoming more popular. It has spikes of white flowers (less compact than those of *M. armeniacum*) in spring. Plant the bulbs in quantities, and close together, for the best display. H 20cm (8in), S 5cm (2in). Hardy/Z 3–9.

## NARCISSUS
### Daffodil

Spring would not be spring without daffodils, probably the largest of the bulb genera, with their distinctive central cups or trumpets. They have one of the longest flowering seasons of almost any bulb, with a few appearing as early as midwinter. Almost without exception, the daffodils grown in gardens today are artificial hybrids. The number of these is so vast that they are usefully categorized in a number of divisions (see right). Daffodils look best when planted en masse, in grass, on banks or beneath deciduous trees and shrubs. Smaller species and hybrids are excellent in sunny rock gardens or alpine troughs.

*Cultivation* Daffodils are tolerant bulbs that will grow in any reasonable garden soil so long as it is well drained. They should be

in sun when in growth, so if planting beneath deciduous trees, choose varieties that die down before the tree is in full leaf. Deadhead after flowering, where practicable, to ensure good flowering in subsequent seasons.

### Trumpet daffodils (Division 1)

The trumpet is the same length as, or longer than, the petals. All are hardy/Z 3–9. The classic **'King Alfred'** is a popular, sturdy hybrid, with bright yellow flowers in mid-spring. H 35cm (14in).

### Large-cupped daffodils (Division 2)

The cup is longer than one-third of, but less than the length of, the petals. All are hardy/Z 3–9. **'Carlton'** has soft yellow flowers with large cups with frilly edges in mid-spring. It is good for naturalizing. H 45cm (18in). One of the best-loved white daffodils, **'Ice Follies'** has flowers, opening in early to mid-spring, with contrasting lemon-yellow coronas that fade to creamy white. It is excellent for naturalizing, especially where strong yellows are not wanted. H 40cm (16in). The strongly coloured **'Pinza'** has rich yellow petals and deep red cups in mid-spring. It is an effective contrast to *Muscari armeniacum*. H 35cm (14in). The vigorous **'Rainbow'**, which flowers in late spring, is an unusual daffodil with white petals surrounding a pink cup. H 45cm (18in). **'Saint Patrick's Day'** is an eye-catching daffodil, flowering in mid-spring, with lime green coronas surrounded by creamy-white petals. H 35cm (14in).

Narcissus 'Carlton'

## Small-cupped daffodils (Division 3)
The cup is less than one-third the length of the petals. All are hardy/Z 3–9. 'Merlin' has pure white petals and pale yellow cups. H 45cm (18in). 'Verona' has white petals and a cream cup that fades to white. H 45cm (18in).

## Double daffodils (Division 4)
The petals or the cup (or both) are doubled, sometimes leading to a muddled appearance. All are hardy/Z 3–9. One of the best-known, 'Rip van Winkle' has bright yellow flowers in early spring. H 25cm (10in). 'White Lion' has unusual flowers, with white outer petals and pale lemon-yellow central segments. Flowering in mid-spring, it is a good choice for naturalizing. H 40cm (16in). The fragrant 'Yellow Cheerfulness' has golden-yellow flowers in mid-spring. It is a good border daffodil. H 45cm (18in).

## Triandrus daffodils (Division 5)
Derived from *N. triandrus*, with usually between two and six flowers on each stem. All are hardy/Z 3–9. 'Hawera' has dainty, canary yellow flowers in mid- to late spring. It is excellent in pots and can be brought indoors when in flower. H 25cm (10in). 'Thalia' is technically a dwarf but is taller than most. It produces shining white flowers in mid-spring, combining well with *Fritillaria meleagris*. H 30cm (12in).

## Cyclamineus daffodils (Division 6)
Derived from *N. cyclamineus*, these

*Narcissus* 'Jetfire'

have solitary flowers with characteristically swept-back petals. They are usually dwarf. All are hardy/Z 3–9. As its name suggests, 'February Gold' produces bright yellow flowers in late winter. It is excellent in containers, windowboxes and in spring borders with primroses. H 30cm (12in). 'Jetfire', which flowers in early spring, has orange cups and rich yellow petals that flex back. It is a good contrast to *Muscari armeniacum*. H 20cm (8in). The vigorous 'Little Witch' has bright yellow flowers. H 20cm (8in). 'Peeping Tom' is sturdy, with golden-yellow flowers that have long trumpets and swept-back petals in early spring. It is an excellent border daffodil. H 25cm (10in).

## Jonquilla daffodils (Division 7)
These have from one to five, usually fragrant, flowers on each stem. All are hardy/Z 3–9. 'Quail' has appealing, clear yellow flowers in mid-spring. H 30cm (12in). 'Suzy' is a strongly scented daffodil, which flowers

in mid-spring. Yellow petals surround flattened orange cups. H 40cm (16in).

## Tazetta daffodils (Division 8)
These have from three to twenty flowers on each stem. Some are half-hardy but the following are both hardy/Z 3–9. The dainty 'Minnow', which flowers in early spring, has three to five flowers on each stem, with rounded, creamy-white petals and short primrose-yellow cups. H 18cm (7in). The fragrant 'Silver Chimes' produces its silver-white flowers in mid- to late spring. It works well with *Fritillaria meleagris*. H 30cm (12in).

## Poeticus daffodils (Division 9)
Related to *N. poeticus*, these have white petals and very shallow cups and are fragrant. They are usually late flowering. All are hardy/Z 3–9. One of the last to flower in late spring, 'Actaea' has glistening white petals surrounding a brilliant orange corona. H 45cm (18in).

## Species (Division 10)
The plants in this group are species and wild variants, few of which are suitable for general garden use.
*N. bulbocodium* (hoop-petticoat daffodil) is a charming species from southern Europe and northern Africa. It has broad, funnel-like cups and pointed petals in mid-spring. Tricky to grow, it needs a site that is moist in spring and dry in summer, so is often easiest in an alpine house. H 10–15cm (4–6in). Hardy/Z 7–9.

*N. cyclamineus* is a distinctive species from Spain and Portugal. The bright yellow flowers, produced in early spring, have swept-back petals (like a cyclamen) and long, narrow cups. H 15–20cm (6–8in). Hardy/Z 3–9.
*N. poeticus* var. *recurvus* (old pheasant's eye) is fragrant and flowers in late spring. It has distinctive, glistening white petals and, short red-edged, yellow cups. It is a parent of 'Actaea' and is excellent for naturalizing in grass. H 35cm (14in). Hardy/Z 3–9.

## Split-corona daffodils (Division 11)
The flowers in this group are usually solitary with cups that are split for more than half their length. All are hardy/Z 3–9. 'Chanterelle' has white petals and yellow cups. H 45cm (18in). 'Orangery' has white petals and orange cups. H 45cm (18in).

## Miscellaneous (Division 12)
Daffodils that do not fit easily into any of the above categories. The following are hardy/Z 3–9. 'Jumblie' is a reliable dwarf for early spring display. Each stem carries several golden-yellow cups whose petals flex back slightly. It is a good choice for a hanging basket. H 20cm (8in). In early to mid-spring 'Quince' has pale yellow petals that sweep back and surround darker yellow cups with frilly edges. H 15cm (6in). The popular 'Tête-à-Tête' produces reliable crops of bright yellow flowers in early spring. It is good for a hanging basket or windowbox. H 15cm (6in).

*Narcissus* 'Rip van Winkle'

*Narcissus* 'Suzy'

*Narcissus* 'Actaea'

*Narcissus bulbocodium*

Nectaroscordum siculum

# NECTAROSCORDUM

The small genus is related to *Allium*, but the flowers are distinctive. It is a quiet, elegant plant that combines well with the neater growing old roses.
*Cultivation* Grow in any reasonable, well-drained soil in sun or light shade.

### N. siculum
(syn. *Allium siculum*)
This species from the eastern Mediterranean has pale greenish-cream flowers that hang from the tops of erect stems in summer; the outsides are flushed with plum red. H to 1.2m (4ft), S 10cm (4in). Hardy/Z 7–10.

# NERINE
Guernsey lily
A well-established clump of nerines will be a focus of attention when the flowers appear in autumn. Each is trumpet-shaped, but the petals curve sharply backwards, giving a most elegant appearance. Usually a clear

Nerine bowdenii

pink, they look as if they have been lightly dusted with sugar.
*Cultivation* Nerines need a hot spot in well-drained soil. Plant the dormant bulbs with the necks just above soil level and leave them undisturbed unless they become very congested and stop flowering well.

### N. bowdenii
The most commonly grown species, this has flowers that appear at the end of the growing season in late summer to autumn, when the foliage (which emerges in spring) has all but died down. H 45cm (18in) or more, S 8cm (3in). Hardy/Z 8–10. 'Alba' has white flowers, occasionally tinged with pink. H 45cm (18in) or more, S 8cm (3in).

# ORNITHOGALUM
Star of Bethlehem
This is a large genus of about 80 species, which are found through Africa, Asia and Europe. Not all are hardy, but the species described are easy to grow. Hardy species naturalize readily. In cold areas, the less hardy species can be grown in containers or treated as annuals and planted in borders in spring. All make long-lasting cut flowers.
*Cultivation* Grow in well-drained soil in sun or light shade.

### O. arabicum
This species produces cup-shaped, fragrant white flowers in early summer. H 30–80cm (12–32in), S 8cm (3in). Half-hardy/Z 7–10.

### O. nutans
From 10 to 20 starry, white flowers, striped with green on the outside, hang from the stems in early to mid-spring. This does best in woodland. H 30–40cm (12–16in), S 5cm (2cm). Hardy/Z 6–10.

### O. thyrsoides
Chincherinchee
This popular species has dense spikes of cup-shaped, white flowers from early spring to summer (depending on the planting time). H to 70cm (28in), S 10cm (4in). Half-hardy/Z 7–10.

Ornithogalum nutans

### O. umbellatum
Later flowering than *O. nutans*, this has starry flowers that open only when the sun is shining, closing during dull weather and showing the green exteriors of their petals. It is excellent for naturalizing. H 20cm (8in), S 10cm (4in). Hardy/Z 7–10.

# SCILLA
Squill
This is a large genus, although some of its species have now been transferred to *Hyacinthoides*. The species described is the best-known. It combines well with *Chionodoxa* (glory of the snow) in borders, rock gardens and under deciduous trees and shrubs.
*Cultivation* Grow in well-drained soil in sun or partial shade.

### S. siberica
Siberian squill
This species, from central Russia, produces nodding, star- to bell-shaped, blue flowers in early spring. H 15cm (6in), S 5cm (2in). Among the selections are 'Alba', a rare white form; and 'Spring Beauty', which has larger flowers and is more robust. H to 20cm (8in), S 5cm (2in). Hardy/Z 1–8.

# TIGRIDIA
Tiger flower, peacock flower
These exotic and distinctive flowers for late summer combine well with dahlias and cannas, and are also suitable for growing in containers. Treat them as annuals in cold areas, planting the bulbs only when all danger of frost has passed.

Tigridia pavonia

*Cultivation* Grow in well-drained, fertile soil in full sun. Alternatively, plant in containers of well-drained compost (soil mix).

### T. pavonia
This is the species most generally grown. It produces several flowers on each spike, in shades of white, cream, yellow, pink or red, each lasting for one day only. The flowers are conspicuously spotted. Single-colour selections are seldom available. H 45–60cm (18–24in), S 10cm (4in). Tender/Z 8–10.

# TULIPA
Tulip
Highly prized by many, but tulips are unlikely to achieve again the degree of popularity they enjoyed in the 17th century, when Tulipomania swept western Europe, bankrupting many. So vast is the number of hybrids, that the genus is split into divisions (see right).

All tulips can be grown in containers. Some of the species are dwarf, modest plants that are best in rock gardens, but the hybrids are more versatile. They should be grown en masse, the strikingly marked ones in isolation, but the self-coloureds combine well with a range of spring-flowering plants, including pulmonarias, winter pansies and polyanthus. Pink tulips with blue forget-me-nots is a classic cottage-garden combination, which also works well in containers. Tulips provide a memorable display, but most are

Tulipa 'Oranje Nassau'

Tulipa 'Golden Melody'

Tulipa 'Striped Bellona'

Tulipa 'Esther'

hard work from the gardener's point of view because they cannot simply be left in situ to flower every year – they need lifting. Many prefer to treat them as annual bedding plants, discarding them after flowering and buying in new stock each autumn – making it possible to try out new varieties. Growing tulips is an addictive but expensive hobby.
*Cultivation* Tulips do well in any ordinary garden soil, provided it is well drained. An open site in full sun is desirable, but some shelter from strong winds is advisable for taller varieties. Most of the hybrids, although perennial, do best if not left in the ground permanently. They should be lifted after they have died back, then cleaned and dried off for storage in a cool, well-ventilated place over summer. In autumn, replant the larger bulbs where they are to flower. Small bulbs will not flower but can be grown on in a nursery bed until they reach flowering size.

**Single early tulips (Division 1)**
The cup-shaped flowers are borne in early to mid-spring. These tulips are suitable for growing in borders or in mixed bedding. All are hardy/Z 3–8. **'Apricot Beauty'** has salmon-pink flowers. H 45cm (18in). **'Brilliant Star'** has scarlet flowers. H 30cm (12in). **'Yokohama'**, one of the best yellows, has lemon-yellow flowers. H 35cm (14in).

**Double early tulips (Division 2)**
These tulips have double, bowl-shaped flowers in mid-spring. They are suitable for bedding. All are hardy/Z 3–8. **'Carlton'** has blood-red flowers. H 40cm (16in). **'Monte Carlo'** has sulphur-yellow flowers. H 30cm (12in). **'Oranje Nassau'** is deep orange. H 25cm (10in). **'Schoonoord'** has pure white flowers. H 25cm (10cm). **'Stockholm'** is bright red. H 30cm (12in). **'Willem van Oranje'** has orange flowers, flushed with copper red. H 25cm (10in). **'Willemsoord'** has red flowers, edged with white. H 25cm (10in).

**Triumph tulips (Division 3)**
The single, cup-shaped flowers are produced from mid- to late spring. They are good for bedding and are rain resistant. All are hardy/Z 3–8. **'Abu Hassan'** has purple-brown flowers edged with yellow. H 50cm (20in). **'Attila'** has purple-violet flowers. H 50cm (20in). **'Barcelona'** has fuchsia-purple flowers. H 50cm (20in). **'Blue Ribbon'** has lilac-purple flowers. H 50cm (20in). **'Couleur Cardinal'** has violet-red

flowers. 35cm (14in). **'Don Quichotte'** is deep pink. H 50cm (20in). The violet flowers of **'Dreaming Maid'** are edged with white. H 55cm (22in). **'Garden Party'** has white and carmine red flowers. H 40cm (16in). **'Golden Melody'** has golden-yellow flowers. H 55cm (22in). **'Lustige Witwe'** (syn. 'Merry Widow') has red flowers, edged with white. H 40cm (16in). The yellow flowers of **'New Design'** fade to pinkish white. H 50cm (20in). **'Passionale'** has purple flowers. H 45cm (18in). **'Pax'** is pure white. H 45cm (18in). **'Prinses Irene'** has orange and red flowers. H 35cm (14in). **'Silver Dollar'** has yellow flowers. H 55cm (22in). **'Striped Bellona'** has yellow flowers striped with red. H 50cm (20in).

**Darwin hybrids (Division 4)**
The large, single, oval flowers are carried at the tops of tall, sturdy stems, making them excellent for cutting. (These should not be

confused with Darwin tulips, now included in division 5.) All are hardy/Z 3–8. **'Ad Rem'** has deep orange flowers. H 60cm (2ft). **'Apeldoorn'** has brilliant vermilion red flowers. H 55cm (22in). **'Golden Apeldoorn'** has lemon-yellow flowers. H 55cm (22in). **'Parade'** has bright red flowers. H 60cm (2ft).

**Single late tulips (Division 5)**
The flowers are cup- or goblet-shaped and are borne in late spring. (Darwin, Breeder and Cottage tulips belong to this group.) All are hardy/Z 3–8. **'Avignon'** has bright red flowers. H 50cm (20in). **'Electra'** has magenta flowers. H 25cm (10in). **'Esther'** has light magenta flowers. H 50cm (20in). **'Menton'** has rose-red flowers with pale orange stripes. H 65cm (26in). **'Pink Lady'** has pink flowers. H 50cm (20in). **'Queen of Night'** has purple-black flowers. H 60cm (2ft). **'Sorbet'** is pinkish-white. H 60cm (2ft).

Tulipa 'Attila'

Tulipa 'Apeldoorn'

Tulipa 'Queen of Night'

Tulipa 'Ballerina'

Tulipa 'West Point'

Tulipa 'Fantasy'

## Lily-flowered tulips (Division 6)

The petals of the slender flowers are often pointed and curve backwards. They are late-flowering tulips and rather susceptible to wind damage. All are hardy/Z 3–8. **'Aladdin'** has deep red flowers edged with yellow. H 55cm (22in). **'Ballerina'** has blood-red flowers. H 55cm (22in). **'Mariette'** is pure pink. H 55cm (22in). **'Mona Lisa'** has yellow streaked with red flowers. H 55cm (22in). **'West Point'** has primrose-yellow flowers that look good with forget-me-nots. H 50cm (20in). **'White Triumphator'** has pure white flowers. H 60cm (2ft).

## Fringed tulips (Division 7)

The petals of the cup-shaped flowers are fringed at the edges (sometimes in a different colour). The flowers appear in late spring. All are hardy/Z 3–8. **'Crystal**

Beauty'** has rose-pink flowers with an orange fringe. H 55cm (22in). **'Red Wing'** has rich red flowers. H 50cm (20in).

## Viridiflora tulips (Division 8)

The flowers, which are produced in late spring, are touched with varying amounts of green. All are hardy/Z 3–8. **'Artist'** has deep orange and green flowers. H 30cm (12in). **'Groenland'** has pink and green flowers. H 55cm (22in). **'Spring Green'** has creamy white flowers with broad green stripes. H 50cm (20in).

## Rembrandt tulips (Division 9)

The cup-shaped flowers, borne in late spring, are dramatically variegated with contrasting colours, usually brown, bronze, black, red, pink or purple on a white, yellow or red ground. (These are the tulips depicted in Dutch old master paintings. Unfortunately, since the breaking

of the flower colour is caused by a virus, few are nowadays produced commercially. The obsolete Bizarre and Bijbloemen tulips belonged to this division.) All are hardy/Z 3–8. **'Gala Beauty'** has red and yellow streaked flowers. H 60cm (2ft). **'Jack Laan'** has purple flowers shaded with brown and feathered with white and yellow. H 55cm (22in).

## Parrot tulips (Division 10)

The cup-shaped flowers, borne in mid- to late spring, have twisted petals, which are irregularly cut and evenly banded with other colours. The flowers gradually open flat, exposing black centres and golden stamens. These tulips are sensitive to cold, wet weather and do best in a sheltered spot. These are sports of tulips from other divisions. All are hardy/Z 3–8. **'Black Parrot'** has violet-black flowers. H 50cm (20in). **'Blue Parrot'** is mauve-blue. H 55cm (22in). **'Estella Rijnveld'** has red and creamy white flowers. H 50cm (20in). **'Fantasy'** has pink flowers crested with green and irregularly crimped petals. H 55cm (22in). **'Texas Flame'** has yellow and red flowers. H 45cm (18in).

## Double late tulips (Division 11)

Sometimes called peony-flowered tulips, these flower in late spring. They have fully double, bowl-shaped flowers and should be planted in a sheltered spot because they do not stand up well to bad weather. They do well in

areas with cold winters and late springs. All are hardy/Z 3–8. **'Allegretto'** has red flowers edged with yellow. H 35cm (14in). The pink flowers of **'Angelique'** are edged with white. H 45cm (18in). **'Casablanca'** has white flowers. H 45cm (18in).

## Kaufmanniana tulips (Division 12)

These small, sturdy tulips are usually very early, often with bicoloured flowers and sometimes with spotted foliage. The flowers open flat in sunshine, hence the name 'waterlily tulips'. All are hardy/Z 3–8. **'Chopin'** has yellow flowers streaked with red and grey-green foliage mottled with brown. H 25cm (10in). **'Giuseppe Verdi'** has carmine-red flowers edged with yellow and mottled foliage. H 30cm (12in). **'Gluck'** has carmine-red flowers edged with bright yellow and spotted foliage. H 20cm (8in).

Tulipa 'Mona Lisa'

Tulipa 'Spring Green'

Tulipa 'Blue Parrot'

Tulipa 'Chopin'

Tulipa linifolia

The salmon-pink flowers of **'Shakespeare'** are flushed with orange and yellow. H 25cm (10in). **'Stresa'** has currant-red and yellow flowers and spotted foliage. H 25cm (10in).

### Fosteriana tulips (Division 13)

The group includes *T. fosteriana* and hybrids developed from it. They are similar to the Kauffmanniana and Greigii tulips but have larger, slender flowers. The leaves are sometimes striped. They are suitable for naturalizing. The group includes many red tulips. All are hardy/Z 3–8. **'Madame Lefeber'** has bright red flowers. H 40cm (16in). **'Orange Emperor'** has bright orange flowers with a yellow base. H 40cm (16in). **'Purissima'** (syn. 'White Emperor') is pure white. H 45cm (18in).

### Greigii tulips (Division 14)

The group includes *T. greigii* and hybrids developed from it. They

have blue-grey leaves, mottled to varying degrees with brownish purple. The flowers open wide in full sun. They are early flowering and good for naturalizing. All are hardy/Z 3–8. **'Ali Baba'** has deep pink flowers and spotted foliage. H 30cm (12in). **'Compostella'** has red flowers. H 30cm (12in). **'Ontario'** has magenta-pink flowers and spotted foliage. H 30cm (12in). **'Toronto'** has red flowers. H 30cm (12in).

### Miscellaneous (Division 15)

The group includes the species, selected forms and hybrids that are not in the other divisions. All are hardy/Z 3–8.

#### *T. clusiana* var. *chrysantha* (syn. *T. chrysantha*, *T. stellata* var. *chrysantha*)

The species, which is from northern Afghanistan, has yellow flowers that open flat, like stars, in mid-spring. H 30–35cm (12–14in).

Tulipa 'Shakespeare'

Tulipa saxatilis

**'Cynthia'** has cream flowers, flushed with coral-red and edged with green.

#### *T. linifolia*

Native to Bukhara and the Pamir Alai mountains, this easy-to-grow species has fluorescent red flowers in late spring. H 20cm (8in).

#### *T. praestans*

A multi-flowered species from Central Asia, this is an excellent subject for naturalizing. It has orange-red flowers in early to mid-spring. H 20–25cm (8–10in). There are several cultivars, including **'Fusilier'**, which is a luminous vermilion red; and **'Unicum'**, which has bright red flowers and yellow-edged leaves.

#### *T. saxatilis*

This species, which is native to Crete, appreciates very well-drained soil. The flowers, which open wide in early spring, are soft lilac-pink with yellow centres and are lightly scented. H 30–40cm (12–16in).

#### *T. tarda*

Native to Central Asia, this is one of the best species for ordinary garden use. The star-shaped flowers, with yellow, white-tipped petals, appear in early spring. It naturalizes easily. H 12–15cm (5–6in).

#### *T. turkestanica*

This Turkish species is one of the first to bloom, the flowers appearing in late winter in a good year. The white flowers have bright yellow centres. H 25–30cm (10–12in).

## ZANTEDESCHIA
### Arum lily

South Africa is home to many fine bulbous plants, but few are as ravishing as this one, with its bold, glossy leaves and flowers of breathtaking purity. Planted en masse, arum lilies can be a breathtaking sight. For bulbs, they have a long flowering season. In cold gardens, the shelter of a warm wall will offer protection for many, but some selections are hardy enough to be grown in the

open border. Arum lilies can also be planted as an aquatic, but although plants undoubtedly look spectacular reflected in water, they are susceptible to rot. A number of tender hybrids have been bred for growing in containers under glass in cold areas.

**Cultivation** Arum lilies need soil that does not dry out in the growing season and a position in full sun. In cold areas, provide winter protection in the form of a mulch of straw or other dry material. When grown as an aquatic, plant in plastic baskets to a depth of 15–30cm (6–12in). Make sure that plants in containers do not dry out in winter.

#### *Z. aethiopica*

The best known species, this is also the hardiest, particularly in the form **'Crowborough'**. This produces pure white, funnel-shaped spathes on long stems, from early to midsummer among the glossy green leaves. H 85cm (33in), S 60cm (2ft). Borderline hardy/Z 8–10. **'Green Goddess'** has spathes splashed with green and is more susceptible to frost. Borderline hardy/Z 8–10.

#### *Z.* hybrids

Among the many hybrids are **'Black-eyed Beauty'**, which has deep creamy-yellow spathes, marked with black inside; **'Cameo'**, which has apricot-coloured spathes; **'Mango'**, with orange spathes; and **'Solfaterre'**, which has yellow and black spathes. H 30–40cm (12–16in), S 15–20cm (6–8in). Tender/Z 9–10.

Zantedeschia aethiopica 'Crowborough'

# Alpines

Alpines are among the gems of the plant kingdom. Small but beautifully formed, they can be found producing their jewel-like blooms from the last days of winter to late autumn, providing a wealth of interest through the seasons. Since the majority are neat and compact-growing, alpines are eminently suited to gardens of restricted size, and are ideal for growing in troughs and containers, or, where space allows, in a dedicated rock garden or raised bed; but many can also be grown in mixed borders alongside bigger plants.

A rock garden is one of the most attractive ways of growing alpines. Here carpets of alpines create a tapestry of form and vivid colour.

# What is an alpine?

Botanically, alpines are no different from other plants, and a precise definition is elusive, since the term "alpine" can mean different things to different gardeners.

On the face of it, "alpine" implies mountain-dwelling plants, but most horticulturists understand it as applying to anything that grows above the tree line in harsh, exposed habitats, a definition in itself elastic. The tree line can be close to sea level in areas near the North and South Poles – if it exists at all – while in the Himalayas it can be at altitudes of up to 4,000m (13,000ft). The common feature is the plants' tolerance of open, exposed situations, on stony if not rocky ground, conditions that invariably have a dwarfing effect. In other words, any small, tough, hardy plant may be considered as being "alpine", and this is the sense in which the word is used here. (However, conifer species that have dwarf variants in exposed situations are included with the rest of the conifers.)

The majority of alpines are perennials, and they are often long lived. (Dwarf bulbs, which are often planted to good effect alongside alpines in gardens, in rockeries and in troughs, are rarely found in alpine regions of the world.) Their compact habit is a response to climate. Alpines can be covered in snow for much of the year, during which time they are dormant. (No plant can survive in areas of permanent ice and snow.) When the snow melts, they burst into life: often their annual growth cycle is vastly accelerated compared to the majority of plants, since they often grow in areas with short summers. Their flowers are usually large in relation to the rest of the plant, and are often jewel-like in the vividness and clarity of their colours. They exhibit a number of characteristic habits.

**Cushion** Many alpines from high altitudes have a dense cushion or bun-like habit. The flowers are carried directly on the surface of the cushion or are held well above the foliage on long stalks. Cushion alpines are typical of high alpine habitats, especially rock slopes and cliffs as well as moraines (glaciated areas covered by rocks and other debris).

**Mat** In high, exposed regions, a creeping, mat-forming habit gives the plant considerable protection from strong winds. The mats, spreading outwards from the centre, consist of numerous low, leafy shoots. They can grow from a central rootstock or can root where the shoots touch the ground. Some have underground runners that throw up topgrowth here and there: in other words, what appears as a colony of separate plants can in fact be a single plant.

**Rosette** Some alpines form symmetrical rosettes, either solitary or bunched together, from the centre of which arise the flower stems.

Typically they occur on cliffs and other rocky ground, but occasionally also on high alpine meadows.

**Shrubs** What shrubs are found in alpine regions tend to be severely dwarfed by the bleak, exposed conditions and are therefore low and mounded or spreading.

**Tuft** This a common form and comprises a low, leafy tuft bearing flowers at the stem tips. The tufts are usually herbaceous, and the stems die down at the end of each season, to be replaced by new shoots the next spring that arise from the old base or from below ground level. Tufted alpines are characteristic of high-altitude alpine meadows and open scrub in the mountains, some occurring on more exposed rocky habitats.

## Alpines in the garden

Many gardeners think of growing alpines as a spectator sport, imagining them to be difficult plants for the enthusiast only. While it is true that some alpines are best grown in a dedicated alpine house, a good many are suitable for growing

Dry-stone retaining walls, such as those at the edge of a lawn or patio, can act like an extra flower bed for alpine crevice dwellers.

This gently sloping gravel or scree garden is an ideal way of displaying some of the more spreading alpines.

in the open garden or in troughs, and it is these that form the basis for the following selections featured in this plant category.

What unites the majority of alpines is their need for good drainage (though some primulas prefer damper conditions). The best garden situation is an open, sunny site that is not shaded by overhanging trees or nearby walls or buildings. Exposure to strong winds, which can be detrimental to many other plants, is not a problem.

Some alpines will tolerate the typical conditions enjoyed by most other plants and can be grown in mixed borders: aubrieta (*Aubrieta deltoidea*) and rock soapwort (*Saponaria ocymoides*) are both excellent edging plants, while some of the sturdier bellflowers (notably the invasive *Campanula portenschlagiana*) and stonecrops (*Sedum*) can be planted alongside other border plants.

Ideally, however, create a rock garden, an artificial outcrop of rocks, preferably on a slope for good drainage. On gently sloping ground you could make an arroyo, in nature a dried-up stream bed or rocky ravine. Either will include numerous ledges, clefts and nooks for a wide variety of alpines. If your ground is flat, you can make what is effectively a rock garden on the horizontal, a scree (basically a gravel garden).

Alternatively, grow your alpines in raised beds, which give you all the advantages of improved drainage besides being of inestimable value to gardeners who experience difficulty in bending down. They can be made with a variety of materials. A dry-stone wall made from the local stone will be beautiful even before it is planted, and will allow you to plant in the gaps between the stones, while eco-friendly gardeners might

Each of these alpine stone troughs, enhanced with small rocky outcrops and dwarf shrubs, is a unique miniature garden of lasting interest over many months of the year.

prefer using reclaimed materials, such as railway sleepers (ties). Bricks and mortar can look uncompromisingly harsh initially, but will soon be softened by trailing plants, such as *Gypsophila repens*, that will cascade down the sides.

All alpines thrive in containers, either individually or as collections in troughs. These also offer you the opportunity of growing acid-loving plants (such as rhododendrons and some gentians) if the soil in the

open garden in alkaline. Really tiny alpines are best appreciated in small troughs; you could add a few dwarf conifers to make a miniature mountainscape. Plants such as houseleeks (*Sempervivum*) which in nature seem to grow in virtually no soil at all, are best in shallow pans.

Both raised beds and troughs should be filled with free-draining soil or special alpine compost (soil mix) and can be topdressed with grit and small stones.

Androsace sempervivoides

Aquilegia alpina

Aquilegia flabellata

## ALCHEMILLA

This large genus contains many plants that are too large for the rock garden, but the species described here are neater and less prone to self-seeding than the familiar *Alchemilla mollis*.
*Cultivation* Grow in fertile, well-drained soil in sun or semi-shade.

### A. alpina
**Alpine lady's mantle**
The dark green, deeply lobed leaves form mats, surmounted by tiny, yellow-green flowers in summer. H to 10cm (4cm), S 45cm (18in). Hardy/Z 3–7.

### A. conjuncta
The lobed leaves are blue-green. Clusters of tiny yellow-green flowers are borne in summer and autumn. H to 40cm (16in), S 30cm (12in). Hardy/Z 4–8.

## ANDROSACE

This genus of about 100 species includes many mat-forming perennials that are ideal for rock gardens or alpine troughs.
*Cultivation* Grow in gritty, well-drained but reliably moist soil in sun.

### A. carnea
The species from the Pyrenees and Alps has rosettes of evergreen, hairy leaves and, in spring, clusters of small, yellow-eyed, pink flowers. H to 5cm (2in), S to 15cm (6in). Hardy/Z 4–7.
*A. carnea* subsp. *laggeri* has pinkish-red flowers and is more densely tufted. H to 5cm (2in), S to 15cm (6in).

### A. sempervivoides
(syn. *A. mucronifolia* of gardens)
This evergreen, mat-forming species, native to the western Himalayas, has small, neatly formed, deep-green rosettes, which produce further rosettes on short, strawberry-like runners. The clusters of small, mauve-pink to mid-pink flowers are held above the rosettes on short stalks. H 5–7.5cm (2–3in), S 15–30cm (6–12in). Hardy/Z 4–7.

## AQUILEGIA
**Columbine**
The genus is best known for the herbaceous perennials grown in the border, but it also includes a number of species suitable for the rock garden.
*Cultivation* Grow in gritty but fertile, well-drained soil in full sun.

### A. alpina
(syn. *A. montana*)
**Alpine columbine**
Too tall for all but the largest rock gardens, this has pretty blue flowers in late spring and blue-green, ferny foliage. H 45cm (18in), S to 30cm (12in). Hardy/Z 4–7.

### A. flabellata
(syn. *A. akitensis*)
This delightful little alpine columbine has neat, grey-green, divided foliage. The typical flowers are purple-blue with white tips to the petals. They are borne in late spring and early summer and will seed around in the garden. H 40–50cm (16–20in), S 15–20cm (6–8in). Hardy/Z

4–9. *A. flabellata* var. *pumila* f. *alba* (syn. *A. flabellata* 'Nana Alba') has up to three white flowers on each stem. H and S 10–15cm (4–6in). Hardy/Z 3–9.

## ARABIS
**Rock cress**
The genus contains more than 100 species of annuals and evergreen perennials with white or purple, four-petalled flowers.
*Cultivation* These plants need well-drained soil and a warm position in full sun.

### A. alpina subsp. caucasica
(syn. *A. caucasica*)
The common arabis of gardens comes from the Balkans and western Asia. It is a mat-forming evergreen with close, rather coarse rosettes of greyish-green leaves and bears clusters of white flowers in spring and early summer. H to 15cm (6in), S 50cm (20in). Hardy/Z 4–8. Selected forms

include 'Flore-Pleno', which has double, pure white flowers; and 'Variegata', which has leaves variegated with creamy yellow. H 15–25cm (6–10in), S 20–40cm (8–16in). Hardy/Z 4–8.

## ARMERIA
**Sea pink, thrift**
The genus of evergreen perennials and subshrubs is distributed across Europe, northern Africa and North America. All species produce the little spherical flowerheads.
*Cultivation* Grow in well-drained soil that is not too rich, in a position in full sun.

### A. maritima
(syn. *A. vulgaris*)
The familiar, tough, evergreen hummocks of slender, deep green leaves bear long-stalked heads of pink to reddish-purple flowers in summer. H and S 15–25cm (6–10in). Hardy/Z 4–7.
'Vindictive' has large, rich pink flowerheads. H to 15cm (6in), S 25cm (10in). Hardy/Z 4–7.

## AUBRIETA

These evergreen perennials are popular and reliable garden plants, ideal for sunny walls, scree beds and all manner of crevices. The forms grown in gardens are derived from *A. deltoidea*.
*Cultivation* Grow in well-drained, neutral to alkaline soil in sun. Shear over after flowering to maintain a neat shape.

### A. deltoidea
This species is the familiar aubrieta of gardens, which is

Arabis alpina subsp. caucasica

Armeria maritima

Aubrieta 'Doctor Mules'

native to south-eastern Europe. It is an evergreen, mat-forming plant with close, deep green or grey-green foliage in lax rosettes. The clusters of reddish-purple, violet, mauve or pink flowers are borne in spring and intermittently through summer. H 10–15cm (4–6in), S 15–50cm (6–20in). Hardy/Z 5–7. Among the many named forms are 'Argenteovariegata' (syn. A. albomarginata), which has single, silver-pink flowers and leaves variegated with cream; 'Doctor Mules', which has deep purple flowers; and 'Joy', which has single, mauve flowers.

## AURINIA

The evergreen perennials in the genus are found in mountainous areas throughout southern and central Europe. The small yellow or white flowers have four petals.
*Cultivation* Grow in a position in full sun in moderately fertile soil.

Aurinia saxatilis

Plants will benefit from being sheared over after flowering to keep them neat.

### A. saxatilis
(syn. *Alyssum saxatile*)
**Gold dust**
The familiar yellow alyssum of gardens is a subshrub with large tufts of greyish- or whitish-green leaves. In spring and through summer the plants produce sprays of tiny, yellow flowers. H 20–30cm (8–12in), S 30–50cm (12–20in). Hardy/Z 4–7.

## BALLOTA

This genus includes shrubs and perennials. The species described here is a compact subshrub for a sunny spot in a scree garden or in a Mediterranean planting.
*Cultivation* This needs well-drained soil, which need not be fertile. Grow in full sun and clip back in spring to keep plants neat.

### B. acetabulosa
The grey-green leaves, the main attraction, are borne in pairs along the upright stems. Tiny purple-pink flowers appear in summer. H and S to 60cm (24in). Hardy/Z 5–9.

## CAMPANULA
**Bellflower**
In addition to the many border perennials in this large genus, there are many species that can be grown in the rock garden.
*Cultivation* Campanulas should be grown in fertile, well-drained soil, ideally neutral to alkaline. Grow in a position in full sun.

Campanula carpatica

### C. 'Birch Hybrid'
This prostrate, evergreen hybrid has mauve-blue, bell-shaped flowers in summer. H to 10cm (4in), S 50cm (20in). Hardy/Z 4–7.

### C. carpatica
This widely grown, herbaceous plant, originally from the Carpathian mountains, forms small tufts with numerous, bright green, oval, sharply toothed leaves. The upright, broadly bell-shaped flowers are violet, purple, blue or white and are borne in summer and autumn. H 15cm (6in), S 30–45cm (12–18in). Hardy/Z 4–7.

### C. cochleariifolia
(syn. *C. bellardii, C. pusilla*)
**Fairies' thimbles**
This dainty little bellflower, native to the mountains of Europe, forms spreading mats by means of underground rhizomes. The small leaves are bright, lustrous green, and the thin stems bear several small, nodding bells in blue, lilac, lavender or, occasionally, white. H 8–13cm (3–5in), S 15–40cm (6–16in). Hardy/Z 5–7.

Campanula portenschlagiana

### C. portenschlagiana
**Dalmatian bellflower**
An excellent plant from Croatia for rock crevices or for colonizing old walls. The tufts of small leaves are bright green, and in early summer the numerous branched stems bear a profusion of lilac-blue, rather narrow, bell-shaped flowers. H 15–25cm (6–10in), S 15–50cm (6–20in). Hardy/Z 4–7.

### C. saxatilis
The spreading species, found in rocky areas of Crete, has round leaves that form rosettes. In summer pale blue, tubular flowers are borne in spikes. H to 8cm (3in), S to 20cm (8in). Hardy/Z 5–8.

## CERASTIUM

The species described, a vigorous, mat-forming plant, can be invasive, and the genus, in fact, includes some weeds. The popular perennial *C. tomentosum* is too vigorous and invasive for a rock garden and should be confined to areas of poor soil where nothing else will grow, or allowed to cascade over a wall or bank.
*Cultivation* Grow in full sun in gritty, well-drained soil.

### C. alpinum
**Alpine chickweed**
The grey-green, evergreen leaves of this European species form compact mats above which clusters of small white flowers are borne in late spring to early summer. H 10cm (4in), S 30cm (12in). Hardy Z 3–8.

Campanula 'Birch Hybrid'

Corydalis flexuosa

## CORYDALIS
There are some 300 species in the genus, including many attractive annuals and biennials and some perennials, suitable for shady, woodland gardens and herbaceous borders.
Cultivation Grow in a semi-shaded spot in moist, humus-rich but well-drained soil.

### C. flexuosa
This widely available herbaceous perennial is native to China. The tufts of grey-green or bright green, fern-like, dissected leaves are present through most of the year except high summer. The sprays of blue or lilac-blue, spurred flowers are borne on wiry stems in spring and early summer. H 30cm (12in), S 20–50cm (8–20in). Hardy/Z 5–8.

### C. lutea
(syn. Pseudofumaria lutea)
This tufted, evergreen perennial has rather fleshy, grey-green,

Daphne cneorum

dissected leaves. The pale stems bear small sprays of yellow, spurred flowers from spring until autumn. An excellent plant for crevices, it often self-sows profusely in the garden. H and S to 30cm (12in). Hardy/Z 5–8.

## DAPHNE
The genus is possibly best known for its wonderfully fragrant shrubs, but it also includes some delightful small species, suitable for rock and scree gardens and alpine troughs. All parts of the plants are poisonous.
Cultivation Daphnes need moist but well-drained, fertile soil and a position in sun or partial shade.

### D. alpina
This upright, deciduous, twiggy shrub with elliptical, greyish leaves bears clusters of fragrant white flowers in late spring and early summer. H and S 40cm (16in). Hardy/Z 6–8.

### D. arbuscula
This very small, extremely slow-growing, twiggy, evergreen shrub has narrow, rather leathery, shiny, deep green leaves. The clusters of fragrant pink flowers appear in late spring. This is an excellent trough plant. H and S 15cm (6in). Hardy/Z 5–7.

### D. blagayana
The trailing stems of this mat-forming, usually evergreen shrub can root where they touch the ground. Clusters of sweet-smelling, white flowers appear in spring. H 10cm (4in), S 30cm (12in) or more.

### D. cneorum
(syn. D. odorata)
Garland flower
This branching and trailing evergreen shrub has fragrant pink flowers in spring and, occasionally, a second flush in autumn. The dark green leaves are greyish on the underside. H 20cm (8in), S 1m (3ft). Hardy/Z 5–8. 'Eximia' is a vigorous cultivar, with narrow, grey-green leaves and small clusters of deep rose pink, sweetly fragrant flowers in late spring. H 20cm (8in), S 1m (3ft).

### D. sericea Collina Group
(syn. D. collina)
Plants sold under this name are dense-growing, with elliptical, rather bristly, grey-green leaves. Pale to mid-pink flowers are borne in dense clusters in late spring and early summer. H and S 60cm (24in). Hardy/Z 7–8.

## DIANTHUS
Pink
This huge genus includes many perennials as well as annuals and biennials. There are also several members of the genus that are ideally suited to raised beds, rock and scree gardens and to alpine troughs.
Cultivation Grow in fertile but gritty, well-drained soil (ideally neutral to alkaline) in full sun.

### D. alpinus
Alpine pink
This delightful pink, which is native to the eastern Alps, forms a small, evergreen mat of deep green, narrow, blunt-tipped leaves. The relatively large, fringed flowers are pink to cerise or purplish-pink, with generous speckling above. H 10cm (4in), S 20cm (8in). Hardy/Z 5–8. 'Joan's Blood' has very dark flowers with almost black centres. H 10cm (4in), S 20cm (8in).

### D. deltoides
Maiden pink
This variable species, native to Europe and western Asia, is a mat-forming, evergreen perennial with numerous narrow, deep green leaves that are often flushed with

Dianthus deltoides

Dianthus alpinus

bronze or purple. The spreading, branched stems bear numerous small, fringed flowers in pink, cerise, crimson or white in summer and autumn. H 15–25cm (6–10in), S 30–50cm (12–20in). Hardy/Z 5–8.

## DODECATHEON
American cowslip, shooting star
The perennial species that comprise this genus are native to North America, where they are found in meadows and woodland. They have cyclamen-like flowers, with swept-back petals.
Cultivation Grow in well-drained, reliably moist and fertile soil in sun or partial shade.

### D. pulchellum
(syn. D. radicatum)
The dark green, oval leaves form rosettes above which the deep pink flowers are borne in mid- to late spring. H 35cm (14in), S 15cm (6in). Hardy/Z 3–8.

## ERIGERON
Fleabane
This genus, which includes annuals and biennials, is best known for the perennial hybrids that bring colour to the summer border, but a number of species are suitable for rock gardens.
Cultivation Grow in well-drained but reliably moist soil in sun.

### E. alpinus
Alpine fleabane
This species, native to central and southern Europe, has narrow, grey-green, hairy leaves. Yellow-centred, mauve, daisy-like flowers

are borne from mid- to late summer. H 25cm (10in), S 20cm (8in). Hardy/Z 5–8.

### E. glaucus
**Beach aster**
This evergreen, leafy sub-shrub is native to western North America. It has rather coarse, pale bluish-green, oval leaves, and in summer numerous pale violet to lavender flowerheads are produced, each with an egg-yolk yellow centre. H to 50cm (20in), S 45–90cm (18–36in). Hardy/Z 5–8.

## ERINUS
The two semi-evergreen or evergreen species that comprise this genus are native to rocky areas in central and southern Europe and northern Africa. Only the species described is in general cultivation.
*Cultivation* Grow in well-drained soil in sun or partial shade.

### E. alpinus
**Fairy foxglove**
This species is found in rocky places in central and southern Europe, where it forms small, evergreen tufts. The neatly toothed foliage is mainly borne in small rosettes, and from late spring to summer the rosy-purple or white flowers are clustered at the ends of short leafy stems. H 15cm (6in), S 20cm (8in). Hardy/Z 4–7.

## EURYOPS
Although there are about 100 species in the genus, only a few are widely grown. The species

Erinus alpinus

Euryops acraeus

described is not reliably hardy and needs a sheltered position in a rock garden or raised bed.
*Cultivation* Grow in fairly rich, well-drained soil in full sun. Shear after flowering to keep plants neat.

### E. acraeus
**(syn. E. evansii of gardens)**
This compact evergreen shrub, which is native to South Africa, has crowded, narrow, silver-grey leaves. The daisy-like flowers are acid-yellow and appear in summer. H and S 40cm (16in). Borderline hardy/Z 9–10.

## GENTIANA
**Gentian**
The genus contains about 400 species of annuals, biennials and perennials, which may be evergreen, semi-evergreen or herbaceous. Some require the specialized cultural conditions best provided in an alpine house, but many other species are suitable for growing in a rock or scree garden or an alpine trough.
*Cultivation* Grow in moist but well-drained soil. Most summer-flowering gentians need a position in full sun and prefer neutral to alkaline soil; most autumn-flowering gentians need acid soil and shelter from hot sun.

### G. acaulis
**(syn. G. excisa, G. kochiana)**
**Trumpet gentian**
One of the most beautiful of alpine plants, the species is from the mountains of central and southern Europe. It forms dense mats of evergreen, leathery leaves.

Gentiana acaulis

In spring, and sometimes also in autumn, large, bell-shaped flowers in rich kingfisher-blue appear. H 10cm (4in), S 40cm (16in). Hardy/Z 4–7.

### G. asclepiadea
**Willow gentian**
This herbaceous perennial is from the mountains of southern and central Europe. In mid- to late summer it bears beautiful, trumpet-shaped, rich blue flowers. The narrow leaves are mid-green. H 75cm (30in) or more, S 45cm (18in). Hardy/Z 6–9.

### G. septemfida
This herbaceous species is from the mountains of western Asia. It forms discreet tufts with spreading stems, which bear pairs of elliptical, deep green leaves. One or several deep blue, bell-shaped flowers are borne at the stem tips in late summer and autumn. H 10–25cm (4–10in), S 20–40cm (8–16in). Hardy/Z 6–8.

### G. sino-ornata
**Autumn gentian**
This, the finest autumn-flowering gentian, comes from western China. It is a herbaceous perennial, forming small tufts of narrow, sharply pointed, deep green, rather glossy leaves. The solitary, deep blue, green- and purple-striped, bell-shaped flowers are held on the ends of the spreading stems. It needs humus-rich, acid soil. H 10–15cm (4–6in), S 15–25cm (6–10in). Hardy/Z 5–7.

### G. verna
**Spring gentian, star gentian**
This evergreen perennial species from mountainous areas across Europe is one of the great delights of the alpine garden. It forms small tufts of bright green, oval foliage. The rich-blue, white-centred flowers appear in spring to early summer. H 8cm (3in), S 10–20cm (4–8in). Hardy/Z 4–7.

## GERANIUM
**Cranesbill**
The large genus includes many perennials, but the dainty species described below are ideal for rock gardens and alpine troughs.
*Cultivation* Grow in any well-drained soil in full sun.

### G. cinereum
The species, which is native to the Pyrenees, is an evergreen or semi-evergreen perennial with rounded, lobed, grey-green leaves. The paired, saucer-shaped flowers are pink with an elaborate network of purple veins and are produced in late spring and summer. H 15cm (6in), S 25cm (10in). Hardy/Z 4–9. **'Ballerina'** has grey leaves and purplish flowers with dark red-purple eyes.

### G. dalmaticum
This clump-forming, evergreen perennial from the western Balkans has rounded, deeply lobed, glossy green leaves. The flowers, borne in masses in early and midsummer, are a rich pink with orange-red anthers. H 15cm (6in), S 50cm (20in). Hardy/Z 5–8.

Geranium cinereum 'Ballerina'

## GYPSOPHILA

The genus is best known for *G. paniculata*, which produces the familiar sprays of tiny white flowers, but the species described is a mat-forming plant, ideal for a rock or scree garden.
*Cultivation* Grow in well-drained, preferably alkaline soil in full sun.

### G. repens

This mat-forming, semi-evergreen perennial is native to central and southern Europe. It has grey-green leaves and, in summer, clouds of tiny white, pink or purplish-pink flowers. H 20cm (8in), S 50cm (20in). Hardy/Z 4–7. **'Dorothy Teacher'** is a neat cultivar, with pale pink flowers. H 5cm (2in), S 40cm (16in). **'Fratensis'** has narrow, grey-green leaves, and the spreading stems bear sprays of small pink flowers. H 8cm (5in), S 30cm (12in).

### G. tenuifolia
(syn. *G. gracilescens*)
This low-growing, hummock-forming, evergreen alpine is native to the Caucasus. It has a mass of grass-like, mid-green foliage, and the small white or pale pink flowers are borne aloft on delicate wiry stems in summer. H 10–15cm (4–6in), S 15–25cm (6–10in). Hardy/Z 5–9.

## IBERIS
Candytuft

These easy-to-grow plants are ideal for sunny rock gardens or walls.
*Cultivation* Grow in any moist, well-drained soil, preferably neutral to alkaline, in sun.

### I. saxatilis

This evergreen species from southern Europe has dark green leaves and clusters of small white (occasionally purplish) flowers in summer. H 15cm (6in), S 20cm (8in). Hardy/Z 4–8.

### I. sempervirens
(syn. *I. commutata*)
A useful plant, this spreading, evergreen subshrub from southern Europe has dark green leaves carrying dense heads of brilliant white flowers in late spring and early summer. H 30cm (12in), S 60cm (24in). Hardy/Z 5–9.

*Gypsophila repens* 'Fratensis'

## LEONTOPODIUM
Edelweiss

The genus contains species from the mountains of Europe and Asia. The insignificant flowers are surrounded by long, narrow bracts. Although some species require the specialized conditions of an alpine house, the species described will grow in rock gardens and raised beds.
*Cultivation* Grow in very well-drained, slightly alkaline soil in full sun. Protect from winter wet.

### L. alpinum

This is the edelweiss of the European mountains. It is a small, short-lived, tufted perennial with narrow, greyish, felted foliage. The small, button-flowerheads are clustered and surrounded by white, woolly bracts, giving a daisy-like appearance. H and S 15cm (6in). Hardy/Z 4–6.
**'Mignon'**, which is more mat-forming, has dark green leaves and smaller flowerheads than the species. H 10cm (4in), S 30cm (12in).

*Leontopodium alpinum*

*Iberis sempervirens*

## LEWISIA

This genus of hardy perennials from North America form rosettes of strap-shaped leaves and showy, colourful flowers. Because they resent winter wet, they are often grown in alpine houses. Where they can be sheltered, they are ideal for rock gardens or walls.
*Cultivation* Grow in neutral to acid soil in light shade. Good drainage is essential.

### L. cotyledon

This evergreen perennial is the most tolerant of the genus, and has spoon-shaped leaves, which form a tight rosette. The flowers, usually pinkish-purple but sometimes white, yellow or pinkish-yellow, are borne in clusters on upright stems. H 30cm (12in), S 25cm (10in). Hardy/Z 6–7.
**Cotyledon Hybrids** have funnel-shaped flowers in shades of pink, magenta, orange and yellow. H to 30cm (12in), S to 40cm (16in). Flower colours of plants in the **Sunset Group** are in the yellow to red range.

*Lychnis alpina*

## LYCHNIS
Campion, catchfly

The genus is familiar in cottage-garden plantings, but the species described here is better suited to an alpine trough or rock garden.

### L. alpina
**Alpine catchfly, alpine campion**
This charming tufted perennial, which is native to a large part of northern and central Europe, has narrow, grassy foliage. Clusters of bright rose-purple flowers are held at the tops of short, leafy stems, each petal neatly notched. H and S 15cm (6in). Hardy/Z 4–7.

## PENSTEMON

This large genus is often represented in gardens by the border perennials, but the species described here are ideal for rock and scree gardens.
*Cultivation* Grow in gritty, well-drained soil in sun.

### P. alpinus

This clump-forming species from North America has broad leaves, which form dense rosettes, and blue or purplish, white-throated flowers from summer to autumn. H 25cm (10in), S 20cm (8in). Hardy/Z 5–9.

### P. hirsutus var. pygmaeus

The typical species is an evergreen subshrub, large enough for a border, but this naturally occurring variety is compact and mat-forming. It has purple-tinged leaves and purplish flowers in summer. H and S 10cm (4in). Hardy/Z 5–8.

## PHLOX

This is a large genus, which includes many perennials, some of which are semi-evergreen or evergreen, grown for summer colour in the border. There are also a number of low-growing, mat-forming species, which can be grown in rock gardens, raised beds and walls.
*Cultivation* The plants described here are best in fertile, moist but well-drained soil in light shade. *P. divaricata* and its forms and *P. subulata* can also be grown in full sun.

Penstemon hirsutus var. pygmaeus

*P. divaricata* subsp. *laphamii* 'Chattahoochee'
(syn. *P.* 'Chattahoochee')
This rather lax perennial, which is native to wooded areas in North America, has spreading stems bearing pairs of elliptical, deep green leaves, which are often flushed with purple. The saucer-shaped flowers, which are deep lavender with a crimson eye, are produced in summer over a long season. H 20cm (8in), S 30cm (12in). Hardy/Z 5–9.

*P. douglasii*
Also from North America, this low mat- or cushion-forming, evergreen perennial has small, tooth-like leaf-pairs. The fragrant, saucer-shaped flowers, borne in late spring and early summer, solitary or several, are clustered together close to the foliage, and they vary in colour from pink to lavender, purple, red or white. H 10cm (4in), S 20cm (8in). Hardy/Z 5–7. 'Boothman's Variety' has violet-pink flowers with dark blue centres. H 8cm (3in), S 20cm (8in). 'Iceberg' is white with a bluish coat.

Phlox divaricata subsp. *laphamii* 'Chattahoochee'

*P. subulata*
**Moss phlox**
This species, which is native to the eastern United States, is a mat-forming, evergreen perennial with much-branched stems and numerous linear, pointed leaf-pairs. The saucer-shaped flowers, in shades of pink, purple, red or white, appear in late spring and early summer and are borne in clusters at the shoot-tips, close to the foliage. H 15cm (6in), S 50cm (20in). Hardy/Z 4–9.

## PLATYCODON
**Balloon flower**
The single species in the genus comes from China, Korea and Japan. The common name derives from the shape of the buds from which the flowers open.
*Cultivation* Grow in fertile, moist but well-drained soil. These plants must have full sun.

*P. grandiflorus*
This clump-forming herbaceous perennial has erect, pale stems and oval to elliptical, toothed leaves. The deep blue flowers open from balloon-like buds. H 60cm (2ft), S 30cm (1ft). Hardy/Z 4–9. There are several selected forms, of which the dwarf 'Apoyama' is particularly suitable for a rock garden. It has deep violet flowers. H and S 20cm (8in).

## PRIMULA
**Primrose**
Besides the many valuable border perennials, the genus includes many species that are suitable for rock gardens or alpine houses.
*Cultivation* Grow in very well-drained, humus-rich soil in a sunny position.

Platycodon grandiflorus

Primula marginata

*P. auricula*
**Bear's ear**
The common auricula, native to the Alps, is a low, tufted perennial with rosettes of deep green, rather fleshy leaves. The scented, yellow flowers, up to 2.5cm (1in) across, are clustered at the stalk-tips in spring. H 7.5–15cm (3–6in), S 10–20cm (4–8in). Hardy/Z 5–7. There are many named forms, including 'Chocolate Soldier', which has double, brownish-purple flowers, the petals edged with golden-yellow; and 'Marie Crousse', which has double, violet flowers edged with white. H to 15cm (6in), S 25cm (10in).

*P. marginata*
This tufted, evergreen perennial from the Alps has rosettes of leathery, green or grey-green leaves, which are coarsely toothed and often have whitish powder along the margin. The pink to bluish-lavender, primrose flowers are clustered at the end of short stalks. H 13cm (5in), S 20cm (8in). Hardy/Z 4–7.

*P. vulgaris*
**Common primrose**
This more or less evergreen perennial, native to Europe and western Asia, has rough, elliptical, bright green leaves borne in lax basal rosettes. The fragrant, yellow flowers are borne in profusion in late winter and spring. H 10–20cm (4–8in), S 35cm (14in). Hardy/Z 3–8. Named selections include 'Alba Plena', with double white flowers, and 'Lilacina Plena', with double lilac flowers. Some plants sold under this name may be hybrids with other species.

## PULSATILLA
**Pasque flower**
These lovely perennials have large, bell-shaped flowers, which are followed by silky seedheads. Plant in a raised bed or rock garden where the exquisite flowers can be appreciated.
*Cultivation* Grow in gritty, well-drained, chalky soil in full sun.

*P. alpina*
**Alpine pasque flower**
The species, which is native to mountainous areas of central Europe, has dark green, finely divided foliage. The white flowers, borne in spring, are tinged with bluish-mauve on the outside and have a central mass of bright yellow stamens. H 30cm (12in), S 20cm (8in). Hardy/Z 3–5.

*P. vernalis*
(syn. *Anemone vernalis*)
The leaves of this clump-forming species, which is native to Europe and Siberia, are dark green and finely divided. The beautiful white flowers, flushed with pale purplish-blue on the outside, have bright yellow centres. Protect from winter wet. H 10cm (4in), S 20cm (8in). Hardy/Z 5–8.

*P. vulgaris*
(syn. *Anemone pulsatilla*)
The species, found across Europe, has tufts of finely divided, deep green, rather feathery leaves. The solitary, half-nodding to erect, bell-shaped flowers, which are borne in spring, may be white, red, violet-blue or purple and have silky hairs on the outside. H 20cm (8in), S 30cm (12in). Hardy/Z 5–7. 'Alba' is the white-flowered form.

Pulsatilla vulgaris

Saponaria ocymoides

## RAMONDA

The small genus includes three species of evergreen perennials. They are suitable for rock gardens, raised beds or walls, where they can be grown sideways on. They resent winter wet and for this reason are often grown in alpine houses.
*Cultivation* Grow in rich but very well-drained soil in partial shade.

### R. myconi
(syn. *R. pyrenaica*)
The species is native to northern Spain. It has dark green, hairy leaves in neat rosettes above which dark purplish-blue, yellow-centred flowers are borne in late spring to early summer. H 10cm (4in), S 20cm (8in). Hardy/Z 5–7.

## SALIX
Willow
Better known for its larger shrubs and trees, the genus also includes dwarf species, which are suitable

Salix 'Boydii'

for rock gardens or alpine troughs.
*Cultivation* Grow in gritty, well-drained soil in full sun.

### S. 'Boydii'
(syn. *S. × boydii*)
This slow-growing, twiggy, deciduous shrub develops a thick trunk, which eventually looks rather gnarled. The rounded and crinkly leaves are grey-green, paler beneath. Small, brownish, upright catkins are produced in spring. H 30cm (12in), S 25cm (10in). Hardy/Z 4–7.

## SAPONARIA
Soapwort
A genus of annuals and perennials from mountainous areas of Europe and south-western Asia. The well-known *S. officinalis* is suitable for a mixed border, but the plants described below can be grown in a rock garden, alpine trough or raised bed.
*Cultivation* Grow in gritty, well-drained soil in full sun.

### S. 'Bressingham'
This mat-forming perennial hybrid has mid-green leaves and clusters of deep pink flowers in summer. H 8cm (3in), S 30cm (12in). Hardy/Z 4–8.

### S. ocymoides
Rock soapwort, tumbling Ted
A mat-forming, evergreen perennial, this is native to central and south-eastern Europe. It has numerous, small, oval, deep green leaves. In late spring and summer, spreading clusters of pink or purplish flowers appear. Cut back

after flowering to keep plants neat. H 10cm (4in), S 30cm (12in). Hardy/Z 4–8.

## SAXIFRAGA
Saxifrage
This is a large genus of more than 400 species of mat- or cushion-forming, evergreen or deciduous perennials that are widely distributed in the northern hemisphere, where they are found in mountainous regions. They show considerable variation in habit and leaf form and are widely grown in rock and scree gardens, raised beds and alpine troughs.
*Cultivation* Grow in rich, gritty, well-drained, neutral to alkaline soil in full sun.

### S. cochlearis
A mound-forming, evergreen perennial from the south-western Alps, this has numerous, crowded rosettes of greyish, lime-encrusted leaf-rosettes. In summer, airy sprays of dainty, white flowers are produced on slender, reddish stems. H 25cm (10in), S 15cm (6in). Hardy/Z 6.

### S. 'Kathleen Pinsent'
The spoon-shaped, silvery leaves form rosettes above which the pink flowers are borne in arching clusters. H and S 20cm (8in). Hardy/Z 5–7.

### S. oppositifolia
Purple saxifrage
This saxifrage, native to many cold regions in the northern hemisphere, is a dense, mat-forming, evergreen alpine. It has

Saxifraga cochlearis

Saxifraga paniculata

deep green, scale-like leaves densely clothing the spreading stems. In late winter and early spring, solitary pale pink to rich purple flowers appear close to the foliage. H 2.5cm (1in), S 20cm (8in). Hardy/Z 2–6.

### S. paniculata
(syn. *S. aizoon*)
This tufted, evergreen perennial, which is native to Europe, Canada and Greenland, has crowded rosettes of grey-green, lime-encrusted leaves. In summer, airy sprays of small, white or cream flowers are borne on stiff, arching stalks. H 15cm (6in), S 30cm (12in). Hardy/Z 4–6.

### S. 'Tumbling Waters'
This slow-growing, mat-forming, evergreen hybrid grows in tight rosettes of narrow, lime-encrusted, silvery leaves. When the plant matures after several years, dense, arching, conical heads of small, open cup-shaped, white flowers are produced, after which the main rosette dies and the small offsets grow on. H 60cm (2ft), S 30cm (12in). Hardy/Z 5–7.

## SEDUM
Stonecrop
The large and diverse genus contains around 400 species including perennials and succulents. They are from the northern hemisphere, where they are found in mountain and arid regions, and they are ideal plants for withstanding drought and strong sunshine. Some of the alpine types have a creeping,

scrambling habit, which will cover rock edges.

*Cultivation* Grow sedums in neutral to slightly alkaline, very well-drained soil in full sun.

### S. acre
**Wallpepper, biting stonecrop**
This species, which is found in Europe, North Africa and western Asia, is a familiar little plant of old walls and rooftops. It is a bright green succulent with tiny, closely overlapping leaves. In summer, the shoot tips burst with flat-topped heads of tiny, star-shaped, yellow-green flowers. H 5cm (2in), S 60cm (2ft) or more. Hardy/Z 4–9.

### S. pulchellum
Native to the south-eastern United States, this is a laxly tufted, succulent perennial with erect to ascending stems adorned with narrow leaves. The starry pink flowers are freely produced in summer. It is often grown as an annual. H 5cm (2in), S 25cm (10in). Hardy/Z 8.

### S. spathulifolium
This compact species from western North America grows into rosettes. It is a mat-forming perennial with spoon-shaped, fleshy, brittle green or silvery leaves, often tinted with bronze and purple. In summer sprays of short-stemmed, tiny, star-shaped bright yellow flowers are produced. H 5cm (2in), S indefinite. Hardy/Z 5–9.

## SEMPERVIVUM
**Houseleek**
The 40 species in the genus are mat-forming, evergreen succulents, largely from mountainous regions of Europe and Asia. There are many hybrids, some differing only slightly (if at all) from each other. They are ideal for rock and scree gardens, alpine troughs, walls and containers.

*Cultivation* Grow in gritty, very well-drained soil in full sun. Protect from winter wet.

### S. arachnoideum
**Cobweb houseleek**
This mat- or mound-forming evergreen perennial is native to

*Sempervivum montanum*

central and south-west Europe. It has numerous, greyish leaf-rosettes, tipped with red and enveloped in a cobweb of whitish hairs. The starry, pinkish-red flowers are clustered at the top of a short, leafy stem in summer. H 10cm (4in), S 10cm (4in). Hardy/Z 5–9.

### S. montanum
(syn. *S. helveticum*)
An evergreen perennial from central and southern Europe, this forms low mounds of dull green, downy, succulent leaf-rosettes. The wine-red, starry flowers are borne at the tips of erect flowering shoots in summer. H 10–20cm (4–8in), S 20–40cm (8–16in). Hardy/Z 5.

### S. tectorum
**Common houseleek**
This rather coarse, evergreen perennial from mountainous areas of central and southern Europe has large, succulent leaf-rosettes, the leaves usually green or grey-green with reddish or purplish

*Sempervivum arachnoideum*

tips. A mass of star-shaped, dull pink to purple flowers is borne on stout, leafy stems in summer. H 20cm (8in), S 50cm (20in). Hardy/Z 5–9.

## VERONICA
**Speedwell, brooklime**
The genus contains about 250 species of diverse plants, originating mainly in Europe, where they are found in a range of habitats. Some are cushion-forming or mat-forming species, which are suitable for the rock garden, where they can be exploited to soften unsightly edges. Others are border perennials. They are easy to grow.

*Cultivation* Grow in fairly poor, well-drained soil in full sun.

### V. prostrata
**Prostrate speedwell**
This mat-forming perennial, from the mountains of Europe, has deep green, narrow-oblong leaves. In summer, spikes of rich blue or purplish flowers are borne above the foliage on stiff, somewhat leafy, stems. 'Trehane' has lime green leaves, a sharp contrast to its darker blue flowers. H 15cm (6in), S 40cm (16in). Hardy/Z 4–7.

## VIOLA
**Pansy, violet**
There are pansies and violas for every position in the garden, from the front of borders to alpine houses. They are ideal for summer bedding, and the smaller species are perfect for rock gardens, raised beds and containers.

### V. cornuta
**Horned violet, viola**
This spreading plant, ideal for groundcover and growing with blue-leafed hostas, has deep violet flowers among the copious leaves in early summer. Shearing these off triggers a second crop in late summer. H 15cm (6in), S 60cm (24in). Hardy/Z 5–8. Plants belonging to the **Alba Group** have white flowers. H 15cm (6in), S 60cm (24in). '**Alba Minor**' is similar but more compact. **Lilacina Group** plants produce flowers in shades of lilac.

### V. lutea
**Mountain pansy**
This tufted perennial, native to the mountains of central and western Europe, has bright green, oval leaves and pansy flowers, which are yellow, violet or bi-coloured and appear in spring and summer. H and S 15cm (6in). Hardy/Z 4–8.

*Veronica prostrata*

*Viola cornuta* Alba Group

# Aquatic, Marginal and Bog Plants

Water is the most mysterious and beguiling of the four elements. There have been few more remarkable phenomena than the upsurge of interest in water features of all kinds in recent years. This is no doubt partly due to care for the environment, for any patch of water is bound to attract beneficial wildlife into the garden. Water plants — both those that grow in water and those that revel in the damp margins of a pool — are mostly easy to grow and maintain, and themselves do much to benefit the ecology of the garden at large.

This series of linked pools makes a calming feature, lushly planted with waterlilies and bordered by moisture-loving plants.

# What are aquatic, marginal and bog plants?

Also called water plants or hydrophytes, aquatics are those plants that are specially adapted to live in water. Here the term is extended to include those plants that grow in water-saturated soils.

Aquatics may be rooted in the mud and have their leaves and flowers above or at the surface of the water. Some kinds grow completely underwater. Submerged water plants often have air bladders or large air pores in their stems and leaves that help the plants stand upright or stay afloat.

Most aquatics are perennials. Only a few woody plants are adapted to thrive in permanently waterlogged conditions. A number of perennials, while thriving in soil that is reliably moist, seem equally happy in ordinary border soil, and in this book these are included with the rest of the perennials. Some of the grasses and bamboos also thrive in wet soil.

The water plants described here are adapted to varying depths of water. Bog plants need soil that is

Water lilies are the aristocrats of the water garden, here sharing the depths with the intriguing water soldier (*Stradiodes aloides*).

Most aquatics are rampant growers, but the water violet (*Hottonia palustris*) will deceive you with its dainty flowers.

permanently wet, such as occurs on the edges of a natural pool or stream. Marginals are plants that like to have water around their ankles, usually to a depth of up to 15cm (6in) above the soil level. Deep-water plants have their roots in the mud at the bottom of the pond and (usually) leaves that float on the surface. This group includes the queen of all water plants, the water lily (*Nymphaea*), and no pond is complete without at least one of these beauties. Surface floaters also have floating leaves, but their roots hang unanchored, feeding on nutrients dissolved in the water. One important group is the so-called oxygenators, usually submerged plants that float just below the surface. These are seldom things of beauty in their own right but contribute much to the ecological balance of the pond.

An important consideration when choosing water plants is whether the water is still or moving. The majority are best in still water, though many of the oxygenators are adapted to tolerate moving water.

## Water in the garden

A water feature brings an extra element into the garden, and for many people nowadays a garden would not be complete without one.

Water features can take many forms. A small bubble fountain or water spout mounted on a wall, attractive though these are, cannot support much plant life beyond the mosses and lichens that may ultimately take a hold. To grow the plants described in this chapter, you need a dedicated pond, ideally as big as possible, since most water plants are rampant growers. It is difficult to maintain an ecological balance in a very small, shallow pond, which will soon be colonized by duckweed and algae. Nevertheless, in a confined space, it is possible to make an attractive feature with a wooden half barrel, or similar deep container, which can be planted with a miniature water lily. Although most water plants are best in still rather than running water, it is perfectly acceptable for a pool to incorporate a fountain or other water-agitating device, provided this is not allowed to play continuously. In fact, it can be beneficial, helping to aerate and cool the water during hot weather.

Ponds are best sited in an open, sunny part of the garden, away from overhanging deciduous trees, which will not only shade the water, but drop their leaves in the pond in autumn, leading to a build-up of noxious gases as they decompose.

Water gardens should incorporate a variety of plant material. Submerged plants such as *Lagarosiphon major* provide the essential function of absorbing the nutrients that encourage algae and releasing oxygen, besides providing shelter for small aquatic invertebrates. Plants with floating leaves, such as water lilies, fulfil the valuable function of shading the surface of the water in summer – important if the water is not to overheat. The aim should be for the surface to be covered by between a half and one-third in summer. Marginals have less impact on water clarity, but soften the edges of the pool, besides providing shelter for wildlife.

In a formal pool, the proportions of which relate to other elements in the garden, it is usually best to keep the planting to the minimum, with perhaps a few well-chosen water lilies and some oxygenators to help keep the water clear. Judiciously placed containers around the edge can help to create symmetry and balance.

Informal pools that are more lushly planted will soon attract all manner of wildlife into the garden, which will mostly be of benefit to the garden at large besides being of interest in its own right. A pool is thus an essential element of any garden planned along ecological, environmentally friendly lines.

Water attracts a host of beneficial insects into the garden, as well as vertebrates that will feed on them. Frogs, toads, birds and hedgehogs, which will be attracted to the water, will help keep down slug and snail populations. If your intention is to maintain a breeding colony of frogs, keep fish out of the pond: they will eat frog spawn and attack tadpoles. It is perfectly possible to have two pools, of course, a strictly ornamental pool for fish and an environmental pool.

In a wild garden, this large pond is host to some of the more vigorous water lilies, with the lush and dense waterside plantings a haven for wildlife.

*Aponogeton distachyos*

## ALISMA
**Water plantain**
There are nine species of aquatics in this genus found across the world, mainly in the northern hemisphere, growing on marsh and lake edges. The seeds, which provide valuable food for wildlife, are produced in abundance.
*Cultivation* Grow in a sunny position in water to 15cm (6in) deep.

### A. plantago-aquatica
This deciduous perennial has rosettes of oval, grey-green, ribbed leaves, carried on tall stalks that emerge well above the water. Tiny, pinkish-white flowers appear in midsummer, with three petals arranged in whorls on a pyramidal spike. H 75cm (30in), S 45cm (18in). Hardy/Z 5–8.

## APONOGETON
The genus contains some 44 species of rhizomatous perennials, mostly with floating leaves, which are found in mainly tropical and subtropical areas, but there is one hardy species, which is used extensively in cold water ponds. It is a tolerant plant, particularly of shade, which extends the flowering season.
*Cultivation* Grow in sun or shade in water to 60cm (2ft).

### A. distachyos
**Water hawthorn, Cape pondweed**
This deep-water aquatic has oblong, bright green leaves, which can be semi-evergreen in mild winters. The white flowers, with purple-brown anthers, are held

above the water. Scented, they can be produced in two flushes, in spring and autumn. S 1.2m (4ft). Borderline hardy/Z 9–10.

## CALLA
A genus containing one species, a perennial marginal from the northern hemisphere, where it is found in swamps, bogs and wet woods. In mild winters it is semi-evergreen.
*Cultivation* Grow in full sun in water that is no deeper than 5cm (2in).

### C. palustris
**Bog arum**
This has conspicuous, long, creeping surface roots and round to heart-shaped, glossy, mid-green leaves, which are firm and leathery. The flowers, which appear in spring, look like miniature arum lilies, and are followed by clusters

*Calla palustris*

*Caltha palustris*

of red or orange berries. H 25cm (10in), S 30cm (12in) or more. Hardy/Z 3–8.

## CALLITRICHE
**Water starwort**
The 25 species in this genus are widely distributed throughout the world. They are small, slender plants, generally growing in a tight mass in a wide range of habitats, but mainly in temperate locations. The species described are valuable oxygenators.
*Cultivation* Grow in sun or partial shade in water to 50cm (20in) deep.

### C. hermaphroditica
(syn. *C. autumnalis*)
**Autumn starwort**
This species has light green, linear leaves, held opposite each other on the thin, branching stems. The intertwined mass of stems is an important habitat for many smaller forms of plant life, and the young leaves are a particular delicacy for goldfish. This species is unique in not forming rosettes of floating leaves. S indefinite. Hardy/Z 4–9.

### C. palustris
(syn. *C. verna*)
A submerged oxygenating plant from north Africa and Europe with cress-like leaves, which die back in winter. S indefinite. Hardy/Z 4–9.

## CALTHA
This widespread and common genus contains ten species of temperate marginals, which are

extremely popular in both ornamental and wildlife ponds.
*Cultivation* Grow in sun or partial shade in water no deeper than 10–15cm (4–6in).

### C. palustris
**Marsh marigold, kingcup**
Indispensable for the pond margins, the marsh marigold has long-stalked lower leaves and stalkless upper leaves, which grow longer at flowering. The glistening yellow, buttercup-like flowers can appear as early as late winter in a mild season but are generally at their peak in mid-spring. H 15–30cm (6–12in), S 45cm (18in). Hardy/Z 4–9.
'Flore Pleno' smothers itself in double yellow flowers in spring, often producing a second flush in the summer, and is more compact. H and S 25cm (10in).

## EICHHORNIA
**Water hyacinth, water orchid**
There are seven species in this genus of tropical, mainly floating plants from South America, where they root in shallow mud and form huge colonies, which can swamp rivers and lakes, becoming a major problem. The species described will not survive winters outdoors in cool climates, but for a few months in hot weather it is a striking sight on the pond surface.
*Cultivation* Grow in full sun and warm water, preferably 18°C (64°F). Overwinter under glass at 10–13°C (50–55°F) on trays of moist soil.

### E. crassipes
(syn. *E. speciosa*)
The shiny, pale green leaves have inflated bases, which act as floats.

*Eichhornia crassipes*

In very warm summers, spikes of pale lilac-blue hyacinth-like flowers appear. Long, feathery, dangling roots, purplish-black in colour, are perfect shelter for spawning goldfish. H 15–23cm (6–9in), S 15–30cm(6–12in), more in favourable conditions. Tender/Z 8–10.

## FONTINALIS
### Water moss
There are more than 50 species of submerged aquatic mosses in the genus, which are found throughout the world. They all form floating mats.
*Cultivation* Grow in sun or partial shade in water to about 40cm (16in) deep. Divide in spring. The species described here is suitable for growing in moving water.

### F. antipyretica
### Willow moss
The slender stems, to 80cm (32in) long, are covered with small, evergreen, dark green leaves. S indefinite. Hardy/Z 4–10.

## GUNNERA
These perennials are widely distributed in the southern hemisphere. Some of them are gigantic plants, producing huge leaves. The sinister-looking *S. mamiata* has the largest of any hardy plant. Plenty of moisture and protection from wind are needed if they are to be seen at their best.
*Cultivation* Grow in sun or partial shade in fertile, moist soil. In cold climates, cover the resting crowns of *S. mamiata* with the old leaves.

### G. magellanica
This mat-forming herbaceous perennial has dark green, rounded to kidney-shaped leaves, which are tinged bronze when young. H 15cm (6in), S 30cm (12in). Borderline hardy/Z 8–9.

### G. manicata
### (syn. G. brasiliensis)
### Giant rhubarb
This dramatic species is the largest in the genus, with vast leaves, 2m (6ft) or more across, carried on bristly stalks. The flower spike is like a red-tinged

Houttuynia cordata 'Chameleon'

bottlebrush to 1m (3ft) tall. H 2.4m (8ft), S 4m (13ft). Borderline hardy/Z 7–10.

## HOTTONIA
The genus contains two species of submerged plants with delicate, primula-like flowers, which are held above the water. They are mainly found in clear ponds or slow-moving ditches in temperate areas of the northern hemisphere.
*Cultivation* Grow in full sun and clear water.

### H. palustris
### Water violet
In summer this oxygenator bears violet or white flowers with yellow throats, held well above the surface of the water. The submerged, bright green leaves are finely divided and are arranged like the teeth of a comb. S indefinite. Hardy/Z 5–9.

Gunnera manicata

Houttuynia cordata 'Flore Pleno'

## HOUTTUYNIA
The genus consists of a single species, which originates in eastern Asia. The plant flourishes in wet soil or the shallow margins of ponds and streams, creeping along pond margins and producing extensive mats of shallow rhizomes.
*Cultivation* Grow in full sun or partial shade in shallow water no deeper than 2.5–5cm (1–2in). This can be invasive and should be grown in a container in a small pond. It can also be grown in borders where the soil does not dry out.

### H. cordata
The straight species has heart-shaped, metallic green leaves that smell of oranges when crushed. In full sun, they redden in autumn. The white flowers, with cone-like, green centres, appear in spring.

Hydrocharis morsus-ranae

H 45–50cm (18–20in), S indefinite. Hardy/Z 5–9. The colourful leaves of 'Chameleon' (syn. 'Tricolor') are splashed with crimson, green and cream. 'Flore Pleno' has fragrant heart-shaped leaves and double flowers.

## HYDROCHARIS
### Frogbit
Frogbits are found in temperate and subtropical parts of Europe, Africa, Asia and Australia. Their short stems form mats just under the water surface.
*Cultivation* Grow in full sun in water to 30cm (12in) deep.

### H. morsus-ranae
Rather like a tiny water lily, this species produces kidney-shaped, shiny green leaves that float on the surface and small white flowers with yellow centres. S indefinite. Hardy/Z 7–10.

## LAGAROSIPHON
### Curly water thyme
These submerged plants are native to central Africa and Madagascar but have established themselves in Europe and New Zealand. The species described is a first-rate oxygenator.
*Cultivation* Grow in full sun.

### L. major
### (syn. Elodea crispa)
This species produces long underwater stems set with thick dark green, recurring leaves. It can form dense masses but is easily reduced in summer. S indefinite. Hardy/Z 4–9.

## LIGULARIA

These imposing bog plants are excellent by the water's edge, but can also be included in mixed plantings where the soil doesn't dry out.

*Cultivation* Grow in reliably moist soil in full sun or partial shade. Divide in spring.

### L. dentata

This handsome species produces its vivid orange daisy flowers in mid- to late summer. H 1.2m (4ft), S 60cm (2ft). Hardy/Z 4–8. **'Desdemona'** is more compact, and has richer orange flowers. **'Othello'** is similar but has leaves flushed with purple.

### L. 'Gregynog Gold'

This hybrid has handsome, richly veined, heart-shaped leaves and huge, conical spires of large, vivid orange-yellow flowers. H 1.2m (4ft), S 1m (3ft). Hardy/Z 4–8.

### L. przewalskii

(syn. *Senecio przewalskii*)
This species has very finely cut, dark green leaves, borne on nearly black stems, and spires of small, yellow daisy flowers in mid- to late summer. H 2m (6ft), S 1m (3ft). Hardy/Z 4–8.

## LYSICHITON
### Skunk cabbage

Grand, if rather coarse, plants for the waterside, these are good for colonizing tracts of wet ground. Site them where reflected light from the water will strike the glossy leaves. The common name

Lysichiton americanus

is a reference to the scent of the flowers.

*Cultivation* Grow in full sun in 2.5cm (1in) of water or in wet soil.

### L. americanus
### Yellow skunk cabbage

This impressive plant provides an early spring display of yellow, arum-like spathes. After flowering, the huge shining, cabbage-like leaves gradually lengthen. H 1.2m (4ft), S 1m (3ft). Hardy/Z 7–9.

### L. camschatcensis
### White skunk cabbage

This white-spathed species is less vigorous than the more common *L. americanus* and is therefore more suitable for the margins of a small pond. H and S 75cm (30in). Hardy/Z 7–9.

## MENTHA
### Mint

Aside from the culinary herbs, there is one species that will thrive in water.

*Cultivation* Grow in full sun or partial shade. It tolerates a wide range of water depths but does best in 15cm (6in) of water.

### M. aquatica
### Water mint

Common in ditches and alongside running water, this has deep lilac-coloured flowers above the mint scented leaves. H 15cm–1m (6in–3ft), S indefinite. Hardy/Z 6.

## MYOSOTIS
### Forget-me-not

With its characteristic blue flowers, the water forget-me-not is as appealing as the plants grown in borders.

*Cultivation* Grow in full sun or light dappled shade in no more than 8cm (3in) of water.

### M. scorpioides
### Water forget-me-not

This attractive species has a slightly looser and more delicate habit of growth than most of the more rampant marginals. It bears typical forget-me-not blue flowers with yellow centres in midsummer. H and S 30cm (12in). Hardy/Z 4–10.

Myosotis scorpioides 'Mermaid'

**'Mermaid'** is an improved, compact cultivar that is more free-flowering than the species.

## NUPHAR
### Cow lily, spatterdock

The 25 species of aquatics in the genus, found in temperate areas of the northern hemisphere, bear some resemblance to water lilies but have tougher floating leaves and will grow in conditions that are either too deep or too shaded for water lilies.

*Cultivation* Grow in sun or partial shade in water 30–60cm (1–2ft) deep.

### N. lutea
(syn. *N. luteum*)
### Yellow pond lily

The leathery floating leaves are large in relation to the bowl-shaped, buttercup yellow flowers that appear in summer. This plant

will survive in deep and slow-moving water. S 2m (6ft). Hardy/Z 5–10.

## NYMPHAEA
### Water lily

The aristocrats of the water garden, water lilies are among the most beautiful of all garden plants. Many fine cultivars have been raised, in every shade from white, through all the shades of pink to deepest red and yellow. Some have double flowers, and many are deliciously fragrant. Tropical water lilies extend the colour range into blue and orange, and although these plants are suitable only for frost-free gardens, they can be treated like summer bedding and the plants discarded after blooming. There are water lilies suitable for every size of pond, from barrels and tubs to lakes, but they will not thrive in moving water.

*Cultivation* All should be grown in a sunny position without any water turbulence. Water depths vary as detailed below.

### N. hybrids

The spread refers to the average area that the leaves will eventually cover. All are hardy/Z 3–11.
**'Amabilis'** has star-like flowers with pink petals with lighter tips surrounding deep yellow stamens. The nearly round leaves are reddish-purple when young. S 1.5–2.3m (5–7.5ft), planting depth 30–45cm (12–18in). The moderately vigorous **'Attraction'** has cup-shaped, red flowers,

Nymphaea 'Attraction'

Nymphaea 'Gladstoneana'

Nymphaea 'Pygmaea Helvola'

opening to a star shape and resting on the bronze-tinged leaves. S 2m (6ft), planting depth 15–45cm (6–18in).
'Gladstoneana' is a free-flowering water lily that does best in a larger pond. The starry flowers have white petals surrounding yellow stamens. Bronzed young leaves mature to almost round, wavy-edged green leaves, with crimped margins along the lobes. S 1.5–2.4m (5–8ft), planting depth 45–60cm (18–24in).
'Hermine' (syn. 'Albatross') is a moderately vigorous water lily for a medium-sized pond. The large white flowers have long petals surrounding deep yellow stamens. The red-tinged young leaves mature to dark green. S to 2m (6ft), planting depth 15–45cm (6–18in). The moderately vigorous 'Marliacea Rosea' is suitable for a medium-sized pond. In summer the rose-red flowers appear among the leaves, which are flushed purple on emergence. S 2m (6ft), planting depth 15–45cm (6–18in). 'Mme Wilfron Gonmère' has double

pink flowers that fade to white. S to 1.5m (5ft), planting depth 30–45cm (12–18in). 'Pygmaea Helvola' (syn. N. × helvola) is a delightful miniature and the perfect water lily for a barrel or sink. The cup-shaped, later star-like flowers have pale yellow petals and darker yellow stamens. The leaves are heavily mottled and blotched with purple and have purple undersides. S 60cm (2ft), planting depth 15–23cm (6–9in).

## ORONTIUM
### Golden club
The genus comprises a single species from temperate areas of eastern North America, where it grows in bogs or shallow water.
*Cultivation* Grow in full sun in water 30–45cm (12–18in) deep. In water deeper than 30cm (12in) the leaves float on the surface.

### O. aquaticum
This species produces large, bluish-green leaves with a silvery sheen on the undersides. The extraordinary flower spikes look like lighted cigarettes: yellow at the tip, white below. They appear from spring to early summer. H 45cm (18in), S 75cm (30in). Hardy/Z 7–10.

## PONTEDERIA
This genus of shallow-water plants contains just five species. The plant described is the most widely grown.
*Cultivation* Grow in full sun with up to 13cm (5in) of water above the crown.

### P. cordata
### Pickerel weed
This perennial marginal has shiny, erect, heart-shaped, olive-green leaves, above which the purplish-blue, bottlebrush-like flowers appear in late summer. H 45–60cm (18–24in), S 75cm (30in). Hardy/Z 4–9.

## POTAMOGETON
### Pondweed
There are 80–100 species of submerged aquatic plants in this genus, but only the species described is of value to gardeners, as an oxygenator.
*Cultivation* Grow in full sun.

### P. crispus
### Curled pondweed
The stems, which are capable of growing to 4m (13ft) or more, bear narrow, stalkless, green to

reddish brown leaves, the whole plant looking like seaweed. S indefinite. Hardy/Z 7–10.

## RANUNCULUS
### Buttercup
Among the many garden plants provided by this genus is the species described, one of the precious few flowering oxygenators.
*Cultivation* Grow in full sun in still or running water to a depth of 15–60cm (6–24in).

### R. aquatilis
### Water crowfoot
This submerged perennial has flat, kidney-shaped, floating leaves and thread-like submerged leaves. The buttercup-shaped, white flowers, which are held above the water, have a yellow base to the petals and appear in spring and summer. S indefinite. Hardy/Z 4–8.

## STRATIOTES
This genus comprises a single species, an intriguing plant that behaves both as an oxygenator and a surface floater.
*Cultivation* Grow in full sun in water over 30cm (12in) deep.

### S. aloides
### Water soldier
Rosettes of sword-shaped leaves are produced on runners. These are usually submerged but rise to the surface in early summer, when the white flowers are produced. Dormant buds rest on the bottom of the pond over winter. S indefinite. Hardy/Z 6–9.

Nymphaea 'Hermine'

Stratiotes aloides

# Cacti and Succulents

Cacti and succulents are mostly undemanding plants that are adapted to certain extremes of climate. The range encompasses small, button-like plants to larger, tree-like plants, though they rarely reach unmanageable proportions in cultivation. Though many have spectacular flowers, most are grown for their often bizarre appearance – some hardly look like plants at all. From barrel-shaped cacti, often ribbed like a concertina, to the huge rosettes of agaves, with their thick, fleshy, often boldly marked leaves, and not forgetting the twining hoyas, with their waxy, scented flowers, there is bound to be one amongst them that catches your eye.

Cacti and succulents provide some of the most arresting plant forms in the plant kingdom.

# What are cacti and succulents?

This section could as well be called simply "Succulents". The term "succulent" actually includes the cacti, and what distinguishes cacti from the rest is not, as might be imagined, the spines, but the presence of areoles, modified axillary buds from which all growth arises. The spines do in fact arise from the areoles, but not all cacti are spiny. Equally, some succulents are distinctly cactus-like in appearance, but lack the tell-tale areoles.

In evolutionary terms, cacti and succulents are the youngest plants on the planet and are uniquely adapted to thrive in conditions that are hostile to nearly all other forms of plant life. They have evolved to cope with low rainfall by growing slowly, and can survive periods of drought by conserving as much moisture as possible in their leaves, stems and roots. Hence their fleshy, bloated appearance. The waxy coatings of the leaves also guard against moisture loss.

Succulents are found throughout much of the world. Many are found in deserts, a habitat that is actually

In a hot, dry climate, succulents can play their part as true garden plants.

surprisingly diverse. Some desert areas experience winter rainfall, while in others it tends to rain in the summer only, and plants from such regions will be active in winter and summer respectively and dormant the rest of the time. Some of the maritime regions where succulents occur are subject to cold Antarctic tidal currents, as on the west coast of Africa and South America, and these plants are therefore hardier than those found further inland. To all intents and purposes, cacti are found exclusively in the New World (colonies of in Africa and Madagascar seem to have been introduced by migratory birds).

Cacti can be split into two main groups: those from the desert and those from the rainforest. They occur in a range from Canada (where they can be covered in snow in winter) down to Chile and Argentina, including offshore islands. They are prevalent in the southern USA, down to northern and central South America.

The shape of desert cacti is a response to climatic conditions. Being spherical or globular

minimizes the surface area and thus the amount of moisture that will be lost in transpiration. The characteristic ribbing of some species enables them to expand as moisture becomes available and then contract, like an accordion, without splitting the outer skin. Nearly all have spines, which are usually quite sharp, presumably as a defence against browsing animals. In some species, however (notably the old man cactus, *Cephalocereus senilis*), they look like hair.

Rainforest cacti can easily be mistaken for succulents, since spines are often absent or are replaced by bristles, only the presence of areoles betraying their true allegiance. They generally have flattened, leaf-like stems. In the wild, they often grow epiphytically in places where dead leaves collect, usually in the hollows or forks of trees.

Most cacti and succulents are grown for the sheer fascination of their shape: they are quite unlike any other group of plants. Some, however, have spectacular, if usually short-lived, flowers. One of the most reliable for flower production is the

The round pads of opuntia contrast well with the spiky, steel blue leaves of the agave behind it.

well-known Christmas cactus (*Schlumbergera*), widely grown as a houseplant.

Cacti and succulents have not been heavily hybridized, and the plants grown are mainly species or naturally occurring forms of the species.

## How to grow cacti and succulents

Most cacti and succulents can be grown outdoors only in frost-free, arid climates. Elsewhere, they have to be grown in containers under glass or as houseplants; in fact, they thrive in the warm dry conditions created by most modern central heating systems. Good light is usually essential for all except rainforest cacti, which are adapted to lower light levels. These can be placed in more humid parts of the house, such as a kitchen or bathroom, in a light position but out of direct sunlight. They can be brought into a position in full light in winter. All can be stood outside during the summer months, or even sunk in their pots into borders to make a temporary succulent garden. In a greenhouse, a

winter minimum temperature of 5°C (41°F) is necessary for most species, rising to 10°C (50°F) for most rainforest cacti. Good air circulation is important for all but rainforest cacti (and even these should not be grown in stagnant conditions).

Globular and low-growing plants are best in shallow containers. Large bonsai bowls are excellent and can be planted up with a range of different species. Tall-growing plants are better in correspondingly deeper pots. Epiphytic cacti and any others with trailing stems are effective in hanging baskets.

All cacti and succulents need to be grown in a free-draining medium. Specially formulated composts for cacti are available, and it is best to use these. Alternatively, mix your own by adding one part grit to three parts loam-based compost (soil mix) or two parts loamless compost. Epiphytes need a compost that is moisture-retentive without becoming waterlogged, and the best mix is made up of three parts potting compost, two parts grit and one part leaf mould. Some succulents can be

Indoor cacti and succulent container plants can benefit from a holiday outdoors over the summer months.

grown in conventional potting compost, provided you add grit or sharp sand to improve the drainage. A top-dressing of grit can help prevent water from collecting around the collar of the plant.

Soils where cacti grow in the wild are actually nutrient-high (though humus-low), so you should feed your plants, either with a cactus fertilizer or with a tomato feed at half strength.

Plants should be watered when in active growth, less frequently when dormant. Dormancy occurs not only during winter but also when the temperature rises above a certain level at the height of summer, so you should take care not to over-water during this period. In a cool situation, most can be kept dry from late winter to early spring, but in a centrally heated room, they may need watering every couple of weeks to prevent the compost from drying out completely. Rainforest plants need more water than desert plants. Water them freely when in active growth and give them enough in winter to prevent them from shrivelling.

This impressive collection of mature cacti and succulents in a dedicated greenhouse features several cacti from the popular *Mammilaria* group, which includes many easy-to-cultivate species.

The heights and spreads indicated relate to five-year-old, container-grown plants.

## AEONIUM
These succulents from the Mediterranean, northern Africa and the Canary Islands are grown for their rosettes of fleshy leaves. *Cultivation* Grow in standard cactus compost (soil mix); in winter, maintain a temperature no lower than 5°C (41°F). The maroon-leaved varieties turn green if overwatered.

### A. arboreum
At the end of each branching stem there is a rosette of shiny, glaucous green leaves. Small, star-shaped yellow flowers appear in spring on 2–3 year old stems. H 1m (3ft), S 60cm (2ft). Tender/Z 9–10. 'Arnold Schwarzkopff' has dark maroon (almost black) and bright green leaves. The glossy leaves of 'Atropurpureum' are flushed with dark purplish-red and maroon.

### A. haworthii
**Pinwheel**
This species from the Canary Islands has bluish-green rosettes, often edged with red in summer. Clusters of cream flowers are produced in spring. H and S 30cm (12in). Tender/Z 10.

## AGAVE
There are more than 200 species of dramatic succulents in the genus. They make virtually stemless, usually solitary, rosettes of leaves from ground level. These usually die after flowering, but a cluster of new rosettes generally develops around the base. *Cultivation* Grow in standard cactus compost (soil mix). The

*Aporocactus flagelliformis*

species described require a minimum winter temperature of 5°C (41°F), but as a rule blue-leaved types are hardier than those with pale green leaves.

### A. americana
**(syn. A. altissima)**
**Century plant, maguey**
This handsome Mexican species is often used in landscaping in warm climates, where it will make a dramatic rosette of spiny edged, sharply pointed, pewter grey leaves up to 2.5m (8ft) long (less if grown as a container plant). H and S 2m (6ft). Tender/Z 9–10. 'Mediopicta Alba' is slower growing and less hardy. The leaves are centrally striped with creamy-white. H and S 30cm (12in).

## ALOE
There are about 35 species of succulents in this genus. They are important plants in the cosmetics industry and are widespread from Africa to the Middle East. *Cultivation* Grow aloes in standard potting compost (soil mix) with added grit. The minimum winter temperature varies across the genus.

*Cephalocereus senilis*

### A. vera
**Medicine plant, burn plant**
This species has been used for its medicinal properties since the time of the pharaohs. The rosettes of dull green leaves are spotted with red on young plants. A winter minimum temperature of 10°C (50°F) is best, although plants have been reported to withstand light frosts. H 30cm (12in), S 10cm (4in). Tender/Z 10.

## APOROCACTUS
**Rat's tail cactus**
These Mexican epiphytic cacti have trailing stems, which make them ideal for growing in hanging baskets. They are one of the first cacti to flower, their red or lilac flowers appearing in spring. *Cultivation* Grow in epiphytic cactus compost (soil mix). In summer water regularly as the compost begins to dry out and keep lightly shaded; in winter keep at 6°C (43°F) and water occasionally.

### A. flagelliformis
**(syn. Cereus flagelliformis)**
One of the easiest species to grow, this has slender, cylindrical,

trailing stems to 2m (6ft) long and double, cerise flowers in spring. S 25cm (10in). Tender/Z 10.

## ASTROPHYTUM
The six or so species of slow-growing cacti in the genus are from Mexico. They are globular at first, becoming columnar as they mature. Large, funnel-shaped, yellow flowers appear in summer. *Cultivation* Use standard cactus compost (soil mix) with added calcium. Take care not to over-water in summer and keep dry in winter, at 6°C (43°F), otherwise they can rot.

### A. myriostigma
**(syn. Echinocactus myriostigma)**
**Bishop's cap**
These squat cacti have ribbed, virtually spineless, grey bodies (although some variants show shades of green). H and S 5cm (2in). Tender/Z 10.

### A. ornatum
**(syn. Echinocactus ornatus)**
The ribs of this species, one of the easiest to grow, have clusters of straw-coloured spines. H and S 5cm (2in). Tender/Z 10.

## CEPHALOCEREUS
Only one species, the distinctive old man cactus from Mexico, is commonly found in collections. *Cultivation* Grow in standard cactus compost (soil mix); *C. senilis* benefits from added calcium. Allow plants to dry out between waterings in summer and keep them completely dry between autumn and spring. Grow in full light and maintain a minimum temperature of 7°C (45°F) in winter.

*Aeonium haworthii*

*Agave americana 'Mediopicta Alba'*

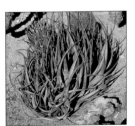
*Aloe vera*

*Astrophytum myriostigma*

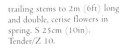

*Crassula ovata*

*Echinocactus grusonii*

### C. senilis
(syn. *Cereus senilis*, *Pilocereus senilis*)
**Old man cactus**
The long white hairs that cover the plant are the distinctive characteristic of this popular species, which is long lived and can reach a height of 2m (6ft) after 50 years. H 8cm (3in), S 2cm (¼in). Tender/Z 10.

## CRASSULA
This extremely diverse genus of succulents includes both small species as well as tree-like plants. On some, the leaves are shiny and glossy; on others they are rough and waxy.
*Cultivation* Grow crassulas in standard cactus compost (soil mix). They need a minimum winter temperature of 5°C (41°F).

### C. ovata
(syn. *C. argentea*)
**Money plant, jade plant**
This species from southern Africa is widely grown as a houseplant, being tolerant of a range of conditions. Mature plants sometimes bear small white flowers in autumn. Ideally, keep at a temperature no lower than 7°C (45°F) in winter, although plants will tolerate short spells at 3°C (37°F). H 45cm (18in), S 30cm (12in). Tender/Z 10.

*Echeveria agavoides*

## ECHEVERIA
With their rosettes of fleshy leaves, these succulents from Central and South America make handsome houseplants and can also be used in summer bedding.
*Cultivation* Standard cactus compost (soil mix) is suitable. The species described needs a minimum winter temperature of 5°C (41°F).

### E. agavoides
The broad, pointed leaves of this distinctive, slow-growing species are pale olive-green, sometimes tinged with red. The flowers, which appear from spring to early summer, are of small ornamental value. H 15cm (6in), S 30cm (12in). Tender/Z 10.

## ECHINOCACTUS
These slow-growing cacti are difficult to grow but are included here because mature specimens are often seen in gardens in California and Mexico and in other hot, dry gardens.
*Cultivation* Use standard cactus compost (soil mix) and maintain a minimum winter temperature of 10°C (50°F).

### E. grusonii
**Golden barrel cactus, mother-in-law's cushion**
The mid-green body of this cactus is covered in distinctive golden spines which shine in full sun. Golden-yellow flowers appear in the crown of mature plants in summer. H 5cm (2in), S 8cm (3in). Tender/Z 10.

## ECHINOPSIS
The easy-to-grow cacti in this genus vary from small, globular plants to tall, columnar ones and are usually free-flowering.

*Cultivation* Grow in standard cactus compost (soil mix). Minimum winter temperature requirements vary; most will endure near-freezing temperatures.

### E. aurea
(syn. *Lobivia echinopsis*)
**Golden lily cactus**
Small, bright yellow flowers are carried on this densely spined species in summer. It needs a minimum winter temperature of 6°C (43°F). H 5cm (2in), S 2.5cm (1in). Tender/Z 10.

### E. 'Gloria'
This hybrid has large scarlet flowers. A minimum winter temperature of 4°C (39°F) is required. H 25cm (10in), S 10cm (4in). Tender/Z 9–10.

### E. smrziana
(syn. *Trichocereus smrziana*)
Mature plants of this Argentinian species bear nocturnal white flowers on thick sturdy stems at various times of year. A minimum winter temperature of 3°C (37°F) is required. H 25cm (10in), S 8cm (3in). Tender/Z 9.

## EPIPHYLLUM
On some species of these rain-forest cacti the flowers, which can be scented, open at night.
*Cultivation* Grow in epiphytic cactus compost (soil mix), in pots or hanging baskets. Keep lightly shaded in summer and in full light in winter with a minimum temperature of 10°C (50°F). Water throughout the year, but sparingly in winter.

### E. anguliger
**Herringbone cactus**
This species from southern Mexico has characteristic notched

*Echinopsis 'Gloria'*

*Epiphyllum anguliger*

stems and small, scented flowers in summer. H 60cm (2ft), S 15cm (6in). Tender/Z 10.

### E. hybrids
Named selections include **'Jennifer Ann'** with yellow flowers; **'King Midas'** with golden-yellow flowers; and **'Wendy May'** with long, pink flowers. H 60cm (2ft), S 15cm (6in). Tender/Z 10.

## ESPOSTOA
These cylindrical cacti from South America have typically woolly stems. The flowers sometimes emit a horrible smell.
*Cultivation* Grow in standard cactus compost (soil mix) with a minimum winter temperature of 7°C (45°F). They are sensitive to overwatering.

### E. lanata
**Snowball cactus**
This is one of the least hairy species in the genus and one of the quickest and easiest to grow. H 10cm (4in), S 2.5cm (1in). Tender/Z 10.

*Espostoa lanata*

Euphorbia milii

Ferocactus glaucescens

# EUPHORBIA

This huge genus is generally represented in gardens by its hardy perennials, but it also includes many succulents, which are diverse in character, some being distinctly cactus-like.
**Cultivation** Use standard potting compost (soil mix) with added grit for the species listed here. The minimum winter temperatures required vary.

### E. milii
**Crown of thorns**
Popular as a houseplant, this species from Madagascar has thorny stems, which are hexagonal in cross-section. It can produce bright red flowers at any time of year. Ideally keep no lower than 16°C (61°F) in winter; at lower temperatures it tends to drop its leaves, although it generally returns to health in spring. H 60cm (2ft), S 30cm (12in). Tender/Z 9–10.

# FEROCACTUS

These large, barbarously armed plants from the southern USA, Mexico and Guatemala are sometimes referred to as barrel cacti, and they can indeed grow to 3m (10ft) in diameter. They usually flower only when they are 25cm (10in) across or more.
**Cultivation** Grow in standard cactus compost. Winter temperature requirements vary.

### F. glaucescens
This species has a ribbed, blue-green body and straight, golden-yellow spines. It needs a minimum winter temperature of 7°C (45°F). H and S 8cm (3in). Tender/Z 10.

### F. herrerae
(syn. *F. wislizeni* var. *herrerae*)
**Candy barrel cactus**
Ultimately a large cactus, to 2m (6ft) tall, this globular species has fishhook-like spines. It flowers only when 30cm (12in) in diameter. Minimum winter temperature 6°C (42°F). H 10cm (4in). S 2.5cm (1in). Tender/Z 10.

# HOYA
**Wax flower**
These succulents, popular as houseplants, have thick, glossy leaves and attractive, sometimes scented, flowers.
**Cultivation** Grow in standard potting compost (soil mix), with added grit or perlite for improved drainage. The temperature should be no lower than 10°C (50°F) in winter, although lows of 5°C (41°F) are tolerated for short periods.

### H. carnosa
Probably the easiest of the hoyas to grow, this climber is however seldom free-flowering in cultivation. The thick, waxy leaves are pointed and bright green; the nectar-rich, highly fragrant flowers appear in summer and can be white or pale pink. H to 3m (10ft), S to 2m (6ft). Tender/Z 10.

### H. lanceolata subsp. bella
(syn. *H. bandaensis*)
This hoya is also easy to grow. Daintier in all its parts than *H. carnosa*, it has sprawling stems set with pointed green leaves and produces quantities of waxy white flowers in hanging clusters in late summer. Its trailing habit makes it ideal for a hanging basket. H and S 30cm (12in). Tender/Z 10.

# KALANCHOE

These perennial succulents, which are widely distributed in the tropics, are grown as houseplants for their foliage and bell-shaped to tubular flowers. They are easy to grow and usually flower readily. There are many hybrids, and not all plants offered for sale are named.
**Cultivation** Grow in standard potting compost (soil mix) with added grit. Winter temperature requirements vary according to species, but the plants described here need a minimum winter temperature of 12°C (54°F).

### K. blossfeldiana
**Flaming Katy**
This familiar species has dark green leaves with scalloped edges, and it can produce its (typically) red flowers at almost any time of year. Short day length triggers flowering, and this can be simulated by keeping the plant in the dark for a few hours a day during the warmer months. Plants sold under this name can have pink, yellow or white flowers. H and S to 30cm (12in). Tender/Z 10.

# LAMPRANTHUS

Originating from South Africa, the succulents in this genus of over 180 species are grown for their profusion of appealing, daisy-like flowers, which make carpets of colour in areas where they can be grown outdoors.
**Cultivation** Grow in standard cactus compost (soil mix) and keep no lower than 1°C (34°F) in winter. Flowers open only in full sun.

### L. haworthii
Deep pink flowers are borne in late spring. Eventually it can make a large bush, but can be clipped to shape. H 60cm (2ft), S 1m (3ft). Tender/Z 10.

# LITHOPS
**Living stone, pebble plants**
These intriguing succulents look just like small stones, an impression entirely destroyed when their spectacular flowers appear. Each plant is composed of a pair of swollen leaves.
**Cultivation** Grow in standard cactus compost (soil mix). Position in a very bright spot and take care not to over-water. In winter keep plants completely dry at a temperature no lower than 1°C (34°F), but preferably 7°C (45°F).

### L. aucampiae
One of the larger species and native to South Africa, this has chocolate-brown leaves with flat upper surfaces. The bright yellow, daisy-like flowers appear in early autumn. H and S 3cm (1in). Tender/Z 10.

# MAMMILLARIA

This genus contains some of the largest and most popular of the globular cacti, since they are easy to grow and to bring into flower. The flowers are carried in rings around the crown of the plant in spring, often with a second (and even third) flush appearing later on.
**Cultivation** Grow in standard cactus compost (soil mix) and maintain a minimum temperature of 6°C (43°F) in winter.

Lampranthus haworthii

Lithops aucampiae

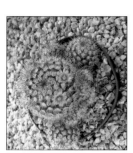
*Mammillaria bombycina*

*Opuntia microdasys*

*Rebutia minuscula* f. *senilis*

### M. bombycina
This Mexican species produces pink flowers after about four years. The spines can be red, brown or yellow. H and S 8cm (3in). Tender/Z 10.

### M. hahniana
**Old lady cactus**
This globular species from Mexico is densely covered with long, curly, hair-like spines, which sometimes grow long and wrap themselves around the body of the plant. The bright red flowers can be followed by even brighter red seedpods. H 5cm (2in), S 8cm (3in). Tender/Z 10.

## OPUNTIA
**Prickly pear**
These fast-growing cacti, widespread from Canada to southern South America, are also a familiar sight in the Mediterranean area, where they have escaped from gardens and become naturalized.
*Cultivation* Grow in standard cactus compost (soil mix). Minimum winter temperatures vary. Take care when handling the plants because the glochids (bristles) are easily embedded in the skin.

### O. microdasys
**Bunny ears**
The flattened pads of this species from Mexico are more or less spineless, but regularly dotted with white areoles filled with glochids. Flowers are produced only on mature plants. This requires a minimum winter temperature of 10°C (50°F). H 15cm (6in), S 10cm (4in). Tender/Z 10.

## OREOCEREUS
**Old man of the Andes**
These slow-growing cacti are found throughout the Andes, where they survive in lower temperatures than they will tolerate in cultivation, probably because of low humidity.
*Cultivation* Grow in standard cactus compost (soil mix). Water with care in summer and keep them dry in winter, allowing the temperature to fall no lower than 6°C (43°F).

### O. celsianus
**(syn. *Borzicactus celsianus*, *Oreocereus neocelsianus*, *Pilocereus celsianus*)**
**Old man of the mountains**
This makes sturdy, upright stems with both thick, straight spines and woolly, white ones. Pale purplish-pink flowers are borne in summer. H 8cm (3in), S 2.5cm (1in). Tender/Z 10.

## PARODIA
Originating from South America, these are some of the easiest cacti to bring into flower.
*Cultivation* Grow in standard cactus compost (soil mix). In winter they are best at a temperature no lower than 10°C (50°F); water occasionally to prevent them from drying out completely.

### P. leninghausii
**(syn. *Eriocactus leninghausii*)**
This distinctive species produces a single stem at first, offsets from the base appearing only as it gets larger. Yellow flowers are produced on plants taller than 15cm (6in). It will tolerate a winter low of 5°C (41°F). H 10cm (4in), S 5cm (2in). Tender/Z 10.

## REBUTIA
These easy-to-grow cacti from South America are among the first to flower in spring.
*Cultivation* Use standard cactus compost (soil mix). They will tolerate temperatures down to near freezing in winter if they are kept dry.

### R. arenacea
**(syn. *Sulcorebutia arenacea*)**
This has a small, rounded body and numerous short spines. The golden-yellow flowers appear in late spring. H 2cm (¼in), S 5cm (2in). Tender/Z 10.

### R. minuscula f. senilis
**Fire crown cactus**
The form differs from the species in having longer, white, hairy spines and brighter red flowers. The squat green body produces offsets slowly, ultimately making clumps. H 2.5cm (1in), S 5cm (2in). Tender/Z 10.

## SCHLUMBERGERA
**Christmas cactus**
These popular rainforest cacti from Brazil have been extensively hybridized to produce a range of easy-to-grow plants. Not all are named. They are valued for their winter flowers, usually produced in abundance.
*Cultivation* Use epiphytic cactus compost (soil mix), and maintain a minimum winter temperature of 5°C (41°F), preferably warmer. Keep out of direct sunlight. Water and feed when in active growth (summer and autumn), but keep the compost barely moist after flowering and for the rest of the year.

### S. hybrids
The arching stems are made up of flattened, bright green segments. At their tips, they produce flowers in winter, the colour range including red (**'Firecracker'**, **'Joanne'**), pale pinkish-orange (**'Gold Charm'**), and lilac (**'Lilac Beauty'**). H 15cm (6in), S 30cm (12in). Tender/Z 10.

## SEDUM
A large genus of succulents which also includes many popular hardy perennials. Sedums range from tiny mats to large, shrubby or even tree-like plants.
*Cultivation* Use standard potting compost (soil mix) with added grit and leaf mould.

### S. rubrotinctum
Short, blunt, fleshy leaves are carried on this arching succulent subshrub. Maintain a minimum winter temperature of 1°C (34°F). H 25cm (10in), S 20cm (8in). Tender/Z 9. The form **'Aurora'** has leaves that are pink to yellow, the colour being more intense in sun. H 20cm (8in), S 1m (3ft).

*Parodia leninghausii*

*Sedum rubrotinctum*

# Orchids

Beautiful, flamboyant, sometimes bizarre: orchids exert a unique appeal. Everything about them is fascinating, from their strange habit of growth, nestling on fallen tree trunks or among rocks or clambering skywards to the tree canopy, to their striking, often intoxicatingly scented flowers. Formerly considered plants for the connoisseur only, nowadays there is a huge range of hybrids that are easy to grow and well within the scope of any gardener. Through careful choice it is possible to make a collection that provides flowers virtually year-round.

Many orchids provide a succesion of impressive flowers over a long period, making them among the most desirable of all plants.

# What is an orchid?

Forming a huge plant family, orchids are primarily herbaceous or evergreen perennials, distinguished from other plant families by the structure of their flowers. Orchids are found throughout the world, in every continent except Antarctica.

Terrestrial orchids, native mainly to temperate regions, are rooted in the ground like most other plants and have either a rhizome (a swollen, horizontal stem) or an underground tuber (a structure with a similar function but without the tendency to grow laterally). Most of these orchids experience a period of dormancy, usually in winter for herbaceous species with rhizomes, while tuberous species are dormant in summer. Evergreens rest either in winter or just after flowering.

Epiphytic orchids, most of which are evergreen, spend their lives above ground and have special aerial roots that allow them to cling to trees or rocks (the latter are more correctly referred to as lithophytic). The roots can absorb nutrients and minerals from any matter that washes down

the tree, but do not derive nourishment from the tree itself, so are not parasites. They are usually dormant in winter, when growth slows down or stops altogether, but tropical species that have their home near the equator will grow and flower virtually continuously. The difference between terrestrial and epiphytic orchids is not as marked as you might think: epiphytes are often to be found with their roots nestling in as deep a layer of leaf litter and other plant debris as is ever to be found on the forest floor, and some terrestrials are quite capable of living epiphytically.

Orchid flowers are composed of six segments, collectively referred to as the perianth. The unopened flower is enclosed by three sepals. These open to reveal three petals. In most other plant families, the sepals are green and are hidden by the open flower. In the case of orchids, they are usually petal-like and are marked and coloured in a similar fashion to the true petals. The lowest of the three petals, called the lip or

labellum, is modified in shape and serves as a landing platform for pollinating insects. This structure represents a peak in plant adaptation to specific pollinators. In some orchids, the lip is inflated and forms a pouch or "slipper", as in the case of *Paphiopedilum*.

Orchid flowers are distinct (though not unique) in that they are symmetrical only from side to side and not from top to bottom. They are produced singly or in a spray (sometimes referred to as a raceme) or on a branched spike.

Different orchids flower at different seasons of the year. Some, however, can flower at any time of year, while others will flower on and off throughout the year. The flower spikes are mostly long-lasting, but in a few species the flowers last for only a day.

Flower size varies. The smallest can be no more than 2mm (0.1in) across, while *Brassia* for instance can be up to 38cm (15in).

## How to grow orchids

All the orchids described on the following pages are suitable for growing indoors, and most of the hybrids have been developed for that very purpose, so in no way can they be described as conventional garden plants. They are usually divided into three broad groups depending on the climate in which the parent species is found.

Cool-growing orchids originate from high altitudes where nights are cool, often dropping to 10°C (50°F). They need a minimum temperature range of 10–13°C (50–55°F) and a maximum of 21–24°C (70–75°F).

Intermediate-growing orchids, from slightly warmer areas, need a minimum temperature of 14–19°C

This *Dendrobium* species is a member of a huge genus, widely distributed in India, south-east Asia, Australia and the Pacific islands.

Cattleyas provide the enthusiast with some of the most flamboyant of all orchid flowers. These orchids show just some of the variations to be found within the genus.

particular genera. Humidity is also important, and the plants should be misted twice daily when in growth, orchids on bark particularly thoroughly, as this is the only means of watering them. Alternatively, stand the pots on trays of special expanded clay pellets. The trays are filled with water, which is then allowed to evaporate.

Water orchids freely during the growing season, but make sure that the containers drain properly and that the plants do not have their feet in water. Water less in winter or when the plants are resting, just enough to keep the growing medium barely moist. Orchids that are more or less permanently in growth can be watered year-round, though less in winter, when growth tends to slow down. Always water directly into the compost, not on to the plant itself – water that collects in the leaves can lead to rotting.

Orchids seem to thrive in collections with others of their kind, so grow as many as you can in the space available.

(57–66°F) with a maximum of 30–33°C (86–91°F).

Warm-growing orchids, originating from steamy rainforests, have a minimum requirement of 20–24°C (68–75°F) and a maximum of 30–33°C (86–91°F).

Light is also an important factor. Orchids from near the equator are adapted to light levels that remain more or less constant throughout the year. In temperate zones, day length fluctuates widely between summer and winter. To persuade the plants that they are nearer home than they are, it is usually necessary to shade them in summer to protect them from hot sun and from scorch: under glass, temperatures can soar much higher than they would in the plants' natural habitat. Conversely, in winter most orchids need maximum light, and the shading should be removed.

Most orchids – even epiphytes – can be grown successfully in containers. Epiphytes are also commonly grown in special wooden or plastic baskets, and this is an especially effective way of displaying those with trailing flower stems,

such as *Stanhopea*. An alternative, for smaller epiphytes, is to tie them to pieces of bark or tree fern fibre, usually with some coconut fibre wrapped around the roots to retain moisture. Bark can be wall mounted or suspended horizontally to make a raft.

Orchids need special composts (soil mix) that are swift-draining; some are specially formulated to suit

Growing orchids in special slatted wooden baskets allows roots access to the air they need, as well as being an effective way of displaying the plants.

# BRASSIA

The mainly epiphytic evergreen orchids in this genus are found in the tropical Americas. They have been much used in hybridizing. **Cultivation** Grow the orchids described below epiphytically in baskets or on bark. Provide light shade in summer and full light in winter.

### B. Rex

Spidery flowers, up to 20cm (8in) long and smelling of musk, appear in summer. The sepals and petals are elongated and are sulphur yellow to lime green, spotted and marked with red-brown to black. The lips are white and are similarly spotted. Flower spike 30cm (12in). Cool-growing/Z 10.

### B. verrucosa
(syn. *B. brachiata*)
**Spider orchid**

The species occurs in a range from southern Mexico to Venezuela. **'Sea Mist'** is a selection with spidery, musky smelling, greenish-yellow flowers in summer, arranged alternately on arching stems. This is an ideal orchid for a growing case. Flower spike to 75cm (30in). Cool-growing/Z 10.

# × BRASSOLAELIO-CATTLEYA

For many growers, these plants, with their huge, dramatic flowers, are the archetypal orchid. They

*Brassia* **Rex**

*Brassia verrucosa* 'Sea Mist'

are also easy to grow. The plants are complex hybrids, involving *Brassavola*, *Cattleya* and *Laelia*.
**Cultivation** Grow these orchids in containers in free-draining compost (soil mix).

### × B. Enid Moore × *Laeliocattleya* Starting Point

One of the showiest of the group, this bears large, creamy-white flowers with ruffled petal edges. The lips are heavily stained with rich rosy purple and have yellow centres lined with purple. Flower spike to 20cm (8in). Cool-growing to intermediate/Z 10.

### × B. Yellow Imp 'Golden Grail'

Bright yellow flowers are borne in spring or autumn. Flower spike to 20cm (8in). Cool-growing to intermediate/Z 10.

# BULBOPHYLLUM

The plants in this large genus of epiphytic orchids, found in a wide range of habitats throughout the tropics, are for the enthusiast rather than for the general grower.
**Cultivation** Grow in epiphytic orchid compost (soil mix) in slatted baskets or on bark.

### B. lobbii

This creeping species is found in tropical regions of north-eastern India, south-eastern Asia and the Philippines. The solitary, pale yellow, red-yellow or ochre flowers appear in summer. They are conspicuously lined with red and brown and can be speckled

× *Brassolaeliocattleya* Enid Moore × *Laeliocattleya* Starting Point

with pink and yellow. Flower spike to 13cm (5in). Intermediate/Z 10.

### B. ornatissimum
(syn. *Cirrhopetalum ornatissimum*)

In autumn this orchid, which is native to India, produces sprays of short-lipped, straw yellow flowers, three to a stem. Each flower is dotted and striped with purple. Flower spike to 10cm (4in). Cool-growing/Z 10.

# CATTLEYA

There are about 40 species in all in the genus, which is possibly the most important to orchid-lovers and probably the most commonly grown. In the wild cattleyas grow epiphytically in Central and South America, but in cultivation they are generally represented by their complex hybrids, which have huge, flamboyant flowers, often with petals with ruffled edges. Cattleyas are familiar flowers, much used by florists.

*Bulbophyllum lobbii*

**Cultivation** Grow in epiphytic orchid compost (soil mix) in containers.

### C. Carla × *Brassolaeliocattleya* Nickie Holguin

In late summer and autumn this hybrid has large, showy, creamy white flowers with lips stained yellow in the centre. Flower spike to 20cm (8in). Cool-growing to intermediate/Z 10.

### C. Enid × *Brassolaeliocattleya* Holiday Inn

Huge, white flowers with pale greenish-yellow centres and lips that are stained rich rosy purple are borne in late summer to autumn. The petal edges are ruffled. Flower spike to 20cm (8in). Cool-growing to intermediate/Z 10.

### C. harrisoniana × Penny Karoda

This desirable and distinctive orchid produces solitary, luminous pink flowers in summer and autumn. The trumpet-like lips are light violet-pink, shading to rich purplish-pink at the edges and with yellow centres. Flower spike to 20cm (8in). Cool-growing to intermediate/Z 10.

### C. labiata × *Brassocattleya* Cutty Sark

The white, yellow-centred flowers appear in summer to autumn. Flower spike to 20cm (8in). Cool-growing to intermediate/Z 10.

### C. loddigesii 'Alba' × Old Whitey

This is a stunning orchid, bearing large, solitary, luminous violet flowers, with ruffled petal edges, in late summer to autumn. The lips are elongated, are marked with rosy purple and have yellow centres. Flower spike 20cm (8in). Cool-growing to intermediate/Z 10.

### C. loddigesii × *Sophrolaeliocattleya* Jeweller's Art 'Carved Coral'

The flowers, which are produced from autumn to spring, are a warm rose-purple with darker purple lips. Flower spike to 20cm (8in). Cool-growing to intermediate/Z 10.

Cattleya loddigesii 'Alba' × Old Whitey

### C. Louis × Carla × *Brassolaeliocattleya* Nickie Holguin

Almost entirely pure white, the flowers, borne from summer to autumn, are stained yellow only at the centre of the lips. Flower spike to 20cm (8in). Cool-growing to intermediate/Z 10.

## COELOGYNE

The genus contains about 200 evergreen, epiphytic orchids, which are found in the mountainous regions of India, south-eastern Asia and the Pacific islands. In spite of their wide spread in the wild, they are not generally well represented in growers' collections. They are easy to grow, but some of the species take up a lot of room. The ones described are modest in size and would make worthwhile additions to any collection, particularly winter-flowering types.
*Cultivation* These are suitable for containers or hanging baskets, unless otherwise indicated.

Cattleya Louis × Carla ×
*Brassolaeliocattleya* Nickie Holguin

Coelogyne Memoria William Micholitz

### C. cristata

In spring this species, which is native to the eastern Himalayas, has dangling stems of fragrant, frosty white flowers, streaked yellow in the throat in spring. It needs a winter rest. Flower spike to 30cm (12in). Cool-growing to intermediate/Z 10.

### C. fimbriata (syn. *Broughtonia linearis*)

This species grows wild in northern India and in a range from Vietnam to Hong Kong. Its solitary, buff yellow flowers, which appear in summer, have white or pale yellow lips marked with dark brown. Flower spike to 5cm (2in). Cool-growing/Z 10.

### C. massangeana

In early spring to summer hanging stems carry up to 20 scented, pale yellow flowers with brown and yellow lips. Native to Malaysia, Sumatra and Java, this orchid needs to be kept dry over winter and is seen at its best when grown hanging from an orchid raft. Flower spike to 45cm (18in). Intermediate/Z 10.

### C. Memoria William Micholitz

The flowers on this hybrid are larger – at 9cm (3½in) across – than those of most coelogynes. Appearing from spring to summer, they are creamy-white and have lips spotted with red and yellow. Flower spike to 45cm (18in). Cool-growing/Z 10.

## CYMBIDIUM

The ideal beginner's orchid, cymbidiums are virtually indestructible plants, bearing impressive spikes of long-lasting, waxy flowers. Unfortunately, they are not the most consistent

Cymbidium erythrostylum

flowerers, and the best way to guarantee reliable flowering is to provide temperatures that fluctuate between night and day in summer and autumn. This is most easily achieved by placing the plants outdoors until as late in the season as possible (in other words, before the first frosts) so that they experience the drop in temperature necessary to trigger flower production. In frost-free climates they are best grown out of doors all year round. The genus, which contains both epiphytes and terrestrials, is found in both temperate and tropical areas of India, the Far East and parts of Australia.
*Cultivation* Grow in epiphytic or

Cymbidium Summer Pearl 'Sonya'

terrestrial orchid compost (growing medium) in containers.

### C. erythrostylum

This compact epiphyte hails from Vietnam and has brilliant white flowers with red striping on the lips in spring and summer. This may also be grown on bark. Flower spike to 60cm (2ft). Cool-growing/Z 9.

### C. Maureen Grapes 'Marilyn'

Erect spikes of greenish-yellow flowers appear mainly in summer on this hybrid. The lips are spotted red towards the edge. Flower spike 60cm (2ft) or more. Cool-growing/Z 9.

### C. nitida (syn. *C. ochracea*)

This epiphyte has very fragrant white flowers, marked with orange and yellow, from spring to early summer. Flower spike to 20cm (8in). Cool-growing/Z 9.

### C. Summer Pearl 'Senna'

Similar in overall appearance and flowering time to *C.* Maureen Grapes 'Marilyn', this hybrid has more greenish, acid-yellow flowers spotted with darker red. Flower spike to 60cm (2ft). Cool-growing/Z 9. The miniature 'Sonya' is a greenish-pink selection from the same hybrid group. The flowers of both orchids stay on the plant for six to eight weeks.

Dendrobium Mousmée

# DENDROBIUM

There are both epiphytes and terrestrials in this large genus of deciduous, semi-evergreen and evergreen orchids. In the wild they occur across a huge area: India, China, south-eastern Asia, Japan, Malaysia, the Philippines, New Guinea, the Pacific islands, Australia and New Zealand. Many are easy to grow, while others need more specialist care. The most popular are hybrids derived from *D. nobile*.
**Cultivation** Grow the following orchids in small pots to restrict the roots or epiphytically on bark. All like bright light; lack of light is usually the cause of failure to produce flowers.

### D. 'Emma Gold'
From summer to autumn the hybrid has tall, upright stems bearing small, greenish-yellow flowers with maroon lips. Support the flower stems with canes if necessary. Flower spike to 60cm (2ft). Cool-growing/Z 10.

### D. loddigesii
This miniature orchid is an epiphyte found in south-western China. The fragrant, rose-pink flowers, with lips lined and fringed yellow, appear in early summer. Flower spike to 15cm (6in). Cool-growing/Z 10.

### D. Mousmée
This is one of the oldest hybrid orchids, but it is still well worth growing. In summer, trusses of white flowers with rich yellow lips hang from strong, upright canes. Flower spike to 40cm (16in). Cool-growing/Z 10.

### D. nobile
An epiphytic species from the Himalayas, southern China and Taiwan, in spring this bears large, pale pink flowers with maroon lips. It needs a winter rest. Flower spike to 45cm (18in). Cool-growing/Z 10.

# ENCYCLIA

The genus, from Central America, contains about 150 species, and the ones in cultivation are mainly from Mexico. These are collector's orchids, rather than for the general grower, but they are highly rewarding. The flowers are often brightly coloured and can be scented. Compact and freely branching, encyclias are suitable for growing outdoors in frost-free areas.
**Cultivation** Good drainage is essential, so grow these orchids in slatted baskets and keep them dry in winter.

### E. brassavolae
This is an evergreen species originating from southern Mexico to western Panama, where it grows epiphytically in forested areas. The racemes of yellowish-green to brown flowers have purple-tipped, white lips and appear from summer to autumn. Flower spike 50cm (25in) or more. Cool-growing/Z 10.

Encyclia fragrans

### E. cochleata
**Cockleshell orchid, clamshell orchid**
The curious, ribbon-like flowers, which are pale green with deep purple lips, can be produced at any time of year on this species, which is distributed from Florida to Mexico, Colombia and Venezuela. Flower spike to 50cm (25in). Cool-growing/Z 10.

### E. fragrans
As its Latin name suggests, this species, from southern Mexico, Central America to Brazil and Greater Antilles, has scented flowers. Cream to greenish-white, with dark maroon striped lips, they are produced in racemes from spring to summer. Flower spike to 20cm (8in). Cool-growing/Z 10.

### E. 'Sunburst'
Racemes of light greenish-yellow flowers with white lips appear in late summer. Flower spike to 15cm (6in). Cool-growing/Z 10.

### E. vitellina 'Burnham Star'
This is a selected form of a species from Mexico and Guatemala. Panicles of vermilion to scarlet flowers with orange to yellow lips are borne from spring to summer. Flower spike to 15cm (6in). Cool-growing/Z 10.

# EPIDENDRUM

This is one of the largest of orchid genera, containing more than 500 species, which are found throughout the tropical Americas, some at high altitudes. A noteworthy feature is that the flowers, sometimes on branching stems, open a few at a time so that individual plants can be in flower for several months. They are all evergreen, some being epiphytes, others terrestrials. They are best displayed so that the flowers are at eye-level.
**Cultivation** These orchids do best in containers. Either provide support for the long stems or allow them to trail down.

### E. 'Pink Cascade'
As befits its name, this hybrid has tall, arching stems with hanging clusters of small, mauve, long-lasting flowers, which are tinged with pink. Flower spike to 60cm (2ft). Cool-growing to intermediate/Z 10.

Encyclia brassavolae

Encyclia vitellina 'Burnham Star'

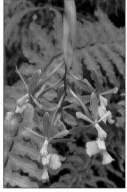

Epidendrum 'Pink Cascade'

*Epidendrum* 'Plastic Doll'

### E. 'Plastic Doll'
An unfortunate name, but this is a pretty plant, with hanging clusters of small, pale green flowers, sometimes marked pink in the centre, with yellow lips. These are carried over a long period in summer. It will flower as a small plant, so it makes a good introduction to the genus for new enthusiasts. Flower spike to 1m (3ft). Cool-growing to intermediate/Z 10.

## LAELIA
This is an important genus, although not many of the 70 species find their way into amateur collections. Their value as parents to intergeneric hybrids (mostly with *Cattleya*) can hardly be overestimated, however. In the wild laelias are found growing both epiphytically and as terrestrials in much of Central and South America from coastal regions to high altitudes.
*L. purpurata* is the national flower of Brazil.
*Cultivation* See individual descriptions for the plants listed.

### L. anceps
This elegant species is an epiphyte originating from central Mexico. The soft lilac flowers have deep mauve, yellow-centred lips veined purple and are produced on tall stems in autumn to winter. Grow in a container or on bark. Rest the plant in winter after flowering. Flower spike to 60cm (2ft). Cool-growing/Z 10.

### L. Pulcherrima 'Alba'
This beautiful hybrid has large, pure white, fragrant flowers in summer. It should be grown in a container. Flower spike to 60cm (2ft). Cool-growing/Z 10.

## × LAELIOCATTLEYA
This hybrid genus consists of crosses between *Laelia* and *Cattleya*, sometimes referred to as cattleyas. It includes some of the most glamorous orchids, which should be represented in any collection.
*Cultivation* Grow in containers or slatted baskets.

### × L. Callistoglossa
From summer to autumn this orchid has very large, pure white flowers that have ruffled petal edges and lips stained yellow at the centre. Flower spike to 30cm (12in). Cool-growing to intermediate/Z 10.

### × L. Canhamiana 'Caerulea'
An orchid that bears large, showy blue flowers with darker lips from winter to spring. Flower spike to 30cm (12in). Cool-growing/Z 10.

### × L. Gila Wilderness 'Majestic'
The large, reddish-purple flowers, which appear in summer, have flared petals. Flower spike to 30cm (12in). Cool-growing/Z 10.

### × L. Love Fantasy 'Sweet Dreams'
From late summer to autumn this orchid produces racemes of sumptuous white flowers with lips that are splashed rosy purple and have yellow centres. Flower spike to 30cm (12in). Cool-growing/Z 10.

*Laelia* Pulcherrima 'Alba'

### × L. Mini Purple 'Pinafore'
An orchid of luminous beauty, this bears large, rosy purple flowers, which have trumpet-like lips stained darker at the tips and yellow at the centre. They are produced from late summer to autumn. Flower spike to 20cm (8in). Cool-growing/Z 10.

### × L. Tiny Treasure × Lake Casitas
Spectacular white flowers, with ruffled petal edges and lips that are stained reddish-purple at the edge and yellow towards the centre, appear in summer and autumn. Flower spike to 20cm (8in). Cool-growing/Z 10.

## MASDEVALLIA
These fascinating orchids have a unique flower structure. They differ from other orchids in that the sepals are very large in comparison with the other parts of the flower, which are so small that they are almost invisible. The 300 or so species occur in the

× *Laeliocattleya* Tiny Treasure × Lake Casitas

wild at high altitudes (mostly in cloud forest) in Mexico, Brazil and Colombia, growing both epiphytically and as terrestrials. They are all evergreen. In the home the hybrids are easier to grow than the species. They do well if underpotted, to restrict the roots.
*Cultivation* Grow in containers of epiphytic compost (soil mix) and do not allow to dry out in winter. They are vulnerable to pesticides and fertilizers, so make sure these are well diluted before applying them.

### M. Whiskers
This unique and distinctive hybrid is notable for the elongated 'tails' that extend from the tips of its sepals. The background colour of these is yellow-orange, but the heavy red spotting predominates. Flower spike to 15cm (6in). Cool-growing/Z 10.

*Laelia anceps*

× *Laeliocattleya* Mini Purple 'Pinafore'

*Masdevallia* Whiskers

Miltonia clowesii

Miltonia warsewiczii 'Alba'

Miltoniopsis Storm

## MILTONIA
### Pansy orchid

Although this is a small genus, the orchids are deservedly popular because of their ease of cultivation. There has been some confusion with the genus *Miltoniopsis*, which it resembles in some ways. There are about 20 species in the genus, and in the wild they are found in forested areas, mainly in Brazil, where they grow epiphytically. (Species found outside Brazil are sometimes included in other genera.) They like to be kept a little pot-bound.
*Cultivation* Grow these orchids in containers or slatted baskets or mounted on bark.

#### M. clowesii
In autumn, each erect stem carries from six to ten greenish-yellow,

star-shaped flowers, which are heavily blotched and barred brown. The lips are white, with a pinkish-mauve blotch on the upper part. Misting in summer can mark the foliage, so provide humidity by other means. It is suitable for growing on a windowsill. Flower spike 60cm (2ft). Cool-growing/Z 10.

#### M. warsewiczii 'Alba'
This is a selection of a species from Peru, Colombia and Costa Rica. In summer it produces fragrant, yellow and white flowers. Flower spike to 50cm (20in). Intermediate/Z 10.

## MILTONIOPSIS

These orchids are also sometimes called pansy orchids because the flowers look like pansies. Their

flat faces, usually with a contrasting 'mask', are just as appealing. Flower colours include white, pink, purple, red and yellow as well as a dramatic blackish-maroon. The five species in the genus are mainly epiphytes, found in the mountains of Central and South America. The hybrids are desirable plants in every respect: vividly coloured, scented, often with two flowering periods a year, and easy to grow.
*Cultivation* Grow in containers. Like miltonias, with which they are often grouped, they like to be kept a little pot-bound and appreciate high humidity.

#### M. Bremen × Lilac Surprise
This hybrid has white flowers, marked deep maroon, which appear mainly in summer but also occasionally at other times. Flower spike to 23cm (9in). Cool-growing/Z 10.

#### M. St Mary
The white flowers are appealingly marked with red and yellow at the centre. As with the other hybrids described, flowering is mainly in summer but can also occur at other times. Flower spike to 23cm (9in). Cool-growing/Z 10.

#### M. Storm
The eye-catching, rich red flowers appear mainly in summer but also at other times. They are blotched with yellow and pink at the base of the lips. Flower spike to 23cm (9in). Cool-growing/Z 10.

## × ODONTIODA

This hybrid group was created by crossing *Odontoglossum* with *Cochlioda*, and in many respects they look like odontoglossums. They do not have a specific flowering season, but can flower at any time when the current season's pseudobulb is mature. The flowers are very showy.
*Cultivation* Grow in containers of epiphytic orchid compost (soil mix).

#### × O. Honiton Lace 'Burnham'
This orchid has tall sprays of large mauve and pink flowers. Flower spike to 45cm (18in). Cool-growing/Z 10.

#### × O. Mont Felard × St Aubin's Bay
A neat-growing orchid, this bears spikes of white flowers spotted with rich pink. The lips are stained the same colour towards the edge and have yellow centres. The petal edges are ruffled and frilled. Flower spike to 45cm (18in). Cool-growing/Z 10.

#### × O. Rialto × Odontocidium Panse
This orchid has sprays of creamy-white flowers, blotched with yellow, and frilled petal edges. Flower spike to 45cm (18in). Cool-growing Z 10.

## × ODONTOCIDIUM

A hybrid group produced by crossing *Odontoglossum* with *Oncidium*. The flowers are often distinctively mottled. Some have definite flowering seasons, while others will flower all year in the right conditions.
*Cultivation* Grow in containers of epiphytic orchid compost (soil mix).

#### × O. Purbeck Gold
Rich yellow flowers mottled with brown are borne mainly in autumn but also occasionally at other times. Flower spike to 50cm (20in). Cool-growing/Z 10.

#### × O. Tiger Hambühren 'Butterfly'
An orchid with impressive spikes of rich yellow flowers mottled with chestnut brown. They appear

Miltoniopsis St Mary

× *Odontocidium* Tiger Hambühren 'Butterfly'

mainly in autumn but also at other times. Flower spike to 45cm (18in). Cool-growing/Z 10.

## ODONTOGLOSSUM

This is an important genus for hybridists and plants from it have been used to create a vast number of excellent, easy-to-grow hybrids. In the wild they are found growing epiphytically, mainly in cool mountain regions of Central and South America. Many of the hybrids can flower at any time of year.
**Cultivation** Grow in containers of epiphytic orchid compost (soil mix).

### O. Geyser Gold

The showy flowers of this orchid, which are carried on upright stems, are rich yellow overlaid with darker gold markings. They can be produced at any time of year. Flower spike to 50cm (20in). Cool-growing/Z 10.

## ONCIDIUM

There are about 450 species of mainly epiphytic orchids in this genus from South America and the West Indies.
**Cultivation** These orchids do best in containers of epiphytic orchid compost (soil mix).

### O. longipes

This small species, from south-eastern Brazil, produces an abundance of short racemes of yellow flowers, spotted and streaked with reddish-brown, in spring and summer. Flower spike to 15cm (6in). Cool-growing to intermediate/Z 10.

### O. macranthum
(syn. *Cyrtolichum macranthum*)

In summer this species, from Colombia, Ecuador and Peru, bears tall, spreading panicles of golden-yellow flowers with lips edged in purple. Flower spike to 1m (3ft). Cool-growing to intermediate/Z 10.

### O. Sharry Baby

From summer to autumn tall, branching stems carry an abundance of dainty, maroon and white flowers that are chocolate-scented. Support the flower stems with canes. Flower spike to 60cm (2ft). Cool-growing/Z 10.

## PAPHIOPEDILUM
### Slipper orchid, Venus' slipper

Paphiopedilums are the well-known slipper orchids, so called because of the flowers' inflated, pouch-like lips (actually designed to trap pollinating insects). Predominantly in shades of green and brown, the flowers can add a rather sinister touch to any orchid collection. The 60 or so evergreen species in the genus are Asian in origin and are mostly terrestrial. There are many hybrids, which are often more sympathetically coloured in white, pink or cream. The leaves can be mottled. Paphiopedilums are robust plants, which tolerate low light levels, making them ideal houseplants. The flowers mainly appear in winter and can last for up to ten weeks on the plant. However, the plants are often slow-growing and reluctant to flower, so they are not the ideal beginner's orchid.
**Cultivation** Grow in terrestrial orchid compost (soil mix) in containers that restrict the roots. Do not mist.

### P. Avalon Mist

Yellowish-green flowers appear from spring to summer on this hybrid. Flower spike to 23cm (9in). Cool-growing to intermediate/Z 10.

### P. Calloso-Argus

This hybrid, which blooms from spring to summer, produces solitary flowers. They are green, striped and spotted with maroon.

*Paphiopedilum* Avalon Mist

The leaves are attractively mottled. Flower spike to 23cm (9in). Cool-growing to intermediate/Z 10.

### P. insigne

From autumn to spring, this species, originating in the eastern Himalayas, carries slipper-like, copper-brown, solitary flowers with yellow dorsal petals. They are spotted with brown. Flower spike to 30cm (12in). Cool-growing to intermediate/Z 10.

### P. philippinense × ciliolare

In autumn and winter, greenish-brown flowers appear on this hybrid. These are heavily spotted and striped with darker brown and have deep pouches. Flower spike to 30cm (12in). Cool-growing to intermediate/Z 10.

*Odontoglossum* Geyser Gold

*Oncidium* Sharry Baby

*Paphiopedilum* Calloso-Argus

Phalaenopsis Lady Sakhara

## PHALAENOPSIS
### Moth orchid

To the orchid-growing community, phalaenopsis hybrids have become as important as laelias once were, largely because of their tolerance of central heating – that is, they will grow in a drier atmosphere than suits most other orchids. This makes them suitable as houseplants. In the wild, they are found growing epiphytically in tropical areas of the Far East, almost always in deep shade. They are of unmatched elegance, which has recently made them a popular choice for bridal bouquets.

*Cultivation* Unless otherwise indicated, these orchids are best grown in slatted baskets or on bark, but they are also suitable for containers if they are free-draining.

#### P. equestris
A compact species from the Philippines and Taiwan, this orchid bears significantly smaller flowers than most of the hybrids. From spring to winter gracefully arching stems carry small, soft pink flowers with darker lips, which are streaked with red. Flower spike to 30cm (12in). Warm-growing/Z 10.

#### P. Lady Sakhara
This gorgeous hybrid has racemes of pink flowers, veined with darker pink and with glowing cerise pink lips. They are produced on arching stems throughout the year. Flower spike 45cm (18in). Warm-growing/Z 10.

#### P. Mystic Golden Leopard
This hybrid can flower throughout the year, producing racemes of soft yellow flowers spotted with maroon. The lips are bright orange. Flower spike 30cm (12in). Warm-growing/Z 10.

#### P. Paifang's Golden Lion
The striking orchid has white flowers that are heavily spotted with rich violet-pink and have glowing pink lips. Flower spike 30cm (12in). Warm-growing/Z 10.

## PHRAGMIPEDIUM
### Lady slipper

Phragmipediums are similar to paphiopedilums, both having the characteristic pouches, but they are less often found in collections because of the difficulty of finding plants in the wild. (Many species are officially designated as endangered, and their importation is prohibited.) The lateral petals are considerably extended and are also twisted. The species are mainly terrestrials, which die back in winter, and are found at low altitudes in Central and South America. There are relatively few hybrids, making them plants for the connoisseur, although they are easy to grow.

*Cultivation* Grow in containers of terrestrial orchid compost (growing medium). Good drainage is essential.

#### P. Eric Young
This hybrid produces a succession of orange-yellow flowers from summer to autumn. Flower spike 45cm (18in). Intermediate/Z 10.

#### P. longifolium
The species comes from Costa Rica, Panama, Colombia and Ecuador. In autumn it produces racemes of light yellowish-green flowers with twisted petal edges margined with purple and sepals veined dark green. The lips are flushed purple. Flower spike to 2m (6ft). Cool-growing/Z 10.

× Sophrolaeliocattleya Marion Fitch 'La Tuilerie'

#### P. schlimmii 'Wilcox'
A selected form of a Colombian species, in summer this produces a succession of white flowers, flushed pink and shading to yellowish green at the centre, with darker lips. Flower spike 45cm (18in). Intermediate/Z 10.

## × SOPHROLAELIO-CATTLEYA

These orchids are of complex parentage, involving *Sophronitis*, *Laelia* and *Cattleya*. The flamboyant flowers, typical of all the cattleyas, can be produced at any time of the year.

*Cultivation* Grow in containers of terrestrial orchid compost (soil mix).

Phalaenopsis Mystic Golden Leopard

Phragmipedium Eric Young

Phragmipedium longifolium

× *S.* Jewel Box 'Dark Waters'
As befits its name, this orchid
produces rich deep red flowers
that have trumpet-like lips. These
are usually borne from autumn
to spring. Flower spike to 30cm
(12in). Cool-growing to
intermediate/Z 10.

× *S.* Marion Fitch 'La Tuilerie'
This orchid can flower at any
time of year. The solitary flowers
are an eye-catching luminous
pinkish-red and have lips that
are ruffled at the edges. Flower
spike 30cm (12in).
Intermediate/Z 10.

× *S.* Rocket Burst 'Deep
Enamel'
The brilliant orange-red
flowers usually appear in spring
and last for a month or so.
Flower spike 30cm (12in).
Intermediate/Z 10.

## STANHOPEA
These epiphytic evergreens from
Central and South America are
orchids for real enthusiasts. The
flowers, which are some of the
most strongly scented of all
orchids, last for only about three
days (in some species only one
day). It is essential to grow
stanhopeas in baskets, because
the flowering stems emerge
from the base of the pseudobulbs
and grow downwards. The species
described is the one most
frequently found in collections.
The shortness of the flowering
season means that the seed (and
hence new plants) are always in
short supply.
*Cultivation* Grow in epiphytic
orchid compost (soil mix) in
special baskets or on bark.

*S. tigrina*
(syn. *S. bernandezii*)
From late summer to autumn
this Mexican species produces
downward-growing stems carrying
substantial, waxy, yellow flowers
splashed with deep red, which are
strongly scented. They last for
only about three days. The plant
sometimes experiences a slow-
down in growth in early summer
before flowering. Flower spike to
45cm (18in). Cool-growing to
intermediate/Z 10.

× *Vuylstekeara* Cambria 'Plush'

## VANDA
Among the most dramatic of all
orchids, these evergreen epiphytes
are widely distributed in China,
the Himalayas, New Guinea and
northern Australia, where they
clamber through tree branches
to reach heights of 2.2m (7ft).
Although usually more modest in
domestic settings, they will still
need plenty of room vertically.
They are, nevertheless, among the
most rewarding orchids, with
flowers produced two or three
times a year (mostly in winter),
and these can last up to four
weeks on the plant. In cold areas
they can be placed outside in the
summer months.
*Cultivation* Grow in slatted
baskets of epiphytic orchid
compost (soil mix).

× *Vuylstekeara* Linda Isler

*V.* Rothschildiana
This remarkable hybrid can
flower at any time of year. The
flowers, carried on long racemes,
are violet-blue with darker veining.
Flower spike 60cm (2ft).
Intermediate/Z 10.

## × VUYLSTEKEARA
These hybridized orchids are
crosses of *Cochlioda*, *Miltonia* and
*Odontoglossum*. The spikes of showy
flowers appear when the
pseudobulb is mature, usually in
autumn. They are easy to grow
and make ideal beginner's orchids.
*Cultivation* Grow these orchids in
containers of epiphytic compost
(soil mix).

× *V.* Cambria 'Plush'
At varying times of the year, when
the pseudobulb is mature, this
hybrid produces long sprays of
vivid crimson flowers, up to 10cm
(4in) across, with large red and
white lips. Flower spike to 50cm
(20in). Cool-growing/Z 10 (but
tolerates warmer conditions).

× *V.* Linda Isler
The tall, sometimes branching
spikes of this orchid carry rust
red flowers, with lips that have
contrasting white borders. Flower
spike to 60cm (2ft). Cool-
growing/Z 10 (but tolerates
warmer conditions).

## × WILSONARA
These hybrids are evergreens,
derived by crossing *Cochlioda*,
*Odontoglossum* and *Oncidium*. The
star-like flowers are generally
produced in large quantities.
*Cultivation* Grow in containers
that constrict the roots, filled
with epiphytic compost
(soil mix).

× *W.* Bonne Nuit
When the pseudobulbs are
mature, this orchid produces
tall, branching spikes that carry
masses of showy, yellow flowers
spotted with brown and with
white lips. Flower spike to 60cm
(2ft). Cool-growing/Z 10.

× *W.* Hambühren Stern
'Cheam'
This epiphytic orchid bears spikes
of warm brown flowers with

× *Wilsonara* Bonne Nuit

yellow lips, which can be
produced at any time of year
when the pseudobulb is mature.
Flower spike to 60cm (2ft).
Cool-growing/Z 10.

× *W.* Widecombe Fair
'Burnham'
This orchid makes an excellent
houseplant, since it tolerates
fluctuating temperatures, and is
therefore suitable for a mixed
collection. When the pseudobulbs
are mature, they produce long
spikes of white and pink flowers.
Flower spike to 60cm (2ft).
Cool-growing/Z 10 (but tolerates
warmer conditions).

× *Wilsonara* Widecombe Fair
'Burnham'

# Ferns

Ferns are a fascinating group of
plants, increasingly valued for their
architectural form, ease of cultivation
and tolerance of conditions
inhospitable to many other plants.
They have a welcome freshness as
their fronds begin to unfurl in
spring, and then develop a
considerable elegance, adding a
subtle, understated note to the
garden. Ravishing in light woodland,
they are also effective near water
or in any other damp, shady part
of the garden.

This mixture of ferns and other perennials brings interest to a shady
corner of the garden.

# What is a fern?

Ferns are primitive plants. The lowest form of plant life grown in gardens, they evolved long before seed-producing plants, some being as old as the Carboniferous Period (beginning 360 million years ago). They belong to the pteridophytes, a class that includes horsetails, club mosses and ground pines. Fossil remains indicate that prehistoric pteridophytes reached the size of large trees, but those that have survived to the present day – apart from the tree ferns of the tropics – are much more modest.

Ferns occur in a variety of habitats. Profuse in the tropics, they are also found – albeit in lesser numbers – as far north as Greenland and as far south as Antarctica, from sea level to high altitudes, but not in deserts or very cold areas. Most – though by no means all – are shade- and moisture-loving. In humid climates, some are epiphytic, clinging to trees like orchids. A few are aquatics.

A few species are widespread to an extraordinary degree: common bracken (*Pteridium aquilinum*), though hardly a garden plant, is found throughout the temperate regions as well as some areas of the tropics, while the maidenhair fern occurs in western Europe, parts of Asia, the Americas and Polynesia.

Like other plants, ferns have well-developed stems, roots and leaves. They can be evergreen or deciduous, and some can be either, depending on the climate. Though they can be long-lived plants, the leaves, or fronds, survive for only one or two years and are replaced by fresh leaves that emerge from the tip of the stem annually.

Ferns do not flower, and thus cannot reproduce in the conventional way by pollination. In fact, the

Few gardening sights are more dramatic than the unfurling fronds of ferns, lit up by early morning sun in spring.

plants we recognize as ferns are actually asexual, and reproduction takes place in two stages. Spores form on the undersides of the mature fronds. These are shed and develop as prothalli, tiny heart-

Here, ferns are used to line a path of stepping stones, strewn with fir cones and decorative masks, through a shady woodland area.

shaped plants that look like liverworts, bearing separate male and female germ cells. Male gametes are able to migrate across the surface of the prothallium to unite with the female gametes, and a new embryo fern is then produced. This absorbs nutrients from the prothallium until its roots penetrate the soil and it is able to survive on its own. The prothallium then dies. Some species are able to reproduce by bulbils that form on the fronds. Hybridization does not seem to occur, but many species show astonishing variation. Some have developed a variety of forms, the fronds being crisped, crested or dwarfed, and these are found both in the wild and in gardens.

Ferns exhibit a wide diversity of size. The tree ferns can reach 15m (50ft) – growing slowly, it is true, often at a rate of no more than 2.5cm (1in) a year – while others are tiny. They can be symmetrical, with the fronds erect and arranged like a shuttlecock, or spread by rhizomes. Some have long stems that twine into trees and other plants, pulling the plants skywards.

The fronds are usually roughly triangular or arrow- or strap-shaped. They can be entire or divided, often very finely, giving a filigree effect. Sometimes they divide like a fish tail or have a feathery appearance. The fronds of all ferns are basically green, but some show red, yellow or grey coloration and have a metallic sheen. Variegation does not occur.

## Ferns in the garden

Formerly very popular, then dismissed as drab and dreary, ferns are finally experiencing a renaissance in gardens. They are unrivalled for bringing dank, dark corners of the garden to life, but it would be a serious underestimation of their value to make that their sole use. Gardeners averse to slug and snail control much prefer them to hostas, which enjoy roughly similar conditions: once established, ferns are virtually indestructible. Gertrude Jekyll was fond of combining hostas and ferns in shady courtyards – an elegant and simple solution to what can be a problem area of the garden.

Ferns can be tricky to place in the open garden, most needing soil that is consistently moist without being waterlogged. Find a cool spot for them, ideally in the shade of deciduous trees, where they are protected from direct sunlight and strong winds – both equally detrimental to most ferns. The traditional fernery – perhaps incorporating a water feature – was essentially a large rockery in shade (sometimes under glass to accommodate tender species), providing conditions that also suit the mosses and lichens that would soon take hold unbidden.

Some of the more architectural ferns, such as the tree fern (*Dicksonia antarctica*), the royal fern (*Osmunda regalis*) and forms of *Polystichum setiferum*, make striking specimens, but are also supremely effective in a massed planting (space permitting) of five or more. Site them where light will filter down on them through the tree canopy above. Many ferns, particularly those with rhizomes, are ideal as ground cover in a shady site or in light woodland. Evergreens can be outstanding features of the winter garden, and even the deciduous species are of value then, as the foliage dies back much later than does that of most other plants.

Unusual but interesting effects can be created by combining some of the sun-tolerant ferns with the usual inhabitants of the mixed border. Forms of the golden male fern (*Dryopteris affinis*) or polypodys (*Polypodium*) would be well worth trying with roses, for example, provided the site is not too open. *Asplenium, Dryopteris* and *Polypodium* are invaluable in so far as they are among the few plants that will tolerate dry shade. Very pleasing effects could be created by combining them with variegated periwinkles (*Vinca*), small-leaved ivies (a form of *Hedera helix*) or hardy cyclamen.

The rhythm of the paving slabs is reflected in the subtle border plantings of ferns and pulmonarias.

Adiantum venustum

## ADIANTUM
### Maidenhair fern
A genus of deciduous, semi-evergreen and evergreen ferns with an elegant overall appearance. The plants described here are hardy, but the genus also includes some tender varieties that can be grown indoors.
*Cultivation* Leafy soil in a shaded spot suits these woodlanders.

### A. aculeatum subsp. subpumilum (syn. A. aculeatum subsp. aleuticum)
### Asiatic maidenhair fern
Originally found in North America and eastern Asia, this is a beautiful fern with a creeping rootstock. It has slender, purplish-black stems with fingered, fan-like blades. It needs fertile, humus-rich soil. H and S 30cm (12in). Hardy/Z 3–8.

### A. venustum
### Himalayan maidenhair fern
The triangular fronds of this evergreen native of China are pink when they first appear in spring, turn soft green and then develop a bluish tinge as they mature. H and S 15–30cm (6–12in). Hardy/Z 3–8.

## ASPLENIUM
### Spleenwort
These evergreen ferns are found worldwide, except in Antarctica. They are ideal for a rock garden.
*Cultivation* Good drainage is essential. Plant them in light shade in crevices between rocks or in gritty soil.

### A. scolopendrium (syn. Phyllitis scolopendrium, Scolopendrium phyllitis)
### Hart's tongue fern
This fern, which is native to western Asia, Europe and North America, is easy to grow and has smooth, leathery, strap-like fronds. H and S 45–60cm (18–24in). Hardy/Z 4–8. It has a number of interesting variants, including **Cristatum Group**, in

which the final third of the frond is divided, giving a tassel-like or crested appearance. H 60cm (2ft), S 80cm (32in).

## ATHYRIUM
### Lady fern
A genus of deciduous, occasionally semi-evergreen, ferns, whose common name apparently relates to their overall elegance and grace. The species are all highly variable, and no two plants are ever quite identical.
*Cultivation* Grow in a moist, shady site, in neutral to acid soil.

### A. filix-femina
### Lady fern
Found throughout the northern hemisphere, this has fine, lacy fronds. There are many selected forms. H 50cm (20in), S 30cm (12in). Hardy/Z 4–9. **'Fieldii'** has long, narrow fronds. H 90cm (3ft), S 30cm (1ft). **'Frizelliae'** (tatting fern) has massed pinnae that are contracted into balls, giving the appearance of a necklace of green beads. H 20cm (8in), S 30cm (12in).

### A. niponicum var. pictum (syn. A. niponicum 'Pictum')
### Japanese painted fern
This beautiful and unusual fern is native to Japan. The broadly triangular fronds are wine red, merging with grey-green. It needs a moist, shady, sheltered position. H and S 45–60cm (18–24in). Hardy/Z 3–8.

Athyrium niponicum var. pictum

### A. otophorum
Originating from eastern Asia, this distinctive fern has fairly broad, triangular fronds, which have dark green segments with purple-red stalks. It does best in a moist, shady, sheltered position. H and S 45–75cm (18–30in). Hardy/Z 3–8.

## CYRTOMIUM
This genus, which was formerly known as *Phanerophlebia*, contains both evergreen and deciduous ferns with distinctive fronds that make an effective contrast to other daintier species in a fernery or a shady rock garden.
*Cultivation* These woodland plants need fertile, moist but well-drained soil in shade.

Asplenium scolopendrium Cristatum Group

Athyrium filix-femina 'Fieldii'

Athyrium filix-femina 'Frizelliae'

Athyrium otophorum

*Cyrtomium fortunei*

## C. fortunei
### Holly fern
This upright, architectural evergreen from eastern Asia has mid-green, leathery fronds with smooth margins. H and S 30–60cm (1–2ft). Hardy/ Z 6–9.

## DICKSONIA
These dramatic tree-like ferns, originating from the temperate and tropical highland forests of Australasia and South America, are ideal as specimens. They can be grown in containers and overwintered indoors.
*Cultivation* Grow in fertile, acid soil in deep to light shade.

### D. antarctica
### Tree fern
This fern, which originates in Australia, is an increasingly popular choice for gardens where a dramatic, exotic-looking feature is wanted. The fronds will reach 2m (6ft) in length on mature specimens. It needs a mild, moist climate. In cool areas it is usually deciduous. Packing the crown loosely with dry straw can help it survive cold winters. H 6m (20ft), S 4m (13ft). Half-hardy/Z 10.

## DRYOPTERIS
### Buckler fern
A genus of (usually) deciduous ferns found by streams and lakes. The common name derives from the kidney-shaped spore covers. They are robust plants, useful for providing large, trouble-free clumps of greenery among flowering perennials.
*Cultivation* Plant in fertile soil in partial shade, although *D. affinis* is tolerant of sun.

### D. affinis
### Golden male fern
The leathery, golden-green fronds of this European fern become progressively darker through the season. H and S up to 1m (3ft). Hardy/Z 4–9. **'Congesta'** is a very pretty dwarf form. H and S 15–23cm (6–9in). **'Cristata'**, rightly known as the king fern, is

*Dryopteris erythrosora*

a truly magnificent plant that makes a bold statement in the garden. The fronds are symmetrically crested. H and S 0.6–1.2m (2–4ft). **'Cristata Angustata'** is less robust, with narrower fronds and a neater habit. H and S 45–60cm (18–24in). **'Polydactyla Mapplebeck'** is equally note-worthy, with crested fronds divided into two terminal crests. H and S 0.6–1.5m (2–5ft).

### D. erythrosora
This fern, which comes from China and Japan, has broadly triangular fronds. They are glossy coppery pink when young,

*Dryopteris filix-mas* 'Crispa Cristata'

maturing to plain green. This may be evergreen in mild winters. H and S 45–60cm (18–24in). Hardy/Z 5–9.

### D. filix-mas
### Male fern
This woodlander, found in Europe and North America, is a good choice for a wild garden. It has tall, upright, lance-shaped but feathery, light green fronds. Although technically deciduous, the male fern does not die back completely in autumn. H and S 1m (3ft). Hardy/Z 4–8. **'Crispa Cristata'** has well-crisped and neatly crested fronds. H 60cm (2ft), S 1m (3ft).

*Dicksonia antarctica*

*Dryopteris affinis* 'Polydactyla Mapplebeck'

*Dryopteris affinis* 'Cristata'

Gymnocarpium dryopteris 'Plumosum'

# GYMNOCARPIUM

This group of deciduous, rhizomatous ferns make excellent groundcover plants.
*Cultivation* Grow in leafy, fertile soil, preferably neutral to acid, in shade.

### G. dryopteris
### Oak fern

This fern, which is found throughout Europe, Asia and in Canada, has soft, golden-green fronds that arise from a creeping rootstock, forming a dense mat. Oak ferns are a good choice for the front of a border in a shady rock garden or in stony soil in woodland. H 23–30cm (9–12in), S indefinite. Hardy/Z 3–8.
'Plumosum' has even lovelier foliage, with triple-headed fronds opening into three delicately laced triangles of vivid green. H 23cm (9in), S indefinite.

# MATTEUCCIA

The moisture-loving deciduous, rhizomatous ferns in this genus, native to the woodlands of North America, eastern Asia and Europe, have a characteristic 'shuttlecock' appearance. They look graceful at the margins of a pond or in damp woodland.
*Cultivation* These ferns need moist, ideally slightly acid, soil in light shade.

### M. struthiopteris
### Shuttlecock fern, ostrich feather fern

This native of Europe, Asia and North America is well known. It has tapering fronds – up to 1.5m (5ft) long – that create an elegant, vase-like structure around a stout rootstock. The creeping rootstock spreads rapidly. H to 1.5m (5ft), S to 1m (3ft) in moist conditions. Hardy/Z 2–8.

# ONOCLEA

This lush deciduous fern makes a good subject for pond margins. An effective use is to stabilize the edges of natural streams. There is only one species in the genus.
*Cultivation* These ferns do best in slightly acid, fertile, moist soil in light shade.

### O. sensibilis
### Sensitive fern, bead fern

This moisture-loving fern, which is native to eastern North America and eastern Asia, bears upright pink-bronze fronds that later become mid-green and arching, with the spores enclosed in bead-like pinnules. It has a creeping rootstock and rapidly colonizes wet areas. H and S 1.2–1.5m (4–5ft). Hardy/Z 4–8.

# OSMUNDA

These large deciduous ferns with upright fronds are widely distributed in the wild. They are distinctive plants for a shady bog garden or for planting at the water's edge.
*Cultivation* They do best in moist, preferably acid, soil in light shade.

### O. regalis
### Royal fern

Found in temperate and subtropical regions around the world, this species does best in very wet conditions, making for a magnificent specimen for a water-side planting. The deep green fronds, with a tough, leathery texture, appear from aerial roots. The tips of the fronds change into long, narrow masses of brownish spore capsules. Royal ferns also make handsome container plants. H and S 0.9–2m/3–6ft. Hardy/Z 3–9.

# PELLAEA

This genus of deciduous, semi-evergreen or evergreen ferns make excellent rock garden plants in sheltered areas.

Onoclea sensibilis

*Cultivation* The species described needs well-drained, alkaline soil in sun, but shaded at midday.

### P. atropurpurea
### Purple cliff brake

Native to North America, this evergreen fern has glaucous green fronds. H and S 30–40cm (12–16in). It makes a good container plant for an alpine house or cool conservatory. Borderline hardy/Z 9–10.

# PLATYCERIUM
### Staghorn fern

The common name of these intriguing tender ferns relates to the shape of the leathery fronds. In the wild, they are rainforest epiphytes.
*Cultivation* Grow in slatted baskets in an epiphytic compost (soil mix) consisting of equal parts leaf mould, perlite or vermiculite, and charcoal. Keep in a lightly shaded spot and mist frequently. In frost-free climates, they can be grown epiphytically in trees.

### P. bifurcatum
### Elkhorn fern

The stiff, antler-like fronds emerge from among heart-shaped basal fronds, which turn brown. H and S 60cm (2ft). Tender/Z 10.

# POLYPODIUM
### Polypody

These evergreen ferns with fleshy rhizomes are good for year-round groundcover.

Matteuccia struthiopteris

Polypodium vulgare

Polypodium vulgare 'Longicaudatum'

Polystichum setiferum 'Pulcherrimum Bevis'

*Cultivation* They do best in stony, but humus-rich soil, in sun or light shade and with protection from cold, dry winds.

### P. vulgare
**Common polypody, wall fern**
This evergreen fern, which is found in Europe and Asia, is a useful plant in the garden, adapting to a range of conditions but preferring stony soil. It has smooth, leathery, deeply cut, lance-shaped green fronds set on either side of a central stem. H 10–45cm (4–18in), S indefinite. Hardy/Z 5–8. The vigorous **'Cornubiense'** is a curious cultivar, with three distinct forms of frond: some are like those of the species; others are very finely cut, consisting of very narrow segments; and some are coarser versions of these. Sometimes all three are incorporated in one frond. H 30–40cm (12–16in), S indefinite. Hardy/Z 5–8. **'Longicaudatum'** (syn. *P. glycyrrhiza* 'Longicaudatum') has more elongated fronds than the species. H and S 23–60cm (9–24in). Hardy/Z 5–8.

## POLYSTICHUM
**Holly fern, shield fern**
This genus of elegant evergreen, semi-evergreen or deciduous ferns usually have a shuttlecock-like appearance. They make good plants for a shady border or a rock garden.
*Cultivation* Grow in preferably alkaline, humus-rich soil in light to deep shade.

### P. setiferum
**Soft shield fern**
This elegant fern, which is native to Europe, has gracefully arching fronds. An evergreen, it is easy to grow, producing large clumps if given shade and moisture. H and S 60cm (2ft), but it can reach 1.5m (5ft). Hardy/Z 5–8.
**Acutilobum Group 'Othello'** has extra-long, elegant fronds, which spread out horizontally. H and S 0.9–1.2m (3–4ft). Hardy/Z 5–8. Plants of the **Divisilobum Group** are variable, but all have large, finely cut fronds. The new growth in spring is densely covered in white scales, which creates an attractive effect. H and S to 1.5m (5ft), but only after several years. Hardy/Z 5–8. **Lineare Group** ferns are prostrate, with long, slender, light green fronds. H and S 0.9–1.2m (3–4ft).
**'Pulcherrimum Bevis'** is an architectural, finely divided fern, with tall, arching fronds. H and S to 1m (3ft). Hardy/Z 5–8.

## THELYPTERIS
This small genus of deciduous ferns is usually represented in gardens by the species described. It is an invasive plant but useful at the margins of a natural pool or stream; it does well at the edge of water.
*Cultivation* Grow in moist or very moist, ideally acid soil in a sunny or lightly shaded spot.

### T. palustris
**Marsh fern**
This fern, which spreads by means of creeping rhizomes, has dainty, erect, finely divided, light green fronds. It is an unassuming plant, but useful to fill damp ground. H and S 50cm–1.5m (20in–5ft). Hardy/Z 5–8.

Polypodium vulgare 'Cornubiense'

Polystichum setiferum Acutilobum Group

# Grasses and Bamboos

This group of plants is becoming increasingly popular with gardeners as their potential is being realized. There is a grass suitable for every soil type and virtually every location in the garden. Some are grand, imposing plants that give height to borders or provide accents, while others are more feathery and can be used in drifts to soften any colour scheme. Some bamboos make good barrier plants, besides providing a wealth of material for use as stakes. Most grasses and bamboos retain their structure over winter, continuing to provide interest during the coldest months.

Grasses add a delicate, feathery texture, in strong contrast to the more formal shape of the dahlias.

# What are grasses and bamboos?

Though they look quite different, grasses and bamboos both belong to the same family, Gramineae (or Poaceae). In fact, close inspection readily reveals the similarities, and it is only the difference in scale that distinguishes them. In the discussion that follows, general references to "grasses" should be understood as including bamboos.

Grasses are among the most important plants on the planet and make up one of the largest and most varied of all the plant families. They are mainly perennial (both evergreen and herbaceous), though there are some annual species. They are found in both swamps and deserts, in the polar regions as well as in the tropics, from coastal areas to near the tops of snow-covered mountains.

Grasses have roots, stems, leaves and flowers like other plants. The stems (called culms, particularly in descriptions of bamboos) are jointed; while the joints are always

solid, the part of the stem in between can be solid or, more usually, hollow. Some have stems that spread sideways. Such stems below ground are referred to as rhizomes, while those above ground are called stolons. Both habits allow many species to colonize great tracts of open ground. In the wild (and indeed in gardens) grasses fulfil the valuable function of preventing soil erosion.

Aside from the important lawn grasses and the ornamentals described in the following pages, grasses encompass food crops such as wheat, oats, barley, corn and cane sugar, while the leaves of some are used in paper manufacture. Others are grown to provide a food source for grazing animals.

Bamboos, generally considered the most primitive of the grasses, are found only in the tropics and warm areas of the temperate zones. Prized for the strength and durability of their hard, woody stems, they have been widely used throughout Asia to make furniture (and even houses), as well as cooking utensils and fishing rods. An interesting feature of bamboos is that the individual culms do not thicken with age once they are mature (as do the stems of other woody plants). Equally extraordinary is the infrequency with which they flower. While other grasses flower annually, bamboos flower only every ten to twenty years (with even longer gaps recorded). After flowering, the plant either dies or is severely weakened, taking some years to recover. (The infrequency of flowering causes botanists difficulties in classification, since relationships among the different species can be established only by studying the inflorescences. This has resulted in a comprehensive revision

of the genera in recent years. Certain genera have been amalgamated, and some species have been reassigned.)

Sedges are similar to grasses in appearance but are distinct in having solid triangular or round stems. They thrive in marshes, swamps, shallow water and water meadows.

## Grasses and bamboos in the garden

Considering the diversity of their natural habitats, it follows that there is a grass for virtually every garden situation. Nothing has been more remarkable than the surge of interest in this group of plants in recent years.

Bamboos have traditionally been regarded as utility plants, but an increasing awareness of their beauty and architectural merits has resulted in more extended use. Excellent for filling "problem" areas of the garden such as ditches or rough, stony ground too difficult to cultivate,

The feathery plums of *Cortaderia selloana* 'Sunningdale Silver' brings interest late in season, along with the sedum and cosmos.

The arching leaves of *Carex elata* 'Aurea' and *Miscanthus sinensis* 'Zebrinus' make for an attractive waterside planting.

they are also valued for providing culms for cutting to make plant supports and screens. As an extension of the latter use, they can themselves be planted to screen one part of the garden from another. They are entirely to the point in a Japanese-style garden and strangely, despite their size (or perhaps because of it), they look superb when planted in a small enclosed town garden. For strictly ornamental use (particularly where space is at a premium), stick to clump-forming species rather than the invasive kinds, or restrict their spread by planting them in large containers sunk in the ground.

Ornamental grasses are grown for the long-lasting appeal both of their leaves and of their plumes of flowers. Beds devoted to grasses alone can be highly effective in a quiet, understated way, but on the whole they are best in mixed company. None are vividly coloured, but they provide an admirable foil for a range of more flamboyant plants. They are especially effective planted in drifts with traditional border perennials and bedding plants, helping to soften potential colour clashes. Many are ideal for a low-maintenance garden, since the tufts of foliage they create are virtually impenetrable to weeds. Larger kinds can be used to "punctuate" borders, used as accent plants as an alternative to yuccas and phormiums, or can be planted as specimens, pampas grass (*Cortaderia selloana*) and *Arundo donax* being among the best. They can also lighten the impression created by the solid lumps of conifers and evergreen shrubs. Both bamboos and the larger grasses are highly effective near water, adding to the calming effect of that element in contrast to

A variety of tufty grasses make an excellent combination in a low-maintenance border scheme such as this one.

busier schemes you may have devised elsewhere. The smaller clump-forming types, such as forms of *Festuca glauca*, are excellent for edging.

Grasses add much to the winter garden. Even though the topgrowth

may be technically dead, they often show pleasing beige coloration and retain their elegant outline, a feature only enhanced by a riming of frost on the bitterest days. The purple moor grass (*Molinia caerulea*) and *Pennisetum alopecuroides* are well worth including in a border for this effect alone.

A highly successful method of growing grasses and bamboos is in containers – in fact this is often the only practical way of enjoying handsome but invasive species. Gardeners with limited time especially appreciate the drought-tolerant ones, since these will withstand a certain amount of neglect. Make sure to keep moisture-loving kinds well watered.

Flower arrangers also value the grasses: not only are they long-lasting and ideal for adding bulk and substance to arrangements, but they can also be dried and used during winter when there is precious little other plant material available.

A fine collection of grasses with mixed planting creates a variety of form and texture, and provides interest over a long period of the year.

*Arundo donax*

## ARUNDO
### Giant reed

The genus of three evergreen grasses is generally represented in gardens by the species described below, which is a plant with bamboo-like foliage that is good in mixed borders and bog gardens.
*Cultivation* Grow this in any reasonable soil, preferably reliably moist, in sun.

### A. donax

One of the most imposing of the grasses, the species, which is native to southern Europe, has stout stems with broad, bluish-green leaves, each about 60cm (2ft) long, that hang down. It seldom flowers in cool climates. H 5m (16ft), S 2m (6ft). Hardy/Z 7–10. *A donax* var. *versicolor* (syn. *A. donax* 'Variegata') has white-striped leaves. H 2m (6ft), S 60cm (2ft). Half-hardy/Z 7–10.

## BRIZA
### Quaking grass

This attractive genus of grasses includes both annuals and perennials suitable for mixed borders. They provide excellent material for drying.
*Cultivation* Grow quaking grass in any well-drained soil in sun or light shade.

### B. minor
#### Lesser quaking grass

This annual species, found across Europe and into western Asia, is easily raised from seed. It produces airy, branching stems of bead-like flowers, which are useful for cutting and drying to use in winter arrangements. H 60cm (2ft), S 30cm (12in). Hardy/ Z 5–8.

## CAREX
### Sedge

This is a large and important genus of sedges, containing about 1000 species, which are distinguished by their triangular stems. They are ideal bog garden plants, but some are also worth trying in mixed borders for their attractive mounds of leaves.
*Cultivation* Sedges have varying needs, but most are best in reliably moist soil in sun or light shade.

### C. comans 'Frosted Curls'

This evergreen hybrid is a compact plant, which makes dense clumps of narrow, pale green leaves that curl at the tips. It is equally tolerant of sun and light shade, but it prefers moist soil, although it is worth trying in drier sites. H and S to 45cm (18in). Hardy/Z 5–9.

### C. conica 'Snowline'
(syn. *C. conica* 'Hime-kan-suge')

The evergreen species, which is from Japan and South Korea, is usually seen in gardens in this attractive form, which makes neat clumps of dark green leaves strikingly margined with white. This does well in ordinary garden soil and is useful for providing long-term interest at the front of a border; it is also effective in

*Briza minor*

*Carex elata 'Aurea'*

gravel. H 30cm (1ft), S 35cm (14in). Hardy/Z 6–8.

### C. elata 'Aurea'
(syn. *C. stricta* 'Aurea', *C. riparia* 'Bowles' Golden')
#### Bowles' golden sedge

This well-known cultivar is a herbaceous sedge with slender, arching, yellowish-green leaves. It is especially effective near water but can also be grown in a container if kept well watered. H 70cm (28in), S 45cm (18in). Hardy/Z 5–9.

### C. flagellifera

This species, native to New Zealand, makes a clump of arching, bronze-brown leaves, which are an excellent foil to green-, silver- or yellow-leaved plants. It will grow in almost any soil. H 2m (6ft), S 1m (3ft). Borderline hardy/Z 8–9.

### C. oshimensis 'Evergold'
(syn. *C. morrowii* 'Evergold')

This outstanding evergreen sedge has arching leaves, centrally banded with cream. It is an excellent plant for lighting up a winter garden. It prefers well-drained soil but will grow in sun or semi-shade. H and S 45cm (18in). Hardy/Z 4–9.

### C. pendula
#### Pendulous sedge, weeping sedge

This is an elegant sedge, found in Europe and northern Africa, which is ideal for a water-side planting. The tall stems, from which the brown, catkin- (pussy willow-) like flowers dangle,

appear in spring and early summer. It will tolerate shade. H 1.2m (4ft), S 1.5m (5ft). Hardy/Z 5–9.

### C. testacea

This evergreen sedge from New Zealand has a subtle appeal. The arching, slender, pale olive-green leaves are tinged with bronze. It will grow in most soils and is effective in containers. H 1.2m (4ft), S 60cm (2ft). Half-hardy/Z 7.

## CHUSQUEA

The genus contains about 120 species of evergreen bamboos from South and Central America. They are handsome plants but many are tender, and only the hardy species described is in general cultivation.
*Cultivation* The species described needs fertile, well-drained soil in sun or light shade.

### C. culeou

One of the most dramatic of all bamboos, this species from Chile makes a splendid specimen. Generally slow-growing, it makes a clump of upright stems with small evergreen leaves. The canes, which are unusual in being solid, are pale olive-green when young, maturing to darker green. H 6m (20ft), S 2.5m (8ft). Hardy/Z 6–9.

## CORTADERIA
### Pampas grass, tussock grass

There are about 24 species of

*Chusquea culeou*

evergreen, tussock-forming grasses in the genus, and some forms are so well known that they have become clichés of suburban gardens. They are, nevertheless, handsome plants, with their richly coloured, glistening plumes. They can be an outstanding feature of the winter garden when rimed with frost. Take care when cutting back the plants in spring: the leaves are lethally sharp.
*Cultivation* Grow pampas grasses in fertile, well-drained soil in sun. Remove dead foliage in early spring.

### C. selloana
**Pampas grass**
Widely grown as a specimen, this perennial species is also excellent for use in mixed borders, where its feathery plumes will tower over lower growing plants in late summer. H 3m (10ft), S 1.5m (5ft). Hardy/Z 7–9. Choose carefully among the many selections, because seed-raised plants are often undistinguished. **'Pumila'** is a desirable compact form, with mid-green leaves and yellow plumes of flowers. H 1.5m (5ft), S 1m (3ft). **'Sunningdale Silver'** is an outstanding form, with generous plumes of silver-cream flowers in late summer and autumn. H 3m (10ft), S 2.5m (8ft). Hardy/Z 7–10.

## CYPERUS
Technically, the 600 or so species belonging to this genus (which includes both annuals and perennials) are sedges not grasses, much though they resemble them in outward appearance. Tender species can be grown as houseplants or 'bedded out' in containers at the margins of a pond. All are good in bog gardens or at the margins of a pool.
*Cultivation* Grow in reliably moist soil or in shallow water in sun or light shade.

### C. involucratus
(**syn.** C. alternifolius, C. flabelliformis)
**Umbrella grass**
This plant, originally from Africa, is widely grown as a houseplant, but it also makes an effective marginal aquatic in warm areas. The tall stems are topped with

sprays of small, pale green flowers surrounded by bracts, which look like the spokes of an umbrella. H 70cm (28in), S 40cm (16in). Tender/ Z 9–10. The dwarf form **'Nanus'** is similar in every respect to the species type but grows to about half its height. H 30cm (12in), S 20cm (8in).

### C. longus
**Galingale**
One of the hardier members of the genus, this species, which is native to Europe and North America, has umbrella-like, greenish-brown flowerheads. It makes an effective marginal aquatic. H 1.5m (5ft), S 1m (3ft). Hardy/Z 7–10.

## DESCHAMPSIA
**Hair grass**
There are about 50 species of evergreen tufted grasses in the genus. They make good border plants and provide a wealth of material for cutting.
*Cultivation* Grow in lime-free soil in sun or light shade.

### D. cespitosa
**Tufted hair grass, tussock grass**
This elegant grass from Europe and Asia and the mountains of Africa makes a fountain of leaves. Stems carrying silky, pale green flowerheads, developing as buff-yellow seedheads, arch gracefully and are effective in flower arrangements, both fresh and dried. H 2m (6ft), S 1.2m (4ft). Hardy/Z 4–7.

*Cyperus involucratus*

## ELYMUS
**Wild rye, lyme grass**
Most of the 150 species of easily pleased grasses in the genus are perennials that are excellent as infill in mixed or herbaceous borders.
*Cultivation* Grow these grasses in any ordinary garden soil in sun or light shade.

### E. magellanicus
This clump-forming species, which is native to Chile and Argentina, has spiky, steel-blue leaves. It is a good container plant. H 15cm (6in), S 45cm (18in).

## FARGESIA
The four species of evergreen bamboos in the genus are native to China and the north-eastern Himalayas. They make fine specimens.

*Cultivation* Grow the species described in reliably moist soil in light shade.

### F. nitida
(**syn.** Arundinaria nitida, Sinarundinaria nitida)
**Fountain bamboo**
The appropriate common name of this evergreen bamboo derives from its arching habit. The canes are generously clothed with narrow green leaves on purplish stems, making an elegant plant despite its size. It can also be grown in a large container, if kept well watered. H 5m (16ft), S 1.5m (5ft). Hardy/Z 4–9.

## FESTUCA
**Fescue**
The genus contains about 300 perennial grasses, which produce attractive tufts of foliage. They are ideal for placing at the front of borders or among rock plants.
*Cultivation* Fescues will grow in garden soils that are well-drained. They prefer a position in sun.

### F. glauca
**Blue fescue, grey fescue**
Rightly one of the most popular of grasses, this evergreen species makes tufts of steely blue leaves. The summer flowers are an added bonus. It can also be grown in containers. H and S 30cm (1ft). Hardy/Z 4–8. The many selections include **'Blaufuchs'** (syn. 'Blue Fox'), which has bright blue leaves. The blue-green leaves of **'Harz'** are tipped purple.

*Cortaderia selloana 'Pumila'*

*Deschampsia cespitosa*

*Festuca glauca*

## GLYCERIA
### Sweet grass, manna grass

The 16 species of perennial grass in the genus are usually grown at the margins of a pond – in the wild, they are found in water to 75cm (30in) deep – but they can also be used to fill gaps in large borders, provided you take measures to restrict their spread. *Cultivation* Grow in shallow water or in any reliably moist soil in a border in sun. To restrict spread, plant in pots or aquatic baskets sunk in the soil.

### G. maxima
### (syn. *G. aquatica*)
### Reed meadow grass, reed sweet grass

This rampant species from temperate regions of Europe and Asia produces deep green leaves, which are flushed with pink when they emerge, and panicles of greenish-purple flowers. H 1m (3ft), S indefinite. Hardy/Z 5–9. The species is generally represented in gardens by the slightly less vigorous *G. maxima* var. *variegata* (syn. *G. aquatica* var. *variegata*, *G. spectabilis* 'Variegata'), which has broad, arching leaves striped creamy white and green. Tinted pink in spring, they die back in winter. Pale green flowers are produced in summer. Excellent near water if space is not a problem but, in some cases, a beautiful menace.

## HAKONECHLOA
### Hakone grass

This genus consists of a single deciduous species, which is native to Japan. It is one of the most desirable of all grasses, equally effective in woodland, in borders and in containers. *Cultivation* Grow hakone grass in fertile, well-drained soil in sun or light shade.

### H. macra 'Aureola'

Hakone is generally represented in gardens by this cultivar, which has broad, arching, yellow leaves narrowly striped with green and flushed with pink or red. The best leaf colour is produced when plants are in a lightly shaded situation. It is an excellent choice for a container. H and S to 45cm (18in). Hardy/Z 5–8.

## HELICTOTRICHON

The 50 or so species of deciduous and evergreen grasses in the genus make excellent border plants and are an effective foil to both grey- and silver-leaved plants. *Cultivation* These grasses will grow in most reasonable, preferably alkaline, soils in sun.

### H. sempervirens
### (syn. *Avena candida*, *A. sempervirens*)
### Blue oat grass

This evergreen species, from central and south-western Europe, is a truly outstanding grass from the gardener's point of view: it has steel-blue, evergreen leaves and loose panicles of straw-coloured flowers in early summer. It is a good choice for a container. H 1.2m (4ft), S 60cm (2ft). Hardy/Z 5–8.

*Hordeum jubatum*

## HORDEUM
### Barley

The genus contains 20 species of annuals and perennials, including *H. vulgare*, the well-known cereal crop, which are mainly of interest to the gardener because of their flowers. They are splendid additions to late summer and autumn borders, combining well with dahlias and Michaelmas daisies. *Cultivation* Grow these grasses in any well-drained soil in sun.

### H. jubatum
### Foxtail barley, squirrel-tail barley

This attractive grass, from north-eastern Asia and North America, is an annual, easily raised from seed. The showy plumes of straw-coloured flowers appear in late summer and autumn, making this excellent for filling gaps in borders towards the end of the season. The flowers can be cut and used in both fresh and dried arrangements. H 50cm (20in), S 30cm (12in). Hardy/Z 5–8.

## IMPERATA

The six species of grass in the genus are grown for the simple beauty of their leaves rather than for their flowers, which appear only in areas with long hot summers. They make a good foil to a range of flowering plants in mixed and herbaceous borders. *Cultivation* Grow in any reasonable soil in sun or light shade. Some winter protection – a dry mulch of straw, for instance – is advisable in cold climates.

*Imperata cylindrica* 'Rubra'

### I. cylindrica 'Rubra'
### (syn. 'Red Baron')
### Japanese blood grass

The upright species is usually found in the form of this attractive cultivar, whose common name refers to the red colouring that the leaves develop from the tip downwards. For the best effect, site it where the sun will shine through the glowing foliage. Remove seedheads to prevent self-seeding because seedlings will almost invariably revert to the plain green of the species. H 1m (3ft), S 60cm (2ft) or more. Half-hardy/Z 5–10.

## LAGURUS
### Hare's tail

The single species in the genus, which is native to the Mediter-ranean, is a real flower arranger's plant that is also effective in beds and borders.

*Glyceria maxima* var. *variegata*

*Helictotrichon sempervirens*

*Lagurus ovatus*

*Cultivation* This grass needs sharply drained, not too fertile soil in sun.

### L. ovatus
**Hare's tail grass**
The familiar species is an annual, making compact clumps of long, narrow and flat leaves but valued principally for its fluffy white oval flowerheads, which are produced throughout summer. These are excellent for drying. H 60cm (2ft), S 15cm (6in). Hardy/Z 6–9.

## LEYMUS
The 40 perennial grasses in the genus are of very striking appearance, but they tend to be invasive. Although they are excellent running through large borders, they can become a menace if not regularly thinned. On the credit side, they are excellent in containers.
*Cultivation* Grow these grasses in any reasonable well-drained soil in sun.

### L. arenarius
**(syn. *Elymus arenarius*)**
**Lyme grass, European dune grass**
This rhizomatous perennial species, native to north and west Europe and western Asia, is one of the most attractive of all grasses, but unfortunately it is too invasive for most gardens. It has arching blue-grey leaves, and, in summer, spikes of blue-grey flowers, which fade to straw yellow. H 1.5m (5ft), S indefinite. Hardy/Z 4–9.

*Leymus arenarius*

*Melica ciliata*

## MELICA
**Melick**
The 70 species of grasses in the genus are widespread in temperate areas. The species described are dainty, elegant grasses, which are good in shady gardens, although they take on their best colour in sun.
*Cultivation* Grow melicks in fertile, well-drained soil in sun or light shade.

### M. altissima
**Siberian melick**
This evergreen perennial species, native to Eastern and Central Europe, has slender upright stems and broad leaves. Spikelets in narrow panicles of pale green flowers are produced during summer. It is useful for flower arrangements and for drying. H 1.2m (4ft), S 60cm (2ft). Hardy/Z 6–9.

*Miscanthus sinensis* 'Zebrinus'

### M. ciliata
**Silky spike melick**
This charming species, which is suitable for most soil types, produces a mound of grey-green leaves and has heads of pale straw-coloured flowers in early summer. H 45cm (18in), S 60cm (2ft). Hardy/Z 6–9.

## MILIUM
There are six species in the genus, all from western Asia, but the grass described below is one of the best of all garden plants, providing a vivid patch of colour throughout the growing season. Use it in mixed beds and borders, in light woodland or in a container.
*Cultivation* This grass will grow in any reasonably fertile, well-drained soil, in sun or (preferably) light shade.

### M. effusum 'Aureum'
**Bowles' golden grass**
This is an outstanding grass that should be in every garden. The fresh, bright yellow leaves are at their best as they emerge in spring, making a charming picture with daffodils and other early bulbs, but maintaining a good colour throughout the season. The yellow flowers in summer are a welcome bonus. H (in flower) 60cm (2ft), S 45cm (18in). Hardy/Z 5–8.

## MISCANTHUS
The 17 species of elegant perennial grasses in the genus are handsome enough to serve as specimens, besides their other uses in beds and borders and for cutting. They sometimes develop pleasing russet tints in autumn.
*Cultivation* These grasses like a sunny site and succeed in both dry and moist soils, although extremes are best avoided.

### M. sinensis
This clump-forming species from eastern Asia has bluish-green leaves and attractive pale grey spikelets, tinged with purple, in autumn. It has given rise to many fine cultivars. H to 4m (13ft), S 1.2m (4ft). Hardy/Z 5–9.
'Gracillimus' (maiden grass) is tall, with narrow leaves, which curl

*Molinia caerulea*

at the tips, and plumes of buff-yellow flowers in autumn. H 1.5m (5ft), S 60cm (2ft). One of the most attractive of the selections from the species is **'Kleine Fontäne'**, which produces upright clumps of leaves and heads of pale pink flowers in late summer. It is an excellent choice in borders with late summer perennials. H 1m (3ft), S 45cm (18in). **'Zebrinus'** is an eye-catching form, with narrow green leaves, banded horizontally with yellow, and silky brown flowers. H 1.5m (5ft), S 60cm (2ft).

## MOLINIA
There are only two or three species in the genus, but these are graceful perennial grasses, which look delightful in herbaceous and mixed borders.
*Cultivation* Molinias need neutral to acid, well-drained soil in sun or light shade.

### M. caerulea
**Purple moor grass**
This species from Europe and south-western Asia has green foliage that turns yellow in autumn. Upright stems are topped with light purplish flowerheads from late summer to autumn. H 1.2m (4ft), S 60cm (2ft). Hardy/Z 5–8. *M. caerulea* subsp. *caerulea* 'Variegata' is an elegant form, with green and white striped leaves, which are sometimes tinged pink, and loose purple-grey flowers on arching stems in late summer and autumn. H and S 60cm (2ft).

Pennisetum alopecuroides

Phalaris arundinacea var. picta 'Picta'

## PENNISETUM

This large genus of about 80 grasses includes annuals as well as the perennials described here. All make excellent border plants and provide material for cutting.
**Cultivation** Grow in well-drained, preferably light, soil in sun.

### P. alopecuroides
(syn. *P. compressum*)
**Fountain grass, swamp foxtail grass**
This species, from western Australia and eastern Asia, makes airy clumps of narrow leaves, which turn reddish-orange in autumn and fade to buff in winter. Purple-brown, bottlebrush-like flowerheads emerge in autumn. H and S 1.2m (4ft). Hardy/Z 5–9.

### P. orientale
Sadly, this beautiful species from Asia and northern India is not reliably hardy in cold areas, where it needs winter protection. It makes clumps of narrow leaves, and bears spikes of soft pinkish-grey summer flowers, which are excellent in arrangements both fresh and dried. H and S 60cm (2ft). Half-hardy/Z 7–9.

### P. villosum
**Feathertop**
This African species is grown principally for its beige-white flowerheads, which are produced from summer to autumn and are much valued by flower arrangers. The leaves are narrow. This species is not fully hardy in cold

climates, where it will need winter protection. H and S 60cm (2ft). Half-hardy/Z 7–9.

## PHALARIS

Although there are about 15 annual and perennial grasses in the genus, to all intents and purposes the species described is the only member of the genus that is generally seen. It can be grown in borders, but is happiest near water.
**Cultivation** The species will grow in any ordinary garden soil, but does best in moist or even boggy ground in sun or light shade.

### P. arundinacea
**Reed canary grass, ribbon grass**
This invasive evergreen species, which is found in the wild in western Asia, southern Africa and North America, has upright, mid-green leaves and, in summer, pale green spikelets, which turn buff. H 1.5m (5ft), S indefinite. Hardy/Z 4–9. The species is usually seen in gardens in the vigorous form *P. arundinacea* var. *picta* 'Picta' (gardener's garters),

Pleioblastus simonii f. variegatus

which has green and white striped, arching leaves. The flower spikes, which appear in summer, can be 1.5m (5ft) high. H 60cm (2ft), S indefinite. '**Tricolor**' is similar except that the leaves have a pink tinge. H 60cm (2ft), S indefinite.

## PHYLLOSTACHYS

The 80 or so evergreen bamboos in the genus are elegant enough for use as specimens in large gardens or at the backs of large borders as a backdrop to other plants. They are also good screening material.
**Cultivation** Grow these bamboos in fertile, well-drained soil in sun or light shade.

### P. bambusoides
**Giant timber bamboo**
Mature specimens of this imposing Chinese bamboo have thick green canes that can be used for building. It has copious, broad, glossy, dark green leaves. H and S 5m (16ft) or more. Hardy/Z 7–10. '**Allgold**' (syn. 'Holochrysa', 'Sulphurea') has golden-yellow canes, sometimes striped with green.

### P. nigra
**Black bamboo**
This dramatic Chinese species has canes that become black with age, a good contrast to the abundant green leaves. It makes an impressive specimen, particularly in an eastern-style garden. H 5m (16ft), S 2m (6ft). Hardy/Z 7–10. The selection '**Boryana**' is shorter and has characteristic brown mottling on its canes once mature. H 4m (13ft), S 2m (6ft).

### P. viridiglaucescens
(syn. *P. edulis* f. *subconvexa*)
This vigorous, elegant species has

Poa labillardieri

smooth, green canes that bend outwards under the weight of the dense, bright green leaves. H and S 4m (13ft). Hardy/Z 7–10.

## PLEIOBLASTUS

The 20 species of dwarf to medium-sized evergreen bamboos in the genus can be rampant and are best used to colonize woodland.
**Cultivation** Grow in moist soil in sun or light shade.

### P. auricomus
(syn. *Arundinaria auricoma*, *A. viridistriata*, *P. viridistriatus*)
This modest species from Japan is useful for small gardens. The leaves are striped with golden yellow and green. It is suitable for growing in containers, provided it is kept well watered. H and S 1m (3ft). Hardy/Z 5–10.

### P. simonii f. variegatus
This attractive form of the Japanese species makes an imposing stand, with broad leaves narrowly striped with green and white, the best colours being on the young leaves. It combines well with other large-leaved plants in an open setting. H and S 4m (13ft). Hardy/Z 7–10.

## POA
**Meadow grass, spear grass**
Some of the 500 species in this genus are lawn grasses, but the one described is a good border plant.
**Cultivation** This grass will grow in most well-drained soils, preferably light ones, in sun or light shade.

### P. labillardieri
This evergreen species from Australia makes dense mounds of fine blue-grey leaves, above which arching stems carry purplish flowerheads in summer. It associates well with red- and purple-leaved plants. H 1.2m (4ft), S 1m (3ft). Hardy/Z 6–9.

## PSEUDOSASA
The six evergreen bamboos in the genus, being very invasive, are principally used as screening material or in a wild garden.
**Cultivation** Grow in fertile, well-drained soil in sun or light shade.

*Pseudosasa japonica*

### P. japonica
(syn. *Arundinaria japonica*)
**Arrow bamboo, metake**
This robust evergreen species from Japan makes a good back-drop to other plants. Its tall, erect canes arch over under the weight of its abundant large, broad, bright green leaves. H and S 4m (13ft) or more. Hardy/Z 7–10.

## SASA
The roughly 40 small to medium-sized bamboos in this genus spread by means of running rootstocks and are potentially far too invasive for general garden use. Provided room, they are excellent for filling large areas and will tolerate deep shade.
*Cultivation* Grow in any reasonable garden soil, in sun or shade.

### S. palmata
(syn. *Arundinaria palmata*)
This attractive, clump-forming evergreen species from Japan has very broad, green leaves. A good plant for colonizing rough areas in a large garden. H 4m (13ft), S indefinite. Hardy/Z 6–10.

*Sasa palmata*

### S. veitchii
(syn. *Arundinaria veitchii*)
An evergreen species from Japan, this has broad green leaves that appear variegated but actually are not. They are solid green when young, but as they age the green retreats from the edges of the leaf, leaving an irregular, creamy buff margin. It is good for creating a thicket. H 1.5m (5ft), S indefinite. Hardy/Z 6–10.

## SCIRPOIDES
**Round-headed clubrush**
This genus consists of a single species, a sedge that is ideal for a bog or stream-side planting.
*Cultivation* This plant needs permanently moist soil (or shallow water) in sun.

### S. holoschoenus
(syn. *Holoschoenus vulgaris*, *Scirpus holoschoenus*)
This dramatic plant has narrow, grass-like foliage that turns tawny brown in autumn and small brown flowers. It is suitable for larger gardens only, where it is most effective when planted at the water's edge. H 1m (3ft), S indefinite. Hardy/Z 7.

## SEMIARUNDINARIA
There are between 10 and 20 species of upright bamboos in the genus, all from China and Japan. They tend to be clumpforming in gardens and as such make fine specimens. Alternatively, use them for screening.
*Cultivation* Reasonably fertile soil is suitable, in sun or light shade.

### S. fastuosa
(syn. *Arundinaria fastuosa*)
**Narihira bamboo**
This imposing bamboo has tall, erect green canes (turning reddish on maturity), topped with masses of airy leaves. This is one of the hardiest bamboos. H 5m (15ft), S indefinite. Hardy/Z 7–10.

## SHIBATAEA
The genus contains eight species of the most manageable evergreen bamboos. The species described can be grown in borders and looks wonderful in gravel. It is also a good container plant.
*Cultivation* Grow in ideally reliably

*Shibataea kumasasa*

moist soil in sun or light shade; the more sun, the wetter the soil should be.

### S. kumasasa
(syn. *Sasa ruscifolia*)
A compact species from Japan, this is suitable for small gardens. H 1m (3ft), S 60cm (2ft). Hardy/Z 6–10.

## STIPA
**Feather grass, needle grass**
There are about 300 species, in the genus. They are lovely grasses that make fine border plants, either in a position of prominence or used in conjunction with summer flowers. Stipas also provide good material for arrangements, both fresh and dried.
*Cultivation* Grow in any reasonably fertile, soil in sun.

### S. arundinacea
**Pheasant's tail grass**
An excellent grass for the autumn garden, this New Zealand species has long, tawny-beige foliage that intensifies in colour as the temperature drops. Thin stems carry brownish flowers in late summer. H and S 1m (3ft). Hardy/Z 7–10.

*Stipa calamagrostis*

### S. calamagrostis
(syn. *S. lasiogrostis*)
This grass, from southern Europe, is good for planting in drifts, and with its narrow, arching leaves, it blends happily with a range of plants. The silky flowerheads, which appear in summer, are initially green with a reddish tinge, fading to pale golden-yellow in late summer. H and S 1m (3ft). Hardy/Z 7–10.

### S. gigantea
**Giant feather grass, golden oats**
Native to Spain and Portugal, this is a large plant, very effective in borders when combined with lower growing plants. It forms tough mounds of leaves from which arise tall stems topped with long-lasting oat-like flowers in summer and autumn. They become golden yellow as they age. H to 2m (6ft), S indefinite. Hardy/Z 7–9.

### S. tenuissima
This well-known species from the southern United States is one of the more handsome of the smaller grasses and is a good choice for use as a specimen in a restricted space. The delicate stems and leaves, which turn blond in summer, move in the slightest breeze, a charming effect when the silky, cream flowers appear in summer. H and S 60cm (2ft). Hardy/Z 6–9.

## TYPHA
**Bulrush, reedmace**
There are 10 species in the genus, which are familiar plants around natural pools and lakes in many parts of the world. Few are of sufficient distinction to find a place in gardens, but the species described is of some merit.
*Cultivation* Grow in shallow water or in the moist soil at the margins of a pond in sun.

### T. latifolia
**Great reedmace, cat's tail**
This invasive species is best used as a marginal aquatic. It has erect stems topped by compact, velvety, brown flowerheads in summer, much valued in flower arrangements. H to 2m (6ft), S indefinite. Hardy/Z 3–10.

# Recommended planting lists

The following lists offer a guide to plants adapted to certain conditions. Most of the entries relate to entire genera. For more detailed information as to preferences of individual species, refer to the relevant entry. Remember that some plants are tolerant of a range of conditions, hence their presence in more than one list.

## PLANTS FOR DRY SOIL IN SUN

TREES
Cercis
Gleditsia

CONIFERS
Juniperus
Pinus
Thuja

SHRUBS
Artemisia
Ballota
Buddleja
Ceanothus
Cistus
Genista
× Halimiocistus
Helianthemum
Hibiscus
Lavandula
Lavatera
Olearia
Perovskia
Phlomis
Potentilla
Rosmarinus
Ruta
Salvia
Santolina

Teucrium
Thymus
Yucca

PERENNIALS
Achillea
Anthemis
Artemisia
Aster
Dianthus
Eryngium
Euphorbia
Helichrysum
Kniphofia
Lychnis
Nepeta
Osteospermum
Papaver
Salvia
Sedum
Stachys
Verbascum
Verbena
Zauschneria

ANNUALS AND BIENNIALS
Calendula
Cleome
Cosmos
Eschscholtzia
Limnanthes
Oenothera

Papaver
Salvia
Tagetes

BULBS, CORMS AND TUBERS
Allium
Crocus
Nerine
Tulipa

ALPINES
Aubrieta
Cerastium
Dianthus
Gypsophila

## PLANTS FOR DRY SOIL IN SHADE

SHRUBS
Buxus
Elaeagnus
Hypericum
Kerria
Sarcococca
Vinca

ANNUALS AND BIENNIALS
Lunaria

CLIMBERS
Hedera

BULBS, CORMS AND TUBERS
Cyclamen

FERNS
Asplenium
Polypodium

Hosta 'Golden Prayers'

## PLANTS FOR MOIST SOIL IN SHADE

TREES
Acer

SHRUBS
Aucuba
Hamamelis
Hydrangea
Kalmia
Mahonia
Sarcococca

PERENNIALS
Aquilegia
Aruncus
Astilbe
Astrantia
Calla
Cimicifuga
Convallaria
Digitalis
Helleborus
Heuchera
Hosta
Lysimachia
Polygonatum

Primula
Pulmonaria
Rheum
Rodgersia
Thalictrum
Tiarella
Tricyrtis
Trillium
Trollius
Viola

## PLANTS FOR EXPOSED SITES

TREES
Acer
Carpinus
Crataegus
Fagus
Fraxinus
Populus
Prunus
Salix
Sorbus

CONIFERS
Chamaecyparis
× Cupressocyparis

Cupressus
Juniperus
Pinus
Thuja

SHRUBS
Berberis
Buddleja
Calluna
Erica
Euonymus
(deciduous)
Ilex
Kalmia
Prunus

PERENNIALS
Achillea
Ajuga
Bergenia
Cimicifuga
Coreopsis
Iris
Persicaria
Primula
Pulmonaria

ANNUALS AND BIENNIALS
Hesperis

BULBS, CORMS AND TUBERS
Allium
Crocus

ALPINES
Campanula
Sempervivum

GRASSES
Miscanthus
Stipa

Stachys byzantina

Sarcococca hookeriana var. dignya

Sempervivum arachnoideum

*Calluna vulgaris* 'My Dream'

*Ceanothus* 'Delight'

*Wisteria* × formosa 'Yae-kokuryū'

## PLANTS FOR ACID OR LIME-FREE SOIL

TREES
*Acacia*
*Arbutus*
*Eucryphia*
*Magnolia*

CONIFERS
*Abies*
*Picea*
*Pinus*

SHRUBS
*Callistemon*
*Calluna*
*Camellia*
*Daboecia*
*Erica*
*Fothergilla*
*Hamamelis*
*Kalmia*
*Magnolia*
*Pieris*
*Rhododendron*

PERENNIALS
*Iris*
*Tricyrtis*
*Trillium*

CLIMBERS
*Lapageria*

BULBS
*Lilium*

ALPINES
*Corydalis*
*Gentiana* (autumn-flowering)
*Lewisia*
*Phlox*
*Primula*

## PLANTS FOR CHALKY SOIL

TREES
*Aesculus*
*Betula*
*Carpinus*
*Cercis*
*Crataegus*
*Fagus*
*Fraxinus*
*Gleditsia*
*Laburnum*
*Laurus*
*Malus*
*Paulownia*
*Prunus*
*Pyrus*
*Robinia*
*Sophora*
*Sorbus*

CONIFERS
*Juniperus*
*Taxus*

*Iris reticulata*

SHRUBS
*Berberis*
*Buxus*
*Ceanothus*
*Cistus*
*Cotoneaster*
*Daphne*
*Deutzia*
*Euonymus*
*Forsythia*
*Fuchsia*
*Genista*
*Hebe*
*Helianthemum*
*Ilex*
*Kerria*
*Lonicera*
*Olearia*
*Osmanthus*
*Paeonia*
*Phillyrea*
*Phlomis*
*Rosmarinus*
*Sarcococca*
*Syringa*
*Viburnum*
*Vinca*
*Weigela*
*Yucca*

PERENNIALS
*Anemone*
*Anthemis*
*Campanula*
*Convallaria*
*Dianthus*
*Iris*
*Paeonia*
*Rudbeckia*
*Salvia*
*Verbascum*
*Viola*

ANNUALS AND BIENNIALS
*Bellis*
*Lobularia*
*Papaver*
*Salvia*
*Viola*

CLIMBERS
*Clematis*
*Hedera*
*Lonicera*
*Parthenocissus*

BULBS, CORMS AND TUBERS
*Anemone*
*Colchicum*
*Crocus*
*Gladiolus*
*Iris*
*Narcissus*
*Tulipa*

ALPINES
*Aubrieta*
*Campanula*
*Dianthus*
*Pulsatilla*
*Saxifraga*

## PLANTS FOR CLAY SOIL

TREES
*Acer*
*Alnus*
*Arbutus*
*Carpinus*
*Fraxinus*
*Salix*

CONIFERS
*Abies*
*Chamaecyparis*
*Cryptomeria*
*Metasequoia*

SHRUBS
*Cornus*
*Magnolia*
*Weigela*

PERENNIALS
*Aconitum*
*Astrantia*
*Digitalis*
*Helenium*
*Hemerocallis*
*Lysimachia*
*Lythrum*
*Persicaria bistorta*
*Rudbeckia*

CLIMBERS
*Lonicera*
*Wisteria*

BULBS, CORMS AND TUBERS
*Anemone*
*Camassia*
*Leucojum*
*Narcissus*

FERNS
*Matteuccia*
*Osmunda*

GRASSES
*Cyperus*

## PLANTS FOR COASTAL SITES

TREES
*Acer*
*Arbutus*
*Ilex*
*Trachycarpus*

CONIFERS
*Chamaecyparis*
*Cupressocyparis*
*Pinus*

SHRUBS
*Artemisia*
*Ceanothus*
*Cistus*
*Cotoneaster*
*Cytisus*
*Elaeagnus*
*Erica*
*Euonymus*
*Fuchsia*
*Genista*
*Halimium*
*Hebe*
*Hydrangea*
*Ilex*
*Lavandula*
*Olearia*
*Phlomis*
*Pittosporum*
*Potentilla*
*Rosmarinus*

*Hakonechloa macra 'Aureola'*

Santolina
Spiraea
Yucca

PERENNIALS
Achillea
Agapanthus
Anthemis
Artemisia
Dianthus
Eryngium
Euphorbia
Geranium

Penstemon
Phormium
Sedum
Stachys

ANNUALS AND
BIENNIALS
Antirrhinum
Matthiola

CLIMBERS
Fallopia
Wisteria

BULBS, CORMS
AND TUBERS
Canna
Chionodoxa
Crocosmia
Crocus
Narcissus
Zantedeschia

ALPINES
Aubrieta
Dianthus
Gypsophila
Sedum
Sempervivum

**PLANTS FOR
AUTUMN AND
WINTER
COLOUR**

TREES
Acer
Aesculus
Arbutus
Betula
Cercidiphyllum

Crataegus
Eucryphia
Malus
Populus
Prunus
Pyrus
Quercus
Robinia
Sorbus

CONIFERS
Cryptomeria
Ginkgo
Larix
Taxodium

SHRUBS
Berberis (deciduous)
Ceratostigma
Calluna
Cornus
Cotinus
Cotoneaster
(deciduous)
Daboecia
Erica
Euonymus

*Narcissus cyclamineus*

Fothergilla
Hamamelis
Paeonia
Photinia
Pyracantha
Spiraea
Viburnum
(deciduous)

PERENNIALS
Helleborus
Ophiopogon
Tiarella

CLIMBERS
Celastrus
Humulus
Parthenocissus
Vitis

FERNS
Osmunda

GRASSES
Festuca
Hakonechloa
Miscanthus

## Plant Hardiness Zones

This map was developed by the Agricultural Research Service of the U.S. Department of Agriculture. Every plant in the directory is given a zone range. The zones 1-11 are based on the average annual minimum temperature. In the zone range, the smaller number indicates the northern-most zone in which a plant can survive the winter and the higher number gives the most southerly area in which it will perform consistently. Bear in mind that factors such as altitude, wind exposure, proximity to water, soil type, snow, night temperature, shade, and the level of water received by a plant may alter a plant's hardiness by as much as two zones.

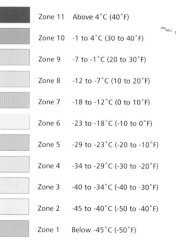

Zone 11   Above 4°C (40°F)
Zone 10   -1 to 4°C (30 to 40°F)
Zone 9   -7 to -1°C (20 to 30°F)
Zone 8   -12 to -7°C (10 to 20°F)
Zone 7   -18 to -12°C (0 to 10°F)
Zone 6   -23 to -18°C (-10 to 0°F)
Zone 5   -29 to -23°C (-20 to -10°F)
Zone 4   -34 to -29°C (-30 to -20°F)
Zone 3   -40 to -34°C (-40 to -30°F)
Zone 2   -45 to -40°C (-50 to -40°F)
Zone 1   Below -45°C (-50°F)

# Index

# Acknowledgements

**Author's acknowledgements**
I would like to thank all the editors who worked on this book, especially Claire Folkard and Penelope Goodare. I would also like to thank all my friends and neighbours who allowed me to invade their gardens in pursuit of those elusive plant portraits.

**Picture acknowledgements**
Photography by Peter Anderson, Jonathan Buckley, Derek Cranch, Helen Fickling, Michelle Garrett, Simon McBride and Marie O'Hara.

The publisher would like to thank the following picture libraries for permission to use their photographs.
**Peter Anderson** 202br.
**A-Z Botanical** 15t, 17tr, 17br, 19tl, 19br, 24br, 26tr, 26br, 92tr, 119bl, 147bl, 202tl, 203tr.
**Jonathan Buckley** 12, 14, 15b, 30, 33t, 42, 44t, 78, 120, 122, 136, 139, 164, 166, 198, 200, 206, 208t, 209t, 226, 228, 229, 234, 236l, 237t.

**Andrew Mikolajski** 6, 10t, 11r, 22tr, 23tl, 70tl, 83tc, 135tl, 138l, 141tr, 169br.
**Peter McHoy** 47tl, 52tl, 52tc, 52tr, 53br, 54tl, 55br, 58b, 60bc, 61br, 63tc, 63tr, 63bl, 64t, 64bl, 65tl, 65tr, 65br, 66tr, 67tc, 67br, 68tl, 68tc, 69tl, 76tc, 76bl, 77br, 82tc, 82br, 83tr, 84tl, 84tc, 85tl, 86bl, 87bl, 88br, 92tl, 93tl, 93tr, 93br, 102br, 103bcl, 104tcl, 104tcr, 104b, 105tl, 105bl, 105br, 106br, 112tl, 112bl, 112bc, 113tr, 113bl, 113bt, 114b, 115tr, 116bc, 117tc, 117tr, 117bl, 118tl, 118tr, 118bl, 118br, 119tr, 124tr, 124bl, 125tl, 125tc, 125bl, 126br, 127tc, 128tc, 129bc, 130b, 131t, 131bl, 131bc, 132br, 135bl, 135br, 140tl, 140tc, 140tr, 140b, 142tc, 144tc, 145tl, 145tc, 146tl, 146tc, 146b, 147tl, 168tl, 168tr, 168bc, 168br, 170tr, 173bl, 182tr, 182b, 190tl, 190tc, 190tr, 190bl, 191tl, 191bl, 191br, 192tr, 192bl, 192br, 193tl, 193tr, 194tr, 194bl, 194br, 195tr, 195bc, 195br, 196tl, 197tl, 197br.

# NOTES

# NOTES

# NOTES

# NOTES